PSYCHO-SOCIAL ASPECTS OF AGING IN INDIA

About the Author

PARAMJEET KAUR DHILLON received her Ph. D. degree from the University of Delhi. She got a W.H.O. fellowship for doing her post-doctoral research in England. She is at present a Reader in the Department of Applied Psychology, University of Delhi, South Campus. Her area of interest is Applied Social Psychology and Organisational Behaviour. She has to her credit a fairly large number of research papers published in professional journals and as book chapters. She is an active researcher and participates in national and international conferences and seminars.

PSYCHO-SOCIAL ASPECTS OF AGING IN INDIA

PARAMJEET KAUR DHILLON
Department of Applied Psychology
University of Delhi, South Campus, New Delhi

Foreword by

Dr. G.G. Mansharamani
Professor of Medicine
Maulana Azad Medical College, New Delhi

CONCEPT PUBLISHING COMPANY PVT. LTD.
NEW DELHI-110059

ISBN: 978-81-7022-426-6

Edition 2022

Published and Printed by

Since 1974

Concept Publishing Company Pvt. Ltd.
A/15-16, Commercial Block, Mohan Garden,
New Delhi-110059 (India)
T: 91 11 41101460
E: publishing@conceptpub.com, *W*: www.conceptpub.com

Cataloging in Publication Data--Courtesy: D.K. Agencies (P) Ltd. <docinfo@dkagencies.com>

Dhillon, Paramjeet Kaur, author.
Psycho-social aspects of aging in India / Paramjeet Kaur Dhillon ; foreword by Dr. G.G. Mansharamani.
pages cm
Reprint. Originally published: 1992.
Includes bibliographical references.
ISBN 9788170224266

1. Aging--India. 2. Aging--India--Psychological aspects. I. Title.

LCC QH529.D55 2022 | DDC 305.260954 23

To

My Mother and Dad

(Mrs. Jagir Dhillon & Major Arjan Singh Dhillon)

Whose generosity and self-sacrifice enabled me

to have what they did not

FOREWORD

Some books are to be tasted,
Other to be swallowed;
And some to be chewed
and digested.

Bacon - of studies

The need for a book on ageing solely written by Indian authors has been a felt need for students and teachers alike for the past so many years. Though the number of old and aged is rapidly rising in our country, not much clinical data and knowledge on the subject is available through books by Indian authors. Numerically, India will have the second largest aged population by the turn of this century.

The problems of the old are multiple, social, economic, psychic, medical, etc. While these have been fully recognised in developed countries and certain well chartered policies have been laid down at official and non-official levels; but not enough attention has been paid in our country so far.

Dr. Paramjeet Kaur Dhillon has done an excellent job in bringing out this book on various Psycho-social aspects of ageing. In twelve chapters she has discussed various aspects of ageing in relation to India's population. Chapters on death anxiety, retirement problems, hospitalisation, institutionalisation are excellent material. Tables have been effectively presented in each chapter which add to the value of the book. Miss Dhillon has exploded various myths regarding retirement. Without activity time becomes void and meaningless. Man will definately live longer, if he is allowed to work longer. In USA the retirement age is 75 years and even when retired, he or she is no extra-burden on the family or the society. Miss Dhillon has effectively dealt with problems on how to cope with retirement. Elders constitute one of our best human resources. They are experienced persons and many of them are eminent in their own fields as doctors, scientists, writers, engineers, etc., and are some of the best assets of the society.

We must develop various programmes and opportunities to utilise their vast expertise and experience.

The elderly are highly vulnerable to loneliness. Depression is common, women are prone to high level of anxiety and depression. In India, depression is not such a common problem because of the joint family system even in its diluted form as it is at present.

This book on socio-psychic aspects of ageing is worth reading by one and all interested in the care of old and the aged. The author has done a good job, I can boldly recommend that this book deserves to be in every library in India. The book is to be cherished, chewed and digested.

DR. G.G. MANSHARAMANI
Professor of Medicine
and
Former President
Geriatric Society of India
Maulana Azad Medical College, New Delhi

PREFACE

To be, infact, is to become and age, and to age is suffering. We are never free of temporality and its bodily analogue, aging, which constantly reminds us of our ultimate condition: death. Joyous moments of life are but beguiling shadows of inevitable old age and its accomplices; disease and death. Old age and the consequent bodily suffering is the destiny of human beings in this world.

—*Milindapanha*, 1890

The early Buddhist text *Milindapanha* identifies old age with suffering. However, the Hindu view emphasises that one should selectively cast away some of the norms and values of middle age and take on a role more suited to old age in order to avoid the suffering. As Young (1989) states that the "Hindu view of the stages of life (*asrama*) attempts to overcome the extreme opposition between this-worldy life (*pravrtti*) and renunciation (*nivrtti*). . . . Hindu thinkers assigned to these stages of life attendant duties and goals to provide, concurrently or serially experiences of this wordly life and renuniciation. And they correlated these stages with the aging process so that by the end of a lifetime a man's experience would have incorporated the poles and made possible, upon deep reflection, their ultimate integration. . . ." However, because this ideal plan of life of . . . a life of engagement (wordly life: *pravrtti*) to renunciation (*nivrtti*) or disengagement, is not actually followed by Hindus these days that old age is becoming psychologically a burden.

Moreover, India is a country of many religions and viewing the basic credo of early Christianity from the gerontological perspective it could be stated as:

"Do not cast me off in the time of old age,
forsake me not when my strength is spent"

– Seventy first Psalm.

This deeply moving and piercing appeal was made centuries ago but unfortunately it received little attention until the twentieth century. Aging, a normal physiological process, has been a source of curiousity and fear from time immemorial but only after the mid-twentieth century has gerontology, the study of aging processes and problems (issues), become the focus of concern and subject of scientific inquiry. So far, research in gerontology and its application has been mainly the concern and interest of biologists, medical scientists and sociologists. For explicable, yet inexecusable reasons the psychologists and behavioural scientists did not enter the field till recently. Gerontology being comparatively a new discipline an interdisciplinary approach would develop a greater understanding of human aging which would provide valuable information for administrators and others who make policies and implement programmes to improve the quantity and quality of life for the millions already aged and the future aged.

The developing countries like India face the most rapidly rising proportion of aged and the accompanying problems. To develop programmes to reduce the problems of the aged and secure a brighter future for them, the need is for research on the aged in these countries.

The present book is an endeavour in this context. Aging is a continuous process influenced by unnumerable factors many of which are so intertwined that if not impossible would be difficult to unravel. However, researchers attempt is always to disentangle these factors and study their effect on the aging processes in order to develop a greater understanding of human aging. The book embodies the contributions of eleven researchers who have examined the psychological and adaptative processes in the aged and the effect of some psychological factors on these processes. The book is an attempt to give a comprehensive view of aging and the aged by presenting research studies on topics selected as representing the main concerns of gerontology from the psychological perspective. The bulk of the contents of *Psycho-social Aspects of Aging in India* deals mainly with different psychological aspects in later life, but these in the middle adult stages of life are also considered. The book provides firstly accumulated information on the state of gerontology and the demographics of aging in India followed by a chapter on theoretical explanations of human behaviour in later life. Furthermore, the book is divided broadly into six sections, each section examining aging from a specific aspect. The first section deals with an introduction to gerontology and theoretical approaches to aging. The two section deals with studies on personality and adjustment patterns, such as psychological needs, reactions to frustration, attitude towards death, etc., of the aged of both sexes in comparison to other age groups of the adult life periods. The three section includes studies investigating the effect of social stratification and age or sex on personality, adjustment patterns and life styles of the aged in India. This section examines how social class alone and in interaction with age or sex effects personality, attitudes toward death, strategies of coping with problems in later years of life and on the perception of old age as held by the community.

Section four includes researchers on retirement and investigate the perceived social supports and causes of stress and anxiety among retired males. Section five deals with institutionalisation of the aged and the effect of institutionalisation on the mental health of the aged with particular emphasis on depression, loneliness, hopelessness and modes of frustration. The concluding section i.e. section six presents the public's perspective on the aged and aging, care of the aged and retirement and conclusions. An extensive list of old age homes in India, state-wise is also included. And finally a comprehensive bibliography is incorporated on aging and the aged.

As always in any venture or project a number of people contribute towards its completion. The book would not have been possible without the input and efforts of my students who are the co-authors of the researches. Professor Mansharamani, former president of the Geriatric Society of India gave the encouragement to incorporate my ideas and researches on aging in the form of a book. I am also grateful to him for writing the foreword for this book. I would like to thank Mr. H.C. Jain, Librarian, University of Delhi South Campus, for help rendered in the location of material for this book.

Helpage India needs a special word of thanks for providing me financial assistance towards finalisation of the manuscript of this book. The moral boost and encouragement provided by Director General of Helpage India, Maj. Gen. R.S. Pannu (Retd.) cannot be expressed in words, especially since it came when I was up against a blank wall. I am grateful to Mr. P.N. Iyer, Head of Research & Development Division of Helpage India, for taking a keen interest and writing the prologomena for this book and thus, highlighting the relevance of the book even for those engaged in extending age-care services.

Finally, I would like to thank my parents who have been very encouraging and supportive in this work and their pride in my efforts has always been a great incentive.

PARAMJEET KAUR DHILLON

PROLEGOMENA

P.N. IYER,
Head of R & D Division, Helpage India

Ageing has always been known to be the final part of the journey in life. The elderly have been bestowed respect and reverance in all societies of the world. Those who have been blessed with a long life, have been considered as fortunate beings and their family has been bestowed greater respect from time immemorial. It is customary for people to dichotomise societies into traditional and non-traditional with respect to the relationship between the older generation and the younger one. History of societies all over the world, however, tell a different story. Anthropologists have described the age-sets as basic structures of primitive society. History of the ancient civilisations show that the elders were accorded special respect, and a high position. Coming to India, the ancient literature dating back to several millenia, are replete with references to the aged persons as the repository and vehicle of dissemination of wisdom, skills and traditions: and in fact, the very values of life which provide sustenance to the society as a whole.

The history of humanity has been witness to sweeping changes in the value systems and the context in which individuals are viewed by the rest of the society. It is unfortunate, and yet it cannot be denied, that the superficialities and external trappings have gradually gained ascendancy over the deeper values of life. This functional change in the value system has come about as a concomitant or side-effect of the Industrial Revolution in the past two Centuries. Even as the pace of 'progress' and 'development' has been accelerating, a remarkable acceleration in the replacement of old values by new ones has been noticed. The position of respect enjoyed by the elders since the beginning of civilisation and emergence of the Man from the caves, has taken a severe beating from the new cultural ethos. In retrospect, it is seen that the position of respect of the aged in society is inversely proportional to the so called 'progress' or 'development' of the human society. The net result is that control over human economic resources, and the possession of youthful vigour and a handsome visage are found to be the desired ends as a universal penchant. It is the expression of this illogical human desire that we find the craze for 'remaining young' assume the proportions of a creed in the Western Societies in the past few decades. The seeds of discontent and maladjustments are thus firmly planted and assidiously cultivated over the life time of those who are now victims of this scourge in their oldage today. It is this discontent and resulting conflict between the self-created illusions and the inevitable empirical realities, which are at the root of intractable socio-psychological problems among a vast majority of the aged in the Western Societies. Growing old with grace, acceptance of the inevitable bio-systemic changes of old-age, reformulation of life-styles and aspirations in keeping with one's own age, are some of the facts of life which lie hidden and submerged today.

Are we in India isolated or protected from this onslaught of illusion over reality? It is not possible to give a categorical reply, in an affirmative or a negative. It is partly true, and partly it is not. There are certain sections of this vast Indian society which have fallen a victim to the philosophy of self-centredness along with the Westernised style of life, and the perspectives and attitudes which go along with it. And yet, the strong bastion of values of life as handed down to all castes, races and religions being practiced in the Indian sub-continent, have proved immune to the alien values. Both these facets are to be found widely dispersed amidst the rural as also among the urban inhabitants. Inroads into the value system affecting the position and status of the aged in the society is not isolated to any particular social cohort, nor has it yet attained a superimposing position in any kind of societal classification scheme in the Indian sub-continent yet, whether on the basis of religion, language, varna, caste or sub-caste, linguistic affinity, city-town-village life, backwardness or forwardness either in terms of caste or education or economy. This is a feature which cannot be ignored when we are considering the 'life perspectives' of the elderly in the Indian Society. Because, it is a self-regulatory and self-correctional mechanism which is available to the society in India and the sub-continent, and has all but disappeared from the affluent societies of the North.

Herein lies a tragic case of the ascendancy of materialism, be it Capitalism or Communism: and, the victim of the tragedy is the old person who is deprived of his status and position, at a time in life when the individual is the weakest and most vulnerable due to the inviolate principles of the processes of biological ageing. This is the root-cause for reaching a state of severe trauma, with no feasible solutions in sight. This is the generalised picture which has been highlighted and projected in the gerontological studies carried out in the Western Societies. Even as the cloud has a silver lining — and, every coin has the other face, similarly, there is an equally uplifting and optimistic picture to be seen in the same Western Societies. There is a sizeable majority of the elderly and the aged in these societies too, which has protected itself from the harmful effects of the present day environment in their own society. This is so, not because some governmental agencies or enactments which have provided them a citadel. The fact is that while some surrender their selves to the prevailing norms, and a good many opt for sitting on the fence, there are also some who are able to stand like a rock unmoved and unaffected by the surge of waves which can only dash themselves and fall back into the ocean. It is this rock which provides a haven and refuge, for the stray boat which has lost its outboard motor. It is this an aspect of human ingenuity and the spirit of definance against all odds which provides sustenance for the growth and continuation of the human society *per se.* Such anchoring rocks are to be found embedded in the Western Societies among the aged, and it is their example which serves as a beacon to all.

Adjustment to the changed context in one's oldage is thus a question of developing an understanding about oneself in the context of societal environment. Perspective of the 'self', as per the change of time in the given milieu, is essential for adjustment in life. This is true for all times, climes and cultures, irrespective of age group to which a person may belong. This situation is compounded in the old age in most of the cases, even as it is universal in early childhood. Adjustment of life in oldage is thus a process of development. It is a myth that ageing provides an exended vacation from learning and development. This aspect has been amply dwelt upon by the sages and seers in India from ancient days, beginning from the *Rigveda* and the *Puranas* through the more recent commentaries and epics composed in all the major languages of India. The ancient Indian texts have highlighted the importance of the essential changes in the persons, as one moves around in the stream of life. This has been defined and elucidated by the division of the life cycle into four stages, called as *Ashram Dharma.* According to this four-fold classification, the first 25 years are for the acquisition of education, 26 to 50 years for performing the functions of a house-holder, 51 to 75 years, as the period of detachment from the human and material acquisitions, and the last 25 years (i.e. upto the age of 100 years) as the period of total renunciation from all attachments and submitting oneself of the pursuit of spiritual freedom. It is not to say that this set of principles has been followed by the majority in the past. However, the fact remains that these principles have continued to guide the Indian psyche as a desirable goal for achieving internal peace and harmony with the societal environment. The unbroken continuation of these traditional values are of immense importance to the social gerontologist, as also to the social workers and social policy-makers. An understanding of this concept is essential for a proper comprehension of the grids of psychological beingness of an elderly or aged Indian. These are the grids, because the perception of empirical existence are viewed through its invisible mesh (though predominating) by an individual, as also by the society with which the individual interacts.

It is an accepted principle of social engineering that social change is best brought about by reformulating and renovating the social organisation of the society within the framework of the prevailing social structures. Society is to be viewed as a dynamic reality and not as a static representation derived from analytical concept dependent upon statistics. It is the element of time which is crucial, not only for understanding a society, but also for understanding even an individual. There can be no controversy, when it is stated that individuals as an interacting whole form a society, and they give a form to it as a collective. Corollary to this statement is equally true. Namely, it is the society which provides the norms for behaviour and conduct of each of its individuals. Disharmony and disorganisation come about when either the individuals do not follow the norms for the common good, or when some sections of the society strike a different path. For the aged individual in India, the relevance of harmony of values is essential for their survival with dignity, respect and honour. The Indian society and the aged in India are mentioned, because, almost 99 per cent of the aged in India are being taken care of by the Society due to the continuity of traditions even today. It is a tragedy that even after 44 years of Independence, the economic conditions have not improved and the society is thereby unable to perform its functions as enjoined by the traditional value systems, towards the aged in their own respective and immediate environs.

The Indian case is an example *par excellence* of the will and intentions incapable of being sustained and practised due to economic restraints. Over 55 per cent of Indian population is below the poverty line, and it is anybody's guess as to how many are far below this invisible poverty line. Empirical evidence forcefully brings home the fact that the aged in India are forced to suffer the most amidst competing demands of other vulnerable and under-privileged sections of the society for a share from the scarce resources. Resource crunch has created a scale for prioritising the vulnerable sections. These priorities are either determined by the conceptualised utility of a designated section of the population, or due to the 'ballot power' of a section of the population. It is a sad commentary that in a land like India the aged find themselves as a neglected lot by the Welfare State, because their conscience cannot permit them to snatch the loaf of bread from a child, a woman, or any other under-privileged. The powers-that-be have decided that a person in India is past utility, at the age of 58 years. The statutory provisions have been undermining the position and status of the elderly, and have caused them immense harm by branding them as 'non-productive', when the available evidence totally negates this conclusion (Table 0.1).

TABLE 0.1: Economically Productive Population by Age Groups

(Percentage: Males only)

Age Group	1950	1975	1990	2000	2025
10-14 yrs.	41.40	21.90	13.63	9.46	2.16
15-19 yrs.	76.95	58.70	52.56	49.75	41.66
20-24 yrs.	93.55	88.60	87.45	86.82	85.00
50-54 yrs.	96.60	95.27	94.46	93.79	91.85
55-59 yrs.	96.00	91.75	89.63	88.06	83.54
60-64 yrs.	89.60	78.37	72.82	69.06	58.20
65 + yrs.	71.65	61.02	53.03	46.75	28.64

Source: World Demographic Estimates and Projections 1950-2025, 1988, page 265; Department of International Economic and Social Affairs, United Nations, New York.

Several societies in the West have seen the emergence of Grey Power. While the Grey Power movements have alleviated the conditions of a sizeable proportion of their ageing population, they have at the same time created a schism between the old and the young, thereby alienating and isolating the former from the latter in the social psyche itself. The inevitable backlash is already to be seen, and perhaps those who attain old age in the twenty first century will have to bear the consequences to an even greater extent. Taking a lesson from the West, India should steer clear of taking a line in advocacy for the aged, which will tend to isolate them from their own kith and kin, who are the *de facto* 'caregivers' to the elders. It is better to strengthen an edifice which has stood the test of time, rather than demolish it to build a new one, which is of doubtful strength and utility.

The aged in India are being increasingly isolated from the main-stream of life due to the rules of superannuation in the organised sector. It is in the unoragnised sector, which comprise of those who sustain themselves by self-employment, entrepreneurship, industriousness and plain hardwork, that persons continue to be productively engaged beyond the 'age of superannuation'. This is a fact which cannot be denied and herein lies a strange paradox. A close analysis of Table 0.2 clearly demonstrates that chronological definition alone is an injustice and a slur on the elderly. A marginal difference of the active population in the 50–54 as compared to 55–59 age group clearly demonstrate that there is no direct relationship between chronological age and activity. The slight fall in the next age cohort 60–64 is probably due to the statutry barriers which render a person inactive, rather than the intrinsic capacity to work.

It is time that the law \givers took a peep into the future and reviewed the superannuation rules in the context of life expectancy (Table 0.2). Unless, this is done, India is going to force upon itself a problem which can be easily avoided, namely perception of the elderly by the society as dependents and as burdens on the younger generation. This is a back-lash which is seen to be raising its head in the Western Society, and it will be wise if we initiate preventive action now, rather than acerbate the situation and face the wrath of a genie by creating it out of nowhere. If the Proverb "Look before you leap" is to be applied anywhere, it is with regard to the superannuation policy and the follow-up measures which need to be looked into.

TABLE 0.2: Life Expectancy in India 1950-55 to 2020-2025 A.D.

Period (A.D.)	Males (in yrs.)	Females (in yrs.)	Total (in yrs.)
1950-55	39.4	38.7	38.6
1960-65	46.2	44.7	45.5
1970-75	51.2	49.3	50.3
1980-85	55.6	55.2	55.4
1990-95	60.1	60.7	60.4
2000-05	64.4	65.9	65.2
2010-15	67.6	70.5	69.0
2020-25	69.6	73.6	71.6

Source: World Demographic Estimates and Projections 1950-2025, 1988, page 264; Department of International Economic and Social Affairs, United Nations, New York.

When we take a look at the future prospects of the aged in India, we have to take into consideration the change in the age structure of the Indian population (Table 0.3). Whereas 60 and above population rose in India from 5.62 per cent of the total population to 6.2 per cent between 1950 and 1975, a much more rapidly accelerating picture emerges in the Quarter Century periods following 1975. The 60 plus population is found to increase from 6,20 per cent to 8.39 per cent by A.D. 2000 and then a giant leap to 14.37 per cent. In other words, whereas the percentage of 60 plus population is expected to rise by 14.01 per cent between 1950 and 2000 A.D., a 14.37 per cent is predicted in half that period between 2000 and 2025 A.D.

TABLE 0.3: Changing Age-structure of Population in India

(Percentage)

Age Groups (in years)	1950 No. in 000s	1975 No. in 000s	1990 No. in 000s	2000 No. in 000s	2025 No. in 000s
0-14 yrs.	139,156 (38.92)	247,062 (39.80)	285,197 (34.48)	290,761 (30.16)	261,293 (21.26)
15-19 yrs.	36,849 (10.31)	63,479 (10.23)	86,970 (10.51)	94,353 (9.79)	89,291 (7.27)
20-49 yrs.	175,435 (49.06)	230,580 (37.15)	335,468 (40.56)	425,988 (44.19)	552,003 (44.92)
50-59 yrs.	22,869 (6.40)	41,089 (6.62)	59,023 (7.14)	72,103 (7.48)	149,709 (12.18)
60-69 yrs.	13,467 (3.77)	25,631 (4.13)	37,732 (4.56)	50,241 (5.21)	104,544 (8.51)
70+ yrs.	6,634 (1.86)	12,860 (2.07)	22,762 (2.75)	30,626 (3.18)	71,989 (5.86)
Total Population	357,561	620,701	827,152	964,072	1,228,829

Source: *World Demographic Estimates and Projections 1950-2025*, 1988, page 265; Department of International Economic and Social Affairs, United Nations, New York.

Note: Figures in the brackets indicate percentage.

It is a strange paradox that whereas longevity is expected to be in the region of 75 years by A.D. 2025 in India, a stage is being set which forebodes ageing to be viewed as a curse in the India of future, rather than be considered as a blessing. Corrective mechanisms are obviously called for. The place to start correctional work in this regard appears to be that the empirically and logically untenable mental constructs and determinants need to be shed unceremoniously without further delay. Second step is to provide for the utilisation of the skill and wisdom of the Grey Skill Banks as human resource potentials for social reconstruction and social developmental tasks, rather than discarding them to the waste-bin of the Nation. This calls for systemic balances, which have gone awry due to short-sighted, simplistic, bureaucratised, and politically motivated approach. This has been the greatest socio-psychological factor responsible for denigrating and dehumanising the prospect of growing old in India in the past few decades. Thirdly, family-support services should be strengthened for providing care for the elderly, especially those who are old among the aged (the Sanskrit term, understood in all Indian langauges of today is, *Vayovriddha*). Fourthly, it is only due to the pre-conceived biases, that the elderly and the aged are not only considered as a separate and distinct group by the policy-makers, but also that any special care made available to them are treated as being at the cost of the other sections of the population. Such an understanding aids the extension of pre-conceived schisms to the society itself. It does not require any elaborate exercise of syllogism to arrive at a conclusion that the current approach of dividing and sub-dividing an organic whole to suit immediate and short-sighted gains needs to be totally overhauled and eschewed. This is essential not only for protecting those who will be entering into the Grey Age in the twenty-first century, but also for protecting the society itself from getting disintegrated.

Psychology as a science of human behaviour has traditionally treated the individual as its subject matter, and sociology has been concerned with the network of human relationships. A meeting point has been found in the psycho-social studies, which are markedly electic in their approach and perspectives. The present attempt is not an exception either. Normal human beings, barring hermits, live in the company of others. The psychological state of an inividual is the product of experiences and influences of the socio-cultural environment to which the individual has been exposed all his life. It is the cumulative effect which creates an individual's psychology. It is a product of immediate experience viewed in the perspective of ingrained past experiences, which taken together, define the psychology at any given point of time. Thus, an individual's psychology is a dynamic process and has to be understood as such. Psycho-social studies enhance their utility when they are tried out in real-life situations for ameliorating the problems of a concerned section of society, by providing an empirical based model. The model for application has to be a dynamic one, as compared to a static model.

Secondly, even as the very term 'psycho-social' implies, the model for application must be multi-dimensional, it cannot be bound within a rigid framework, even as the immediate society of interaction of an individual itself is constantly exposed to the influence of the larger whole. Definition of 'society' is thereby an analytical construct in the main, rather than an 'empirical reality' in finite terms. Fourthly, it must be understood that the individual and the society are 'living' and 'developiong' organisms, and any attempt to withdraw this element from a model can only render it ineffective and non-operative. May be, the fate of many a well-intentioned schemes of the bureaucracy end up as dead-ducks due to this reason. One may well ask as to how can one steer clear of the pitfalls, and come up with a living model? The answer is simple. As long as an inquirer or a field worker is alive to the multiplex realities that surround the subject of study or work, the model will stay alive. Rigidity of approach leads to *rigor motis* of even the most dynamic model. On the other hand, deep-rooted empathy in an inquirer or field worker enables the model to come alive even if it had been delivered as a still-born. This is a miracle within the reach of everyone, the researcher not excluded. The miracle lies in increasing one's own capacities to get into the psyche of others. Though not easy, yet, not impossible either. The development of such a trait is essential when we are dealing with the elderly, because 'withdrawal', overt or covert, is more likely to be present among them.

A few more important considerations concerning the pyscho-social well being of the elderly in India remain to be high-lighted. First among these is the fact that the women in old age in India are found to be widowed much more, in comparison to the aged men. This is so despite the fact that the number and percentage of the aged males has continued to be higher as compared to the women upto the year 1991. Widowhood among women is due to the fact that there is an age difference at marriage, ranging from 5 to 10 years, between husband and wife. While the death rate as per sex is almost equal for men and women in the 50 plus years age-group, the mortality of the husband in his sixties often renders his wife a widow when she enters the sixties. Widowhood in oldage renders the women fully dependent upon the younger members of the family. And the situation is further worsened due to the social custom of headship of the family being confined to the oldest male member. The multi-faceted psycho-social dimensions of aged women needs to be studied in detail, and the implications for the individual are yet to be empirically investigated. The changes attendant upon widowhood can be understood only when a dynamic model is used. The model has to cater to those who own a property, as also for those who do not possess any. It has also to take into consideration the migration pattern as effecting the subject of enquiry in question.

The low literacy rates which are to be found among the elderly population of India today, adds to the complexity of any solution of their problems, including adjustment to the changing situation, and the identification and acceptance of new roles in later life. Illiteracy is a major contingent variable for a variety of psycho-social dimensions of life. This has to be constantly kept in mind by the researcher, and even more by the field worker, who has taken on the role of an 'agent of social change'

It is usual, at least it is customary, that all persons aged 60 and above in India are grouped together in the same compartment. Such an approach is not only violative of the empirical evidence, but it also leads to erroneous conclusions. It is empirically incorrect, because the processes of degeneration of the human orgnism continue to accelerate as an inevitable process in ageing. The sensory perceptions go on diminishing with the passage of time, once the regeneration of cells and tissues of the human body is not able to keep-up with degeneration. Loss of sight, loss of hearing, loss of suppleness and the strength of limbs, decrease in the rate and capacity of the digestive system, impaired functioning of the vasculo-circulatory system and the uninary system, are but a few examples to illustrate the point, that : Even among the 60 plus years age group, further classification and categorisation are required as per the health status of the individual. To press the point further the old among the aged, or the *Vayovriddha*, must be provided with special care and services, because they are the most vulnerable even amongst the vulnerable ones.

CONTENTS

Foreword
– Dr. G.G. Mansharamani 7
Preface 9
Prolegomena
– P.N. Iyer 13
List of Tables 25

PART I
AGING

Introduction 31
1. An Introduction to Gerontology 33
2. Theoretical Approaches to Aging 49

PART II
AGE, SEX AND AGING

Introduction 61
3. The Effect of Age and Sex on Needs, Social Adjustment and Reactions to Frustration
– *Paramjeet Kaur Dhillon* and *Sheila D'Souza* 63
4. Religiosity and Death Anxiety Across Age and Sex: An Inferential Analysis
– *Paramjeet Kaur Dhillon* and *Deepa Mathur* 81
Comments 95

PART III
SOCIAL CLASS AND AGING

Introduction 99
5. The Meaning of the Concept 'Old Age' as held by the Community
– *Paramjeet Kaur Dhillon* and *Anita Gupta* 103
6. Personality, Anxiety and Self Concept: A Study Across Age Variations and Social Class
– *Paramjeet Kaur Dhillon* and *Anju Jasra* 119

7. The Impact of Socio-economic Status and Sex on Emotional Maturity, Life Styles, Death Anxiety, and Religiosity of the Aged
– *Paramjeet Kaur Dhillon* and *Roma Kumar* 137
8. Coping Strategies Across Socio-economic Class: A Study of the Aged
– *Paramjeet Kaur Dhillon* and *Seema Chhabra* 167
Comments 179

PART IV
RETIREMENT AND AGING

Introduction 183
9. Anxiety Among Retired and Working Class I Officers: A Comparative Study
– *Paramjeet Kaur Dhillon* and *Seema Mitbander* 185
10. Perceived Social Support and Effect of Life Events: A Comparative Study of Retired Working and Non-working Males
– *Paramjeet Kaur Dhillon* and *Madhu Arora* 195
Comments 203

PART V
INSTITUTIONALISATION AND THE AGED

Introduction 207
11. Attitude Towards Institutionalisation of the Aged
– *Paramjeet Kaur Dhillon* and *Geeta Poduwal* 209
12. Emotional States of the Institutionalised Aged
– *Paramjeet Kaur Dhillon* and *Shalini Samat* 215
Comments 241

PART VI
PUBLIC VIEW OF THE AGED AND CONCLUSION

13. Public View of the Aged and Aging 245
14. Conclusions 289

Appendix:
Old Age Homes in India 291
Bibliography 307
Index 351

LIST OF TABLES

0.1: Economically Productive Population by Age Groups **17**

0.2: Life Expectancy in India 1950-55 to 2020-2025 A.D. **18**

0.3: Changing age-structure of Population in India **19**

1.1 Percentage Distribution of the Elderly in India's Population (1911 to 1991) **37**

1.2 Age Distribution of the Population, India, 1961-1981 **38**

1.3 Life Expectancy at Birth in India 1941-1981 **38**

1.4 Mortality Rates by Sex in the Age Groups 60+, India, 1975 and 1984 **39**

1.5 Trends in Population, India, 1901-1981 **40**

1.6 Percentage Distribution of India's Population by Age Groups (1911 to 1981) **41**

1.7 Percentage of Married, Widowed, Divorced or Separated population in each Age Group by Sex, India: 1971 and 1981 **43**

1.8 Distribution of population 60+ years by age, sex and completed level of education, India 1981 **44**

3.1 Summary of the ANOVA's for Frustration, Social Adjustment and Needs **71**

3.2 Mean and Standard Deviation on Frustration and its Modes, Social Adjustment and Needs in Relation to Age and Sex **72**

4.1 Schematic Presentation of the Sample **84**

4.2 Summary of the ANOVA for Religiosity and Death Anxiety **86**

4.3 Mean, Standard Deviation and Correlation between Religiosity and Death Anxiety in relation to going/not going to the temple **90**

4.4 Relationship of Demographic Variables to Religiosity and Death Anxiety for going/not going to the temple and for two age groups **92**

5.1 Summary of the Two-Way Analysis of Variance **109**

5.2 Mean and Standard Deviation on the Concept of Old Age and its Factors in Relation to Age **109**

5.3 Comparison of Means on Concept of Old Age and its Factors in Relation to Age: t-Values **111**

5.4 Mean and Standard Deviation on Concept of 'Old Age' and its Factors in Relation of Socio-economic Status and Age **115**

6.1 Mean and Standard Deviation on Personality Traits **128**

6.2 Summary of the ANOVA for the Personality Traits **129**

6.3 Mean and SD for Anxiety and Self-Concept **134**

6.4 Summary of the ANOVA for Anxiety and Self Concept **136**

7.1 Summary of the Two-way Analysis of Variance for Emotional Maturity and its Dimensions **150**

7.2 Mean and Standard Deviation on Emotional Maturity and its Dimension **152**

7.3 Summary of the Two-Way Analysis of variance for Life Styles **156**

7.4 Mean and Standard Deviation on Life Styles **158**

7.5 Significance of Mean Difference of the Comparison Groups on Significant Life Styles: t-values **159**

7.6 Summary of the Two-Way Analysis of Variance for Death Anxiety, Religiosity and Locus of Control **162**

7.7 Mean and Standard Deviation on Death anxiety, Religiosity and Locus of Control **164**

8.1 Schematic representation of the sample **171**

8.2 Mean, S.D., F Value and Response Percentage for each of the six Coping Strategies in relation to Socio-economic Status **175**

9.1 Mean Anxiety Scores on Overt and Covert Anxiety of the Retired and Working Men **189**

9.2 Analysis of Variance on the Five Components of Anxiety for the Working and Retired Groups **190**

9.3 Significance of Difference between Mean Scores of Working and Retired Groups along 5 Dimensions of Anxiety **192**

9.4 Responses of the Working and Retired Group on 5 Areas of Concern for Retirement **193**

10.1 Mean and Standard Deviation on Perceived Social Support for Retired Working and Non-Working Males **198**

10.2 Mean and Standard Deviation on Perceived Effect of Life Events for Retired, Working and Non-working Males **199**

10.3 Product-moment Correlations between Perceived Social Support and Perceived Effect of Life Events for Retired Working and Non-working Males **201**

11.1 Mean, SD and Significance of Mean Difference between Comparison Groups on Attitude towards Institutionalisation of the Aged **213**

12.1 Description of the Sample **225**

12.2 Summary of the ANOVAS for Loneliness, Depression and Hopelessness **230**

12.3 Mean and Standard Deviation for Institutionalised and Non-Institutionalised Aged on Loneliness, Depression and Hopelessness **231**

12.4 Correlation of Psychological and Demographic Variables in the Institutionalised and Non-Institutionalised Aged **232**

12.5 Mean and Standard Deviation on Frustration and its Dimensions **233**

12.6 Summary of the ANOVAS on Frustration and its Dimensions **236**

PART I
AGING

INTRODUCTION

Aging the process of growing old regardless of chronological age, is a continuous process that begins at conception and eventually ends with death. It refers to the regular changes that occur in mature genetically representative organisms living under representative environmental conditions as they advance in chronological age (Birren, 1959). A different and somewhat narrower viewpoint on aging has been expressed by Maynard-Smith and Comfort. Maynard-Smith (1962) defines aging processes as those which render individuals more suspectible as they grow older to the various factors, intrinsic or extrinsic, which may cause death, recognising that death may arise from a decline in the individual organism's ability to maintain its intrinsic function in the face of physiological stress from an extrinsic source such as accident or disease. Comfort (1960) describes aging as an increased ability to die, or an increasing loss of vigour, with increasing chronological age, or with the passage of the life cycle. Strehler (1962) proposed four criteria of aging that are widely accepted:

(1) Aging is universal, in that it occurs in all members of the population (unlike disease);
(2) Aging is 'progressive', a continuous process;
(3) Aging is intrinsic to the organism; and
(4) Aging is degenerative (as opposed to developmental or maturational changes).

Therefore, it can be stated that aging and death are fundamental, intrinsic biological properties of living organisms including humans.

'Aging' and 'Senescence' are often used interchangeably but 'Senescence' is a term which describes the group of deleterious effects that lead to a decrease in the efficient functioning of an organism with increasing age, and leads to an increased probability of death. Although 'Senescence' and 'aging' both describe the same process, senescence is often used in a restrictive sense to refer to the state of old age characteristic of the late years of the life span and infers to pathological effects. 'Senility' refers to the physical and mental deterioration often associated with old age.

Although people are classified as elderly after the age of 60, all organs of an individual do not age at the same rate and any specific organ does not necessarily age at the same rate in different individuals. As a result, different individuals undergo aging at different rates and some individuals may have symptoms of aging in their 40s, whereas others may not feel old even in their 70s.

However, signs of aging tend to start becoming noticeable after the age of forty. Aging is characterised by a general reduction in functional capacities and structural changes in the body for instance, gradual increase in body weight, degeneration of the elastic tissues of the skin resulting in wrinkling, deterioration in the hearing ability and vision, decline in muscle power, bone less and bladder control, deterioration of the muscles of the shoulders – shoulder width decreases, diameter of the hips increases, loss of elasticity in the lungs results in breathing problems, reduced efficiency of heart and circulation of blood, hormone imbalance, deterioration in some areas of the brain effecting learning and memory, etc. The apparent effects of physical and functional decline due to aging seem to be related to the psychological functioning and mental health of the elderly. For instance among the elderly raised blood pressure, cerebrovascular and cardiovascular disorders and lowered functional capacity are related to slower reactions (Birren *et al.*, 1979), many activities not performed as well as they were, less mobility and inability to respond to various stimuli. The decline in the ability to divide attention (try to do two things at once) results in difficulty in participating in group conversation, etc.

The interpretation of aging from the Adlerian (1870-1937) psychological perspective can be stated as 'physical decline, loss of status, beauty and other abilities result in feelings of inferiority and loss of self-esteem in later life which probably make the elderly not only more vulnerable and receptive to socially induced ageist attitudes of being incompetent, but also bring about changes in attitudes, life styles, coping strategies, personality and mental health of the elderly'.

The increase in the number of older people in every country has resulted in the study of human aging focusing on understanding the processes of aging in general and problems of old age in particular. So as to make the life of the elderly more fulfilling, satisfying and meaningful.

1

AN INTRODUCTION TO GERONTOLOGY

Grow old along with me
The best is yet to be,
The last of life for which the first was made.
– R. Browning
(*Rabbi Ben Ezra*)

As a white candle in a holy place
So is the beauty of an aged face
– Joseph Campbell
(*The Old Woman*)

Human beings proceed through a predictable course of biological development – leading from infancy to childhood, on to adolescence and youth, then to adulthood and middle age and finally to old age and ultimate extinction. This developmental sequence, according to McKee and Robertson (1975) 'is not simply a biological one; it is also a social process, because the nature of the life cycle – its length, its stages, its problems, its rewards – varies in accordance with the historical and social location of each individual and generation'.

The review of literature indicates that some stages of human development have been studied and researched more thoroughly than others. One stage of human development that had not received much attention until recently was old age. However, during the past two decades or so aging and the field of gerontology have become the focus of extensive concern, discussion, research, writing, and political action particularly, in the developed countries but also in the developing countries. To-day aging has become on issue and a subject of study and research as people in the medical and nursing professions and sociologists, psychologists, social workers, architects, policy-makers, as well as the general public are becoming sensitive to the issues and problems of the elderly.

Problems of the Aged: Traditional vs Western Societies

In most traditional societies of Asia, the process of the life cycle presented relatively few problems for in these societies roles and statuses were prescribed by the age and sex in a fairly rigid pattern, there were few significant options open to the individual as he or she proceeded through the life cycle, and the comparatively static nature of the culture provided stability in the roles and mutual interactions of the generations. These traditional societies usually accorded a respectable and an honoured place to the old who, because of their years of experience, were regarded the repository of the knowledge and wisdom of the community. Simmons (1945) in a study of traditional societies found that these communities offered such a satisfactory role to the elderly that many people looked forward to old age rather than fearing it. The old people were often the dominant member of the family, wielded considerable political power in the community and were expected to remain active in the community and to perform some forms of light labour. However, these traditional societies are now undergoing rapid changes because of modernisation, industrialisation and urbanisation and are adopting the western culture and philosophy, particularly that of the American Society. On the other hand the western society is oriented towards youth, mobility and activity and the aged have no honourable or useful place in society. The knowledge of aging and the aged, in this society, was dominated by myths, stereotypes, prejudices, ignorance and personal fears of growing old. Such myths and stereotypes could be dangerous and damaging to both the aging and the aged.

Crandall (1980) to emphasise this point has, given an illustration "if some one believes that 'senility' is an inevitable consequence of aging (it is not) then a relative who is old may be treated as though he or she were, in fact, senile. For example, if grandfather cannot remember something that took place forty years ago and his relatives believe that senility and aging are synonymous, then grandfather's forgetfulness may be interpreted as senility. If this happens, the concept of senility may be forced on him. His questions will be ignored since they will be seen as babbling. When he does not respond to questions or commands, it will reinforce the fact that he is senile, and not simply hard of hearing. When he has trouble in buttoning his shirt, it will be because his mind is 'gone' and not because he has arthritis. In time all of his behaviour will be defined as that of a senile old man. In an atmosphere in which individuals tell him he is senile ('let me do it for you') and act towards him as though he were senile, he may eventually begin to play the role of a senile individual. Infact, grandfather will either play the role expected of him or be severely chastised or worse drugged and put in an institution."

In western societies, in contrast to the traditional societies, the aged are deprived of defined roles and statuses and are poorly integrated into the social structure. They can no longer take it for granted to lay claim on their children or kin for support and social participation, and any advice given is likely to go unheeded for it would be considered irrelevant. There is a stigma associated with old age for the western society has created a way of life that emphasises youth, beauty, knowledge and intelligence are often associated with youth and even the accepted values of society are those of the young.

In old age physical and biological changes take place like hardening of the arteries and changes in the bone structure which lead to some medical problems, such as lack of mobility, problems in thinking, strokes, prostate and heart problems, bone fractures, eye diseases, arthritis and many more. These in turn effect the individual psychologically and result in changes in life style, emotional problems and poor health. In western countries the elderly have to face these problems by themselves with little help from children and relatives.

The impact of retirement is tremendous as it results in loss of role, status, power, opportunities for interaction and as Miller (1965) states "loss of an occupational identity", with the result the individual withdraws from society and has little social interaction. Therefore, retirement the point demarcating middle age from old age can lead to low morale, decreased levels of satisfaction, depression, feelings of loneliness and hopelessness.

Economics is another important problem in the lives of the aged. In summarising the impact of income on the aged in America the White House Conference on Aging (1971) setforth the following statement:

> "Only when their incomes are adequate and secure can the aged be expected to lead meaningful, self-respecting and independent lives."

Perhaps the most important problem confronting the aged to-day, particularly in the western countries, is how they are viewed by the general population. The elderly are perceived in negative if not in derogatory terms by other groups in society making old age to seem all the more dreadful.

Therefore, people particularly in the western world do not grow old gracefully, they try to maintain the appearance of youth even as it vanishes for old age is dreaded as a crises as it deprives a person of work opportunities, goals, roles, status and the onset of problems of adjustment. What are the reasons for the sudden interest in aging and the field of gerontology in India and other traditional societies? A number of factors can account for it – factors that stem from individual experience and from the changes taking place in society as a whole. The increasing number of people and percentage of the total population to age 60 and beyond have made the problems of aging more widespread, visible and ultimately more widely known. The transition of societies from traditional to modern industrialised societies, especially in countries like India, is also highlighting the problems faced by older people to the general public, government and researchers.

A Demographic Profile of the Aged

A profile of the aged will be given by examining a number of demographic variables of the Indian population. The demographic characteristics examined will be such as changing sex and age composition, life expectancy, urban/rural growth, birth rate, etc. The pronounced changes in demographic characteristics over the years and decades whether they may have come about as a result of physical factors such as epidemics, floods, drought or as a result of social factors such as changing ideas about children, marriage, migrating to urban areas, have resulted in tremendous changes in the social structure of the society. In the proceeding pages the demographic variables as they relate to the aged will be examined, specifically the growth of the elderly population in India and a social demographic profile of the aged.

Growth of the Elderly Population in India

In 1911, there were 2.52 million Indians over the age of 60, comprising 1.4 per cent of the total population. In 1971, 32.593 millions were over age 60, comprising approximately 5.95 per cent of the total population.

In 1981 there were 42,840,000. Indians over 60 years, comprising approximately 6.2 per cent of the population. Today there are approximately over 50 million Indian over the age of 60 (Provisional estimates : *India Today* 1991). Table 1.1 presents the percentage distribution of India's elderly in the population and depicts how rapidly the 60+ age group is growing compared to the population since 1911.

TABLE 1.1: Percentage Distribution of the Elderly in India's Population (1911 to 1991)

Year	Population in millions	% 60 and above	60 and above population in million
1911	252	1.0	2.52
1921	251	1.2	3.012
1931	279	1.5	4.185
1951	361	5.57	19.855
1961	439	5.64	24.79
1971	548	5.95	32.59
1981	685	6.21	42.53
1991	843.9		50.00 + (Provisional estimates)

Source: Census of India 1981, Part IV-A; Social and Cultural Tables; C-2 Table; IAMR Fact Book on Manpower, P. 12; and Aggarwala, S.N. 1973, *Population In India*.

Not only are more people living to age 60 but once they reach that age they live longer. In 1961 there were 2.56 per cent persons in the age group 60-64, 1.11 per cent in the age group 65-69 and 1.96 per cent in the age 70+ but in 1981 the figures for the elderly changed and there were 2.73 per cent persons in the age group 60-64 years, 1.43 per cent in the age group 65-69 years and 2.33 per cent in the age group 70+. Table 1.2 shows the increase in the population in the age groups of the elderly during 1961-1981.

The changes in the elderly population in India are mainly due to the mortality rate and life expectancy. These factors will be examined (See also Chapter 13).

Life Expectancy

The life expectancy is the factor responsible for the greatest growth of the aged population. In India life expectancy at birth was 32.1 years for the decade 1941-51, 32.5 years for the males and 31.7 years for females. Compared to the figures of earlier decades, the average expectation of life improved considerably. It was 54 years in 1981 and today the provisional estimate is that it is almost 62 years (*India Today*, 1991) Table 1.3 shows the changes in the life expectancy at birth during the last couple of decades. There are almost an equal number of males and females in age groups of the population above age 60.

TABLE 1.2: Age Distribution of the Population, India, 1961-1981

Age group	1961			1971			1981		
	Persons	Males	Females	Persons	Males	Females	Persons	Males	Females
0- 4	15.06	14.68	15.47	14.51	14.15	14.90	2.55	12.28	12.85
5- 9	14.73	14.63	14.86	14.96	14.86	15.07	14.08	14.03	14.13
10-14	11.23	11.62	10.82	12.55	12.85	12.22	12.92	13.16	12.65
15-19	8.18	8.22	8.12	8.66	8.88	8.42	9.64	9.89	9.37
20-24	8.51	8.05	8.99	7.86	7.60	8.15	8.62	8.43	8.82
25-29	8.33	8.19	8.48	7.45	7.16	7.75	7.62	7.49	7.77
30-34	7.03	7.07	6.98	6.60	6.45	6.77	6.37	6.28	6.47
35-39	5.80	6.02	5.57	6.00	6.07	5.93	5.84	5.79	5.90
40-44	5.21	5.34	5.06	5.16	5.30	5.01	5.14	5.24	5.03
45-49	4.11	4.31	3.91	4.18	4.39	3.94	4.39	4.47	4.31
50-54	3.90	4.04	3.75	3.75	3.91	3.57	3.82	4.02	3.61
55-59	2.24	2.34	2.14	2.34	2.42	2.25	2.47	2.47	2.46
60-64	2.56	2.52	2.60	2.62	2.64	2.61	2.73	2.73	2.73
65-69	1.11	1.09	1.12	1.28	1.28	1.27	1.43	1.39	1.47
70+	1.96	1.84	2.09	2.06	2.02	2.12	2.33	2.28	2.38
Age not stated	0.04	0.04	0.04	0.02	0.02	0.02	0.05	0.05	0.05
Total	100.00	100.00	100.00	100.00	100.00	100.00	100.00	100.00	100.00

TABLE 1.3: Life Expectancy at Birth in India (In years) 1941-1981

Period	Males	Female	Overall
1941-51	32.5	31.7	32.1
1951-61	41.9	40.6	41.2
1961-71	47.1	45.6	46.4
1971-81	54.1	54.7	54.0

Source: Census of India, 1971, Age and Life Tables, and Census of India, Paper I of 1984.

Life expectancy is dependent on the incidence of mortality rates which is turn depend on a large number of factors such as the occurrence of epidemics, the prevalence of diseases, the level of nutrition attained by the people of a country, the conditions of living, care of women, infant mortality rates, etc. While poverty of the Indian people is at the root of the phenomenon of short life span, the discovery of wonder medicines to control epidemics, the general improvement in medical assistance, the public health measures taken under the various plans have further reduced death rates. Even then, the present level of life expectancy in India does not compare favourably with America where the life expectancy is over 72 years.

Mortality Rate

The rate of growth of population is a function of birth rate and death rate. The death rate stood at 36.3 years per thousand in 1921-30 and it came down to 18.9 years during 1961-70. It further showed a decline during 1971-80 and became 15.0 per thousand.

There is a decline in the death rate not only in the population as a whole but also in the age group 60+, though the mortality rate is still very high in the older age group as compared to other age groups.

TABLE 1.4: Mortality Rates by Sex in the Age Groups 60+, India, 1975 and 1984

Year		60-64	65-69	70 & over
1975	Total	38.5	56.3	113.2
	Male	39.6	59.0	120.3
	Female	33.3	53.7	106.4
1984	Total	39.3	46.2	107.1
	Male	36.1	50.6	110.8
	Female	30.4	41.9	103.4

Source: Verma, 1988. Handbook of population statistics, Census of India.

The decline in mortality in India, both for the population as a whole and the aged in particular has meant greater longevity of the aged and thus, helped to increase their number in the total population.

Profile of the Aged

The composition of the population can have a tremendous impact on the social structure of a society. Some of the social demographic characteristics of the aged such as sex ratio, dependency, marital status, place of residence and education will be examined.

TABLE 1.5: Trends in Population, India, 1901-1981

Census year	Population			Sex ratio (Females per 1,000 males)	Rural	Urban	% age of urban population to total population
	Persons	Males	Females				
1901	238,396,327	120,791,301	117,358,672	972	979	910	10.84
1911	252,093,390	128,385,368	123,708,022	964	975	872	10.29
1921	251,321,213	128,546,225	122,774,988	955	970	846	11.18
1931	278,977,238	142,929,689	135,788,921	950	966	838	11.99
1941	318,660,580	163,685,302	154,690,267	945	965	831	13.86
1951	361,088,090	185,528,462	175,559,626	946	965	860	17.29
1961	439,234,771	226,293,201	212,941,570	941	963	845	17.97
1971	548,159,652	284,049,276	264,110,376	930	949	858	19.91
1981	685,184,692	354,397,884	330,786,808	933			23.31

1981 figures of India include the projected population of Assam where Census could not be held owing to disturbed conditions prevailing there at the time of 1981 Census.

Sex Ratio

There is a variation in the sex rates between the western and the Asian countries. In the western countries the trend has been in favour of a feminine population whereas, in Asia, in general, and in India in particular, the trend has been in favour of a masculine population and this trend still persists. In fact, the number of females per thousand males are on the decrease, both in the rural and urban India. In India the death of more females in comparison to males is due to social and economic factors which explain the fact why the otherwise biologically superior female cannot reverse the trend of excess males to females.

The sex ratio indicates an unequal distribution between the sexes in the different age groups (Table 1.2).

However, it is noticed (Table 1.2) that the trend of males in favour of females in the age groups of the elderly has changed if not actually reversed.

There are almost an equal number of males and females in the age groups of the population above age 60.

Dependency Ratio

The dependency ratio compares the number of economically productive versus economically non-productive individuals. The working age of the population in India is considered as 15-60 years. The aged dependency percentage is on the increase since the past few decades. Table 1.1 shows that in 1971 there were 32.59 million aged dependents whereas, in 1981 the figure of the aged dependents became 42.53 million. Today the provisional estimate is that there are approximately over 50 million aged dependents.

Since India is not a highly industrialised society the burden of the aged dependents would to a large extent fall on the productive population.

Place of Residence and Living Arrangements

About 76.69 per cent of India's population still resides in rural areas (Table 1.5). Thus, a large majority of India's aged also reside in the villages which lack medical facilities, mass transportation and community facilities. The aged residing in rural areas, particularly the men have comparatively more leisurely life style and companionship than the aged living in the urban areas.

The elderly in the rural areas reside usually with their son's family and are still to a large extent integrated in the village society. The aged living in the urban areas also to a large extent reside with their children or children reside with them and it is only a small percentage of the elderly who live independently from their children.

TABLE 1.6: Percentage Distribution of India's Population by Age Groups (1911 to 1981)

Year	0-14	15-60	60 and above
1911	38.8	60.2	1.0
1921	39.2	59.6	1.2
1931	38.3	60.2	1.5
1951	37.4	57.1	5.5**
1961	41.0	53.3	5.7
1971	40.65	53.4	5.95
1981	39.5	54.3	6.2

* For age group 15-64

** For the age group 65 and above.

Source: IAMR Fact Book on Manpower, p.12 and Census of 1981, Part IV-A, Social and Cultural Tables, C-2 Table; and S.N. Aggarwal, 1973, *Population in India*.

Marital Status

In 1971 about 79.3 per cent older men in the age group 60-64 years were married as compared with 36.7 per cent older women, 62.5 per cent older women were widowed by the age 64 years as compared with 17.6 per cent older men. The same trend in observed in 1981, though the percentage of older women widowed by the age 64 years decreased by 6.52 per cent during the decade 1971-81 (Table 1.7).

This trend would indirectly have a tremendous influence on the structure of the society and the degree of dependency for majority of the older women who were not in employment would have to depend entirely on their son's for survival as they may not have independent income.

Education

The total number of persons of age 60+ according to the 1981 census, were 43,167,386 of which 22,022,868 were males and 21,144,518 were

TABLE 1.7: Percentage of Married, Widowed, Divorced or Separated Population in each Age Group by Sex. India; 1971 and 1981

Age group	Male Female	Total			Rural			Urban		
		Married	Widowed	Divorced/ Separated	Married	Widowed	Divorced/ Separated	Married	Widowed	Divorced/ Separated
1971										
60—64	M	79.3	17.6	0.3	78.8	18.1	0.3	81.9	14.7	0.3
	F	36.7	62.5	0.4	37.1	62.2	0.4	34.9	64.0	0.4
65—69	M	76.7	20.2	0.3	76.1	21.0	0.3	79.4	16.8	0.2
	F	34.7	64.1	0.3	35.1	64.1	0.3	32.6	66.8	0.3
70 +	M	66.8	30.0	0.3	66.3	30.5	0.3	69.5	27.0	0.4
	F	19.5	79.6	0.3	19.8	79.4	0.2	18.4	80.2	0.3
1981										
60—64	M	83.44	14.12	0.39	82.73	14.87	0.42	86.37	11.09	0.27
	F	43.17	55.98	0.48	43.67	55.57	0.49	41.13	57.69	0.46
65—69	M	80.58	17.06	0.38	89.87	17.82	0.40	83.49	13.95	0.30
	F	40.79	58.41	0.41	41.72	57.56	0.42	37.04	61.83	0.35
70 +	M	70.45	27.12	0.39	69.81	27.82	0.40	73.19	24.14	0.32
	F	21.72	77.57	0.30	22.16	77.22	0.31	20.01	78.95	0.29
15—44	F	80.43	2.89	0.75	83.71	3.02	0.83	73.43	2.50	0.52
15—49	F	80.68	4.05	0.75	83.69	4.19	0.82	74.11	3.62	0.53

females. Out of the total males and female of age 60+ only 7,662,473 males and 1,667,519 females were literate and the rest were illiterate (Table 1.8).

The lower levels of education for the aged reflect the fact that in the past occupation was not as dependent on higher education as it is today. In the past, only a very small percentage of women were gainfully employed outside the house and still a smaller percentage were employed in jobs where higher education was essential. In the past low levels of education did not work against the aged, as they often do in the contemporary society.

TABLE 1.8: Distribution of Population 60+ Years by Age, Sex and Completed Level of Education, India, 1981

	Males	Females
Total literate population	7,66,243	1,667,519
Non Formal	400,145	100,231
Formal	2,416,398	635,367
Primary	2,574,759	637,493
Middle	1,083,293	182,372
Matriculation/Secondary	758,692	74,396
Higher Secondary/Intermediate	1,39,105	11,184
Non-Technical diploma/certificate	9,286	2,309
Technical diploma/Certificate	40,057	7,299
Graduate & above	240,739	16,868

Source: Verma (1988), A Handbook of population statistics, Census of India 1981.

Concepts/Terms used in the Study of Older People

The study of aging and the aged has created a new vocabulary, some of the words commonly used are: Gerontology, Social Gerontology, Aging and the Aged.

Gerontology: The study of old age comes from the Greek words '*Geras*' meaning 'Old age' and '*logos*' referring to a study or description of something. Gerontology is a broad term and encompasses the psychological, socio-economic and physiological aspects of aging (Reed, 1966). Though gerontology was recognised during the 1940s, but it was not until the late 1970s that interest was first shown by writers, social reformers, medical personnel and psychologists, on the physical and mental limitations of people during the early, middle and late adult years.

Zarit (1977) discussing the scope of gerontology stated that it is especially concerned with "differences in aging, how some people may age successfully, how others may experience increasing difficulties, how one person may continue learning and growing while others get stuck, lost in the past. . . . Gerontology is not concerned merely with problems but also with the possibility of continuing growth in older people. Overall it is the study of 'the whole person' and the aging process as reflected in all aspects of life functioning."

Social Gerontology, is a subfield of gerontology and is concerned with the reciprocal relationship between the individual and society, such as the effects of physical changes on the individual as determined by the societal values placed on those physical conditions.

Aging refers to the process of growing old, or developing qualities of the old: maturing, changes that occur as the result of the passing of time. According to Birren (1959) "aging refers to the regular changes that occur in mature genetically representative organism living under representative environmental conditions as they advance in chronological age." Aging is experienced as an inevitable and life long process. Scientifically, all organisms can be said to be aging from the moment of conception. Aging can thus, be viewed on a continuum, with conception at one end and death on the other. Indivicuals are considered to be in the growth period for the first 25-30 years of their life and after that in the period of decline or aging. Generally the aging process is very slow and gradual, individuals are not socially defined as aging until the aging process produces noticeable effects such as balding, greying hair, wearing bifocals, etc., (Crandall, 1980). However, not all aspects of the human organism are necessarily in close synchrony in the process of aging. While an individual may be declining physically in the later years he may show an expansion in the psychological domain. Aging is often defined biologically, chronologically, socially and psychologically (Neugarten and Datan, 1973)

1. *Biological Age*: The central feature of biological aging is how long the individual of the species will live. Thus, the biological age of a person is his present position relative to his potential life span. Biological age, thus defined is closely related to chronological age but

is not identical with it, since it is derived from a different set of measurements.

2. *Chronological Age*: The term chronological means in order of time. Chronological age is measured for each person from the time of birth in a socially determined way. According to Treichel (1980) chronological aging refers to the time that elapses from birth, providing others with some clue to the roles and patterns of behaviour that are to be expected to us as members of a particular age group. The behaviour of a five-year old child is quite different from that of a 45 year old. Thus, chronological age assumes importance in the human life cycle. Since old age is negatively defined many people invest large sums of money and go to great lengths to look young. Treichel (1980) distinguishes between chronological aging, primary aging and secondary aging. Primary aging refers to biochemical changes that accompany chronological aging. These are considered to include the daily loss of thousand of cells in the individual's brain, a tendency for facial skin to dry out by age 30, and gradual deterioration of parts of the body, until finally death occurs. Primary aging is considered to be to some extent genetically determined. Secondary aging, is primary aging that has been accelerated as a result of a lifetime of stresses – emotional tension, physical trauma, disease or other insults to the body.

3. *Social Age*: Social age is a system of segregating people into different levels of maturation according to social factors. It refers to the social habits and roles of the individual relative to the expectation of his group and society.

4. *Psychological Age* is a system whereby maturity is measured in terms of capabilities, adjustment, and knowledge. It refers to the adaptive capacities of individuals as observed from their behaviour but may also refer to subjective reactions or self-awareness.

Aged: The term 'aged' refers to 'Old, Elderly, Ancient, Antiquated'. *The Chamber's Twentieth Century Dictionary* (1964) defined aged as 'advanced in age'. Crandall (1980) states that the term aged is harder to define. A ten-year old is likely to think of someone as aged after age thirty. On the other hand, a 65-year old may think as aged those individuals 75+ years of age. It is thus difficult for researchers to decide when an individual is aged. Generally the term 'aged' refers to 'those individuals who are 65+ years of age'. The terms, 'aged', 'older' and 'elderly' are often used synonymously. In India the age of retirement for government employees in 58 years and in semi-government institutions it is 60 years. Therefore, in India the term 'aged' could refer to those individuals who are 60+ years of age for re-employment after super annuation for a period of 5 years is given only to a chosen few.

Conclusion

The scientific study of aging and the aged is comparatively of recent origin. The interest in the field of gerontology is growing very rapidly not only in the developed countries of the world but also in the developing countries, particularly India, where the aging population is on the increase.

A demographic analysis shows that the aged population in India represents 6.4 per cent of the total population, are living mainly in rural areas in joint families with their children and grand children, have a high percentage of illiterates, and a greater number of aged widows than widowers. However, there is an increase in the growth of the urban population over the decades and there is a rapid transition of the urban society from traditional to modern and western which will increase the problems for the aged.

The increasing concern and interest in aging and the aged has led to the creation of new concepts such as gerontology, social gerontology, aging, aged and many others.

2

THEORETICAL APPROACHES TO AGING

Human have always been intrigued by the process of aging and the possibility of controlling it and perhaps even of eliminating death. Despite centuries of profound human concern, however, aging remains poorly understood yet excessively theorised about. Theories that explain human behaviour during the later years of life are as follows:

Disengagement Theory

This theory is the most persistent influential, and controversial in gerontology. Disengagement theory contains three basic propositions according to two of its proponents (Cumming and Henry, 1961):

(i) A process of mutual withdrawal of aging individuals and society from each other is a usual occurrence.
(ii) This process of withdrawal is inevitable.
(iii) It is also necessary for successful aging.

In its simplest form this theory states that aging involves an inevitable withdrawal or disengagement, resulting in decreased interaction between the aging person and others in the social milieu to which he or she belongs.

Atchley (1972) stated that disengagement is not usually a single event but instead a gradual process that involves the separation of an individual from several of his or her regular social roles and activities. The disengagement theorists recognise that although the process of disengagement is inevitable, variations will occur because of difference in health and personality. These theorists believe that high levels of life satisfaction are associated with the aged person's reducing of the number and importance of his roles. Thus, happiness in old age consists of individuals recognising the fact that they are no longer young and that there are more competent individuals to fill their roles.

This theory was formulated from the Kansas city studies. In these early studies a significant decline in social interaction, current role activity, age involvement in current roles and activity change was noted with increasing age. The disengagement theorists felt that the decline in various functions was logical, since it brought about a natural, normal satisfying process called disengagement.

The theory maintains that those entering old age must gradually be phased out of important roles in order for society to function. Society must be able to replace persons whose ability to perform adequately in an important position becomes questionable through old age or otherwise. If old age is a problem (which this theory says it is) than it is necessary to be able to move the aged person out of the key position and into a less important one. The disengagement of the society from the individual is only half of the disengagement theory, the other half of the theory maintains that the individual himself withdraws from certain social roles when he becomes old. The more roles an older person withdraws from the less that person is bound to society's norms. The disengaged person is thus, able to play a particular social role that allows him or her to become increasingly more self centered and more preoccupied with personal interests. To the extent that the disengagement process allows the aged person to assume such a role, the more successful the aged person will be in retirement. The basic assumption of the theory is that both the individual and society are gratified by the process. For the individual, the withdrawal brings a release from societal pressures for continued high level productivity and performance. For society, the withdrawal of the older members presumably allows younger, more energetic, competent and recently trained persons to assume the roles that must be filled in the social system.

Activity Theory

Activity theory is the antithesis of the disengagement theory. This theory, as suggested by Havighurst (1963), is primarily an action theory for successful aging. It consists of three basic premises:

(i) the majority of the normally aging persons will maintain fairly constant levels of activity;

(ii) the amount of engagement or disengagement will be influenced by past life styles and by socio-economic considerations rather than by some intrinsic inevitable process; and

(iii) that it is necessary to maintain or develop substantial levels of social, physical and mental activity if aging experience is to be successful.

The assumption of the activity theory is that the relationship between the social system and the personality system remains fairly stable as an individual passes from the status of middle age to that of old age. It holds that the norms for old age are the same as those for middle age, and that the older person should be judged in terms of middle age criteria of success.

Successful aging consists of being or behaving as much as possible like a middle aged person. According to activity theorists, any exhibition of behaviour by older persons that would not be appropriate in middle aged persons is considered maladjustment. This theory might be referred to as the "golden-years" concept of aging. It claims that to be happy in old age individuals need to keep active. Happiness is achieved by denying the onset of old age and by maintaining the middle-aged way of life, values and beliefs for as long as possible. Activity theorists believe that if existing roles or relationships are lost, it is important to replace them. Replacement of roles and relationships is necessary because when activity drops, there is corresponding drop in level of life satisfaction. Thus, this theory emphasises the stability of personality system orientations as an individual ages, and ignores any need for societal structured alternatives to compensate for losses that the individual experiences as part of the aging process.

There is research that supports the activity theory. In a longitudinal study, carried over a period of 10 years, Palmore (1968) found that older men tended to show almost no overall reduction in their activities or life satisfaction while older women tended to have a small reduction in their activities or life satisfaction. He pointed out that his data were obtained from persons who were relatively healthy and therefore, disengagement may be more typical of the less healthy. His point was that disengagement by the elderly is not an inevitable product of aging. It was found that activity was significantly related to high morale and life satisfaction.

One of the major criticism of this theory is that it may not be role activity that determines high morale, rather it may be that those with high morale can form friendships and have a greater probability of staying active than those with low morale. Another problem is that many older individual's happiness is not obtained by staying active for many older individuals prefer what might be called a rocking chair approach to old age.

Continuity Theory

This theory is somewhat more recent than the others and is based on the premise that the various stages of the life cycle are characterised by a high degree of continuity. As a person grows to maturity and passes to the stages of later maturity and old age the individual develops rather stable values, attitude, norms, habits that become an integral part of his or her personality. The manner in which an individual will react to the aging process will thus be influenced by that person's attempts to maintain characteristic traits and predispoitions. The predispositions to act in certain ways are always subject to change or modification because of the ongoing and sometimes complex forms of interactions people have with others and with the environment during all stages of the life cycle. Thus, although there is a tendency towards consistency, the theory admits that people also change by adapting to new situations. In other words continuity theory starts with the single premise that the individual will try to maintain as long as possible his or her preferred life style, and than holds that adaptation can go in several different directions depending on how the individual perceives his or her changing status and attempts to adjust to this change. Continuity theory does not assert that one must be disengaged or active in order to be well adjusted in the later years but rather, that the decision regarding which roles are to be discarded and which maintained, will in large part be determined by the individual's past history and preferred style of life.

Age Stratification Model

Age stratification has been set forth as a model to explain the behaviour of the aged (Riley, Johnson & Fonner, 1972). The age stratification model perceives age as an important determinant of behaviour for two reasons. First, age may limit the ability of the individual to perform certain roles. Second, society differentially allocates rights, roles, privileges and opportunities on the basis of age.

Age is a variable that determines the types of roles and options available to individuals. Chronological age can effect role performance because of biological, legal or social restrictions, that is, biological age limits role alternatives. Thus, this theory states that as stratification of society is on the basis of classes, castes or social strata, according to this perspective age is the basis of stratification of society. Children, teenagers, young adults, mature adults and older persons could be identified as the distinct status groups in the society, each acquiring different roles on the basis of their age. Persons of different age groups are viewed and treated differentially in all societies. Thus, age is a significant factor in social stratification and the basis of qualifying or disqualifying individuals for different roles.

Although the age stratification model has been well received by researchers, it has some problems. The first problem is that the theory does not take into account different social classes, or racial, or ethnic groups and their perceptions and expectations. Society everywhere is stratified not only on the basis of age but also on the basis of race, ethnicity and other variables.

The Exchange Theory

This theory offers a new perspective from which to view the process of aging and the interaction between the individual and the social system. Dowd (1975) believes that the decreased social interaction in older age can perhaps best be explained in terms of an intricate process of exchange between society and its older population resulting from the older people's power dependent relationship. The basic premises of the exchange theory are: (i) society is made up of social actors in pursuit of common goals. (ii) Pursuing these goals, actors enter into social relations with other actors; these entail some costs in the form of time, energy, effort and wealth. (iii) Actors expect to reap as their reward the achievement of desired goals; for this they are willing to assume the necessary costs. (iv) Regardless of the nature of the exchange relationship, each actor will attempt to maximise rewards and minimise costs. (v) Exchange processes are more than an economic transaction, since they involve intrinsic psychological satisfaction and need gratification. (vi) Only those activities that are economical will be repeated. Power enters the exchange relationship when one of the participants in the exchange values the rewards gained in the relationship more than the other participant does. The exchange theorists view of power is that it is derived from imbalances in the social exchange. Blau's (1964) perspective is that much of social life is an intricate exchange in which every participant in social interaction approaches and withdraws in patterns that add to or subtract from his or her store of power and prestige.

In viewing aging as exchange Dowd argued that decreased social interaction is the eventual result of a series of exchange relationships in which the power of older persons relative to their social environment is gradually diminished until all that remains of their power resources is the humble capacity to comply. Thus, from this perspective aging workers primarily face a problem of decreasing power resources, as there particular skill or expertise becomes out moded or its value reduced and thus, have to exchange that is of value. The exchange theory states that older person's disengagement is not mutually satisfying for the individual and society as claimed by the proponents of the disengagement theory, but rather in the exchange relationship between older persons and society, society enjoys a distinct advantage.

Labelling Theory

This theory has been traditionally used by sociologists to explain criminal behaviour and mental illness. Bengtson (1973) has suggested that this theory can be used to explain some of the behaviour of the aged. The basic assertion of labelling theory is that one derives the concept of self from the interaction with other people in one's social milieu. One tends to think of oneself in terms of how other people define her/him and react to her/him. The behavioural corollary of the labeling theory is that once others have defined her/him into distinct categories, they react to her/him on the basis of these categories; and as a result the self concept and behaviour changes of the labelled person. Thus, from the labelling perspective, the behaviour of older persons may largely depend on the reactions of significant others in their immediate social milieu. The reactions of these significant others depend on how they define and categorise the elderly. In essence, the theory states that through the process of labelling, individuals are forced into acting out specific roles.

Labelling theory suggests that when a label such as "senile" or "old", is given, it has a significant impact on the way individuals will be treated and perceived by others. As labelled individuals they take on new identities, positions and roles. Often the new identity becomes what is called a "master status". The master status is simply the status that over rides all others. It is the status that others are quick to notice and respond. This theory does not maintain that most or all individuals who have the label "senile" are in fact "normal". The theory simply points out the fact that labels can have a tremendous impact on the way in which one reacts to others.

Personality Theory

This theory attempts to explain the contradictions reported in the disengagement theory and activity theory.

One of the major proponents of this theory is Havighurst. He claims that both disengagement and activity theories are inadequate to explain the data. He claims that disengagement and activity theorists have incorrectly focused on the amount of activity as the important variable in determining the life satisfaction. He believes that it is not the level of activity but rather the personality type that is the pivotal variables in determining life satisfaction. In other words, different personality types need different levels of activity for high life satisfaction.

Subculture Theory

Rose and Peterson (1965) proposed that the aged form a subculture and that it is this subculture that defines and gives direction to their behaviour.

Rose believes that a subculture among age groups emerges when the group members interact with each other significantly more than they interact with persons in other age categories. This, he asserts, occurs when the members (i) have a positive affinity for each other due to such factors as long-standing friendship or common problems, interests or concerns, and (ii) are excluded from interaction with other groups in the population to some significant extent. Both sets of circumstances, according to Rose and Peterson (1965), apply to the elderly of most societies in which most often the elderly are not actively involved in an occupation or career, are dependent on others for their income, and are generally excluded from the mainstream of life.

The proponents of the subculture theory recognise that many of the distinctive behaviours of the aged result from factors other than the aged subculture, for example biological changes, social norms, and generational changes. However, subculture theorists generally believe that of all the subcultures to which an aged individual belongs, the age subculture is the most powerful. In other words, the ethnic, religious, gender, social class, or occupational subculture are over ridden by age subculture.

Role Theory

Several writers have setforth the belief that behaviour in old age can be explained through role theory (Phillips, 1975; Cavan 1962). A role, is behaviour expected from individuals who occupy certain positions (e.g. father, teacher) or a certain status. Most role theorists use what is called the dramaturgical model. The major idea behind the dramaturgical model is that just as actors play different roles on the stage, so individuals play different roles in everyday life.

In "real" life, the behaviour of an individual is determined by the roles he occupies in society. The roles one holds in society have what might be called "Social Scripts" attached to them .

In everyday life there are numerous directors; that is, there are many individuals who have the power to make another act in what they consider to be an appropriate manner. These directors have power and can supply sanctions in order to make certain that one performs one's roles according to the standards they lay down for them. The directors of everyday life play roles such as mother, teacher, boss, coach, or wife.

Because an individual interacts with others in everyday life, he/she has reciprocal influence on others. The position of those who are interacting, as well as their behaviours and moods, are generally taken into consideration in interaction. Thus, in everyday life one's behaviour is determined by the roles of those with whom one interacts and the way in which the individuals in those roles are behaving.

Although a very general theory of old age, role theory can be used to explain the wide fluctuations of behaviour seen among the aged. These variations result from the fact that individuals have defined, the situations differently, have interpreted and responded to the looking glass self in different ways, or have considered different selves to be appropriate for certain situations (Thomas & Biddle, 1966).

Phenomenological Theory

This theory first appeared in the *American Behavioural Science Journal* in the form of an article by Snygg (1941) and was later elaborated by Combs & Snygg (1959). The basic idea behind phenomenological theory is that to understand human behaviour one must understand the individual's perceptual world. It has been recognised that individuals see the world very differently from one another. The major idea is that through life experience and socialisation, one develops a perceptual framework through which he/she selectively perceives and interprets the world. Thus, individuals can perceive the same phenomena very differently. For example, aged individuals may respond differently to such phenomena as retirement, health changes, or widowhood. The differences in their responses is not due to the phenomenon in and of itself but to the individual's interpretation or perception of the phenomena.

Conclusion

The hidden purpose behind these theories has been the design of interventions either to help individuals age successfully or to stop the aging process entirely. Because of methodological difficulties, pre-experimental biases, and lack of multidisciplinary focus, there is no one theory that unifies the biological, psychological and social perspective on aging. Aging is a multidirectional approach. Various theories explain and predict limited aspects of aging, but even these theories view aging as a static condition rather than as a dynamic process. Theoretical approaches to aging, however, have the potential for refinement, enhancement and synthesis.

PART II

AGE, SEX AND AGING

INTRODUCTION

Chronological age is an important variable in all societies for on its basis all societies make assumptions about the appropriate behaviours and level of functioning of different age groups. Individuals have rights, roles, opportunities and responsibilities, assigned or denied to them on the basis of their age. Thus, there are societal norms and expectations about how one is to respond and behave at any age in life. In India a mother may scold her seventeen-year old son "to grow up and act his age" and a man who has grown up children and is 55+ of age will be referred to as a "wicked man" if he shows an interest in the opposite sex when Indian society generally believes that he is at an age when he should no longer be interested in sex.

On the basis of age grading the life span is divided into different periods or developmental stages. Generally speaking there are three life periods: Infancy, Juvenile period and Adulthood, each further subdivided into different stages (Bromley 1974). The life-period or developmental stage approach illustrates that as individuals grow old, they go through periods that are separate and distinct from other periods in regard to rights, roles, responsibilities, physical characteristics, capabilities, psychological and social needs and patterns of behaviour. Individuals throughout their life in almost all societies, move into and out of life periods as a result of chronological age, though the age of the onset of the life period may vary from society to society. Gerontologists are generally interested in studying the physical, social and psychological characteristics of the life periods that fall after age 60+ and compare them with other life periods to understand the nature of the changes and the cause of these changes.

The first study in this part is in the same direction, that is, it investigates the social and psychological needs, social and emotional adjustment levels and the modes of reactions to frustrating situations of the age group 60+ and compares it with two other age groups 30–40 years and 45–55 years.

Death and dying is another variable which is often associated with old age, for death in industrialised societies is most common among those who have retired from work, have fulfilled their parental responsibilities and are beyond the age of 60. The industrial revolution and the ever-advancing medical technology has significantly reduced death among children, teenagers and the young adults. Thus, death is often thought of as happening to someone who is very old. According to Cox (1984) the young often think that it is not going to happen to me today, tomorrow, or even next year or for twenty, thirty years from now. I may die but that's so far off, Why worry about it?

The most prevalent attitude towards death is fear and Bengston *et al.* (1977) found age to be a critical factor in explaining one's fear of death. They observed that young perceive death as so far in the future that it evokes little or no concern. The middle-aged are likely to be increasingly aware of the slowing of certain biological functions and the finiteness of their lives but often have not had time to think of and fear death. The old have most frequently come to accept death as inevitable. The elderly develop coping mechanisms to deal with this undesirable and inevitable reality of death. Malinowski (1948) believes that hope for a life after death is the only thing that makes the fear of death manageable. In other words, religion reduces the fear of death and Malinowski (1948) in this regards states, "religion steps in selecting the positive creed, the comforting view, the culturally valuable belief in immortality in the spirit of the body and in the continuance of life after death." No wonder then, that the aged consider religion to be more important in their lives than other age groups. Harris (1975) in a study observed that religion was considered to be very important in the lives of 34 per cent of those 18–24, 45 per cent of those 25–39, 58 per cent of those 40–54, 65 per cent of those 55–64, 69 per cent of those 65–69, 71 per cent of those 70–79, and 73 per cent of those 80+.

The study on religiosity and death anxiety is an attempt to investigate the degree of religiosity and fear of death in the age groups 60+ and compare it with the age groups 50–60 years. The study also tries to ascertain the relationship of religiosity and death anxiety in the two age groups and the sexes.

3

THE EFFECT OF AGE AND SEX ON NEEDS, SOCIAL ADJUSTMENT AND REACTIONS TO FRUSTRATION

PARAMJEET KAUR DHILLON and SHEILA D'SOUZA

The declaration of 1982 as the year of the aged has resulted in highlighting various issues of the aged and the aging process, with special emphasis on individual differences in growth and experience, learning and capacity to live successfully. Aging refers to the regular changes that occur in mature genetically representative organisms living under representative environmental conditions as they advance in chronological age (Birren, 1959). Elaborating the changes within the life cycle Kuhlen (1968) emphasised change in the motivational factors. He proposed that motives change during the life course because certain needs (achievement power, self-actualisation, creativity) have been fulfilled and because of interim changes in social position. There is a shift from active direct gratification . . . to gratification obtained in more indirect and vicarious fashion in the later half of life. Neugarten (1972) found that as people grow old, sex role reversal occurs: while men become passive, withdrawn and reserved, women move in the opposite direction, their need dominance and need affiliation becomes stronger than compared to men. The aging men come to accept their changing social emotional needs, while aging women are unable to do so. Apart from changes in self concept (Monge, 1971) and the need to avoid risk (Botwinnick, 1966), there are also changes in emotionality (Yunus, 1960; Willoughby, 1935), life satisfaction (Tobin & Neugarten, 1961) and frustration tolerance (Cumming & Henry, 1961).

An individual's emotional adjustment, social maturity, flexibility, need patterns, frustration tolerance and coping strategies affect his social adjustment, which is a social equilibrium with low conflict. It is true that, as a person grows older and his experience widens, he learns from them so as to be able to cope with problems and conflict situations in a consistent, positive and mature manner, with greater compatibility of responses, and greater variety of coping styles, resulting in a higher level of social adjustment.

The above mentioned findings of investigators indicate that social adjustment and some psychological variables affecting social adjustment are age related. Therefore, it seems essential to review the literature on social adjustment, needs and reactions to frustration in relation to age and sex.

Needs

A need is a motivational concept and is equivalent to such terms as motive, wish, drive and urge. Needs almost always refer to some want or lack or deficit in an organism involving a physiological disequilibrium or a psychological tension. Needs form the core of personality and behaviour.

Studies related to Needs.

Ahammer and Baltes (1972) conducted a study on three age groups – adolescents (15–18 years), adults (34–40 years) and older people (64–74 years). The Jackson personality inventory was administered to them to study how adults, adolescents and older people view themselves and each other by asking them how desirable it is to be affiliative, nurturing, autonomous and achieving. Data were analysed by analysis of variance. Results indicated that both adolescents and older people felt that being affiliative was desirable than middle aged people. Middle aged adults were more concerned about achievement than the younger and older men. On need for autonomy and independence, and need for nurturance there were no significant differences between the three age groups but the younger and middle aged men perceived the older men to be more nurturant and less independent than they perceived themselves.

Smith (1970) investigated the relationship of age and achievement motivation. Subjects were 89 male volunteers distributed by decade intervals between 21–69 years. Results revealed that there was little systematic relationship between age and achievement.

Davis (1966) studied the aspiration tendency in three different age groups 20–30 years, 40–58 years and 66–85 years. Baseline level was obtained using the Rotter Level of Aspiration Board and change in aspiration after the introduction of a fictitious peer group norm was measured. Results indicated that older men maintained as high a baseline of aspiration as did younger ones and were equally responsive to socially determined failure. After the experience of success however, they decreased their aspiration level while the young men increased theirs.

Neugarten *et al.* (1964) conducted a sequence of inter-related studies over a period of 10 years on samples of persons ranging in age from 40–80 years. The results showed consistent age differences in intrapsychic dimensions, e.g., a change from active to passive mastery in relating to the environment and a change from outer world to inner world orientation which was described as increased inferiority. As related differences were apparent, older men seemed more receptive than younger men to their affiliative, nurturant and sensual promptings.

Social Adjustment

Social adjustment is commonly defined as the changes in habitual conduct or behaviour which an individual must make in order to fit into the community in which he lives (Warren, 1962). The term also indicates the process by which an individual or a group reaches a state of social equilibrium in the sense of experiencing no conflict. Social adjustment has two major components: Emotional adjustment and Social maturity.

Studies related to Social Adjustment

Douglas and Arenberg (1978) studied the relationship between age and temperament using the Guilford Zimmerman Temperament Scale. The scale was administered to 915 men from 17–98 years of age. Results showed that general activity declined only after the age of 50. Thoughtfulness and personal relations showed a short-term cultural decline, whereas, friendliness showed a long-term cultural decline.

Cameron (1967) conducted a study on 320 subjects, half young adults and half over the age of 59 years. They were administered the Eysenck Extraversion Scale to test for age difference in ego-centricity and introversion. Results indicated that typical aged females are more egocentric and introverted than young adult females. But no difference between young and aged males along either dimension was found.

The results of a study by Willoughby (1935) on 500 unmarried women, 325 unmarried men and 275 couples within the age group of 15–75 showed that women were significantly more emotional than men. The trend for males showed evidence of peaks of emotionality in early maturity and old age and relative freedom from emotionality in adolescence and middle life.

Phillips (1961) in a study of 257 individuals 60 years of age or older and their close associates, analysed the relationship between role changes, various aspects of subjective age and adjustment. Findings indicate that the relationship between aspects of subjective age and adjustment are most consistent. The results of a study by Bhatia (1983) on four age groups: 20–30 years; 30–50 years; 50–60 years and 60 and above, showed that there were no consistent changes in values and self concept with increase in age.

Frustration

Frustration has been defined as the condition of being thwarted in the satisfaction of a motive (Harriman, 1947), or 'as any interference with a goal response or with instrumental act leading to it, (Sears, 1946). Frustration has been taken as a motivational determinant (Bower, 1962; Parney 1960), an inhibitor (Doob & Gross, 1968; Estes 1958), and a primary-oriented phenomenon (Sargent, 1948). However, frustration once aroused gets expressed in various modes, such as aggression, fixation, regression and resignation.

Studies related to Frustration

Brichacek (1980) administered a satisfaction and frustration questionnaire to 1,968 males aged 20–60 years. The results indicated that in life frustration culminates between 30 and 40 years. In younger and older subjects it is markedly lower and in the 6th decade of life it is the lowest. The differences are not due to changes in value orientation, which is relatively independent of age, but rather to the feeling of less satisfaction.

Cason and Dean (1963) compared four age groups within the age range of 10–90 years on annoyability as reported by men and women. The results indicated that annoyability was highest in the age group 40–60 years and lowest in the age group 60–90 years. The extent of anger expressed by aged subjects is also shown to have a relationship to the degree of boredom and to whether or not the subject was employed.

Cumming and Henry (1966) in a study of over 200 men and women, within the age group of 50–59, tested the hypothesis that frequency and intensity with which people experience certain active emotional states such as anger and irritation decline with age. The results proved the hypothesis.

Devi (1967) carried out a study on sex differences in reaction to frustrating situations. The sample consisted of 220 subjects (110 males and 110 females) from the middle socio-economic background. The chi-square test was applied for testing significance. The results showed a significant difference between males and females in their reaction pattern to normal frustrating situations. Female subjects appeared to be regressive and liked withdrawal behaviour as compared to male subjects. Males were found to be more aggressive.

The review of literature shows that there is a scarcity of research both in India and abroad on the modes of frustration, social adjustment and needs of people in different stages of the life cycle. Taking the aforesaid observation in view a study was conducted to ascertain the level of frustration, degree of social adjustment and the need patterns of three age levels (comprising both males and females): 30–40 years, 45–55 years, and 60 years and above; belonging to the middle social class.

METHODOLOGY

The objective of the study was to determine the effect of age and sex on level of frustration experienced, modes of frustration, social adjustment and the need patterns. Hypotheses: The following hypotheses were formulated:

1. The three age groups and the sexes will differ significantly in the degree of frustration experienced.

    (a) With increase in age there will be an increase in the use of resigned and fixated responses to frustrating situations.

    (b) Women will use more resigned and fixated responses to frustration than men.

    (c) The younger age groups will use more regressive and

aggressive reactions to frustration in comparison to the older age groups.

(d) Males will resort more to aggressive reactions and woman to more regressive reactions to frustrating situations.

2. There will be a significant difference in the level of social adjustment of the three age group and the sexes:

   (a) With increase in age social adjustment, social maturity and emotional adjustment will increase.
   (b) Men will be more socially mature, socially and emotionally adjusted than women.

3. The three age groups and the sexes will differ significantly in their higher order needs:

   (a) Younger the age group greater the need for achievement, affiliation and succorance in comparison to the older age group.
   (b) Males will have a greater need for achievement than females, whereas females will have a greater need for affiliation and succorance.
   (c) With increase in age the need for nurturance will increase.
   (d) Women will have greater need for nurturance than males.

Sample

The sample consisted of 240 married men and women, belonging to the middle socio-economic class. These 240 subjects comprised of three age groups: 30–40 years, 45–55 years and 60 and above years with mean ages of 34.5 years, 49.3 years and 64.5 years respectively. Each age group consisted of 40 married men and 40 married women from various occupations/professions. In all three age groups, the male respondents comprised of engineers, doctors, lecturers, bank officers, executives and businessmen having medium size business, women respondents on the other hand comprised of doctors, nurses, lecturers, bank officers, or wives of officials.

Tools

1. Frustration was assessed by Chauhan and Tiwari's Frustration

test (1972). This test measures the behaviour mechanism of frustration and makes frustration accessible to quantitative analysis. The intense cathecticity and conativeness of frustration gets expressed in various modes such as aggression, fixation, regression and resignation. Aggression has been defined as 'an act whose response is injurious to an organism' (Dollard *et al*, 1939). Fixation has been taken as a defense against anxiety by stopping the process of development (Symonds, 1946). Regression means a return to an earlier mode of adjustment. Resignation is an emotionally tinged attitude shown by cessation of active response to a situation where previously efforts were made to alter the situation. The test consists of 40 items, 10 items for each of the four modes of frustration: Aggression, Fixation, Regression and Resignation. Each of the 40 items have five alternative answers (multiple choice) graded on a 5 point scale on the positive dimension and a zero point on the negative dimension. A total score and a score for each mode of frustration can be obtained from the test. Higher the score more the frustration potential and lower the score more the frustration free behaviour. The test-retest reliability coefficients for the four modes ranged between .78 to .92. Reliability of the test according to age, sex, grade and culture has also been calculated.

2. Social adjustment was measured by Deva's Social Adjustment Inventory (1982). In this inventory social adjustment is assessed by two components: Emotional Adjustment and Social Maturity. The inventory consists of 85 items scaled according to the Thurstone's technique of 'equal appearing intervals'. An emotional adjustment score and a social maturity score can be obtained from the inventory. The social adjustment score of an individual is obtained by adding the emotional adjustment and social maturity scores. High scores indicate poor adjustment and low scores good adjustment. The inventory yields satisfactory reliability and validity indices. The test-retest reliability coefficient was .91 and the validity coefficients of the two scales 'emotional adjustment' and 'social maturity' were .81 and .79 respectively.
3. Needs were assessed by Edwards Personal Preference Schedule (1959) adapted by Tripathi (1973). This schedule provides a quick measure of a number of relatively independent

personality variables. These variables originate from a list of manifest needs presented by Murray. Of the 15 needs measured by the TPPS, only four needs: Affiliation, Succorance, Achievement and Nurturance, have been measured for the purpose of this study.

4. A personal data schedule was devised to obtain relevant information about the respondents's age, educational level, sex, marital status, profession, etc.

Procedure

The subjects were approached personally and rapport was established. On assurance of strict confidentiality the personal data schedule along with other scales was administered to the respondents. The respondents were requested to give the first response that came to mind and to complete all the questions in each scale.

Results and Discussion

In order to test the hypotheses both descriptive and inferential analyses were computed. Table 3.1 shows the summary of the ANOVA'S for frustration. The ANOVA table shows that the main effect of age on frustration is not significant. Table 3.2 shows that the mean scores of the three age groups are almost similar. This means that the amount of frustration perceived by the three age groups is almost the same. The main effect of sex is significant on frustration experienced ($F = 18.53$, $p < .01$). The mean score (Table 3.2) of males is higher than that of females. This implies that males experience a greater amount of frustration than females. The explanation for this finding seems to lie in the socialisation of females, particularly in India, where girls are taught to tolerate frustration. The interaction effect of age and sex is also significant ($F = 540.08$, $p < .01$). The cell means reveal that females in the age group 30–40 years and 45–55 years experience if not more almost the same amount of frustration as males in these age groups, but in the age group 60 years and above males experience a greater degree of frustration than females. The hypothesis stating that the three age group and the sexes will differ significantly in the degree of frustration experienced has been only partially proved.

TABLE 3.1: Summary of the ANOVA's for Frustration, Social Adjustment and Needs

Variables	Sources of Variation										
	Age Groups			Sex			Age Groups × Sex			Error	(Within Cell)
	df	s^2	F	df	s^2	F	df	s^2	F	df	s^2
1. *Frustration*	2	104.76	2.77	1	700.41	18.53**	2	20409.63	540.08**	234	37.79
i. Regression	2	43.21	1.15	1	18.15	.483	2	97.82	5.27**	234	37.57
ii. Fixation	2	29.205	.944	1	57.04	1.84	2	2.57	.081	234	30.95
iii. Resignation	2	194.88	4.41*	1	123.27	2.79	2	150.06	3.39*	234	44.27
iv. Aggression	2	401.4	11.84**	1	650.11	19.18**	2	107.96	3.19	234	33.89
2. *Social Adjustment*	2	1190.85	0.819	1	15746.4	10.83**	2	3983.75	2.74	234	1453.43
i. Social maturity	2	234919.85	381.0**	1	476583.06	772.96**	2	231692.95	375.78**	234	616.57
ii. Emotional adjustment	2	1989.54	7.36**	1	614.4	2.27	2	838.14	3.10	234	270.25
3. *Needs*											
i. Achievement	2	4.212	.400	1	2.816	.267	2	20.205	1.92	234	10.53
ii Succorance	2	2.72	.193	1	51.34	3.65	2	14.79	2.10	234	14.08
iii. Affiliation	2	92.47	6.10**	1	160.02	10.56**	2	26.11	1.72	234	15.15
iv. Nurtimance	2	18.25	1.143	1	113.44	7.11**	2	35.78	2.24	234	15.96

** $p < .01$ level; * $p < .05$ level.

TABLE 3.2: Mean and Standard Deviation on Frustration and its Modes, Social Adjustment and Needs in Relations Age and Sex

Variables		Age Groups										
		30—40 years			45—55 years			60 & above years			Total	
		Males	Females	Total	Males	Females	Total	Males	Females	Total	Males	Females
1. *Frustration*	$\bar{X}$	103.35	104.26	103.81	100.65	102.46	101.56	109.55	96.55	103.05	104.52	101.1
Modes:	SD	17.09	15.09	16.13	14.28	13.99	14.17	12.53	9.79	12.99	13.20	12.30
i. Regression	$\bar{X}$	29.58	30.65	30.11	29.15	30.6	29.88	30.83	26.65	28.74	29.85	29.30
	SD	5.11	4.32	4.76	4.75	8.36	6.84	5.06	7.55	6.75	5.03	7.21
ii. Fixation	$\bar{X}$	27.10	27.68	27.39	26.85	28.10	27.48	27.95	29.03	28.48	27.29	28.27
	SD	5.23	6.02	5.65	4.09	6.19	5.29	5.96	5.17	5.61	5.17	5.84
iii. Resignation	$\bar{X}$	22.00	20.68	21.34	20.93	22.23	21.60	26.28	22.05	24.16	23.80	21.65
	SD	8.97	6.61	7.90	6.78	6.57	6.70	6.52	1.73	5.21	7.85	5.52
iv. Aggression	$\bar{X}$	26.55	25.33	25.94	23.90	21.08	22.49	24.65	18.83	21.74	25.03	21.74
	SD	5.75	5.38	5.59	5.91	7.43	6.86	5.73	3.63	5.61	5.90	6.30
2. *Social Adjustment*	$\bar{X}$	90.36	88.38	89.35	96.50	79.89	88.19	97.18	67.15	82.16	94.67	78.47
Dimensions:	SD	34.25	36.00	35.15	46.18	33.18	41.06	40.09	34.53	40.32	44.30	32.20
i. Social Maturity	$\bar{X}$	47.08	40.83	43.95	56.78	47.08	51.93	55.55	32.60	44.08	53.13	40.17
	SD	26.66	21.24	27.39	25.84	25.87	26.31	26.54	24.21	27.87	26.89	24.58
ii. Emotional	$\bar{X}$	43.28	47.55	45.41	39.48	32.55	36.01	41.30	34.35	37.83	41.35	38.15
Adjustment	SD	15.87	19.92	18.13	19.15	13.24	16.82	14.69	13.21	14.39	16.75	17.14
3. *Needs:*	$\bar{X}$	14.66	14.78	14.73	14.15	15.43	14.79	14.73	14.0	14.36	14.52	14.73
i. Achievement	SD	3.82	2.92	3.40	3.02	3.24	3.19	3.76	2.17	3.09	3.56	2.87
ii. Succorance	$\bar{X}$	12.98	12.98	12.98	12.45	14.15	13.30	12.45	13.53	12.99	12.63	13.55
	SD	3.39	4.07	3.74	4.82	3.03	4.12	4.14	2.18	3.35	4.17	3.22
iii. Affiliation	$\bar{X}$	12.43	12.93	12.68	13.73	15.93	14.83	12.55	14.90	13.73	12.90	14.58
	SD	4.71	4.08	4.41	3.43	3.47	3.59	4.17	2.99	3.81	4.18	3.74
iv. Nurturance	$\bar{X}$	14.48	15.30	14.89	14.83	15.23	15.03	14.33	17.23	15.78	14.54	15.92
	SD	3.34	3.87	3.64	4.14	3.88	4.02	3.88	4.47	4.48	3.31	4.19

The total score on frustration was the aggregate of the separate scores on the different modes of frustration. Therefore, the investigators felt that separate analysis should be computed for the four modes of frustration. The two-way analysis shows that the main effects of age and sex are not significant on Regression and Fixation. However, the interaction effect of age and sex is significant on the regressive mode of frustration ($F = 5.27$, $p < .01$). The cell means (Table 3.2) reveal that though females in the age groups 30–40 years and 45–55 years use regression as a mode of expressing frustration more than males but in the age group 60 years and above males use regression more than females.

The hypotheses stating that the younger age group and women will resort more to regressive behaviour than the older age groups and males have not been accepted. The results of the study also reject the hypotheses stating that fixated responses will increase with advancing age and females will resort more to fixated responses than males.

The ANOVA table indicates a significant main effect of age on Resignation ($F = 4.41$, $p < .05$). A glance at the mean scores (Table 3.2) shows that people in the age group 60 years and above make the maximum use of resignation ($\bar{X} = 24.16$) as a mode of frustration followed by the age group 45–55 years ($\bar{X} = 24.16$, $\bar{X} = 21.60$, $t = 2.69$ $p < .01$) and 30–40 years ($\bar{X} = 24.16$, $\bar{X} = 21.34$, $t = 2.66$, $p < .01$). The main effect of sex is not significant on resignation ($F = 2.79$ NS). Table 3.2 however, shows that the mean score of males is higher than that of females but the difference is not large enough to be statistically significant. The interaction effect is significant ($F = 3.39$, $p < .05$). The cell means show that males in the age groups 30–40 years and 60 years and above use resignation as a mode of frustration more than females in these age groups, but in the age group 45–55 years females use resignation more than males. This means that the use of a mode of frustration depends upon the sex of the individual and the age group to which one belongs rather than simply on chronological age. The hypothesis stating that with increase in age there will be an increase in use of resignation responses has been accepted but the hypothesis regarding women using more resigned responses to frustration than males has been rejected.

The analysis of variance shows that the main effect of age is significant on Aggression ($F = 11.84$; $p < .01$). The mean scores indicate that subjects in the age group 30–40 years use aggressive reactions to frustration more than those in the age groups 45–55 years

($\bar{X}$ = 25.94, $\bar{X}$ = 22.49, t = 3.48 p < .01) and 60 years and above ($\bar{X}$ = 25.94, $\bar{X}$ = 21.74, t = 4.77, p < .01). This means that with increase in age aggressive reactions decrease. The explanation for this finding seems to be that the young being more hot blooded and impulsive, therefore, react in a more aggressive manner, whereas, with age impulsiveness decreases and reasoning becomes more predominant, thereby, decreasing aggressive reactions. The main effect of sex is also significant on aggressive reactions to frustration (F = 19.18, p < .01). A glance at Table 3.2 shows that males have a higher mean score than females. This indicates that males make more use of aggressive reactions to frustration than females. The plausible explanation of this finding lies in the socialisation of males and females in the Indian society, where it is accepted that males can use aggressive reactions to frustration but not females.

The interaction effect of age and sex is also significant on aggression (F = 3.19, p < .05). The cell means reveal (Table 3.2) that males are more aggressive than females in all the three age groups but the difference between the sexes in the use of aggressive reactions to frustration becomes larger with increase in age, that is, males in the age group 60 years and above use much more aggressive reactions ($\bar{X}$ = 24.65) than females ($\bar{X}$ = 18.83) of this group, as compared to males of the other two groups.

The results prove the hypotheses that younger age groups make more use of aggressive reactions than older age groups and that males resort to more aggressive reactions that females. The findings on frustration reveal that (a) age does not significantly effect the overall frustration level, nor the modes of regression and fixation. Age significantly effects the use of the modes of resignation and aggression. Males in the age group 60 years and above use resignation more as a means of coping with frustration as compared to males of the other two age groups; (b) females experience less amount of frustration and make less use of resignation and aggression as a means of dealing with frustration in comparison to males; and (3) the interaction effect of age and sex is significant on overall frustration, modes of Regression, Resignation and Aggression.

SOCIAL ADJUSTMENT

To test the second hypothesis two-way analysis of variance was computed and Table 3.1 shows that age has no significant effect on social adjustment. The mean scores (Table 3.2) do show a slight difference between the three age groups on social adjustment but the difference in the mean scores in not large enough to be statistically significant. However, the results reveal a tendency for the older age group to be better adjusted ($\bar{X}$ = 82.16) than the younger age groups 45–55 years ($\bar{X}$ = 88.19) and 30–40 years, ($\bar{X}$ = 89.35).

The results indicate that the main effect of sex is significant (F = 772.96, p < .001) on social adjustment. Males have obtained a higher mean score ($\bar{X}$ = 94.67) than females ($\bar{X}$ = 78.47) implying that females have a better social adjustment than males. The interaction effect is not significant. However, the cell means (Table 3.2) indicate that the mean scores of males in all the three age groups is higher than females, implying that females have a better social adjustment than males, irrespective of age. The explication for this finding lies in the process of socialisation, where women are taught to adjust and accommodate to situations more than men, and in the prevailing Indian social conditions, women generally have little identity of their own.

The results reject the hypotheses that males are more socially adjusted than females and younger age groups are more socially adjusted than older age groups.

The two components of social adjustment: Social Maturity and Emotional adjustment were analysed separately, and the results are presented in Tables 3.1 and 3.2. The ANOVA results show that age has a significant effect on Social Maturity (F = 381.00; p < .001). A glance at the mean (Table 3.2) scores shows that the age group 45–55 years has the highest mean score followed by the age groups 60 years and above and 30–40 years. This implies that people in the age group 45–55 are the least socially mature ($\bar{X}$ = 51.93, $\bar{X}$ = 43.95, t = 1.88, p < .05; $\bar{X}$ = 51.93; $\bar{X}$ = 44.08, t = 1.83, p < .05) as compared to the other two age groups. This means that people in this group feel more insecure probably because of the middle-age problems that they face and have still not acquired the coping strategies of the older group and the coping skills of the younger group are no longer of much use to them. This is probably the reason why they feel less confident, more insecure and more is need of help and attention which makes them socially immature.

The main effect of sex on social maturity is also significant (F = 772.96; p < .01). The mean scores indicate that females are more socially mature ($\bar{X}$ = 40.17) than males ($\bar{X}$ = 53.13). The interaction effect of age and sex is also significant. The cell means (Table 3.2) show that though females are more mature than males in all the age groups (mean scores are lower) the difference in the level of social maturity between the sexes increases with age. The results of the study do not prove the hypotheses that with increase in age social maturity increases, and that males are more socially mature than females.

On Emotional adjustment age has been found to have a significant effect ($F = 7.36$, $p < .01$). The mean scores show that people of the age group 45–55 years have a better emotional adjustment than people of the age group 30–40 years ($\bar{X} = 37.83$; $\bar{X} = 45.41$; $t = 3.39$, $p < .01$). There is no significant difference in the mean scores between the age groups 45–55 years and 60 years and above. The results indicate that people of the age-group 30–40 years are the least emotionally adjusted ($\bar{X} = 45.41$, $\bar{X} = 37.83$; $t = 2.93$, $p < .01$) which implies that people of this age group are more emotional, get more emotionally upset and frustrated. This could probably be due to the reason that people in this age are still hot blooded and impulsive than people in the older age groups and secondly, people in this age group are trying to find a place for themselves in society and advance their career which further gives rise to tension and frustration.

The main effect of sex has no significant effect on emotional adjustment. The interaction effect is however, significant ($F = 3.10$, $p < .05$). The cell means reveal that males in the age group 30–40 years are slightly better emotionally adjusted than females of this age group, whereas, in the other two age groups (45–55 years and 60 years and above) females are better emotionally adjusted than males. This could be probably because firstly, during this period women in India particularly, have too much workload: looking after the house, small children, cooking, etc., and also their professional role. Men in India seldom help their wives in doing domestic work; and secondly, as women physically age earlier than men, therefore, their middle age also starts earlier bringing along with it its emotional problems. The results of the study reject the hypothesis that younger age groups will be more emotionally adjusted than older age groups. The hypothesis stating that males will be more emotionally adjusted than females has also not been proved.

Needs

The summary of the two-way analysis of variance presented in Table 3.1 shows that age and sex have no significant effect on the need for achievement and succorance. A glance at the mean scores (Table 3.2) shows that the three age groups (30–40 years, 45–55 years, 60 years and above) have almost an equal need for achievement and succorance. This means that people at all ages desire to accomplish tasks requiring skill successfully, to be recognised as good in one's work, and to do things better than others.

Regarding the need for succorance it also seems that people at all ages need sympathy, affection, encouragement, etc., from others, to the same degree.

The non-significant effect of sex on need for achievement can be explained according to the present day situation, where both men and women are equally achievement oriented and are striving to occupy equally prestigious jobs. No sex differences in the need for succorance is contrary to popular belief which states that women want more sympathy, affection, encouragement and kindness from others, than men. This may be because women probably express their need for succorance more openly and men do not express this need for it is thought of as a weakness and a feminine trait.

The interaction effect of age and sex on need for achievement and succorance is also not significant. The results of the study reject the hypotheses that younger the age greater the need for achievement and older the age greater the need for succorance. The results also reject the hypotheses that men will have a greater need for achievement and women will have a greater need for succorance.

The analysis of variance indicates that the main affect of age is significant on the need for affiliation ($F = 6.10$, $p < .01$). The mean scores show (Table 3.2) that people in the age group 45–55 years have a higher need for affiliation than the age groups 60 years and above ($\bar{X} = 14.83$, $\bar{X} = 13.73$, $t = 1.90$, $p < .05$) and 30–40 years ($\bar{X} = 14.83$, $\bar{X} = 12.68$, $t = 3.41$, $p < .01$). The greater need for affiliation for 45–55 age group may be due to the fact that at this stage in the life cycle people lose their youth and thus, their bearing. They start realising that they are no longer young but have still not accepted this fact, which makes them feel insecure and probably, in order to over come this feeling they form strong attachments, new friends, and share things with friends etc. which gives them a feeling of belongingness. Whereas, the 30–40 years age group have a lower need for affiliation because their priority is their career and in the present day competitive society they are trying to find a place for themselves. The main effect of sex is also significant on the need for affiliation ($F = 10.56$, $p < .01$).

The mean scores show that females have a greater need for affiliation ($\bar{X}$ = 14.58) than males ($\bar{X}$ = 12.90). This may probably be due to the differences in the basic personality structure of the sexes. Women by nature are more loyal, do things for others and form strong attachments as compared to men. The interaction effect is not significant on the need for affiliation. The findings of this study reject the hypothesis that younger the age greater the need for affiliation. The results, however, prove the hypothesis that females have a greater need for affiliation than males.

On the need for nurturance age has been found to have a non-significant affect (F = 1.143). A glance at the mean scores (Table 3.2) shows that there is a slight increase in the mean score with increase in age ($\bar{X}$ = 14.89; $\bar{X}$ = 15.03; $\bar{X}$ = 15.78) but the difference is not large enough to be statistically significant. It seems that the need for nurturance does not increase with advancing are. The main effect of sex is significant on the need for nurturance (F = 7.11, $p < .01$). The higher mean score of females ($\bar{X}$ = 15.92) than males ($\bar{X}$ = 14.54) implies that females have a greater need for nurturance than males. These findings can be explained to some extent in terms of socialisation, roles and the basic nature of the sexes.

Females are taught to be nurturant as they have to become mothers and look after the young children. Women are also expected to look after the aged and sick. The higher need for nurturance in women compared to men could also be due to her basic nature to sympathise with others, help others in need, treat others with kindness and sympathy, etc. The interaction effect of age and sex is not significant on the need for nurturance.

The findings of the study do not prove the hypothesis that the need for nurturance increases with age, but the results do indicate a slight trend in this direction. The results, however, prove the hypothesis that women have a greater need for nurturance than men.

The following conclusions could be drawn from the results of the study:

(1) Age significantly effects resignation and aggression modes of coping with frustration, social maturity, emotional adjustment, and need for affiliation. Use of aggression as a strategy of coping with frustration decreases with age and people above age 60 years use resignation more as a way of coping with frustration than people of younger age groups. People of age

group 30–40 years are more socially mature, have a greater need for affiliation but are less emotionally adjusted than people of age groups 45–55 years and 60 years and above.

(2) Women in India, irrespective of age, experience a lower level of frustration, make less use of resignation and aggression as modes of coping with frustration, are better socially adjusted, more socially mature with a greater need for affiliation and nurturance than men.

(3) The interaction of age and sex is significant on the level of frustration, three modes of coping with frustration: regression, resignation and aggression, social maturity and emotional adjustment.

4

RELIGIOSITY AND DEATH ANXIETY ACROSS AGE AND SEX : An Inferential Analysis

PARAMJEET KAUR DHILLON and DEEPA MATHUR

Religion becomes increasingly important with the onset of late life and inevitable approach of death. Mathiasen (1955) has asserted that religion is 'the key to a happy life in old age. A sense of all encompassing love of God is the basic emotional security and firm spiritual foundation for people who face the end of life'. The older generation is more likely to be religious than others in the population as there is a turning toward religion in old age. As Gail (1974) states that the individual in the middle years of life begins the gradual process of coming to terms with the inevitability of his or her own death, an event which earlier had seemed impossibly distant. This awareness of death probably makes the person turn towards religion for consolation and emotional security.

Religion and religious organisations perform many functions in the lives of the aged. Some of these functions are: providing companionship and counselling (McDonald, 1973), giving meaning to the lives of the individuals, comforting the sick, suffering, bereaved and dying (Moberg, 1970; Ailor, 1973) and supplying social services and functions (Jacobs, 1974). Wolff (1959) reported that religious belief, prayer and faith in God, all help the aged to overcome many of the common problems in the old such as loneliness, grief and unhappiness.

Religion may also help in the reduction of the fear of death. Research studies (Swenson, 1959, 1961; Blazer & Palmore, 1976) have found that those who have conservative religious views were less afraid of death than other groups. Hinton (1967) found that religious individuals were relatively free of anxiety in regard to dying. Ross (1974) has also claimed that individuals who are 'tepid' believers have greater difficulty in accepting death.

Treanton (1961) however, held different views and claimed that the differences in the fear of death may not be due to religion itself, but rather to the fact that religious individuals are more likely to have a reference group that will support them when they are dying.

Research evidence indicates that the aged who are church members are better adjusted than non-members and that those who read religious books and attend religious services often adjust better than those who read religious books and attend religious services less frequently. Riley & Fonner (1968) and Moberg (1965) reported that religious indicators such as attending church frequently, reading Bible at home, believing in a life after death, listening to religious programmes, correlated with high personal adjustment high, morale and high life satisfaction.

Blazer and Palmore (1976) in their studies have also confirmed the fact that there is a strong relationship between religious activities and feelings of happiness, usefulness and adjustment in old age. It could also be possible that individuals who are well adjusted are more religiously active. Thus, it implies that religion is an important aspect in the lives of older individuals. Religion offers many individuals an 'alternative reality', i.e. a reality different from that forced on them by health or economic circumstances. An alternative reality may be necessary for those living in 'desperate circumstances'. Religion can offer these individuals an escape from earthly existence and the hope of a better life. In this way, religion may be a primary factor in having a happy old age (Blazer and Palmore, 1976).

Holcomb (1975) noted that crisis situations were faced better by those with some type of religious orientation. The reason was that individuals could view and understand the crisis more clearly and ultimately enable them to survive the crisis with fewer emotional scars.

Several studies have been conducted on religiosity in old age. Attendance at religious services is associated with several variables. One of the variables is gender. Studies conducted by Riley and Foner (1968) have indicated that women of all ages attend religious services more frequently than men. When asked if they had attended religious services within the last seven days, 46 per cent of women surveyed and 36 per cent of the men surveyed, replied affirmatively.

Wingrove and Alston (1971) in a study on 120 aged found that 46 per cent of the white collar workers and 38 per cent of the blue collar reported frequent attendance at religious services. The result was confirmed in a study conducted by Blazer and Palmore (1976) who found that those in manual occupations were less active in religion than those in non-manual occupations.

In a retrospective study on attendance at religious services Riley and Foner (1968) found that 30 per cent of those who were above 60 years of age reported that their attendance had increased, and the remainder reported no change in their attendance pattern. Blazer and Palmore (1976) in their study noted a fairly constant decline over time in religious service attendance. These studies indicate that after the age of 65, the older one becomes the greater the likelihood of reduced attendance at religious services.

METHODOLOGY

Keeping in view the importance of religion in the lives of the aged the present study was designed to examine:

(1) The difference in Religiosity and Death Anxiety between groups going/not going to the temple according to age and sex.
(2) The interaction effect of going/not going to the temple, age and sex on Religiosity and Death Anxiety.
(3) The relationship between Religiosity and Death Anxiety in groups going/not going to the temple, age and sex, and
(4) The relationship between Religiosity, Death anxiety and Demographic variables (Personal income, education, occupation and death of spouse) in groups going/not going to the temple in relation to age.

Sample

To study religiosity and death anxiety in the aged in relation to temple attendance, age and sex, a sample of 160 subjects was selected. Of these 160 subjects, 80 subjects (40 males, 40 females) belonged to the group who visited the temple at least once a week and 80 subjects (40 males, 40 females) belonged to the group who never went to the temple at all. The two group (80 subjects-going/not going to the temple) were further divided into two age groups: 50–60 years, and 61 years and above with 40 subjects (20 males, and 20 females) in each age group. The mean age of the group 50–60 years was 56 years and the mean age of the group 61 years and above was 78 years. The mean personal income of the age group 50–60 years was Rs. 2500 whereas, the mean income of the age group 61 years and above was Rs. 790. The educational level of the majority of the subjects in the group going to the temple was post graduation and above, whereas, the educational level of the subjects in the group not going to the temple was graduation. The occupation of the majority of the subjects going to the temple was business/chartered accountancy, etc., whereas the occupation of those not going to the temple was social work/clerical. The description of the sample is presented in Table 4.1.

TABLE 4.1: Schematic Presentation of the Sample

Variables	Going to the Temple N=80				Not going to the Temple N=80			
	50–60 years (N=40)		61 & above yrs (N=40)		50–60 years (N=40)		61 & above yrs. (N=40)	
Sex	Male	Female	Male	Female	Male	Female	Male	Female
	20	20	20	20	20	20	20	20

Tools Used

The tools used for the study were the following:

(1) A personal information schedule was devised seeking information such as: name, age, going/not going to the temple once a week, personal income, occupation, education, spouse dead/alive, etc.

(2) Religiosity was measured with the Religiosity Scale developed by Bhushan (1971). This scale consists of 32 items which elicit a degree of emotional involvement of the subject in giving expression of his/her faith in God and Religious acts. Each statement has five response categories ranging from totally agree to totally disagree with a neutral response as 'cant say'. The reliability co-efficients were calculated by split-half method (.89) and the test retest method (.78). The content, predictive and concurrent validity was calculated for the scale. Judgement of each item of the scale by experts was taken as the content validity. The predictive validity was calculated on 46 identified, religious Hindu male regular worshippers and 46

Hindu male non-worshippers ($t = 8.47$, $p < .001$). For concurrent validity the test was validated against Allport - Vernon-Lindzey's Study of values ($r = .57$).

(3) Death anxiety was assessed with the Death Anxiety Scale developed by Templer (1970). This scale measures anxiety related to death. The scale consists of 15 items, each item has two alternative responses: true, and false. The test-retest reliability co-efficient on 31 Hoppins-Ville community college students with three weeks interval was estimated as .83. The construct validity of the Death Anxiety Scale was investigated by:

(a) Comparing Death Anxiety scores of psychiatric patients with control patients and

(b) Correlating Boyar's Fear of Death Scale (FODS) scores with Templer's Death Anxiety Scores.

Results and Discussion

Taking the objectives of the study into consideration the data were analysed by both descriptive and inferential statistics. Table 4.1 presents the summary of the three-way ANOVA for Religiosity and Death anxiety. The ANOVA results indicate that the main effect of going/not going to the temple is significant for religiosity ($F = 10.74$, $p < .01$). The mean scores (Table 4.2) reveal that those who go to the temple are more religious ($\bar{X} = 125.59$) than those who do not go to the temple ($\bar{X} = 120.07$).

The main effect of age has also been found to be significant for religiosity ($F = 78.61$, $p < .01$). Table 4.2 shows that people in the age group 61 years and above are more religious ($\bar{X} = 150.63$) than those in the age group 50–60 years ($\bar{X} = 134.32$). The analysis indicates that as age increases religiosity also increases. This result has been supported by the findings of Deoras and Jana Bandhu (1970) who found that in 86 per cent subjects religiosity increased due to age. The traditional model of religiosity also states that church attendance reaches a low level in the age group 30–35 years and then gradually increases untill old age which also supports the findings of the present study that religiosity increases with age.

The main effect of sex is also statistically significant ($F = 79.73$, $p < .001$) for religiosity. A glance at the mean scores indicate that females are more religious ($\bar{X} = 133.93$) than males ($\bar{X} = 118.67$). This

TABLE 4.2: Summary of the ANOVA for Religiosity and Death Anxiety

Variables		Source of Variance							
		A (Going/not going to the temple)	B (Age groups)	C (Sex)	A×B	B×C	A×C	A×B×C	Error
Religiosity	df	1	1	1	1	1	1	1	152
	MS	13653.3	99315.1	100667.2	5017.6	71289	2592.1	12957.1	1263.33
	F	10.74**	78.61**	79.73**	3.97*	56.43**	2.05	10.26**	
Death Anxiety	df	1	1	1	1	1	1	1	152
	MS	57.005	112.25	70.25	27.23	5.63	5.63	4.16	5.32
	F	10.72**	21.09**	13.20**	5.12*	1.06	1.06	.78	

** $p < .01$ level; * $p < .05$ level.

finding is in agreement with the results of Wingrove and Alston (1971) and Riley and Foner (1968), who observed that greater percentage of women in contrast to men surveyed attend religious services and are therefore, more religious.

The interaction effect of temple attendance by age (A × B) on religiosity is significant ($F = 3.97$, $p < .05$). The results show that as age increases (from below 60 years to 61 years and above) religiosity also increases in both groups, going and not going to the temple, but increase in religiosity due to age is more in the group going to the temple (mean difference = 16.31) as compared to the group not going to the temple. This may be due to religious practices, such as reading religious books or watching religious programmes on television, etc., and going to the temple, which together account for high scores on religiosity in this group.

The interaction effect of age by sex (B × C) on religiosity is again found to be statistically significant ($F = 56.43$, $p < .01$) (Table 4.2). It is evident from Table 4.3 that females (irrespective) of going/not going to the temple) are more religious than males and the difference in religiosity between the sexes is greater in the age group 50–60 years than in the age group 61 years and above. This means that temple going females are more religious than males at a younger age (50–60 years) but as age increases (61 years and above) the difference between the degree of religiosity decreases and they become almost equally religious. The explanation for this seems to be that females are consistently religious but males after the age of 61 years or so suddenly become more religious probably they start feeling old and face reality and so turn to religion.

The interaction effect of going/not going to the temple and sex (A × B) on religiosity is however, not significant (Table 4.2). The cell means indicates that females whether going or not going to the temple are consistently more religious than males of both conditions/situations going/not going to the temple.

The interaction effect of going/not going to the temple, age and sex (A × B × C). Table 4.2 has been found to be significant. Females going to the temple in the age group 50–60 years are more religious than males ($t = 2.75$, $p < .01$ level) whereas, there is no significant difference in the degree of religiosity between the sexes in the age group 61 years and above ($t = 1.51$). Females not going to the temple in the age group 50–60 years are more religious than males (mean difference = 22.90, $t = 2.74$, $p < .01$ level), whereas, there is no significant difference in religiosity between the males and females in the age group 61 years and above (t = .66). Males after the age of 61 suddenly turn to religion and become almost as religious as females.

Death Anxiety

The ANOVA results indicate that the main effect of going/not going to the temple is significant for death anxiety ($F = 10.72$, $p < .01$) (Table 4.2). Death anxiety has been found to be more in the aged going to the temple (Table 4.3: $\bar{X} = 12.20$) than those not going to the temple ($\bar{X} = 10.33$). This particular finding is contradictory to the previous findings which indicate that religious individuals are relatively free of anxiety in regard to dying (Swenson, 1959; Blazer and Palmore, 1976; Hinton, 1967 and Kubler-Ross, 1974). This may probably be due to the fact that subjects of this study do not have a strong faith in God but are rather 'tepid' believers, therefore, they have greater difficulty in accepting death. Moreover, as Treanton (1961) pointed out that differences in the fear of death may not be due to religion in and of itself but rather to the fact that religious individuals are more likely to have a reference group that will support them when they are dying. It is possible that subjects in this study do not have a satisfactory reference group and therefore, even though they seem to be more religious, are still afraid of death.

The main effect of age has also been found to be significant for death anxiety ($F = 21.09$, $p < .01$; Table 4.2). The aged in the age group 61 and above ($\bar{X} = 13.98$) have been found to have more death anxiety than those in the age group 50–60 years ($\bar{X} = 10.96$: Table 4.3). The explanation could be that at younger age death often comes unexpectedly whereas, in old age its inevitability is recognised (Peck, 1968) and thus the fear of confronting death increases with age.

The third main effect viz., sex is also found to be significant on death anxiety ($F = 13.20$, $p < .01$: Table 4.2). Females have been found to have more death anxiety ($\bar{X} = 11.99$) than males ($\bar{X} = 9.97$) irrespective of going/not going to the temple and age. This may be because females are the weaker sex and also the socialisation of females in the Indian society particularly, conditions them to fear anything which is unseen.

The interaction effect of going/not going to the temple and age on death anxiety has been found to be significant ($F = 5.12$, $p < .05$) (Table 4.2). It is observed that death anxiety in the age group 61 and above is greater for the aged (going and not going to the temple) as compared to those in the age group 50–60 years. But the difference in death anxiety in the two age groups (50–60 years 61 years and above) within the group not going to the temple is more ($t = 2.01$ $p < .05$) than the difference in the age groups (50–60 years and 61 years and above) within the group going to the temple (Table 4.3 : $t = 1.93$ NS).

However, the interaction effects of A × C, B × C and A × B × C on death anxiety have not been found to be significant.

Relationship of Religiosity and Death Anxiety

Significant positive relationships have been observed between religiosity and death anxiety for the aged going to the temple ($r = .72$, $p < .001$) and not going to the temple ($r = .67$, $p < .001$) as well as age groups 50–60 years ($r = .64$, $p < .01$; $r = .59$, $p < .01$) and 61 years and above ($r = .93$, $p < .001$; $r =.82$, $p < .001$). This means that going or not going to the temple does not make a person fear death less for it is possible that those people who do not go to the temple are religious as one has to have faith in God in order to be religious and not mere temple attendance.

Religiosity and death anxiety have also been found to be related positively for males going ($r = .53$, $p < .05$) and not going to the temple ($r = .50$, $p < .05$) as well as for the females going ($r = .66$, $p < .001$) not going to the temple ($r = .58$, $p < .01$). These results indicate that irrespective of temple attendance and sex an increase in religiosity results in increase in death anxiety. This finding of the study is contrary to popular belief and religious preachings, according to which religion helps an individual to look beyond life after death and this in the process reduces anxiety about death. The plausible explanation for this finding of the study seems to be that probably the instrument used in the study for measuring religiosity could not tap an individuals religiosity or religious feelings but probably could only assess an individual's religious ritual life which is only a part of religiosity. Table 4.4 shows the relationship of Religiosity and Death anxiety to demographic variables in relation to age and temple attendance/non-attendance.

Personal income and religiosity have been found to be related positively and significantly for the aged going and not going to the temple in the age group 50–60 years (going $r = +.96$, $p < .001$; not going $r =.84$, $p < .001$) as well as in the age group 61 years and above

TABLE 4.3: Mean, Standard Deviation and Correlation Between Religiosity and Death Anxiety in Relation to Going/Not Going to the Temple (n=80 in each), age (n=40 in each group) and sex (n=40 for each)

Age Group		Temple Attendance									
		Going to the temple					Not going to the temple				
		Religiosity		Death Anxiety		r	Religiosity		Death Anxiety		r
		$\bar{X}$	SD	$\bar{X}$	SD		$\bar{X}$	SD	$\bar{X}$	SD	
50—60 years	Males	112.35	33.20	10.03	4.27	.50*	93.15	41.02	8.47	4.17	.43*
	Females	129.65	23.33	11.64	3.96	.69***	116.05	39.06	10.01	4.01	.57**
	Total	134.32	17.01	12.67	2.11	.64**	127.92	20.63	10.88	3.92	.59**
61 & above years	Males	139.95	31.06	12.01	2.32	.54*	128.80	43.36	9.98	4.09	.49*
	Females	148.85	20.45	13.08	2.14	.87***	134.32	30.15	11.67	2.36	.78***
	Total	150.63	15.72	14.31	4.93	.93***	140.02	19.73	12.43	2.98	.82***
Grand Total		133.14	25.11	12.20	2.96	.72***	120.07	37.40	10.33	3.96	.67***
Total Sex-wise	Males	125.59	32.33	11.13	3.05	.53*	111.75	40.01	9.52	4.33	.50*
	Females	140.02	21.19	12.92	2.95	.66***	127.85	32.50	11.05	3.58	.58**

*** $p < .001$ level; ** $p < .01$ level; * $p < .05$ level.

(going $r = +.94$, $p < .001$; not going $r = +.89$). This probably implies that as personal income increases religiosity also increases in the aged. This is because the aged with higher personal income have more opportunities and facilities to engage in external religious practices and derive satisfaction from them. Education is also found to be related positively and significantly to religiosity for the aged going and not going to the temple in the age group 50–60 years (going $r = .78$, $p < .001$; not going $r = .40$, $p < .01$) and 61 and above (going $r =.63$, $p < .001$; not going $r = .82$, $p < .001$). Occupation and religiosity have also been found to be related positively and significantly for the aged going and not going to the temple in the age group 50–60 years (going $r =.72$, $p < .001$; not going $r = .43$, $p < .01$). This indicates that higher the occupational status, greater is the religiosity. This result is indirectly in keeping with the findings of Wingrove and Alston (1971) who found that 46 per cent of white collar workers and 38 per cent blue collar workers claimed that they frequently attended religious services. In another study Blazer and Palmore (1976) found that those in manual occupations were less active in religion than those in non-manual occupations. Death of spouse has been found to be related positively to religiosity for the aged going and not going to the temple in both the age groups 50–60 years (going $r = +.90$, $p < .001$; not going $r = +.96$, $p < .001$) and 61 and above years (going $r = .96$, $p < .001$; not going $r = .96$, $p < .001$). This probably means that death of spouse increases religiosity. The reason could be that religiosity provides companionship and gives meaning to life to the elderly person whose spouse is dead. Here religion may be considered as a source of solace to the individual. Moreover, Holcomb (1975) has stated that religion helps individuals to understand crises more clearly and ultimately enables them to cope with these crises with fewer emotional scares.

Personal income is found to be related negatively and significantly to death anxiety for the aged going to the temple in the age group 50–60 years ($r = -.84$, $p < .001$) and 61 years and above ($r = -.84$, $p < .001$). This means that higher personal income reduces death anxiety among those going to the temple. Those who go to the temple also seem to be more religious and their higher personal income enables them to spend some of their money for religious purposes. The utilisation of some of their money for pious work probably helps them to fear death less which reduces their death anxiety. However, for people in the age group 50–60 years ($r = +.73$, $p < .001$) and 61 years and above ($r = .76$, $p < .001$) and belonging to the group not going to the temple, personal income is found to be related positively and significantly to death anxiety. Thus, in the group not going to the temple higher personal income is associated with more death anxiety. This may be because these rich people have lived in luxury and reduced all types of pain by what money can buy and material wealth can compensate, and the process of dying and life after death is unknown which makes these people more apprehensive about death, as they do not even go to the temple for solace, which probably causes anxiety about death.

TABLE 4.4: Relationship of Demographic Variables to Religiosity and Death Anxiety for going/not going to the temple and for two age groups

Age Groups	Demographic Variables	Temple Attendance			
		Going to the temple		Not going to the temple	
		Religiosity	Death Anxiety	Religiosity	Death Anxiety
50–60	Personal Income	+ .96***	− .84***	+ .84***	+ .73***
	Education	+ .78***	+ .72***	+ .40**	+ .61***
	Occupation	+ .72***	+ .69***	+ .49***	+ .67***
	Death of Spouse	+ .90***	+ .94***	+ .96***	+ .94***
61 & above	Personal Income	+ .94***	− .84***	+ .89***	+ .76***
	Education	+ .63***	+ .50***	+ .82***	+ .80***
	Occupation	+ .72***	+ .67***	+ .43**	+ .49***
	Death of Spouse	+ .96***	+ .94***	+ .96***	+ .94***

Death anxiety and education are also found to be related positively and significantly for those going and not going to the temple in the age group 50–60 years (going $r = .72$, $p < .001$; not going $r = .61$ $p < .001$), and 61 years and above (going $r = .50$, $p < .001$; not going $r = .80$ $p < .001$). This result indicates that higher the education higher is the religiosity and death anxiety for the aged.

Occupation is also found to be related positively and significantly to death anxiety for the aged going and not going to the temple in the age group 50–60 years (going $r = .69$, $p < .001$; not going $r = .49$, $p < .001$) as well as in the age group 61 years and above (going $r = .72$, $p < .001$, not going $r = .43$, $p < .01$), implying that people higher in the occupational hierarchy have more death anxiety.

Death of spouse has also been found to be related positively to death anxiety among those going and not going to the temple in the age group 50–60 years (going $r = .94$, $p < .001$; not going $r = .94$, $p < .001$) and 61 years and above (going $r = .94$ $p < .001$; not going $r = .94$, $p < .001$). Death of one's spouse is a great life event which affects an individual emotionally and psychologically and leaves a vacuum in one's life. But death of a spouse in old age hits an individual even harder and the person starts feeling lonely, insecure and loses purpose in life. Such an individual thinks of death and probably about his/her own death which causes fear and anxiety in the aged.

COMMENTS

Developmental Psychologists and Gerontologists utilise cohort (i.e., different age group) analysis to compare groups of people born during specific time periods (usually separated by five-year to 10 year intervals) as they move through the life cycle. It is assumed that these people generally experience particular historical events at approximately the same time in their biological, psychological and sociological development and are effected by these events in more or less a similar manner. Studies comparing different age groups are carried out on the assumption that differences among such groups are the result of developmental changes. The two studies presented in this section are also an attempt in this direction.

In the first study people of three age groups 30–40 years, 45–55 years and 60 years and above and the sexes have been compared on psychological needs, social adjustment and reactions to frustration. The results exhibit a significant main effect of age group differences on need for affiliation, social maturity, emotional adjustment, and two reactions to frustration (resignation and aggression). People of age group 45–55 years manifest a greater need for affiliation and greater social immaturity than people of age groups 60 years and above and 30–40 years. People within the age group 30–40 years have a lesser need for affiliation, are more socially mature but less emotionally adjusted, and make greater use of aggressive reactions to frustration than people of the two age groups: 45–55 years and 60 years and above. The aged 60 years and above confront frustrating situations with less aggressive reactions and more resignated reactions as compared to both age groups 45–55 years and 30–40 years. The main effect of sex has also been found to be significant on these psychological variables, Males display a greater amount of frustration and aggressive reactions to frustration than females. They also show a lesser degree of social adjustment, social maturity, need for affiliation and nurturance in comparison to females. The interaction effect of different age groups and sex has also been found to be significant on amount of frustration experienced, reactions to frustration, degree of social maturity and emotional adjustment.

The results of the second study indicate a significant effect of age group difference on religiosity and death anxiety. Among people frequently going to the temple, the age group 61 years and above is found to have more religiosity and death anxiety than people of the age group 50–60 years. Among people never going to the temple, again the age group 61 years and above exhibits more religiosity and more death anxiety than the age group 50–60 years. Religiosity and death anxiety has been found to be related significantly and positively in both age groups under both the situations frequently/never going to the temple. Religiosity and death anxiety are also seen to be related positively and significantly to education, occupation and death of spouse in both the age groups under both situations: frequently/never going to the temple. However, death anxiety is found to be related significantly and negatively to personal income in both age groups under the situation frequently going to the temple and positively significantly related in both age groups under the situation never going to the temple.

The empirical findings of the studies in this section reveal considerable differences between cohorts (i.e., different age groups) on psychological variables such as religiosity, death anxiety, need for affiliation, social adjustment and reactions to frustration.

PART III

SOCIAL CLASS AND AGING

INTRODUCTION

Social stratification of some kind exists in all societies of the world over and in the words of Barber (1968) it means that both individuals and groups of individuals are conceived of as constituting higher and lower differentiated strata, or classes, in terms of some specific or generalised characteristic or set of characteristics. Differentiation can be in authority relationships, income, prestige, social status, economic power position, class consciousness, degree of inequality of rewards and privileges.

Society for most purposes is stratified in three strata or classes: Upper, Middle and Lower. Several objective indicators have been established according to which society can be stratified, however, the ones that are generally used are: occupation, education, income, socio-cultural background of the parents, place of residence, material possessions, etc. These factors contribute towards making a social class and also tend to produce different kinds of socio-psychological environments or 'ecology' that sustains not only due to external circumstances but also by internal systems of values, preferences, inter and intrapersonal relationships that have validity of their own and persist even after the external circumstances change.

A good deal has been written about the culture or subculture of the social classes: lower-class, middle-class and upper-class. Barber (1968) states that the upper-class culture is marked by group interaction, consciousness of its position in society and certain subcultural customs that set the upper class off from the rest of society. Baltzell (1958) refers to the distinct speech patterns and style of living of this class which set this class somewhat apart from other classes. Kahl (1957) elaborates this view and points out "the skills of graceful living' of this class and states that tradition, familism, and lineage are the main attributes of this class. The middle class culture or subculture, according to Gans (1962), emphasises the importance of the nuclear family, child rearing, the husband's career, and education in terms of its contribution to career advancement. Kahl (1957) distinguishes between the lower-middle class and the upper middle class. He asserts that the lower-middle class is concerned about respectability, which is manifested by a desire for children to attend college, a strong interest in religion and home ownership. On the other hand, the upper-middle-class lays greater stress upon success in a career, the style of living of the family, individual initiative combined with smooth group functioning, planning for the future, on activity, accomplishment and practical results.

The lower-class subculture, according to Miller (1958) has six major concerns: concerns that revolve around "trouble; toughness; smartness; excitement; fate; and autonomy". Rainwater (1966) reports that in the lower-class subculture three kinds of survival strategies are prevalent: an expressive strategy (leading to immediate gratification); a violent strategy; and a depressive strategy. Further elaborating on the survival strategies he states that "when the expressive strategy fails or when it is unavailable, there is . . . great temptation to adopt a violent strategy in which you force others to give you what you need. . . . Finally there is the depressive strategy in which goals are increasingly constricted to the bare necessities for survival. . . ." Lewis (1967) also documents a variety of life styles found among the lower-class people and asserts that much of the behaviour of this class can be seen as a pragmatic response to the stresses and deprivations of life. The aforesaid observations about the different social classes by investigators seem to imply that each socio-economic class depicts its unique characteristics, viz., the affluence of the upper class, struggles of the middle, and the chronic deprivation of the lower class, which influence the family structure, child rearing practices, experiences of life, etc., and which in turn effect the value patterns, attitudes, needs, expectations, cognitive and motivational patterns, coping mechanisms, style of life and the character structure. People born and socialised, in the ecology of the different social classes would experience different kinds of deprivations, problems, tensions, etc, and would thus develop different cognitive, affective and motivational behavioural patterns. As a result these people would probably differ in their perception of the life events and reactions to them, anxiety and stress levels experienced, and in their personality patterns. There is however, a paucity of research in India ascertaining the effects of social class on the cognitive, motivational and behavioural patterns of people of different ages. The research undertaken and reported in this section is an attempt to overcome this drawback.

The first study aims to examine the perception and meaning of old age as held by six age groups of the upper-middle class and the lower-middle class.

The second investigation studies different dimensions of personality, anxiety level and self concept of adults of two age-groups: 45–50 years and 55–59 years; belonging to three social classes: Low, Middle and High.

The next study ascertains the effect of social class on the level of emotional maturity, anxiety about death, Locus of control and degree of religiosity, of people in the age group 65+.

Strategies used by the aged (60+) of three social classes: High, middle and low, to cope with life stresses, is the fourth topic of research reported in this section.

5

THE MEANING OF THE CONCEPT 'OLD AGE' AS HELD BY THE COMMUNITY

PARAMJEET KAUR DHILLON and ANITA GUPTA

Aging is a natural phenomenon which has not only profound personal implications for the individual but also implications for the society. Man has throughout the ages reflected upon changes occurring in behaviour and temperament with advancing age. With the life saving drugs, to-day there is a large increase in the proportion of old people in every country. No doubt one feels love and affection and a sense of responsibility for one's parents, grand parents and elderly relatives, but one could also have hostile attitudes the roots of which lie either in early parent-child relationships or restrictions in leisure activities due to the presence of old or sick elderly at home, or burdens of looking after sick parents/grand parents or financial dependence of the elders or the authority and wealth that the elders are slow to relinquish. Whatever the reasons, people differ widely in their beliefs about and attitudes towards old people. In India, the large majority of older people still live with their children and grand children but the well-being of this older population is determined to a large extent by how they are defined and categorised by others in the social environment. Most often people behave the way the significant others in the social world expect them to behave, because only a very strong and determined person can resist the social definition placed on him by others and carve out a new image for himself. Therefore, one of the problems confronting older people to-day is how they are perceived by the others in the community. There is research evidence which indicates that the elders are viewed negatively by young, middle and older adults. Furthermore, research has also indicated that age becomes the most significant factor in the perception of the elderly while other factors, such as sex, education or ethnicity, are less important. Review of research studies show that children and adolescents hold negative attitude towards the elderly. Seefeldt (1984) compared the attitudes of children towards the elderly in four diverse cultures. The semantic differential subtest of the CATE (Children's Attitudes Towards the Elderly) was administered to 4th 5th and 6th grade children. The results indicate that the children in the Alentian Islands, Paraguay and Australia rated young people more positively than they did old people while children in mainland United States rated old and young people alike. There were no differences between cultures in the children's rating of the concept 'Old people', but children in Alentian Island rated old people more negatively than those in other cultures on several items of the semantic differential scale. Miller *et al.* (1984) examined pre-school children's understanding of attitude towards aging as well as their ability to differentiate older and younger people and their comparative attitudes towards them. To assess the child's attitudes towards elderly persons, three sets of artists drawings were used. Each set contained pictures of a young adult, an elderly man, a young woman and an elderly woman, all drawn with the same basic facial expressions and some bodily stance to control the extranenous factors. The results indicated that children more significantly chose pictures of young people over older people. The age of the child was a significant factor in the child's discrimination of age differences. Galper and Seefeldt (1980) examined the attitudes of 180 children 3 to 11 years of age towards the elderly. Most children disliked the idea of aging themselves and stereotyped the elderly as ugly, tired and sick. In contrast, Burkee (1981) found that in general, children did not have a negative attitude towards older persons that stereotypically are held by the society. On the evaluative factor of a semantic differential measure old persons were rated more positively than younger people.

Kastenbaum and Burhee (1964) found that adolescents and young adults had a predominately negative attitude towards aged persons. Old people were seen as bound to the past, and old age was viewed as an unpleasant experience. Mickey and Kalish (1968) also found that older adults were being viewed more negatively than younger adults by pre-adolescents, adolescents and college students. Weinberger and Millam (1975) observed that college students possessed more negative view of the elderly. Contrary results were obtained by Cameron (1972) in a study in which the sample included young adults, middle aged and old persons. He reported that middle aged persons were frequently considered to be the happiest and young adults had more chances and greater desire for fun, whereas, the aged had the least. In support of these findings, Borges and Dulton (1979) surveyed attitude towards aging among seven groups of respondents ranging in age from 6 to over 65 years of age. The results revealed that the year selected as the 'best year' of life increased with the age of the respondent and the younger respondents did not rate their future life to be as good as older persons. Also the young did not see the potential satisfaction of middle and later years.

Doka (1985) found that adolescents had considerable misinformation about aging and anxiety about the later stages of the life cycle. They also had negative stereotypes about the elderly. Ivester and King (1977) carried out a study on high school students and found a positive attitude towards the aged. Festinga (1964) has suggested that attitudes usually become more congruent with reality when people are exposed to groups of persons about whom they have negative attitudes.

Ivester and King (1977) have explained the results in terms of a more effective resource pool for people to work with the aged, as the sample was from a rural community, where the extended family tends to remain more intact than in urban areas and hence provided more opportunities for adolescents to have contact with the elderly.

Bassili and Reil (1981) found that young adults stereotype old people mainly in terms of age. The 'old age' stereotype that emerged consisted mainly of the following attitudes: conservative, traditional, present-oriented and moral. Whether a person thinks of himself as young, middle-aged or old will depend upon many things-not merely his calendar age, but also his physical health and outward appearance, the way he is treated by other people and the prevailing social norms and attitudes regarding age differences.

Pratt (1976) carried out a study, on college students, middle aged adults and elderly adults, to investigate devaluation of old age in comparison to old age in general. Devaluation was predicted from attitude towards: (1) cultural values, (2) negative concomitants of old age, (3) demographic variables, and (4) self reported intergenerational contact. Semantic differential scales were used: good-bad, optimistic-pessimistic, complete-incomplete, timely-untimely, positive-negative, successful-unsuccessful, important-unimportant. Factors identified as possibly affecting attitude towards and/or devaluation of age were: (1) poor health, (2) social isolation, (3) death, (4) financial-security, (5) achievement, (6) independence, and (7) personal-productivity. Results indicated no significant differences due to age on sex or age-sex interaction were found in attitude towards three cultural value concepts. Significant age differences were found for attitude towards poor health, social isolation, financial insecurity, death, youth, middle age, old age in general and devaluation of old age. The elderly subjects were more positive towards these concepts. For all other concepts except social isolation and financial insecurity the young subjects were most negative. Middle aged subjects were most negative towards social isolation and financial insecurity. Significant differences due to sex were found only for attitude towards death, the females being more positive than males in all age groups.

Research evidence, cited above, reveals that the attitude of various age groups towards the elderly are not clear-cut. Some studies show that children or adolescents or young adults hold negative attitude towards the elderly, while others found that they hold positive attitude towards them. Furthermore, most of these studies have been carried out in those countries where the nuclear family has completely replaced the joint family system thereby, depriving children, adolescents and young adults of the opportunity of contact with and objective assessment of the elderly. Keeping these observations in view, a study on the meaning of the concept 'Old Age' as held by the Indian urban community was undertaken by the investigators to ascertain how the perception of and attitude towards the elderly is effected by age and social class.

METHODOLOGY

The sub-objectives of the study were:

(1) To find out the meaning of the concept 'Old Age' as held by different age groups.
(2) To assess the effect of socio-economic status on the meaning of the concept 'Old Age'
(3) To study the interaction effect of age and socio-economic status on the meaning of the concept 'Old Age'.

Sample

The sample comprised of 96 male respondents belonging to the Upper-middle (N=48) and Lower-middle (N = 48) socioeconomic status. The sample consisted of six age groups: 10–19 years, 20–29 years, 30–39 years, 40–49 years, 50–59 years and 60 years and above. Each age group comprised of 16 males, eight from the Upper-middle class and eight from the Lower-middle class. The socio-economic class was determined by Kuppuswamy's modified socio-economic scale. The respondents were sampled from different colonies of South Delhi: Gulmohar Park, Neeti Bagh, Uday Park, Anand Lok, Sadik Nagar and Yusuf Sarai.

Tools Used

The following tools were used in the study.

1. The socio-economic status was measured by a modified version of Kuppuswamy's (1962) 'Socio-Economic Status Scale' (Urban).
2. To assess the meaning of the concept 'Old Age' a scale based on the semantic differential technique was constructed by Gupta and Dhillon (1987). The scale consists of 26 bipolar adjectives comprising five factors or dimensions of meaning; Receptivity, Stability, Activity, Potency and Evaluation. The bipolar adjectives were selected from Osgood *et al's* (1975) list of adjectives and each adjective is scored on a 7-point scale. Each bipolar adjective has a negative and a positive extreme point. The positive extreme is given a score of 7 and the extreme negative point a score of one. The maximum score possible on the scale is 182 and the minimum is 26.

Osgood et al. (1957) describes the 'Receptivity factor' as the individual's perception of the receptivity (capability of receiving accepting) of the object or concept. The 'Stability factor' as the individual's perception of the stability (state of being stable: steadiness; fixity, etc,) of the object or concept. The 'Activity factor' as the individual's perception of the activity (efficiency, agility, alertness) of the object or concept. The 'Potency factor' as the individual's perception of the potency (power, might, strength) of the objects or concept. The 'Evaluative factor' as the individual's evaluation (value, worth) of the object or concept being rated. The evaluation factor corresponds to the favourable/unfavourable dimension of the more traditional attitude scales. The scales were translated into Hindi for the Hindi speaking subjects.

Procedure

The respondents were approached individually at home. After establishing rapport and assuring the respondents of confidentiality they were administered the semantic differential scale and the personal data schedule. Generally the respondents of the Upper-middle class gave their responses in writing and the respondents of the Lower-middle class gave their responses orally and the investigators recorded them. In all 130 respondents were administered the schedule, of which only 96 respondents were taken for this study according to the criterion of the two social classes: Upper-middle and Lower-middle.

Results and Discussion

The data were analysed by two-way analysis of variance and Table 5.1 shows the summary of the ANOVAS for six age groups and social class on the concept 'Old Age' and its five dimensions; Receptivity, Stability, Activity, Potency and Evaluation. Tables 5.2 and 5.4 present the mean scores and standard deviation on the concept 'old age' and its five dimensions in relation to age and social class.

1. Age and the Concept 'Old Age'

The analysis of variance shows that age is a significant factor ($F = 54.96$, $p < .01$) in the perception of old age. A perusal of Table 5.2 shows that there is a difference between the scores of the various age groups. The age groups rank ordered according to the degree of unfavourable perception of old age are as follows: 30–39 years ($\bar{X} = 67.73$); 40–49 years ($\bar{X} = 79.13$); 10–19 years ($\bar{X} = 81.50$); 60 years and above ($\bar{X} = 102.63$); 20–29 years ($\bar{X} = 105.25$) and 50–59 years ($\bar{X} = 106.19$). The age group 30–39 years has obtained the lowest mean score indicating that people of this age–group perceive old age most unfavourably. The age group 50–59 years has obtained the highest score implying that people of this age-group perceive old age most favourable in comparison to people of other age groups.

In order to find out if the mean difference between various age groups was significant, 't-values' were computed. Table 5.3 shows the comparison of mean scores on the concept old age in relation to age. Comparing the mean score of the age group 10–19 years with the mean

TABLE 5.1: Summary of the Two-way Analysis of Variance

Concept of 'Old Age'	Source of Variance										
	Age Groups (C)			SES (R)			C × R			Within Cells	
	df	s^2	F	df	s^2	F	df	s^2	F	df	s^2
Concept of 'Old Age' (Total)	5	4301.61	54.96**	1	68213.34	871.51**	5	1428.05	18.24**	84	78.27
Dimensions											
1. Receptivity	5	136.02	24.73**	1	782.03	142.19**	5	16.65	3.03*	84	5.50
2. Stability	5	88.40	28.42**	1	748.16	240.57**	5	21.33	6.86**	84	3.11
3. Activity	5	195.03	24.81**	1	2614.59	332.65**	5	74.28	9.45**	84	7.86
4. Potency	5	152.99	24.21**	1	1600.66	253.27**	5	100.10	15.84**	84	6.32
5. Evaluation	5	455.14	23.80**	1	13160.16	688.29**	5	289.55	15.14**	84	19.12

** $p < .01$ level; * $p < .05$ level.

TABLE 5.2: Mean and Standard Deviation on the Concept of Old Age and its Factors in Relation to Age

Age groups	Factors											
	Receptivity		Stability		Activity		Potency		Evaluation		Total	
	$\bar{X}$	SD	$\bar{X}$	SD	$\bar{X}$	SD	$\bar{X}$	SD	$\bar{X}$	SD	$\bar{X}$	SD
10—19 Years	8.81	3.59	7.69	2.23	15.31	5.09	12.63	2.83	37.06	11.80	81.5	22.13
20—29 Years	12.50	4.72	12.63	3.52	21.00	7.21	15.88	2.83	43.25	12.75	105.25	29.59
30—39 Years	7.31	2.39	8.19	2.90	11.94	3.44	12.50	4.24	28.31	5.49	67.63	15.72
40—49 Years	9.13	2.78	8.69	2.99	14.63	4.33	13.06	4.29	34.38	12.15	79.13	24.04
50—59 Years	14.69	3.60	12.75	3.21	18.25	6.36	19.50	7.51	41.0	16.35	106.19	35.21
60 & above	13.19	4.63	11.69	4.88	20.06	8.88	18.44	7.47	39.25	16.32	102.63	41.11
Total	10.94	4.57	10.27	3.99	16.86	6.94	15.33	5.95	37.21	13.88	90.39	32.82

scores of the other five age groups on the concept old age, it is observed that the adolescents perceive old age more favourably ($\bar{X}$ = 81.50) than people of the age group 30–39 years ($\bar{X}$ = 67.63, t = 2.06, p < .05). There is no significant difference in the perception of old age between adolescents of the age group 10–19 years and adults of the age group 40–49 years ($\bar{X}$ = 79.13, t = .29). On the whole people of these three age groups (10–19 years, 30–39 years and 40–49 years) perceive old age quite unfavourably as their mean scores lie far below the neutral or average group score (neither favourable nor unfavourable score $\bar{X}$ = 104), whereas, people of the other three age groups, 20–29 years, 50–59 years and 60 years and above perceive old age quite favourably ($\bar{X}$ = 105.25; $\bar{X}$ = 106.19; $\bar{X}$ = 102.63). The results show that there is no significant difference in the mean scores of these three age groups (Table 5.3), which means that people of these age groups have more or less a similar perception of old age. Moreover, people of these three age groups also do not really have a favourable perception of old age but rather an ambivalent perception of old age as their mean score ($\bar{X}$ = 104) lies in the uncertain or neutral category.

On the five dimensions of the concept 'Old Age' the ANOVA results indicate that age is a significant factor for all the five dimensions of the concept old age. Table 5.2 shows that on the dimension of Receptivity, the mean score of age groups 10–19 years, 30–39, and 40–49 years ($\bar{X}$ = 8.81; $\bar{X}$ = 7.31; $\bar{X}$ = 9.13) lie quite below the average score ($\bar{X}$ = 12.00). This means that people of these age groups perceive old age as to having little receptivity i.e. having little capability of receiving or accepting, etc. They perceive old age as to be less sensitive, interesting and contended. However, people of age-group 20–29 years, 50–59 years and 60 years and above ($\bar{X}$ = 12.50; $\bar{X}$ =14.69; $\bar{X}$ = 13.19) perceive old age to be quite receptive, or at least receptive to an average degree.

On the dimension of stability, the mean scores of the age groups 20–29 years, 50–59 years, 60 years and above ($\bar{X}$ = 12.63; $\bar{X}$ = 12.75; $\bar{X}$ = 11.69) lie in the average range of stability ($\bar{X}$ = 12.00). This means that people of these age groups perceive old age as to be neither very stable, steady, secure nor very unstable. They associate old age with an average degree of sanity, carefulness, security, etc. However, the age groups 10–19 years, 30–39 years, 40–49 years ($\bar{X}$ = 7.79; $\bar{X}$ = 8.19) associate old age with a lesser degree of stability, viz., more of carelessness, changeability and insanity.

TABLE 5.3: Comparison of Means on Concept of Old Age and its Factors in Relation to age: t-values

Comparison Groups	t-Values					
	Total Concept	Factor A	Factor B	Factor C	Factor D	Factor E
10–19 years-20–29 years	2.59**	2.51**	4.79**	2.61**	3.28**	1.44
10–19 years-30–39 years	2.06*	1.40	0.55	2.22*	0.10	2.72**
10–19 years-40–49 years	0.29	0.29	1.09	0.41	0.34	0.64
10–19 years-50–59 years	2.39*	4.67**	5.27**	1.46	3.45**	0.79
10–19 years-60 & above	1.83*	3.02**	3.01**	1.88*	2.93**	0.44
20–29 years-30–39 years	4.54**	3.96**	3.93**	4.58**	2.68**	4.34**
20–29 years-40–49 years	2.77**	2.48**	3.46**	3.06**	2.22*	2.03*
20–29 years-50–59 years	0.08	1.49	0.10	1.16	1.82*	0.44
20–29 years 60 & above	0.21	0.42	0.63	0.33	1.29	0.78
30–39 years-40–49 years	1.61	2.00*	0.48	1.96*.	0.38	1.84
30–39 years-50–59 years	4.04**	6.90**	4.26**	3.53**	3.29**	2.97**
30–39 years-60 & above	3.21**	4.56**	2.50**	3.44**	2.79**	2.57**
40–49 years-50–59 years	2.56**	4.92**	3.72**	1.90*	3.01**	1.31
40–49 years-60 & above	1.99*	3.03**	2.11*	2.22*	2.53**	0.97
50–59 years-60 & above	00000.27	1.03	0.73	0.67	0.40	0.31

** $p < .01$; * $p < .05$ level.

On the dimension of activity, people of age groups 10–19 years, 30–39 years, 40–49 years ($\bar{X}$ = 15.31; $\bar{X}$ = 11.94; $\bar{X}$ = 14.63) and to some extent 50–59 years ($\bar{X}$ =18.25) perceive old age with less than an average degree of activity, agility and alertness ($\bar{X}$ = 20.00). They associate old age with passivity, relaxation, peacefulness, calmness and unemotionality. Only the age groups 20–29 years, and 60 years and above ($\bar{X}$ = 21.00; $\bar{X}$ = 20.06) associate old age with an average degree of activity ($\bar{X}$ = 20.00), viz., emotionality, excitability, efficiency, alertness, tension, etc.

On the dimension of potency, Tables 5.2 and 5.3 show that there is a significant difference between the mean scores of age groups 10–19 years, 30–39 years, 40–49 years and age groups 20–29 years, 50–59 years and 60 years and above. This indicates that people of these age groups perceive old age to be associated with different degrees of potency. A comparison of all age groups shows that the age group 30–39 years perceives old age with the least amount of potency ($\bar{X}$ = 12.50) and the age group 50–59 years with the maximum amount of potency ($\bar{X}$ = 19.50). But the results also show that the mean scores for all the age groups lie below the average score ($\bar{X}$ = 20.00), which means that none of the age groups really associate old age with strength, health, and power. They associate old age with varying degrees of weakness, sickness, timidity, softness, etc.

On the Evaluation dimension, it is observed that people of the age groups 20–29 years ($\bar{X}$ = 43.25), 50–59 years ($\bar{X}$ = 41.00) and 60 years and above ($\bar{X}$ = 39.25) have neither a favourable nor an unfavourable attitude towards old age ($\bar{X}$ = 40.00). The age groups 10–19 years ($\bar{X}$ = 37.06) and 40–49 years ($\bar{X}$ = 34.38) can be stated to have a lightly unfavourable attitude towards old age. However, it is only people of the age group 30–39 years ($\bar{X}$ = 28.31) which really evaluate old age unfavourably and associate the following attributes with old age: dirty, bad, unkind, worthless, foolish, ungrateful, etc.

The results of the present study indicate that none of the age groups really have a favourable meaning of the concept old age. But nevertheless, people of the age groups 20–29 years, 50–59 years, and 60 years and above do associate old age with an average degree of receptivity, stability, activity and evaluation, whereas, people of the age groups 30–39 years, 40–49 years and 10–19 years have an unfavourable perception of old age in varying degrees. If the life span is roughly divided into three broad phases: (1) adolescence and youth (10–22 years); (2) declining of youth and approaching middle age (30 to 49 years); and (3) declining middle age and approaching old age (50 years and above); the findings show that subjects in the second phase of life have the most unfavourable perception of old age. A plausible explanation for the unfavourable perception of old age in this phase may be due to the interaction of a number of factors, such as, personal fears and insecurity of occupational achievement and finding a place in society, problems of the aged parents and fears of the impending middle age and loss of youth and attraction. The fears and insecurity of this age is reflected in the unfavourable perception of old age. The results indicate that there is a great variation in the perception of old age during the first phase of life which includes two decades: 10–19 years and 20–29 years. The first decade which ranges from 10–19 years shows an unfavourable perception of old age, whereas, the second decade which ranges from 20–29 years depicts comparatively a more favourable perception of old age on almost all its dimensions. The reasons for the difference in perception seems to be due to the fact that the young subjects of the first phase of life (10–19 years) being in the adolescent period have their own personal problems of growing up and their difficulty in trying to cope with them. Besides these personal problems, other situations like serious clashes of opinion with the parents and grand parents, restrictions imposed by the elders, and the criticism of the elderly all get expressed in an unfavourable perception of old age. On the other hand, subjects in the second decade (20–29 years) have passed the critical adolescent age and its problems, have become more confident of themselves, are busy planning a career, and have probably become more tolerant of difference of opinion and criticism of the elders, which together account for comparatively a more favourable perception of old age.

In the third phase, which includes age groups: 50–59 years and 60 years and above, subjects start perceiving old age with less disfavour in comparison to the second phase. This is because respondents of the two age groups slowly start accepting the facts of life, such as loss of youth and vitality as the middle age crises being almost over, their career is also usually at its peak and people in this phase have normally attained their maximum status in society, as a result they develop an ambivalent perception of old age.

2. Social Class and Perception of Old Age

The two-way analysis of variance (Table 5.1) shows that social class significantly ($F = 871.51$; $p < .01$) effects the way old age is perceived. Table 5.4 presents the mean scores and standard deviation on the concept old age and its dimensions in relation to social class and age. A glance at the mean scores of the upper-middle ($\bar{X} = 177.04$) and lower-middle class ($\bar{X} = 63.73$) also shows a significant difference in their perception of old age. On the whole, irrespective of age, people of the upper-middle class have a favourable perception of old age, whereas, people of the lower-middle class have an unfavourable perception of old age.

The different dimensions of the concept 'old age' were analysed separately in relation to social class and the results are presented in Tables 5.1 and 5.4. The two-way analysis of variance (Table 5.1) shows that the main effect of social class is significant on all the five dimensions: Receptivity ($F = 142.19$; $p < .01$); Stability ($F = 240.57$; $p < .01$); Activity ($F = 332.65$; $p < .01$); Potency ($F = 253.27$; $p < .01$) and Evaluation ($F = 688.29$; $p < .01$).

A perusal of Table 5.4 indicates that on the dimension of Receptivity the mean score of the upper-middle class ($\bar{X} = 13.79$) is greater than that of the lower-middle class ($\bar{X} = 8.08$). This implies that the upper-middle class perceives old age to be more receptive than the lower-middle class. The people of the upper-middle class associate more attributes like contended, sensitive and interesting to old age, whereas, the lower-middle class associates more attributes like discontended, insensitive and boring to old age.

On the dimension of Stability the greater mean score of the upper-middle class ($\bar{X} = 13.04$) in comparison to the lower-middle social class ($\bar{X} = 7.46$), means that this class perceives old age as more stable, sane and careful, etc., than the lower-middle class. The lower-middle class perceives old age as more changeable, insane and careless.

The upper-middle class associates old age ($\bar{X} = 22.08$) with more activity than the lower-middle class ($\bar{X} = 11.65$). This means that the upper-middle social class perceives old age as more active, agile, tense, excitable, emotional, etc., whereas, the lower-middle class perceives old age to be more passive, unemotional, calm and peaceful.

Old age is associated with more strength, power and potency by the upper-middle class ($\bar{X} = 19.42$) as compared to the lower-middle class ($\bar{X} = 11.25$). The upper-middle class perceives old age to be moderately healthy, strong, aggressive, hard, etc., and the lower-middle class perceives old age more with sickness, weakness, timidity, softness, etc.

On the dimension of Evaluation, it is observed that the upper-middle class has obtained a greater mean score ($\bar{X} = 48.92$) as compared to the lower-middle class ($\bar{X} = 25.50$). This means that the lower-middle class evaluates old age more as ugly, worthless, sad, unkind, unpleasant, bad, dirty, ungrateful, etc., in comparison to the upper-middle social class.

TABLE 5.4: Mean and Standard Deviation on Concept of 'Old Age' and its Factors in relation to Socio-Economic Status and Age

Age group	Socio-Economic Status											
	Receptivity (A)				Stability (B)				Activity (C)			
	High SES		Low SES		High SES		Low SES		High SES		Low SES	
	$\bar{X}$	SD	$\bar{X}$	SD	$\bar{X}$	SD	$\bar{X}$	SD	$\bar{X}$	SD	$\bar{X}$	SD
1	2	3	4	5	6	7	8	9	10	11	12	13
10—19 years	11.88	1.05	5.75	2.44	9.0	1.87	6.38	1.73	19.50	3.61	11.13	1.96
20—29 years	16.50	1.50	8.50	3.20	16.00	1.00	9.25	0.97	27.25	1.79	14.75	4.79
30—39 years	9.0	1.73	5.62	1.65	10.38	2.29	6.00	1.41	14.88	2.37	9.00	0.87
40—49 years	11.13	1.89	7.13	1.96	11.38	1.32	5.75	1.48	17.88	2.80	11.38	2.91
50—59 years	17.00	2.06	12.38	3.31	15.13	1.69	10.38	2.55	24.38	0.99	12.13	2.20
60 & above	17.25	1.85	9.13	2.25	16.38	1.50	7.00	1.22	28.63	1.58	11.50	2.92
Total	13.79	3.67	8.08	3.47	13.04	3.34	7.46	2.39	22.08	5.54	11.65	3.32

Contd.

TABLE 5.4 *Contd.*

Age group	Socio-Economic Status											
	Potency (D)				Evaluation (E)				Total			
	High SES		Low SES		High SES		Low SES		High SES		Low SES	
	$\bar{X}$	SD	$\bar{X}$	SD	$\bar{X}$	SD	$\bar{X}$	SD	$\bar{X}$	SD	$\bar{X}$	SD
1	14	15	16	17	18	19	20	21	22	23	24	25
10—19 years	13.88	2.93	11.34	2.06	47.38	4.72	26.75	6.61	101.63	10.17	61.38	8.14
20—29 years	18.25	1.71	13.50	1.32	55.50	1.58	31.00	4.71	133.50	2.92	77.00	12.11
30—39 years	15.50	3.97	9.50	1.50	32.88	2.76	23.75	3.31	82.63	4.47	52.63	4.90
40—49 years	16.63	2.39	9.50	2.40	45.50	4.70	23.25	5.09	101.25	9.01	57.00	9.77
50—59 years	26.63	1.11	12.38	3.16	57.00	1.87	25.00	4.39	140.13	3.69	72.25	12.74
60 & above	25.63	1.73	11.25	2.28	55.25	2.05	23.25	4.09	143.12	2.20	62.13	9.77
Total	19.42	5.52	11.25	2.63	48.92	8.96	25.50	5.54				

The results show that people of the lower-middle class, irrespective of the age group to which they belong, perceive old age unfavourably, whereas, people of the upper-middle class perceive old age quite favourably. Upper-middle class denotes more affluency, facilities, education, authority, etc., than the lower-middle class, as a result, the elderly of the upper-middle class maintain themselves in every possible way and try to remain healthy, strong, active and happy. Therefore, when respondents of different age groups of the upper-middle class perceive their old people their perception of old age becomes quite favourable. On the other hand, the lower-middle class is always striving to maintain respectability and a standard of living where old people also have to work and contribute towards the upkeep of the family. When the elderly of this class due to ill health cannot contribute, either financially or otherwise, they are generally neglected by their family, with the result these elderly become sad, disgruntled and sometimes quarrelsome. When people of different age groups of this class see the plight of the elderly they probably develop an unfavourable attitude towards old age.

3. Interaction of Age and Social Class on the Concept 'Old Age'

The ANOVA results (Table 5.1) show that the interaction effect is significant on the concept "old age' ($F = 18.24$; $p < .01$) and on all its dimensions: Receptivity ($F = 3.03$; $p < .0$); Stability ($F = 6.86$, $p < .01$); Activity ($F = 9.45$; $p < .01$); Potency ($F = 15.84$, $p < .01$) and Evaluation ($F = 15.14$, $p < .01$). A perusal of Table 5.4 reveals that though on the whole the upper-middle class perceives old age quite favourably ($\bar{X} = 117.04$) but still people of different age groups perceive old age with varying degrees of favourability. People of age groups 60 years and above ($\bar{X} = 143.12$), 50–59 years ($\bar{X} = 140.13$) and 20–29 years ($\bar{X} = 133.50$) perceive old age favourably, whereas, people of age groups 10–19 years ($\bar{X} = 101.63$) and 40–49 years ($\bar{X} = 101.25$) perceive old age neither favourably nor unfavourably but people of age group 30–39 years ($\bar{X} = 82.63$) perceive old age unfavourably.

Similarly, even though the lower-middle class on the whole perceives old age disapprovingly ($\bar{X} = 63.73$) but still within the class people of various age groups perceive old age with different degrees of disapproval. The rank order of the age groups in degrees of disapproval of old age is as follows:

(1) 20–29 years ($\bar{X} = 77.00$); (2) 50–59 years ($\bar{X} = 72.25$);
(3) 60 years and above ($\bar{X} = 62.13$); (4) 10–19 years ($\bar{X} = 61.38$);
(5) 40–49 years ($\bar{X} = 57.00$) and (6) 30–39 years ($\bar{X} = 52.63$).

The separate analysis of the dimensions of the concept old age also shows the same trend, that is, within each social class different age groups associate old age with different degrees of receptivity, stability, activity, potency and evaluation. The results of the study indicate that in the upper-middle class the three groups: 60 years and above, 50–59 years, and 20–29 years associate old age with almost an equally favourable degree of receptivity, stability, activity, potency and evaluation. In the lower-middle class also the age groups 20–29 years and 50–59 years, comparatively, perceive old age with less disfavour than the other age groups on the dimensions of receptivity, stability, activity, potency and evaluation. It is observed that in the upper-middle class people of the age group 60 years and above associate old age more with attributes like contended, sensitive, emotional, stable, active, healthy, strong, happy, pleasant, wise, and clean, whereas, in the lower-middle class the same age group associates the opposite attributes to old age.

Looking at the effects of age, social class and interaction of age and social class on perception of old age, it is observed that when age was considered, irrespective of social class, people of age groups 20–29 years, 50–59 years and 60 years and above were found to have an ambivalent (neutral) perception of old age. But when age and social class were taken together into consideration these same age groups in the upper-middle class were found to have a favourable perception of old age and in the lower-middle class an unfavourable perception of old age.

The following conclusions can be drawn from the findings of the present study:

1. Age is a significant factor effecting the concept 'old age' and its dimensions; Receptivity, Stability, Activity, Potency and Evaluation. People of the age groups 20–29 years, 50–59 years and 60 years and above, have been found comparatively to perceive old age more favourably than people of the age groups 10–19 years, 30–39 years and 40–49 years.
2. Socio-economic status significantly effects the meaning of the concept old age and all its dimensions. Respondents of the upper-middle class, irrespective of age, perceive old age much more favourably than respondents of the lower-middle class.
3. The interaction of age and socio-economic status has also been found to significantly effect the perception of old age.

6

PERSONALITY, ANXIETY AND SELF CONCEPT: A Study Across Age Variations and Social Class

PARAMJEET KAUR DHILLON and ANJU JASRA

Introduction

An individual's personality may develop and change as he goes through different phases of life — infancy, childhood, adolescence, adulthood, middle age and old age. The bulk of evidence and the theories of personality suggest that the basic personality character, as distinct from more peripheral character, once established, is relatively persistent across the years (Bower, 1974). But there is research evidence (Schaie and Katty, 1978) which suggests that adult personality changes can occur either as a result of systematic developmental modifications in adulthood or through significant environmental influences manifested within the individual's work and family life. Tendency towards stability or change is not necessarily built in, but relate to people's social environment. Adults undergo a certain mellowing in middle years. The masculine mid-life crises has been viewed as a time of inner and outer change with constructive or destructive consequences depending on the individual's personal and cultural circumstances (Crutmann, 1972). Orville (1976) on the other hand, reviewing literature that challenges the prevalent view that nothing of consequence occurs in the person during middle age, states that evidence does not support the existence of age specific crises, rather it suggests that transition may assume different dimensions if accompanied by multiple simultaneous demands for personality change. Data do not indicate that middle stages of life form an invariant profession of events in the life cycle. Changes are instead characterised as transitions from one comparatively steady stage to another.

When does middle age begin? Middle age has no generally accepted boundaries, some United States census reports define it as covering ages 45 to 64 years, while other studies date it from 30 to 70 years. Definitions of middle age may involve life developments. Middle age may be defined as the period when the children leave home and the parental bread winner retire from his job (Kerch Koff, 1976). Middle age may also be defined in terms of the way people perceive themselves.

Middle age, especially that part of middle age which is nearer to the onset of old age is a time which creates changes in the life pattern of both males and females. This is the time when in individual has either settled down comfortably in life or is still struggling to settle down. It is at this time when the individual starts thinking about making his life secure before retirement so that he may face no problems after retirement, and as a parent he/she is busy trying to get the children settled in life. On the other hand, a few physical changes are also visible such as greying, and the beginning of realisation that youth is over, middle age is in its last stages and old age is near. The individual, therefore, in this period of life due to these factors may experience more tension and anxiety. The physical changes occurring and the fear that someday he/she may have to become dependent on someone, and the loosing of control over children, may effect the self concept. Moreover, how the individual views old age will also influence the self concept.

Taking into consideration the controversy regarding the changes occurring in the life cycle and personality of males during the middle age, literature was reviewed on some personality variables such as anxiety, self concept and personality traits in relation to age. On each variable some studies with their relevant findings are presented in the following paragraph.

Self Concept

Psychologists, sociologists, theologists and philosophers are all interested in the investigation of the self concept. James (1890) analysed the self in terms of its constituent part as the sum total of what the individual considers himself to possess, including his body traits, characteristics, abilities, assumptions, family work, possessions, friends and other affiliations. Jesild explained the self concept as a composite of the thoughts and feelings which constitute a person's awareness of his individual existence, his conception of who and what he is, and the individual qualities he attributes to himself. To some extent the individuals' evaluation of himself is determined by his social experience.

Lorrie (1979) assessed the validity of the self acceptance construct in mapping the evaluative dimension of self concept. Three constructs: self acceptance, self description and acceptance of others — were each measured by seven different methods. The sample consisted of 137 subjects in the age range 14–82 years. The average convergent validity values were .55 for self acceptance, .42 for self description and .41 for acceptance of others. Both of the self-constructs had strong discriminant validity from acceptance of others, the average correlation of .22 between self acceptance and acceptance of others was consistent with their theoretical relationship. Perry and Slemp (1980) conducted a study on 90 men and women, to investigate the attitude of young adults (19–25; $\bar{X}$ = 23 years), middle aged (35–55; $\bar{X}$ = 46 years), and elderly (65 and over; $\bar{X}$ = 74 years) persons, towards themselves and towards others in each age group. The results indicated that the older group rated life to be much less meaningful than either of the younger groups, both when rating themselves and their peers. The younger groups rated their peers lives as even less meaningful than their own. Family was rated more important by both the young adult and middle aged groups than by the older group, both when rating the importance of family to themselves and others. The two young groups tended to see health as more important, both to themselves and to the elderly, than did those in the over 65 age group. The younger group characterised the elderly as having a great desire to be needed, while the elderly group rated themselves significantly lower on this variables. All age groups rated the elderly group as 'poor dears'.

Collter (1975) investigated the self concept in an active middle class population, 55–86 years of age, that was mobile and living independently. The results of this study show that age did not seem to depress the self concept of the subjects. If there was any trend in the data it was in the positive direction. All self concept scores increased with increasing age, notably the scores of the global self concept. The results of this study suggested that any assessment of persons in the later years must complement objective with the subjective dimension in order to secure a balanced picture of what is really happening in the third age or culminating years of life. One of the conclusions drawn from this study was that age-integration and age-segregation did not appear to influence the level of self concept.

Monge (1975) studied the structure of the self concept from adolescence through old age on 4,500 individuals. The results revealed significant main effect of age and sex on four factors; Achievement — Leadership; Congeniality — Sociability; Adjustment; and Masculinity — Femininity. Czaja (1975) compared 10 males and 10 female volunteers from 6 age groups (20–25, 30–35, 40–45, 50–55, 60–65 and 70–75) to study age differences in life satisfaction as a function of discrepancy between real and ideal self concept. Significant differences were found among age groups for real and ideal self concept scores. Age significantly correlated with real and ideal self concept, and discrepancy between real and ideal self concept and life satisfaction. Younger subject (20–25 years) had a lower real and ideal self ratings and were less satisfied with their lives than the elderly subjects (60–75 years).

Anxiety

Anxiety is both a concept and a personality trait. It is a pervasive and significant motivational dimension in personality and has been found to be a factor of considerable importance in influencing and directing human behaviour and performance.

Anxiety is unique among personality variables in its constructive and destructive potential. Without it the organism can not survive, yet can perpetuate the most primitive and bizzare behaviour. On the opposite side, anxiety raises an individual's level of motivation and enables him to make maximum use of his resources.

The concept of anxiety has played a key role in human behaviour and adjustment. No condition has been as widely held to be at the root of human misery in the form of adjustive failures or even the positive accomplishment of mankind, as anxiety. It has been found to be an important independent variable in explaining may features of human behaviour and psychopathological problems. It is also an important construct influencing social interactions.

Karen Horney (1937) made basic anxiety central to her theory. She believed that this anxiety arises from social influences in the development of man rather than from the conflict between biological motives and the ego or super ego. Basic anxiety is first aroused in the person by any social situation which tends to make him fearful. It can be instigated by tension or conflict between close ones, by criticism, coldness, indifference and so on. Once anxiety is aroused the person attempts to alleviate it by trial and error behaviour which in turn forms certain patterns of neurotic needs. A neurotic need is thus, a learned need which the person acquires to reduce anxiety. Almost everyone possesses neurotic needs to some degree but when a person is unable to resolve conflicts between them, some needs tend to dominate his or her life. Horney further stated that anxiety is not biological or instinctual in origin. It is social and arises from culturally induced disturbances in the child's development.

Mickore, Amrith and Deshpande (1967) studied the anxiety levels and personality of a sample of 100 males. They found that anxiety levels do effect personality functions. Further individuals with low anxiety levels scored higher on the traits of self reliance, sense of personal worth and feeling of belongingness as compared to those who had high anxiety level.

Stuart (1974) reported that growth from middle age to old age focusses on stage formation and the final stage permits the complete integration of personality. To investigate this difference, 65 university faculty and 35 auto workers aged 40–85 years, balanced by sex and employment/retirement, were selected. He concluded from his study that there was a significant relation of age and stage score, a relation that is independent of longevity.

Robert and Rance (1976) investigated the relationship between change in individual life circumstances, perceived rate of social change and anxiety level. These relationships were examined in 2 samples: 130, 17–66 years old subjects (predominately college students and teachers) in England and 648, 17–52 years old subjects in the U.S. Results indicated a positive correlation between both kinds of change and anxiety level, with the perceived rate of social change being more significant as a prediction of anxiety level than change in life circumstances. In both societies the data support the notion that a high rate of change generates psychological reactions which requires adjustments on the part of the individuals, with the reaction moderated when the changes are perceived as desirable.

Cumming (1944) found that anxiety tends to increase with age and girls on the whole tend to experience greater anxiety than boys.

Costa and McCrae (1976) used a cluster analytic approach to determine possible age differences in the structure of personality and 3 cognitive factors. The subjects were 969 adult male volunteers divided into 3 age groups: 25–34, 35–54 and 55–82 years. The results show no age differences in the two clusters: anxiety — adjustment, and introversion — extraversion. However, significant age differences were observed in the third cluster termed 'Openness to experience'. Young subjects showed openness to feeling, middle aged subjects showed openness to ideas and the older subjects showed a balanced openness to both feelings and ideas. The results also indicate that older subjects performed less well than younger ones on Manual Dexterity and Pattern Analysis capability but not on Information Processing ability.

Collette (1974) in a multigenerational sample (young subjects: mean = 22.9 years, N = 123; middle aged subjects: Mean = 42.2 years, N = 90; older subjects: mean = 72.9 years, N = 180) studied attitudes towards independence, achievement, personal productivity, poor health, social isolation, financial insecurity and death. All subjects devalued old age, viz., held negative attitudes towards the concomittants of old age such as poor health, social isolation and financial insecurity. The middle aged and young subjects devalued old age more than did the elderly. Significant age differences were found for all attitudes measured.

Paintal (1976) examined social relationships and activities that distinguish well adjusted from maladjusted 45–74 year old males. The subjects were 94 Hindu registered medical practitioners representing lower, middle and upper socio-economic status. Results show that (a) well adjusted subjects had more friends than poorly adjusted subjects, (b) the frequency of meeting friends and participation in organisation decreased with increasing age, and (c) poorly adjusted subjects reported feeling more bored and lonely than well adjusted subjects.

The review of literature indicates that there are not many studies investigating age differences in self concept, anxiety and personality. Furthermore, it also shows that in India, there is a dearth of research exploring the relationship between age and these personality variables. Taking the above stated observations into consideration the present study was designed to investigate the effect of variations in age, during the middle years of life, and social class on personality traits, self concept and anxiety of males.

METHODOLOGY

Hypotheses

The following hypotheses were formulated:

1. There will be no significant difference in neurotic tendency, self

sufficiency, introversion-extraversion, dominance-submission, confidence and sociability between the two age groups (45–50 years, and 57–59 years).

2. The three socio-economic classes will differ in the degree of neurotic tendency, self sufficiency, introversion-extroversion, dominance-submission, confidence and sociability, exhibited by them.

   (a) The higher social class will exhibit a greater degree of neurotic tendency, self sufficiency, extroversion, dominance, confidence and sociability than the middle and lower socio-economic groups.

3. Subject of the two age groups will differ significantly in the amount of perceived total anxiety, overt and overt anxiety.

   (a) The age group 57–59 years will exhibit a higher level of global anxiety, covert and overt anxiety than the age group 45–50 years.

4. There will be a significant difference in the amount of perceived global anxiety among the three socio-economic classes.

   (a) Subjects of the high socio-economic class will perceive the least degree of global anxiety, both covert and overt anxiety as compared to the middle and lower socio-economic classes.

5. The two age groups will differ significantly in their self-esteem.

   (a) The age group 57–59 years will have a lower self concept than the age group 45–50 years.

6. The three socio-economic classes will differ significantly in their perceived self concept.

   (a) Subjects of the high social class will have a higher self concept than subjects of the middle and lower social classes.

7. The interaction effect of age and socio-economic status will be significant on self concept, anxiety and personality traits.

Design

A 2 × 3 factorial design was used in the present study. The 2 factors are the two age groups and 3 factors are the socio-economic levels.

Sample

The sample of the present study comprosed of 240 male subjects, belonging to two age groups: 45–50 years (Mean age = 48.3 years) and 57.59 years (Mean age = 57.5 years from three socio-economic classes. High, Middle and low. The lower socio-economic groups comprised of subjects whose income was below Rs. 1,000 (Mean income = Rs. 625); The middle socio-economic group had an income of Rs. 1,500 Rs. 3,500 (Mean income = Rs. 2,900) and the income of the higher socio-economic group was above Rs. 4,000 ($\bar{X}$ = Rs. 4,250) per month. The people in the lower socio-economic group were working as peons, *daftaris*, sweepers, waterboys, drivers and clerks. The subjects of the middle socio-economic group were officers and the subjects of the higher socio-economic group were highly placed managers, directors, etc. Each age group comprised of 120 subjects, 40 subject from each of the three socio-economic classes. The sample was selected from various offices in Delhi: Reserve Bank of India, Delhi High Court, Punjab National Bank, Hindustan Petroleum, Hoechst Pharmaceuticals and DCM group.

Tools Used

1. The self concept was measured by the 'Self Concept Inventory' constructed by Deo (1961). The author has taken self concept in this inventory to be synonymous with self perception (i.e. the individual as is known to the individual). The inventory consists of 75 trait names divided into three dimensions; the physical self, intellectual self, and the socio-emotional self. Each trait adjective and its antonyms are presented on a 5-point response scale. The scale consists of pairs of adjectives classified into positive and negative, on the basis of the first adjective. A low score on the scale indicates a positive self concept while the

high score on the scale indicates a negative self concept. The possible range of scores is from 75–375.

2. Personality traits were measured by the Personality Inventory devised by Bernreuter (1961). The inventory consists of items divided into six scales measuring neurotic tendency, self sufficiency, introversion-extroversion, dominance-submission, self confidence and sociability. The scale provides six separate scores, one for each trait. The reliability coefficients were computed by the split half method for each of the six scales. The reliability coefficients range from .85 to .92. The author has reported validating the test by correlating it with previously validated tests. Norms are provided for school students, college students and adults.
3. Anxiety was assessed by the IPAT Anxiety scale Questionnaire devised by Cattell and Scheier (1963). The anxiety scale consists of 40 questions with three alternative response answers. The scale provides three kinds of scores: a total anxiety score, a covert anxiety score and an overt anxiety score. The authors in this scale have taken anxiety as comprising of five personality components: Defective Integration, lack of self sentiment; ego weakness, lack of ego strength; suspiciousness or paranoid insecurity; Guilt proneness; Frustrative tension or Id pressure. The reliability coefficients reported for the test by the test-retest method, split-half method and Kuder-Richardson method are high, ranging from .80 to .93. The authors have reported calculating Construct validity and Concrete validity. Norms have been provided for men, women and general population.
4. Personal data schedule was devised to get the necessary information regarding the subjects' age, education, position (status), income, etc.

Procedure

The subjects were approached personally at their work place and rapport was established. After gaining their confidence the three scales and the personal data schedule were administered. The subjects were requested to fill the questionnaires and provide the necessary information annonymously. The scale were translated into Hindi for those who could not understand English.

Results and Discussion

To test the first two hypotheses, means, standard deviation and ANOVA were calculated for the personality traits and the results are presented in Tables 6.1 and 6.2.

TABLE 6.1: Mean and Standards Deviation on Personality Traits

Personality traits	Socio-Economic Status	Age Groups 45–50		Age Groups 57–59		Total	
		$\bar{X}$	SD	$\bar{X}$	SD	$\bar{X}$	SD
Neurotic Tendency	Low SES	78.97	10.65	75.72	7.03	77.33	9.16
	Middle SES	90.97	4.00	73.07	16.61	82.02	14.85
	High SES	70.75	21.36	73.62	13.06	72.18	17.76
	Total	80.23	16.25	74.14	12.08		
Self-Sufficiency	Low SES	35.12	21.92	51.0	9.42	43.06	18.64
	Middle SES	48.65	33.40	47.25	23.91	47.95	29.23
	High SES	64.52	20.41	33.85	13.17	49.18	21.15
	Total	49.43	27.76	44.03	18.22		
Introversion-Extroversion	Low SES	80.25	16.98	76.30	14.76	78.28	16.75
	Middle SES	65.02	37.94	32.62	21.12	48.82	31.46
	High SES	63.25	26.98	68.30	12.03	65.77	21.00
	Total	69.50	29.61	59.07	17.41		
Dominance Submission	Low SES	31.37	18.40	28.30	14.76	29.83	16.75
	Middle SES	35.07	23.80	32.62	21.12	33.85	22.53
	High SES	29.50	16.02	24.47	12.82	26.98	19.66
	Total	31.98	9.05	28.46	17.77		
Confidence	Low SES	85.10	7.16	78.65	6.52	81.87	6.19
	Middle SES	85.55	15.15	72.10	19.11	78.82	19.32
	High SES	71.60	20.60	75.15	12.61	73.37	17.17
	Total	80.75	16.04	75.30	14.00		
Sociability	Low SES	55.72	10.05	72.83	13.79	64.27	14.75
	Middle SES	51.32	28.83	54.05	29.09	52.68	28.99
	High SES	50.82	22.66	48.32	22.56	49.57	22.64
	Total	52.62	22.06	58.40	24.97		

TABLE 6.2: Summary of the ANOVA for the Personality Traits

Personality Variables	Source of Variance										
	Age			SES			Age × SES			WC	
	df	Ms	F	Df	Ms	F	df	Ms	F	df	Ms
Neurotic Tendency	1	298133	614 **	2	96591.7	198.98**	2	47289.31	97.41**	234	485.43
Self-Sufficiency	1	193183	397.96**	2	78575.21	161.86**	2	47114.23	97.05**	234	485.43
Introversion-Extroversion	1	201158	392.02**	2	89615.8	174.64**	2	49128.65	95.74**	234	513.12
Dominance-Submission	1	742.01	1.80	2	950.88	2.30	2	36.07	.08	234	412.18
Confidence	1	83401	182.76**	2	7508.9	16.45**	2	3697.05	8.10**	234	456.33
Sociability	1	116.20	7.93**	2	43.93	2.94	2	65.95	4.50*	234	14.66

** P < .01 level; * P < .05 level.

The ANOVA analysis shows (Table 6.2) that age has a significant effect on five of the six traits of personality viz., Neurotic Tendency, Self-sufficiency, Introversion-Extroversion, Confidence and Sociability. A close perusal of Table 6.1 reveals that males of age group 45–50 years ($\bar{X}$ = 80.23) have a slight more neurotic tendency as compared to males of the age group 57–59 years ($\bar{X}$ = 74.14). This difference in neurotic tendency could be explained on the basis of mid-life crises. As Gutmann (1972) states that it is a time of inner and outer change with constructive and destructiive consequences depending on the individual's personal and cultural circumstances. In India males besides facing the mid-life personal and emotional problems, has to face problems of grown up children and these together may contribute to the slight neurotic tendency exhibited by this age group.

Males of the age group 57-59 years are less self sufficient ($\bar{X}$ = 44.03) than males of the age group 45–50 years ($\bar{X}$ = 49.43). The difference in self sufficiency can probably be attributed to job and financial security, hope of attainment of high professional status and meaning in life. On the other hand, males of the age 57–59 years are facing retirement which implies insecurity and therefore, do not feel so self sufficient.

However, comparing the results of Indian adult males with that of their American counterparts, it is observed that Indian males feel far less self sufficient than American males. This may probably be due to greater feelings of financial insecurity, dependency, and emotional insecurity among Indian males.

On the dimension of Introversion-Extraversion males of the age group 57–59 years ($\bar{X}$ = 59.07) have a less tendency towards introversion as compared to the males of the age group 45–50 years ($\bar{X}$ = 69.50). The explanation seems to be that the younger group being more self-sufficient tend towards introversion. This finding is in contradiction with the results of Gauth (1975) and Costa and McCrae (1976) who found that one tends to mellow down with age, becomes more observant and less participative, and less open to feelings. Indian adult males when compared with the American males on the Introversion-Extraversion dimension showed no significant differences were observed. Males of the age group 57–59 years have been observed to have more self confidence ($\bar{X}$ = 75.30) than males of the age group 45–50 years ($\bar{X}$ = 80.75). The results are in the expected direction as people of the older age group have made a place for themselves in society, and profession and are therefore, more confident of themselves. Whereas, people of the age group 45–50 years are still struggling to climb the ladder of success, are facing the mid-life crises, and are thus, less self confident. The Indian adult males seem to be more self confident than their American counterparts probably because of differences in the pace and demands of life in the two cultures. On the trait of Sociability, males of the age group 45–50 years tend to be more sociable ($\bar{X}$ = 52.62) than males of the age group 57–59 years ($\bar{X}$ = 58.40). This may be because with age one tends to be less boisterous, more sober and thoughtful.

The ANOVA reveals a non-significant effect of age on the dimension of dominance-submission. However, the mean scores reveal a tendency towards less dominance with increase in age but the difference is not large enough to be significant. The Indian adult males when compared with their American counterparts seen to be more dominant. The plausible explanation seems to be differences in the encouragement of different traits during socialisation of males in the two cultures.

Personality Traits and Socio-Economic Status

To study the effect of socio-economic status on the above-mentioned personality traits analysis of variance was computed (Table 6.2). The ANOVAS indicate that social status has a significant effect on neurotic tendency, self sufficiency, introversion-extraversion and confidence. A glance at the mean scores (Table 6.1) reveals that males of the middle social class have a greater neurotic tendency ($\bar{X}$ = 82.02) than males of the lower ($\bar{X}$ = 77.33) and high social class ($\bar{X}$ = 72.18). The lesser emotional stability of the middle class males could be attributed to high ambitions, striving for higher class standards, but still trying to maintain the values of the middle class, such as respectability, strong religious faith and moral standards.

The lower social class does not strive hard to raise their standard of living as they feel it is practically impossible, whereas, the upper class does not need to strive nor conform to norms as it sets the standards and norms for the other social classes.

The males of the higher social class are observed to more self sufficient ($\bar{X}$ = 49.18) than males of the middle ($\bar{X}$ = 47.95) and lower social class ($\bar{X}$ = 43.06). Males of the high social class being more financially secure and confident prefer to be alone and rarely ask for sympathy or encouragement. Whereas males of the lower social class prefer not to be alone and ask for advice and encouragement from others.

On the dimension of Introversion — Extraversion it is observed that males of the lower class have a greater tendency ($\bar{X}$ = 89.28) towards introversion than males of the middle ($\bar{X}$ = 48.82) and high social class ($\bar{X}$ = 65.77). The greater tendency of the lower social class males towards introversion may be due to financial and emotional insecurity and inferiority which makes them more imaginative and to live within themselves.

A significant effect of social class on confidence (F = 16.45, $P < .01$) is noticeable in Table 6.2. The mean confidence scores reveal that males of the higher social class have more confidence ($\bar{X}$ = 73.73) than males of the middle ($\bar{X}$ = 78.82) and lower social class ($\bar{X}$ = 81.87). The confidence of the higher class can be attributed to its status in society and affluency.

The interaction effect of Age and Social class has been found to be significant on Neurotic tendency, Self Sufficiency, Introversion-Extraversion, Confidence and Sociability. (Table 6.2). Examination of the cell means (Table 6.1) shows that males of the age group 45–50 years and of the middle class have a greater neurotic tendency than males of the other two classes and those of the age group 57–59 years. Males of the high social class and belonging to the age group 45–50 years exhibit more self sufficiency than males of the other two classes, whereas, males of the low social class and belonging to the age group 57–59 years exhibit more self sufficiency than males of the middle and high social classes.

A close perusal of Table 6.1 also reveals that males of the age group 45–50 years and belonging to the low social class show more introverted tendency than males of the middle and high social classes. Males of the high social class and belonging to the age group 45–50 years have more self confidence than males of the other two social classes, whereas, males of the age group 57–59 years and belonging to the middle class have more self confidence than males of both the lower and high social classes.

The cell means also show that males of the age group 57–59 years and belonging to the low social class are more non-social and prefer to be solitary than males of middle and high social classes. Whereas, in the age group 45–50 years males of all the social classes tend to be equally sociable.

The findings on personality indicate that (1) age effects significantly the tendency of Neuroticism, Self sufficiency, Introversion, Confidence and Sociability, (2) Social class also effect significantly the tendency to be Neurotic, Self sufficient, Introverted, and Self Confident and, (3) the interaction effect of age and social class is significant on the tendency to be neurotic, self sufficient, introverted, confident and sociable.

Hypothesis 1 stating no significant difference between the two age groups on personality traits has been rejected. Hypothesis 2 has been partially proved as males of the high class do exhibit a greater amount of self sufficiency and confidence than males of the other two social classes.

To test hypotheses 3–7 the data on Anxiety, and Self Concept were analysed and mean and standard deviation are presented in Table 6.3 and Summary of the ANOVA is presented in Table 6.4.

The ANOVA results show (Table 6.4) that age has no significant effect on overall anxiety experienced. The mean overall anxiety scores (Table 6.3) also show that males of both the age groups 40–50 years, and 57–59 years, experience almost the same degree of anxiety ($\bar{X}$ = 31.14 and $\bar{X}$ = 32.06). The findings of the present study are contrary to the results obtained by Cumming (1944) who found that anxiety tends to increase with age.

However, age has been found to effect significant the amount of Covert anxiety and Overt anxiety experienced. A glance at the mean covert and overt anxiety scores shows that males of the age group 45–50 year ($\bar{X}$ = 15.57) experience more covert anxiety than males of the age group 57–59 years ($\bar{X}$ = 14.16). Whereas, males of the age group 57–59 years experience a greater amount of overt anxiety than the age group 45–50 years. The age group 45–50 years experience more anxiety not only due to the mid-life crises but also in trying to achieve a high professional status, etc but are reluctant to admit or show anxiety as expression of anxiety would be taken as a weakness and a feminine trait (Sarason *et al*, 1979) and males at this age are already facing ego problems and therefore, have greater covert anxiety. Males of the age group 57–59 years have greater overt anxiety is probably because expression and manifestation of anxiety at this age is not directly related to the ego of the person but taken as a part of life. Males of the age group are on the verge of retirement and manifestation of anxiety is probably taken as related to the impending retirement.

TABLE 6.3: Mean and SD for Anxiety and Self-Concept

Variables	Socio-Economic Status	Age Groups				Total	
		45–50		57–59			
		$\bar{X}$	SD	$\bar{X}$	SD	$\bar{X}$	SD
Overall Anxiety	Low SES	29.39	3.19	31.00	6.15	30.19	5.92
	Middle SES	32.90	4.70	31.60	3.81	32.25	4.55
	High SES	31.12	4.99	33.57	4.09	32.34	4.13
	Total	31.14	5.25	32.06	5.68		
Covert Anxiety	Low SES	14.97	2.93	13.00	4.43	13.99	3.92
	Middle SES	16.80	4.60	13.90	2.89	15.35	4.06
	High SES	14.95	5.62	15.57	4.18	15.26	3.79
	Total	15.57	3.70	14.16	4.03		
Overt Anxiety	Low SES	14.42	3.80	18.00	7.28	16.21	6.08
	Middle SES	16.10	4.60	17.70	4.49	16.90	4.51
	High SES	16.17	5.62	18.00	4.94	17.08	5.37
	Total	15.56	4.80	17.90	5.70		
Self Concept	Low SES	182.30	24.75	186.80	7.47	184.55	19.40
	Middle SES	184.95	14.41	173.57	20.80	179.26	19.56
	High SES	179.25	13.91	159.45	16.56.	169.35	14.43
	Total	182.17	16.03	173.27	14.72		

Socio-economic status has no significant effect on overall anxiety experienced, or covert or overt anxiety. However, the interaction effect (Age × Sex) is significant on covert anxiety ($F = 4.50$, $P < .05$). The cell means (Table 6.3) shows that males of the age group 45–50 years and belonging to the middle social class experience more covert anxiety than males of the other two classes, whereas, males of the age group 57–59 years and belonging to the high social class experience greater covert anxiety than males of the other two classes. The finding indicates that the two age groups experience almost the same degree of overall anxiety but the younger age group (45–50 years) has more covert anxiety and the older age group (57–59 years) has greater overt anxiety.

The analysis of variance shows a significant effect of age on self concept ($F = 147.32$, $P < .01$). The mean self concept scores indicate that males of the age group 45–50 years ($\bar{X} = 182.17$) have a lower self concept than males of the age group 57–59 years ($\bar{X} = 173.27$). Self concept in this study covers three aspects of self: Physical, Intellectual and Socio-emotional. The age group 45–50 years because of mid-life age is facing a crises from all the three fronts. Males are trying hard to maintain their youthful looks and at the same time trying to keep the fast approaching old age away. This conflict, along with the obstacles faced in achieving high status results in a lower self-concept among males of this age group. Perry and Slemp (1980) also observed that age group 35–55 years rated health to be more important to themselves as compared to the age group 65 years and above. This finding is in line with the results obtained by Collter (1975) who observed that self concept increased with age. Monge (1975) found that the main effect of age was significant on achievement, adjustment, and congeniality-sociability. Czajo (1975) also observed that the younger subjects had a lower real and ideal self ratings than the elderly subjects.

The main effect of social class has also been found to be significant on Self Concept ($F = 73.78$, $P < .01$). The mean self concept scores of the three social classes reveal that males of the low social class have a lower self concept ($\bar{X} = 184.55$) followed by the middle ($\bar{X} = 179.26$) and the high social class ($\bar{X} = 169.35$). One of the obvious reasons for the lower self concept of the lower social class seems to be their low status and state of poverty, which implies financial and emotional insecurity, helplessness and dependency and the higher self concept of the higher social class is due to their affluency and perception of power.

The interaction effect (Age × SES) is also significant on Self concept ($F = 66.49$, $P < .01$). The examination of the cell means shows that males of the three social classes and belonging to the age group 45–50 years have more or less a similar self concept. However, it is observed that with increase in age the self concept of the males in the three social classes undergoes drastic change. Males of the age group 57–59 years and belonging to the low social class start developing a lower self concept, whereas, males of the middle and high social classes start developing a higher self concept.

Thus, it can be stated that with increase in age there is an increase in the self concept in the males of the middle and higher social classes but in the lower class with increase in age the self concept becomes lower.

The following conclusions can be drawn from the results of the present study:

1. Personality traits such as neurotic tendency, self sufficiency, introversion-extraversion, confidence and sociability are effected by age and socio-economic status.
2. Age has a significant effect on the manifestation of anxiety (Overt and Covert anxiety).
3. Age and Social class significantly effect the self concept.

Thus, it can be stated that after the early forties, age and social class effect personality traits, manifestation of anxiety and self concept among males.

TABLE 6.4: Summary of the ANOVA for Anxiety and Self Concept

Variables	Source of Variance										
	Age			SES			Age × SES			WC	
	df	s^2	F	df	s^2	F	df	s^2	F	df	s^2
Overall Anxiety	1	228.0	1.98	2	79.45	.69	2	35.98	.31	234	114.97
Covert Anxiety	1	116.20	7.92**	2	43.93	2.99	2	65.95	4.50*	234	14.66
Overt Anxiety	1	326.67	11.56**	2	33.96	1.20	2	23.37	.83	234	28.24
Self Concept	1	71459.60	147.32**	2	35790.98	73.78**	2	32252.47	66.49**	234	485.04

** $P < .01$; * $P < .05$

7

THE IMPACT OF SOCIO-ECONOMIC STATUS AND SEX ON EMOTIONAL MATURITY, LIFE STYLES, DEATH ANXIETY AND RELIGIOSITY OF THE AGED

PARAMJEET K. DHILLON and ROMA KUMAR

"What shall I do with this absurdity—
O heart, O troubled heart — this caricature,
Decrepit age that has been tied to me
As to a dog's tail. . . ."

– W.B. Yeats

The poet laments the inevitability of aging and growing old. It is a process that all are undergoing but most people are not aware of it till some marked event, such as the first grey hair, a wrinkle or an achy twinge, reminds them of it. The only consolation in this awareness is the realisation that it is inevitable and everyone else is moving along in the same direction and therefore, aging generally does not have too great an adverse effect psychologically on the aging individuals in most societies. The society in every country, the world over, has a social structure which can broadly be divided into three social classes namely the high, middle and low. Research studies have revealed that socio-economic status is a significant determinant of ideals and values (Pillai, 1975), needs (Dhillon and Acharya, 1984), motives (Tripathi, 1983), cognitive development (Sinha and Shukla, 1974) and personality (Dixit and Moorjani, 1983 and others.)

Research evidence on the significant impact of social class on human development and behaviour inspired the investigators to examine emotional maturity, life styles, death anxiety, locus of control and religiosity among the aged belonging to different social classes.

The review of literature on the elderly in relation to the above-mentioned variables is presented below.

Emotional Maturity

Emotional maturity is not only the effective determiner of the personality pattern but it also helps to control the growth of an individual's development. The concept 'mature' emotional behaviour at any level is that which reflects the fruits of normal emotional development. Smitson (1974) explains emotional maturity as a process in which the personality is continuously striving for greater sense of emotional health, both intra-psychically and intra-personally.

Kaplan (1940) elaboratising the characteristics of an emotionally mature person, states that he has the capacity of withstand delay in satisfaction of needs, ability to tolerate a reasonable amount of frustration, belief in long-term planning and is capable of delaying or revising his expectations in terms of demands of the situation.

Welford (1980) relating emotions and biological aging, states that with age the central nervous system becomes more prone to over activity and that its normal homeostatic feedback mechanisms are not as efficient as they were at younger ages. Applied to emotionality, this suggests that the intensity and duration of emotional experiences may increase with age. However, Malatesta and Kalnok (1984) in a study on 40 males and 40 females in each of the 3 age groups (17–34, 35–56 and 57–88 years) found no support for the claim that there is a drift towards more negative effect with age, nor was there evidence that emotion was less salient or important to older subjects (Ss).

Cameron (1975) conducted a study on the mood states of 6,452 persons aged 4 to 99 in four different situations : leisure, home, school and work, social class, sex and situational differences in mood were found but no significant age differences were discovered.

Reviewing 30 years of research on the subjective, well-being of older Americans, Larson (1978) found that subjective well-being was related most strongly to health, followed by socio-economic status, degree of social interaction and marital status.

McCrae and Costa (1983) in a study on 240 men (aged 35–85 years) concluded that there is no association of emotional maturity with well being and proposed that age level may determine the occasions or interpretations of happiness or unhappiness but that the quality and quantity of the experience of subjective well-being itself is independent of maturity.

George (1978) tested a sample of 380 white males and females, aged 50–76, to question the presence of a significant and predictable relationship between levels of activity and psychological well-being. The findings indicate a weak correlation between levels of activity and psychological well being. The findings support that higher levels of well-being are associated with higher SES, good health, and being married. The social status factors are important predictors of individual differences in levels of activity and psychological well-being.

Life Style

People in modern complex societies often enjoy some options in selecting and changing their "life style" — the overall pattern of living, whereby, an individual attempts to meet his or her biological, social and emotional needs. A life style provides the context in which the individual confronts the crisis of intimacy versus isolation described by Eric Erikson (Newman & Newman, 1975).

The personality theory of Adler (1929, 1931) describes the 'Style of life' as the system principle by which the individual personality functions, it is the whole that commands the parts and explains the uniqueness of the person. He further explains that every person has the same goal, that of attaining superiority. But there are innumerable ways of striving for this goal. One person tries to become superior through developing the intellect, while another bends all of his or her efforts to achieving muscular perfection. The intellectual has one style of life, the athlete another. Everything is done with an eye to the ultimate goal of achieving superiority. All of a person's behaviour springs from his or her style of life. The person perceives, learns and retains what fits the style of life and ignores everything else.

Neugarten, Havighurst and Tobin (1968) refer to eight patterns of aging that they observed emerging in a group of 70 to 79-year olds. They named these categories of behaviour patterns as: the Reorganisers, the Focussed, the Disengaged, the Holding or the Constricted, the Succorance, the Seeking, the Apathetic and the Disorganised.

Sachie (1984) presents evidence from a longitudinal study with 120 persons followed from middle (mean age 46 years) to old (mean age 67 years) age to show that cognitive style and other life style variables in midlife can predict individual differences in pattern and rate of ability decline in old age. The results suggest that during early middle age, attitudinal flexibility maintains high level of function on the fluid abilities and on motor-cognitive flexibility. High performance on the latter variables at midlife, in addition to an engaged life style and the absence of family dissolution, is critical for maintenance of high levels of ability performance from middle to old age. The longitudinal study of Maas and Kuypers (1974) focused on 30–70 years olds as they grew old. The results of the study distinguished four major life-styles among their aging subjects : the family centred persons, hobbyist, the remotely sociable persons and the unwell or disorganised persons. The first two patterns are the most adaptive in that they bring continued life satisfaction and personal fulfillment.

Death Anxiety

A major transition that people face in their later years is a change in self perception from a healthy active, person to an unhealthy, inactive person closer to death. Death and the bereavement it brings to survivors is, therefore, a reality for aging persons. Death is very personal, people may rage against it, deny it or accept it but their reaction always relates to themselves and those they value. Death occurs to persons to individuals who deal with it in their own unique ways. However, members of different age groups and social classes may have common fears, expectations about and experience with death.

Death occurs with greater frequency in old age than at any other time in the life cycle, the young may die whereas, the old person must die. However, death and dying are a normal part of the role of the aged. Kastenbaum (1965) has found that although society may expect and even try to hasten the death of the aged through cursory medical care, there exists within most of the aged a strong desire to live. Kubler-Ross (1974) has echoed the same sentiment when she asserts that "old age is not synonymous with being glad to die." Thus, although old age is a time of loneliness and despair for many older individuals, it is not necessarily a time when they feel that their lives have lost all meaning and that death is better than life. A few expectations to this general rule may be found among the aged who are socially isolated. Carpenter and Wylie (1974) found that there was a low will to live among 48 per cent of those who were socially isolated. There is a common belief that older individuals fear death more than younger individuals. However, Marshall (1975) claims that with increasing age the fear of death decreases and that older individuals generally face death with a calm and accepting attitude. Hinton (1967) has noted that young terminal patients are much more anxious than older patients about their illness. Kalish (1976) has also claimed that the lowered fear of death in the aged stems from three factors. Firstly, the aged perceive themselves as having less value and fewer prospects for the future, secondly, many aged feel that they have lived longer than expected and that they are therefore, on borrowed time and thirdly, the aged have had to deal with the deaths of friends, peers, family members and colleagues and so have come to accept death.

Keller *et al.* (1984) administrated a questionnaire on attitude towards death on 874 — 18–87-year olds, categorised into six age groups. The analysis indicated that there was no difference by sex on 'evaluation of death in general'. However, females expressed a significantly greater 'belief in life hereafter' and more 'death anxiety related to self' than males. Age was significant for 'evaluation of death in general', 'belief in the life hereafter' and 'death anxieties related to self'. The old age group exhibited less death anxiety related to self than their younger counterparts. No significant interaction between sex and age was observed for the three factors.

Ryan (1984) examined the process of dying in a squamish Indian society, a plains Indian society and an Irish society. The results show that the concepts and processes surrounding death are mediated by socio-economic, political and religious factors.

Robinson and Wood (1983) administered a death anxiety scale, a fear of death scale and a threat index to 100 people ranging in age from 17–79 years, with varying health conditions, to assess personal orientation towards death. Multiple repression analysis indicated that older Ss were significantly less death anxious, less fearful of their own death and more integrated, in that they showed less self death discrepancy than younger Ss. Further analysis revealed no differences between any of the groups on fear of death or death anxiety, indicting that the current state of a S's health was not related to his/her death orientation.

Flint *et al.* (1983) in a study on 69 females (mean age 69 years) and 22 males (mean age 67 years) tested whether older individuals with high satisfaction with life have more acceptance of death than individuals with low life satisfaction. The results supported the hypothesis that life satisfaction and death acceptance are related for older persons.

Kurlychek and Trepper (1982) examined the purpose in life and fear of death, on 23 college students and 21 Ss of 60 years and above, both subjectively (self reporting) and how they felt the Ss of the other generation would respond. The older Ss reported significantly higher purpose in life and less fear of personal death. Both groups related to other as having less purpose in life and more fear of death and dying.

Rubio Herrera (1981) on a study of 300 Ss (age 65–95 years) found that the acceptance of death increased with age of the subject, but was greatly influenced by personal history, residency and cultural and economic level.

Stevens *et al.* (1980) on a study of 295 : 16–83 years olds found that older subjects (60–83 years) had significantly lower death anxiety than younger subjects.

Keily and Dudetk (1977) interviewed 100 : 65–90 years old Ss with reference to their feelings about their own life and their attitude towards death. From the results it was concluded that when elderly people remain in good health they are active and preserve a sense of personal worth, and are not likely to have greater problems in old age than they did at a younger age.

Locus of Control

Rotter, Seeman and Liverant (1962) defined locus of control as the 'degree to which the individual accepts personal responsibility for what happens to him or her'. Lefcount (1966) defined it more explicitly as "an individual's perception of the location of responsibility for events (negative or positive) which happen to that person". Rotter (1966) introduced the Internal — External scale as a measure of individual differences in a generalised belief that a person can control his own destiny. He states that people acquire generalised expectancies to perceive reinforcing events either as dependent upon their own control or occur as a result of displaying their skills. The internal participants have a generalised expectancy that the outcome of events is contingent upon their own behaviour, while externals see little or no connection between behaviour and outcome but view what happens to them as a result of fate, luck or competence, powerlessness, helplessness, mastery and alienation.

Review of the literature on internal – external construct (Lefcourt 1967 and Rotter 1966) reports that external subjects are slower than internal subjects on learning a variety of tasks. Externality has been linked to depression (Abrahamawitz, 1969) and anxiety (Joe 1971; Phras, 1973). Ryckman and Malikiosi (1975) compared scores of college students, middle aged, and elderty persons on the Levenson Locus of control scales. They concluded that there was no decrease in internality with old age and that the elderly perceived themselves as free of control by powerful others and as living in a predictable environment.

The result of a study by Molinari and Niederche (1985), on 117 community — elderly and 305 college under graduates, suggest that the elderly sampled had a more external locus of control than the young. There was a significant relationship linking pattern of high internality and low belief in powerful others with low depression in the elderly, but not in the young. They reached some conclusions on locus of control literature with the elderly: (1) There are no consistent sex differences in locus of control nor does sex consistently interact with adjustment of locus of control in the elderly, and (2) their is a positive relationship between internality and adjustment in non-institutionalised elderly.

Lumpkins (1985) in a study on 601 subjects (mean age 72.5 years) observed that as subjects aged their health declined and they became more external in their locus of control. Even after partialing out the effect of age and health, SS with less activity were more external in their locus of control.

Tiwari and Tripathi (1981) examined the relationship between socio-economic status (SES), sex and components of perceived locus of control on 240 subjects. A NOVA indicated significant effects of SES and sex on the subjects perceived locus of control. Results indicate that low — SES Ss are more internally controlled than high SES subjects.

Mehrke, Hulicka and Morganti (1980) administered Rotter's I — E Locus of control scale, the life satisfaction scale and a measure of self concept to 99 domiciliary residents — 33 in each of the 3 age groups (50–59, 60–69, and 70 years and above). A significant age difference was found with Ss over age 70, they were more positive on the composite of the three measures. Univariate analysis, however, resulted in significant age differences in self-concept and life satisfaction but not in locus of control. Results suggest that the older Ss resolved the ego integrity Vs despair crisis more adequately inspite of having lived for a longer period of time in what has been conceived as sterile environment.

Religiosity

Religion is a powerful institution which plays an important role in shaping social behaviour. The term religiosity refers to religious faith. Galloway(1956) defines religiosity as "faith on a power beyond himself, whereby he seeks to satisfy emotional need and gain stability of life and which he expresses in acts of worship and service." He further states that religiosity has three important aspects : theoretical, practical and emotional. Theoretically it refers to an individual's faith in God or some superordinate force, experience of or belief in nearness to God and constitutes three important dimensions: communion, partnership and identification with God. The practical aspect constitutes an individual's faith in observance of ethical and moral duties and rituals as divine commands. The emotional aspect is reflected in the feeling of devotion and dedication to God and experience of pleasure, delight and satisfaction in observance of religious practices. Glock's (1962) comprehensive analysis of the "core dimensions of religiosity" provides a frame of reference within which not only the three dimensions of Galloway (1956) but also "all of the many diverse manifestations of religiosity prescribed by the different religions of the world can be ordered." He further elaborates that within each of the five dimensions there are distinctions both in kind and in degree, thus, making each of its dimensions complex and multidimensional.

Covalt (1960) found no evidence to support the common assumption that people turn to religion as they grow older. Jeffers and Nichols (1961) however, found in their study, on 251 persons of North Carolina past the age of 60, that religion means more to most subjects as the years go by and the end of life approaches.

A large study of 1700 elderly Minnesotons found that 52 to 55 per cent of the men and 66 to 71 per cent of the women reported that religion was the most important thing in their lives (Taves & Hansen, 1963).

Wolff (1961) summarising psychological aspects of aging states that geriatric patients who have ambivalent feelings towards life and death may turn toward religion which "gives them emotional support and tends to relieve them from the fear that everything soon will come to an end."

A higher proportion of old people believe that there is a life after death, there is a God and apparently are more inclined to hold traditional and conservative beliefs of their religion (Gray & Moberg, 1962). A study by Riley and Forner (1968) showed that 86 per cent of the aged were absolutely certain that a God existed. Harris *et al.* (1975) from a study reported that religion was considered to be very important in the lives of 34 per cent of those 18–24 years, 45 per cent of those 25–39 years, 58 per cent of those 40–54 years, 65 per cent of those 55–64 years, 69 per cent of those 65–69 years, 71 per cent of those 70–79 years and 73 per cent of those 80+ years.

Some studies have revealed increase in religious practices in old age. Public opinion data indicate consistently higher figures for church attendance, *Bible* reading, and prayer among persons aged 50 and over than among young groups (Tach, 1953). Age, among 597 institutional women aged 65 or older living in Protestant houses for the aged, was positively correlated with increased religious activities as well as with increased dependence upon religion (Pan 1954). However, Fiske (1961) observed that persons aged 60+ years were found to attend church less frequently than at age 50, and few attended more often than before.

Orbach's (1961) in a study on 6911 adults, residing in the Detroit Metropolitan area, found that age was unrelated to changes in church attendance; there was no indication of an increase in attendance in the later years, although the data suggests that there is a polarising effect in which intermediary categories of 'casuals' and 'cursory' church goers tend to shift into a dichotomous distribution of regular church attenders and non-attenders.

Ainlay and Smith (1984) investigated the multidimensional conceptualisation of religious participation among the aged. Data on attitudes towards religious participation and on the frequency of public and private religious behaviour were obtained on 947 church members (age 50+ years). The results revealed that religious attitudes and behaviours became more homogeneous as age increased. Secondly, the dimension of participation became more distinct with advancing age, showing an increase in private religious behaviours and a decrease in public religious behaviour.

The review of literature on the elderly in relation to Emotional maturity, Life styles, Death anxiety, Locus of control and Religiosity shows that most of the studies have been conducted abroad and that there is a dearth of information about the elderly in this context in India. Therefore, the present study was designed to fill this vacuum and to investigate the effect of socio-economic status and sex on emotional maturity, life styles, death anxiety, locus of control and religiosity of the aged (60+).

METHODOLOGY

The objective of the present study was to investigate the effect of social class and sex on Personality, Death anxiety and Religiosity in the age group 65 years and above.

Hypotheses

The following hypotheses were formulated:

(1) (a) There will be a significant difference among the three social classes in the degree of emotional maturity. The elderly of the high class will exhibit more emotional maturity than those of the middle and lower classes.
(b) Women will exhibit significantly a higher degree of emotional maturity than men.
(c) The interaction effect of social class and sex will be significant on emotional maturity.

(2) (a) The aged in the high, middle and lower class will differ significantly in their life styles.
(b) The life styles of aged women will be significantly different from aged men.
(c) The interaction effect of social class and sex will be significant on life styles.

(3) (a) The aged in the three social classes will differ significantly in their locus of control. The high class will exhibit more internal locus of control than middle and lower class.
(b) Men will exhibit more an internal locus of control and women an external locus of control.
(c) The interaction effect of social class and sex will be significant on locus of control.

(4) (a) There would be a significant difference among the three social classes in the amount of perceived death anxiety. The

high class will perceive a greater amount of death anxiety than middle and lower class.

(b) Men will perceive a greater amount of death anxiety than women.

(c) The interaction effect of social class and sex will be significant on death anxiety.

(5) (a) The high, middle and lower class will exhibit significant differences in the degree of perceived religiosity. The lower class will exhibit a greater degree of perceived religiosity than the high and middle classes.

(b) Women will perceive a greater degree of religiosity than men.

(c) The interaction effect of social class and sex on religiosity will be significant.

Design

In the present study a 3 × 2 factorial design was used. The 3 factors being the three social classes and 2, the sex. The independent variables are the social class and sex. The control variable is age, subjects belonging to the age group 65 years and above and residing in Delhi.

Sample

The total sample comprised of 240 subjects in the age group 65 years and above and belonging to three social classes. High, Middle and Low. Of these 240 subjects, 80 subjects (40 males and 40 females) represented each of three social classes. The sample was selected from different localities of Delhi representing different social classes.

Tools

1. The socio-economic status was determined by using Narain Rao's (1973) 'The Socio-Economic Status Rating Scale'. The instrument contains items on the following seven areas: (1) Community, (2) Income, (3) Occupation, (4) Education. (5) Individual's self rating of his/her own economic status, (6) Individual's self rating of his own social status and the (7) the locality from which the subject hails. Items in almost all areas of this scale were modified to suit the present times and the

urban Delhi population. The items on community were deleted to determine the social class of the subject. The author has reported using several indices of reliability such as intra judge, inter judge and test and retest reliability and the coefficients obtained range from .81 to .96.

2. Emotional maturity was measured by Singh and Bhargava's (1984) "The Emotional Maturity Scale". It contains 48 statements rated on a five point scale ranging from very much to never. The scale measures five dimensions of emotional maturity: emotional unstability, emotional regression, emotional maladjustment, personality disintegration and lack of independence. It gives an overall emotional maturity score and separate scores for the five dimensions. High scores indicate emotional immaturity. The range of possible scores for the overall emotional maturity is 48 to 240. The reliability coefficients as reported by the authors by the test-retest method was .75 and by the internal consistency method the coefficients ranged from .42 to .86. The validity co-efficient 'calculated against external criteria was found to be .64.
3. Life styles were assessed by Thorne's (1975) 'The Life Style Analysis Scale'. The scale consists of 100 items having two response categories : True/False. The questionnaire measures ten life styles, each represented by 10 items. The ten life styles are : Normal coping; Individualistic; Exploitive; Pampared-Spoiled; Defiant-Resistive; Domineering — Authoritarian; Conforming; Escapist; Oneupmanship and Evasive-Ignoring. The maximum score possible on each life style is ten and the minimum is 0. The author reports high reliability and validity for the scale.
4. Death anxiety was measured by Templer's (1972) 'Death Anxiety Scale'. The scale comprises of 15 items with two response categories. True and False. The maximum possible score is 15 and the minimum is 0. The author reports a test-retest reliability of .83 and a high construct validity.
5. Locus of control was measured by Menon, Wig and Varma's (1980) 'The P.G.I. Locus of Control Scale'. The scale comprises of seven items with three alternative response. The maximum possible score is 14 and the minimum is 0. A high score implies belief in internal control. The rest-retest and the inter-scorer reliability coefficients are reported as .77 and .99

respectively. The validity coefficient obtained by external criteria was found to be .79.

6. Religiosity was measured by Bhushan's (1970). 'The Religiosity Scale'. The instrument consists of 36 statements related on a five points scale, ranging from totally Agree to Totally Disagree. The range of possible scores is 36 to 180 and higher score indicating a greater degree of religiosity. The split half reliability of the scale is reported as .82 and the test-retest reliability as .78. The scale has high content and predictive validity.

Results and Discussion

To test the first hypothesis data on Emotional Maturity was analysed and Table 7.1 presents the summary of the ANOVA's for overall emotional maturity and its five dimensions.

The ANOVA reveals that the main effect of SES is not significant on overall emotional maturity (F = 0.85) and its four dimensions : emotional unstability (F = 1.22), emotional regression (F = 2.92), personality disintegration (F = 0.37) and lack of independence (F = 0.30).

Emotional maturity implies an ability to keep one's emotions under control, delay gratification of needs and suffer without self pity.

A glance at the overall emotional maturity scores (Table 7.2) of the aged of the three social classes ($\bar{X}$ = 79.67, $\bar{X}$ = 79.18, $\bar{X}$ = 77.13) shows that the differences amongst them is only negligible, and that the aged of all the three social classes are emotionally mature for the mean scores according to the norms lie in the extremely emotionally mature category. This finding of the study is contrary to the results of George (1978) who observed that psychological well being and activity were best predicted by social status factors and personality. Higher levels of well being were associated with higher SES and good health.

Emotional unstability represents a syndrome which includes a lack of capacity to dispose off problems, irritability, need of constant help for ones day to day work, vulnerability, stubbornness, and temper tantrums.

The mean emotional unstability scores of the three social classes ($\bar{X}$ = 14.25), ($\bar{X}$ = 15.37, $\bar{X}$ = 15.58) according to the norms lie in the 'Moderately stable category'. This implies that the elderly, irrespective of social class, have the capacity to dispose of problems and are

TABLE 7.1: Summary of the Two-way Analysis of Variance for Emotional Maturity and its Dimensions

Emotional Maturity	Source of Variance										
	Socio-Economic Status (A)			Sex (B)			A × B			Within Cells	
	df	s^2	F	df	s^2	F	df	s^2	F	df	S^2
Overall Emotional Maturity	2	145.07	0.85	1	2124.15	12.37**	2	292.33	1.70	234	171.71
Emotional Unstability	2	38.05	1.22	1	152	4.90*	2	82.89	2.67	234	31.00
Emotional Regression	2	90.08	2.92	1	281.66	9.55**	2	181.80	5.90**	234	30.77
Social Maladjustment	2	103.61	4.13*	1	53.20	2.12	2	75.18	3.00	234	25.03
Personality Disintegration	2	9.5	0.37	1	1586.20	63.22**	2	219.3	8.74**	234	25.09
Lack of Independence	2	22.21	.30	1	624.04	8.63**	2	8789.05	121.62**	234	72.26

** $P < .01$ level; * $P < .05$ level.

therefore, less irritable, vulnerable, stubborn and prone to temper tantrums. This finding is contrary to the results of Cameron (1975) who found that the frequency of happy, sad and netural moods were dependent on the social class, leisure and work. The results of the present study are also contrary to the results of Larsen (1978) who found that subjective well-being was strongly related to health, SES, housing, etc. Emotional regression denotes a broad group of factors representing feelings of inferiority, restlessness, hostility, aggressiveness and self-centredness. A glance at the mean scores on emotional regression of the three social classes (Table 7.2, $\bar{X}$ = 16.82, $\bar{X}$ = 14.79; $\bar{X}$ = 15. 26) when compared with the norms indicate that the aged use regression less often as a means to solve problems and do not feel inferior, restless, hostile, aggressive and self centered but behave as mature adults.

Personality disintegration includes all those symptoms which represent disintegration of personality, like the reaction formation, phobias, rationalisation, pessimism, immorality, etc. Such a person suffers from inferiorities and hence reacts to the environment through aggressiveness, destruction and has a distorted sense of reality. On the dimension of personality disintegration also the mean scores of the aged in all the social classes ($\bar{X}$ = 15.37, $\bar{X}$ = 14.95, $\bar{X}$ = 15.41) lie in the 'moderately integrated personality' category. This indicates that the aged do not suffer from reaction of phobic formation, pessimism, immorality and a distorted sense of reality but have a fairly good integrated personality.

Lack of independence means a parasitic dependence on others, egoism and lack of objective interests. The mean independence scores of the three social classes ($\bar{X}$ = 20.97, $\bar{X}$ = 20.04, $\bar{X}$ = 20.07) when compared with the norms reveal that the aged in all the social classes lack independence to a fair degree; in other words, according to Bhargava (1984), the aged to quite an extent are dependent on others, egoistic and lack objective interests. This finding of the study is in line with the conclusions drawn by Ebaugh (1956) that the aged are financially as well as emotionally dependent on others because of loss of friends, family members, fear of useless loneliness and indifference of children.

Social maladjustment implies lack of adaptability, feeling of hatred, seclusion, boasting tendencies, telling lies and shirking responsibility and work.

TABLE 7.2: Mean and Standard Deviation on Emotional Maturity and its Dimension

Emotional Maturity	Social Class																	
	High						Middle						Low						Total			
	Males		Females		Total		Males		Females		Total		Males		Females		Total		Males		Females	
	$\bar{X}$	SD	$\bar{X}$	SD	$\bar{X}$	SD	$\bar{X}$	SD	$\bar{X}$	SD	$\bar{X}$	SD	$\bar{X}$	SD	$\bar{X}$	SD	$\bar{X}$	SD	$\bar{X}$	SD	$\bar{X}$	SD
Overall Emotional Maturity	80.45	13.18	78.90	13.19	79.67	13.20	83.10	13.33	75.27	12.17	79.18	13.35	81.37	13.80	72.90	11.85	77.13	13.54	81.64	13.48	75.69	12.66
Emotional-Unstability	13.20	4.94	15.30	6.19	14.25	5.63	13.70	5.64	17.03	4.53	15.37	5.32	14.43	4.94	16.74	6.83	15.58	5.89	13.78	5.14	16.35	6.00
Emotional Regression	15.80	4.20	17.83	4.82	16.82	4.56	15.18	5.67	14.40	5.31	14.79	5.43	12.63	5.62	17.88	7.21	15.26	6.90	14.54	5.32	16.70	6.02
Social Maladjustment	12.73	4.74	12.05	5.33	12.39	4.99	13.88	5.20	14.73	3.92	14.31	4.57	13.78	5.57	10.78	5.08	12.28	5.47	13.46	5.14	12.52	5.03
Personality Disintegration	16.03	4.74	14.70	4.42	15.37	4.58	18.40	2.99	11.50	5.31	14.95	5.59	18.83	5.76	11.98	6.19	15.41	6.82	17.75	4.74	12.73	5.50
Lack of Independence	22.73	4.97	19.20	8.56	20.97	6.97	21.85	9.03	18.23	7.79	20.04	8.52	21.33	9.50	18.80	10.39	20.07	9.91	21.97	7.91	18.74	8.88

The ANOVA table reveals a significant effect of socio-economic status on social maladjustment ($F = 4.13$, $p < .05$). A close perusal of Table 7.2 reveals that there is a difference between the mean social maladjustment scores of the three social classes. The aged of the middle class show slightly more social maladjustment ($\bar{X} = 14.31$) than the elderly of the high ($\bar{X} = 12.39$) and low social classes ($\bar{X} = 12.28$). However, the mean social maladjustment scores of the three social classes according to the norm lie in the 'good adjustment' category, which means that they have a fairly good capacity for social adaptability, are not seclusives and shirkers of responsibility. The reason for good social adaptability among the aged seems to lie in the type of socialisation and the family structure prevalent in India where the young and the elderly live in a joint or extended family and therefore, the capacity for social adaptability develops early in life and thus, continues throughout life.

The ANOVA table also shows that the main effect of sex is significant on overall emotional maturity ($F = 42.37$, $p < .01$), emotional unstability ($F = 4.90$, $p < .50$), emotional regression ($F = 9.55$, $p < .01$), personality disintegration ($F = 63.22$, $p < .01$) and lack of independence ($F = 8.63$, $p < .01$). A close perusal of Table 7.2 shows that there is a difference in the mean overall emotional maturity scores of males and females. Males having a higher mean score ($\bar{X} = 81.64$) than females ($\bar{X} = 75.69$) indicate that females tend to be more emotionally mature than males. According to Bhargava (1984) greater emotional maturity means having a greater sense of emotional health, both intra psychically and intra personally. The degree of emotional maturity being higher in women in comparison to men could be due only partially to her biological makeup but mainly it is due to her roles as a wife, mother and homemaker.

Males are more emotionally stable ($\bar{X} = 13.78$) than females ($\bar{X} = 16.35$) which means that women in comparison to men lack the capacity to dispose of problems, are more irritable, vulnerable, stubborn and prone to temper tantrums. This findings seems indirectly in agreement with the findings of Malatesta and Kalnok (1984) who found that emotion was important to the lives of women than men and they engaged in more emotional masking than men. Cochran and Hale (1984) reported that the connection between health and psychological distress levels seem relatively pronounced for the elderly males than females.

On the dimension of emotional regression it is observed that females use regression much more ($\bar{X}$ = 16.70) than males ($\bar{X}$ = 14.54). This means that women comparatively feel more inferior, restless, hostile and aggressive than men and therefore, in difficult situations use regression as a strategy to cope with the situation. The explanation for women regressing more than men seems to lie mainly in the kind of socialisation of Indian girls. The nurturance and rearing of girls is such that they develop feelings of inferiority and weakness. Regressive behaviour in girls in India is accepted if not actually approved by society, but such behaviour is not acceptable in males.

The mean personality disintegration scores indicate that males ($\bar{X}$ = 17.75) have a greater tendency towards reaction and phobic formation, pessimism, aggression, destruction and a distorted sense of reality, viz., towards neuroticism than females ($\bar{X}$=12.73). These findings are indirectly in agreement with Cochran and Hale's results (1984) that relationship between psychological distress levels and health are relatively more pronounced for males than females. Thus, under psychological distress women break down and cry and therefore, giving expression to their emotions. Men in order to prove to themselves and others that they are a symbol of strength do not express their emotions but try to hide them and this may be one of the reasons for a greater tendency towards personality disintegration .

On the dimension of lack of independence, it is observed that Indian women have a lesser inclination towards dependency on others ($\bar{X}$ = 18.74) than Indian males ($\bar{X}$ = 21.97) in old age. These findings seem to be contrary to expectation but on closer observation of the Indian society it is apparent that the tendency is of the aged males towards dependency rather than the females. Women even in old age continue to perform household duties even in the presence of young daughter's and grand daughter's-in-law but elderly males start depending on their sons and grandsons.

No sex differences were observed on the dimension of social maladjustment (F = 2.12). The mean scores indicate that the aged of both the sexes ($\bar{X}$ = 13.46, $\bar{X}$ = 12.52) have a good capacity for social adaptability. The plausible explanation for the good adjustment of the aged of both sexes, irrespective of social class, seems to lie in the process of socialisation, the Indian family structure and the Indian society.

The analysis of Variance (Table 7.1) shows a significant interaction effect of social class and sex on the dimensions of emotional regression (F = 5.90, $p < .01$), personality disintegration (F = 8.74, $p < .01$) and lack of independence ($F = 121.62, p < .01$). The examination of the cell means indicates that females of the high and low social classes resort to regressive behaviour more often than males of these classes. On the other hand, males of the lower class make use of regressive behaviour the least as compared to males of the other two classes and females of all the social classes.

On personality disintegration the cell means show that males of the middle and lower social class have a greater tendency for personality disintegration than females of these classes and males of the high class. Whereas, females of the high social class have a greater tendency towards personality disintegration than females of the other two social classes. These findings are in agreement with results of Cameron (1975) who reported that social class and sex were determinants of differences in needs among the aged.

The examination of cell mean scores on independence reveals that males in all the social classes lack independence more than females in the age group 65+.

The summary of the findings on Emotional Maturity is as follows:

(1) Social class does not significantly effect the degree of emotional maturity of the elderly in the age group 65+. The elderly in India exhibit a high degree of emotional maturity;

(2) Females have significantly a greater degree of emotional maturity than males, irrespective of social class; and

(3) The interaction effect of social class and sex is significant on three dimensions of emotional maturity: emotional regression, personality disintegration and lack of independence.

Life Styles

To test the second hypothesis Two-way analysis of variance was computed for the ten life styles and Table 7.3, 7.4 and 7.5 present the results.

The ANOVA table reveals that SES has a significant effect on five of the ten life styles used by the aged. Social class significantly effects the use of the normal coping style ($F = 5.23, p < .01$). A glance at the mean normal coping style scores (Table 7.4) of the three social classes shows that the aged of the high social class use this style to cope with their biological, social and emotional needs more than the aged of the lower class ($\bar{X} = 3.13$) and the aged of the middle class ($\bar{X} = 2.94$). The

TABLE 7.3:. Summary of the Two-way Analysis of variance for Life Styles

Life Styles	Source of Variance										
	Socio-Economic Status (A)			Sex (B)			A × B			Within Cells	
	df	s^2	F	df	s^2	F	df	s^2	F	df	S^2
Normal Coping Style	2	35.59	5.23**	1	30.10	4.43*	2	4.02	0.6	234	6.80
Individualistic Style	2	56.27	8.46**	1	8.07	1.21	2	143.32	21.55**	234	6.65
Exploitive Style	2	16.54	1.95	1	71.50	8.44**	2	2.84	0.34	234	8.47
Pampered-Spoiled Style	2	8.87	1.11	1	5.71	0.71	2	36.83	4.59*	234	8.03
Defiant-Resistive Style	2	21.38	2.18	1	0.70	0.07	2	2.66	0.80	234	9.80
Domineering-Authoritarian Style	2	37.09	4.57*	1	67.198	8.28**	2	52.17	6.42**	234	8.12
Conforming Style	2	35.39	5.75**	1	0.21	0.03	2	17.71	2.88	234	6.16
Escapist Style	2	85.29	10.98**	1	14.50	1.87	2	2.31	0.30	234	7.77
Oneupmanship Style	2	4.78	0.94	1	30.81	6.06*	2	0.35	0.70	234	5.08
Evasive-Ignoring Style	2	0.82	0.09	1	15.00	1.80	2	10.96	1.31	234	8.34

** $p < .01$ level; * $p < .05$ level.

significance of difference between means (Table 7.5) also reveals that the aged of the high class use this style significantly to a greater degree than the aged of the lower ($t = 2.63, p < .03$) and middle class ($t = 3.33, p < .01$). The aged of the middle and lower class do not differ significantly in the use of this style. The normal style of coping reflects the normal methods of earning or getting what is wanted by paying for it. However, the aged of the middle and lower class use this style rarely, whereas, the aged of the high class use this style comparatively more frequently.

On the Individualistic life style social class has been observed to have a significant effect ($F = 8.46, p < .01$). The mean individualistic style scores (Table 7.4) of these social classes reflect the use of this style in varying degrees. The significance of mean difference reveals (Table 7.5) that the aged of the high social class use this life style to a greater degree than the aged of the lower class ($\bar{X} = 4.33$, $\bar{X} = 2.83$, $t = 3.48, p < .01$) and the middle class ($\bar{X} = 2.93$, $t = 3.03, p < .01$). There is no significant difference in the use of this life style between the aged of the middle and lower class. The aged of the middle and lower class use the individualistic life style rarely, whereas, the aged of the high class use it more frequently. The individualistic life style reflects the need to be distinctively individualised and different to meet their biological, social and emotional needs. The reason for the high class aged to use this style frequently to meet ones needs is probably because they are resourceful and can financially afford to be distinctive in their dress, living and also behaviour, whereas, the aged of the middle and lower class due to lack of resources cannot afford to have a distinctive individualised life style even if they desire such a life style.

The significant effect of social class on the Domineering-Authoritarian life style ($F = 4.57, p < .05$) indicates that the aged of the different social classes differ in the use of this life style. The mean scores and the significance of mean difference (Tables 7.4 and 7.5) shows that the aged of the middle class use this life style more than the aged of the lower class ($\bar{X} = 5.44$, $\bar{X} = 4.13$, $t = 2.91, p < .01$). There is no significant difference between the aged of the high and middle, and high and lower class in the use of the domineering-authoritarian life style. This style is used most by the aged of the middle class. However, the aged of all the three social classes use this life style quite frequently. The domineering-authoritarian life style reflects that the attitudes of authority and 'I know best', 'You should do what I say'. The explanation for the use of this life style by the aged in general, is

TABLE 7.4: Mean and Standard Deviation of Life Styles

Life Styles	Socio-economic Status																					
	High						Middle						Low						Total			
	Males		Females		Total		Males		Females		Total		Males		Females		Total		Males		Females	
	$\bar{X}$	SD	$\bar{X}$	SD	$\bar{X}$	SD	$\bar{X}$	SD	$\bar{X}$	SD	$\bar{X}$	SD	$\bar{X}$	SD	$\bar{X}$	SD	$\bar{X}$	SD	$\bar{X}$	SD	$\bar{X}$	SD
Normal Coping Style	3.88	2.30	4.48	3.11	4.18	2.76	2.78	2.00	3.10	2.08	2.94	2.05	2.53	2.07	3.73	2.25	3.13	2.24	3.06	2.19	3.77	2.50
Individualistic Style	3.70	2.42	4.95	3.12	4.33	2.86	2.68	2.12	3.18	2.10	2.93	2.11	3.15	2.67	2.50	2.01	2.83	2.34	3.18	2.40	3.54	2.41
Exploitive Style	4.00	2.44	3.30	2.45	3.65	2.47	4.78	3.57	3.65	2.69	4.22	3.29	5.28	3.12	3.83	2.81	4.56	3.29	4.69	3.12	3.59	2.66
Pampered-Spoiled Style	4.18	2.88	3.70	2.73	3.94	2.82	2.80	2.01	4.68	3.05	3.74	2.55	4.63	2.93	4.15	2.86	4.39	2.90	3.87	2.62	4.18	2.91
Defiant-Resistive Style	3.68	2.43	4.08	3.13	3.88	2.81	3.83	2.88	4.05	3.19	3.94	3.04	4.95	3.23	4.65	3.56	4.80	3.40	4.15	2.92	4.26	3.31
Domineering-Authoritarian Style	6.05	2.49	3.10	2.37	4.58	2.85	5.55	3.29	5.33	2.77	5.44	3.04	4.13	1.89	4.13	2.25	4.13	2.93	5.24	2.95	4.19	2.94
Conforming Style	4.20	2.23	3.40	2.25	3.80	2.24	1.98	1.00	2.98	2.07	2.48	1.54	3.23	2.40	2.85	2.09	3.04	2.25	3.14	1.90	3.08	2.16
Escapist Style	4.40	2.31	4.85	3.30	4.63	2.86	4.55	2.31	5.49	4.48	5.02	3.42	2.95	2.32	3.13	2.09	3.04	2.20	3.97	2.77	4.46	2.99
Oneupmanship Style	3.65	2.67	3.08	2.29	3.37	2.51	3.23	1.79	2.53	1.95	2.88	1.80	3.58	1.97	2.70	2.05	3.14	2.00	3.49	2.19	2.77	2.09
Evasive-Ignoring Style	3.83	2.76	3.48	2.74	3.66	2.74	3.15	2.67	4.00	2.89	3.58	2.81	2.95	2.07	3.95	2.84	3.45	2.50	3.31	2.55	3.81	2.83

probably due to their being the breadwinners of the family during their younger days and also due to the respect and importance accorded to them in the Indian family, especially, in the middle class families.

TABLE 7.5: Significance of Mean Difference of the Comparison Groups on Significant Life Styls: t-values

Life Styles	Comparison Groups		
	High Class – Low Class	Middle Class – Low Class	High Class – Middle Class
Normal Style	2.63*	0.95	3.33**
Individualistic Style	3.48**	0.23	3.03**
Domineering-Authoritarian Style	1.02	2.91**	1.87
Conforming Style	2.71*	1.87	3.38**
Escapist Style	3.96**	4.62**	0.74

** $p < .01$; * $p < .05$.

Socio-economic status has been observed to have a significant effect on the conforming life style ($F = 5.75$, $p < .01$) of the aged. The mean conforming life style scores show that the aged of the high social class comparatively use this style more than the aged of the lower class ($\bar{X} = 3.80$, $\bar{X} = 3.04$, $t = 2.17$, $p < .05$) and the middle class ($\bar{X} = 2.48$, $t = 3.38$, $p < .05$). There is no significant difference in the use of this style between the aged of the middle class and the low class ($t = 1.87$). The conforming life style implies the level of adjustment by 'going along with people', viz., doing what the majority expects or conforming to the rules and norms of society. Comparing the aged of the three social classes it is observed that the aged of the high class comparatively make the maximum use of the conforming life style and the aged of the middle class make the minimum use of it. However, in spite of differences in the conforming life style among the social classes the mean scores when compared with the norms indicate that this life style is not used often, in fact it is used rarely. The plausible explanation for using this life style 'only sometimes' by the aged seems to be that either they are disillusioned by the present rules and norms of society, or the norms are no longer functional and important for them. A significant effect of SES is observed on the Escapist life style ($F = 10.98$, $p < .01$) implying that the aged of the different social classes differ in the use of this style of life. A glance at the mean scores (Table 7.4) and the significant difference between means, reveals that the aged of the middle class use this style to cope with life problems and their needs more than the aged of the lower class ($\bar{X} = 5.02$, $\bar{X} = 3.04$, $t = 4.62$, $p < .01$). Similarly, aged of the high class also use the escapist style more than the aged of the lower class ($\bar{X} = 4.63$, $\bar{X} = 3.04$, $t = 3.96$, $p < .01$). There is no significant difference between aged of the high and middle classes in the use of this life style. The aged of the high and middle social classes use the escapist style quite frequently, whereas, the aged of the lower class use it rarely to deal with life problems and needs. The results are not surprising for it is observed that high and middle classes try to evaded unpleasant stressful situations for they are thought to be soft and weak, but the lower class has learnt that they cannot avoid unpleasant situations and so have learnt to confront them and in the process have become hard and strong emotionally.

No significant effect of SES has been observed on the Exploitive style, Pampared-spoiled style, Defiant-resistive style, Oneupmanship style and the Evasive-Ignoring style, implying that the aged in the three social classes do not differ in the use of these life styles to gratify their needs and solve the problems of life. The finding regarding the significant effect of social class on five life styles in this study are consistant with the results of Mass and Kuypers (1974) who reported that health and SES are the most salient features influencing both life styles and personality.

The two-way analysis as variance (Table 7.3) indicates the main effect of sex to be significant on four life styles: Normal coping style ($F = 4.43$, $p < .05$), Exploitive style ($F = 8.44$, $p < .01$), Domineering-Authoritarian style ($F = 8.28$, $p < .01$) and Oneupmanship style ($F = 6.06$, $p < .05$). A close perusal of Table 7.4 reveals that females ($\bar{X} = 3.77$) use normal coping style slightly more than males ($\bar{X} = 3.06$), but this life style when compared with the norms shows that this style is used by both sexes only occasionally.

Males use the exploitive style ($\bar{X} = 4.69$), domineering-authoritarian style ($\bar{X} = 5.24$) and Oneupmanship style ($\bar{X} = 3.49$) more than females ($\bar{X} = 3.59$, $\bar{X} = 4.19$, $\bar{X} = 2.77$, respectively). This implies that males attempt to get ahead by exploiting others, have attitude of authority, and 'I know best', and use their wits to get the better of people more than females. The plausible explanation for the aged men to use these life styles more than aged women seems to be that they have been the breadwinners in the family, have faced the struggles of life and survived in the cut threat competitive world probably by the use of these life styles. On the other hand, women having led a sheltered life did not need to use these life styles to the same extent. However, it is noticed that the aged males use these life styles in different degrees with the domineering-authoritarian style being the most often used, followed by the exploitive style and the oneupmanship style. No significant differences were observed between the sexes in the use of the Individualistic, Pampered-Spoiled, Defiant-Resistive, Conforming, Escapist, Evasive-Ignoring styles. Aged of both sexes use these life styles occasionally and almost to the same degree.

The analysis of variance (Table 7.3) reveals that the interaction effect of SES and sex is significant on three life styles : Individualistic, Pampered-Spoiled and Domineering-Authoritarian. The examination of the cell means shows that females of the high and middle classes use the individualistic life style more than males of these classes but males of the lower class use this style more than females of this class. On the pampered-spoiled style females of the middle social class use this style far more than the males of this class, whereas, there is no significant difference between males and females of the high and low social classes in the use of the pampared-spoiled style. The males of the middle social class use the pampared-spoiled style rarely as compared to the males of the other two classes and females of the three social classes.

A close perusal of the mean scores (Table 7.4) reveals that males of the high class use the domineering-authoritarian style far more than females of this class, whereas, no significant difference is observed between the males and females of the middle and lower classes in the use of this life style.

The findings indicate that: (1) Socio-economic status has a significant effect on some life styles of the aged; (2) Sex significantly effects the use of some life styles and that also probably due to differences in the roles of the present aged in their life. The aged males and females do not exhibit any particular dominating life style to cope with life situations; and (3) the interaction effect of social class and sex is significant on a few life styles of the aged.

Death Anxiety, Locus of Control and Religiosity

To test hypotheses 3-5, data on Death Anxiety, Locus of Control and Religiosity was analysed and Table 7.6 present the summary of the ANOVA's and Table 7.7 the mean scores and standard deviation.

TABLE 7.6: Summary of the Two-way Analysis of Variance for Death Anxiety, Religiosity and Locus of Control.

Psychological Variables	Source of Variance										
	Socio-Economic Status (A)			Sex (B)			A × B			Within Cells	
	df	s^2	F	df	s^2	F	df	s^2	F	df	S^2
Death Anxiety	2	4.07	0.56	1	4.82	0.67	2	22.47	3.12	234	7.21
Religiosity	2	4438.06	6.10**	1	17136.60	23.55**	2	1368.77	1.88	234	727.61
Locus of Control	2	7.21	1.04	1	91.27	13.13**	2	5.58	.80	234	6.95

** $p < .01$.

The ANOVA table shows no significant effect of social class on amount of perceived death anxiety (F = .56) of the aged. The mean scores (Table 7.7) show that the aged, irrespective of the social class, have almost the same amount of anxiety about death ($\bar{X}$ = 8.75, $\bar{X}$ = 8.55, $\bar{X}$ = 9.00). The results of the present study are in contradiction with the findings of Ryan (1984), who found that the concepts and processes surrounding death are mediated by socio-economic factors. The results are also contrary to Herrera's (1981) findings that acceptance of death was greatly influenced by personal history, residency, cultural and economic level. The plausible explanation, for the non significant difference in the amount of perceived death anxiety among the aged, of all the three social classes, may be because death in the elderly is a reality and as Kalish (1976) states 'death is a biological event, a rite of passage, an inevitability and a natural occurrence' and with age a growing awareness that death is near, probably, results in similar attitude towards and apprehensions about death in the aged, irrespective of social class.

A nonsignificant difference has been observed in the amount of perceived death anxiety between the sexes (males $\bar{X}$ = 8.63; females $\bar{X}$ = 8.91). The reason seems to be, that with increase in age the awareness of death brings about a similar degree of anxiety in males and females. This finding of the study is consistent with Rhudick and Dibner's (1961) results showing no demonstrable relationship between type of death attitudes and sex, age and occupational status. The results of the study reveal that the aged in India, irrespective of social class and sex, perceive more or less an average degree of death anxiety.

On Locus of Control it is observed that social class has no significant effect (Table 7.6, F = 1.04). The mean locus of control scores ($\bar{X}$ = 6.68, $\bar{X}$ = 6.29, $\bar{X}$ = 6.76), reveal that the aged in India have an ambivalence about the location of responsibility for events, both negative and positive, as the mean scores lie near the neutral score 7. This finding of the study is in contradiction with the result obtained by Tiwari and Tripathi (1981), who found that low SES individuals are internally controlled than high SES individuals. The results are also contrary to Lumpkins (1985) findings that the aged people have more external locus of control.

The ANOVA shows that the main effect of sex is significant on locus of control (F = 13.13, $p < .01$). Aged females showing ambivalence of locus of control ($\bar{X}$ = 7.02) whereas, the males showing an inclination towards an external locus of control ($\bar{X}$ = 6.13). Teski,

TABLE 7.7: Mean and Standard Deviation on Death Anxiety, Religiosity and Locus of Control

Psycological Variables	Socio-Economic Status																					
	High SES						Middle SES						Low SES						Total			
	Males		Females		Total		Males		Females		Total		Males		Females		Total		Males		Females	
	$\bar{X}$	SD	$\bar{X}$	SD	$\bar{X}$	SD	$\bar{X}$	SD	$\bar{X}$	SD	$\bar{X}$	SD	$\bar{X}$	SD	$\bar{X}$	SD	$\bar{X}$	SD	$\bar{X}$	SD	$\bar{X}$	SD
Death Anxiety	8.13	2.67	9.38	2.24	8.75	2.54	8.98	2.69	8.13	2.72	8.55	2.74	8.78	2.39	9.22	3.10	9.00	2.78	8.63	2.61	8.91	2.71
Locus of Control	5.93	2.75	7.43	2.22	6.68	2.56	6.55	2.31	6.03	2.81	6.29	2.45	5.93	2.44	7.61	2.98	6.76	3.00	6.13	2.68	7.02	2.57
Religiosity	69.50	25.79	94.90	17.30	82.20	25.37	74.47	22.63	90.90	25.14	82.68	25.29	90.90	34.14	99.77	31.33	95.33	33.06	78.29	29.40	95.19	25.51

Arcuri and Lester (1980) have also reported females to have comparatively a more internal locus of control, especially housewives who had worked, showed significantly higher belief in internal control. The results of the present study are however, contrary to the findings of Thomas and Hooper (1983) and Molinari and Niederche (1984) who reported no significant difference between the sexes on locus of control.

No significant interaction effect of socio-economic status and sex is observed on locus of control.

The results indicate that the perception of the aged in all the three social classes is ambivalent on locus of control, probably, because of the socio-cultural religious milieu in India.

On Religiosity the main effect of social class is significant ($F = 6.10$, $p < .01$, Table 7.6). The mean religiosity scores (Table 7.7) show that the aged of the lower social class are more religious than the aged of the middle ($\bar{X} = 95.33$, $\bar{X} = 82.68$, $t = 2.71$, $p < .01$) and the high classes ($\bar{X} = 82.20$, $t = 2.82$, $p < .01$). The lower class aged being more religious, may be due to the greater insecurities and struggles of life, where a strong belief in Fate and God probably, provides some solace to them. This findings is in agreement with the results of Wingrove and Alston (1971), who reported a strong impact of social environment on church attendance. However, the results are contradictory to the earlier findings (Kivett, 1979) which state that religious motivation is not effected by age, education and occupation.

Females differ significantly from males on Religiosity ($F = 23.55$, $p < .01$). Females are observed to be more religious ($\bar{X} = 95.10$) than males ($\bar{X} = 78.29$). Wingrove and Alston (1971) also obtained similar results, viz., they found females to be more religious than males at nearly all ages. This implies that women in most cultures are more religious than males probably, because of their greater emotional insecurity, physical weakness and vulnerability, and faith in a power beyond provides emotional satisfaction and stability in their life. No significant interaction effect was observed on perceived religiosity. The results of the study imply, that those groups who are disadvantaged in society, such as, lower class and females, are more religious than the advantaged groups.

Thus, the following conclusion can be drawn from the findings of the present study:

(1) Socio-economic status is a significant factor influencing life

styles and religiosity among the aged in India.

(2) Sex significantly effects overall emotional maturity, emotional unstability, emotional regression, personality disintegration and lack of independence; the normal coping, exploitive, domineering-authoritarian and oneupmanship styles of life; religiosity and locus of control; and

(3) The interaction effect is significant only on emotional regression, personality disintegration, lack of independence; and the individualistic, pampared-spoiled and domineering-authoritarian life styles.

8

COPING STRATEGIES ACROSS SOCIO-ECONOMIC CLASS: A Study of the Aged

PARAMJEET KAUR DHILLON and SEEMA CHHABRA

Introduction

Human aging is a pattern of changes in the structure and functioning of the body and the adjustment of the person. A human being throughout his life desires self respect, respect from others, to be useful, to be able to enjoy new pleasures, accept new challenges, be a part of the present and future, to free oneself from over-powering physical needs, excessive stress and anxiety and to function up to one's potential and capacity. It seems, however, that old people have more than their share of all these stresses and the accompanying strain. The role of stress in human functioning is of great significance as it effects satisfaction, morale, adaptive functioning, physical health, mental health and well being.

Stress during old age can arise from a number of sources. Birren (1964) states the following six sources of stress that are age-related in society and that may also vary with the social class:

i) adverse physiological changes and restrictions on activity;
ii) occupational redundancy or failure to progress;
iii) failure to keep pace with cultural, social and scientific developments leading to the feeling of being out of data and out of touch;
iv) loss of youthful vigour and freedom coupled with the uninviting prospect of growing old, usually reinforced by prevailing social attitudes;

v) loss of values or stabilising emotional relationships through bereavement, loss of employment or departure of children and,

vi) the 'no-solution' problem of being caught up in a web of unsatisfactory circumstances, especially those not of one's own making, from which escape seems impossible, such as, marital ties, shortage of money and unsatisfactory employment.

People come to terms with life in old age in various ways. There is no standard or 'best' mode of adjustment and elderly people evolve strategies of personal adjustment, which enable them to avoid emotionally disturbing situations or strategies which enable them to cope with the stressful situation. Lee *et al.* (1984) regarded coping as a critical strategy that allows the older population to appraise their situations, assess needed skills, and face critical, radically distinct life tasks.

Craik (1965) observed that older people differ widely but many become more cautious and less confident. Cautiousness becomes more prominent with age, that is, older people seem to be less discriminating with respect to the particular hazards of different situations, while the young are confident in some situations but not in others.

In a study by Reichard *et al.* (1962), cluster analysis was applied to 115 ratings of the personal characteristics of 40 well adjusted and 30 poorly adjusted subjects. It revealed five fairly distinct ways of 'coming to terms' with the problems of old age. These five strategies were: Constructive approach; Dependency; Defensiveness; Hostility; and Self-hate.

Friedman and Garnick (1962) in a study, conducted on a heterogeneous sample of 140 subjects, divided into two age groups 45–65 years (young) and 65–86 years (old), and tested the hypothesis that the aged tend to regard anger as undesirable but yet perceive themselves free to show such feelings. The subjects were given the Clyde Mood Scale and had to answer the question: Is it right to be angry? The results confirmed the hypothesis. The frequency of 'yes' responses to the question: It is right to be angry ? was significantly greater in young than the older group. No sex differences were found in the age groups. Self-descriptions, derived from the Clyde Mood Scale, showed that the young group more often thought themselves as rebellious but the old group more often thought themselves as furious.

McCrae (1980) carried out two cross sectional studies which

attempted to assess the influence of age on the use of 28 coping mechanisms. In the first study 255 men and women aged 24–91 years completed a questionnaire on three stresses as perceived by them. Results indicated that the older people coped in much the same way as younger people and that where they employed different mechanisms, it appeared to be largely because of the different types of stress they faced. However, middle aged and older persons were consistently less inclined than younger persons to rely on hostile reactions and escapist fantasy, regardless of the type of stress.

West and Simmons (1983) examined the relationship between life changes and illness for each sex, to determine if elderly men and women differ in their vulnerability to life change stress and to identify differences in what serves as a coping resource. 132 men and 167 women over the age of 65 years completed a battery of questionnaires that focussed on nine variables: Life change, illness, marital status, confidence, social resources, self-efficacy, religiosity, occupational status and income. Results suggest that elderly women are more responsive to life changes. This may be due to the tendency for males to be less emotional and to suppress feelings. For women, marriage and self efficacy were exacerbators, for men, having a condigned exacerbated illness. Resources functioning as coping facilitators for young age groups (such as high occupational status) may function as coping inhibitors when related to the largely negative or uncontrollable events of old age. In addition, the sexes were found to differ in the factors that serve as coping resources.

Preston and Mansfield (1984) too explored the relationship among stress, coping and health through interviews with 200 elderly (aged 60–92 years), residents of small communities in central Pennsylvania. Subjects were asked to indicate stress associated with life changes and events, the size of their social networks, coping styles, health status and whether health inhibited daily activities. Using cluster analysis, four groups were identified with different degrees of stress and health and with distinct patterns of coping. Group 1 (26% of Ss) led stress-free lives and had good health; group 2 (41%) experienced higher life stress and reasonably good health and used coping styles based on keeping active and managing without much outside help; Group 3 (27%) subjects had similar stress and health scores compared to Group 2, but were more likely to feel that their health inhibited their activity, employed the largest repertoire of coping mechanisms, and had a larger helping network than Groups 1 and 2; and Group 4 (6%) was characterised by life stress, poor health and limited activity suggesting a loss control over their bodies and problems with independent living. Group 4, it is noteworthy was the smallest in size.

Review of literature indicates that a number of studies have been conducted in India on adjustment trends of middle and old age individuals and on the factors related to adjustment in old age but hardly, any study on the modes of adjustment or coping strategies of the elderly. Ramamurti (1968, 1971) found that among the urban aged men there was a deterioration in adjustment with increasing age.

Jamuna (1984) in a study of rural women also observed a similar deterioration of adjustment with age in the later years. Some of the variables found to contribute to good adjustment in old age were good husband-wife communication, spouse living, good marital satisfaction, high role availability and involvement. Individuals living in joint families were found to have better adjustment than individuals living in nuclear families (Jamuna, 1984). Individuals from higher socio-economic classes (Ramamurti, 1970 & 1978) and individuals of higher educational status (Ramamurti, 1968, 1970; Jamuna 1984) showed better adjustment. Anantharamah (1979) studied 172 subjects (55–89 years) from Bangalore using an adjustment inventory. The results showed that adjustment was positively correlated to education, occupation, income and social class but negatively with age in later years.

Keeping in view the scarcity of studies in India on how the elderly 'come to terms' with the problems of old age, the present study was designed with the purpose to examine and compare the coping strategies of the aged belonging to different socio-economic classes.

METHODOLOGY

Objectives

The objectives of the study were as follow:

(1) To determine the coping strategies of the aged in each of the three socio-economic status groups: Low, Middle and High.

(2) To compare the coping strategies of the aged of the three SES groups.

Sample

The sample consisted of 90 males in the age group 60+ years. Of these 90 elderly males, 30 males were selected from each of the three socio-economic classes: High, Middle and Low. Table 8.1 shows the schematic representation of the sample.

TABLE 8.1: Schematic Representation of the Sample

Variables	Socio-economic Class		
	LIG	MIG	HIG
N	30	30	30
Sex	Male	Male	Male
Average Age	68 yrs.	66 yrs.	70 yrs.
Average Income	Rs. 350/p.m.	Rs. 1000/p.m.	Rs. 2200/p.m.
Residential Colony	Delhi Cantonment	West Delhi	South Delhi

Tools

The following tools were used in the study:

(i) The socio-economic status was measured by a modified version of Kuppuswamy's (1962) Socio-Economic Status Scale (Urban). The item referring to income was modified according to the government pay scales as applicable before the 1986 revision of pay scales.

(ii) Coping strategies were assessed by Westbrook's (1979) 'Coping Strategies Scale'. Westbrook developed a classification of coping based on people's cognition of the domain by a multi-dimensional scaling of 87 similarity ratings of 30 coping strategies from a selection of coping strategies listed by Mechanic (1970), and Adams and Preston (1969). A representative sample of 30 items were selected for the coping strategies scale. These 30 items covered six coping strategies: Action, Escape; Optimism; Seeking Interpersonal help; Fatalism and Passivism; and Control. The scale provides a five point response category ranging from always true to never true. Higher the score greater the use of the coping strategy.

Procedure for Data Collection

The data were collected from various colonies of New Delhi and the process of data collection was the same for each of the three socio-economic classes. After establishing good rapport with the respondents and assuring them of complete confidentiality, the Socio-Economic Status scale was administered. This ascertained the subject's relative socio-economic rating. On the basis of the socio-economic status rating 30 respondents were selected from each of the three social classes and the coping strategies scale was administered. Both the scales were translated into Hindi for those who could not understand English.

Results and Discussion

Keeping in mind the objectives of the study, the data were analysed by Descriptive statistics, ANOVA and *t*-test. The discussion is presented in two parts, keeping in view the objectives of the study:

(1) Profile of the coping strategies of the aged in each socio-economic class.

Lower Socio-economic Class: A perusal of Table 8.2 reveals that the lower social class makes the maximum use of the strategy of 'seeking interpersonal help' (86%), followed by the strategies of 'Fatalism' (82%) and 'Escapism' (72.57%). This implies that the lower social class, in coping with various stresses of day to day life, seeks help, comfort and sympathy from others. This class also makes great use of the strategy of 'Fatalism and Passivism', i.e. an acceptance that much of life is difficult and problematic. It also exhibits a tendency of escapism, implying a strategy of avoidance or lack of mastery either by emotional reaction (crying) or getting away to keep one's mind of the problem.

The aged of the lower social class relatively employ least the 'Control strategy'. They employ the strategies of 'Optimism' and 'Action' to a moderate degree. The findings regarding the use of these coping strategies by the lower class aged can be explained by the psychology of poverty. Pareek (1964) defined poverty psychologically in terms of deprivation, helplessness and powerlessness. Poverty as a structural component produces a three fold motivational pattern characterised by low need for achievement, extension and high need for dependency. It is contented that dependency motive is expressed through a lack of initiative, avoidance syndrome, excessive fear of failure, seeking favours and almost lack of self help. The present study conforms to this view with respect to the coping patterns of the aged from the lower social class.

Middle Socio-economic Class: Table 8.2 shows that the aged of the middle class also employ the strategy of 'Seeking interpersonal help' (75.15%) the maximum, but they also use the strategy of 'Action' almost equally (74.94%). The third strategy used in order of preference is 'Fatalism and Passivism (67.53%). This means that the aged of the middle social class too have a tendency to seek help, sympathy and comfort from friends and relatives about family, professional and personal problems.

Besides seeking help, these aged also personally take positive action, try to find the cause of the problem, its solution and ways of coping with it. At the same time the aged of this class also accept that life is difficult and there will be problems. The strategy of 'Control' to cope with stresses of life is used to a moderate degree (52.3%), whereas, the strategies of 'Optimism' and 'Escapism' (31.67%) are relatively used less often.

High Socio-economic Class: The aged of the high social class cope with the day to day problems by employing the strategy of 'Optimism' (87.57%) the maximum, followed closely by the strategy of 'Seeking interpersonal help'(81.85%) and 'Control' (71.65%). This implies that the aged of this class have a tendency to remain optimistic and cheerful about the future and do not worry unduely with respect to the present and the past. They talk to friends and relatives about their problems and seek advice, sympathy and comfort but they also perceive themselves capable of controlling their feelings and the situation, accepting the limitations and compromising. A close perusal of Table 8.2 reveals that to cope with life problems the aged of this class also employ the strategies of 'Escapism' (63.23%) and 'Action' (62.37%) almost equally. The strategy of 'Fatalism' and 'Passivism' is also employed to a moderate degree (52.33%).

A glance at the profile of the coping strategies of the high class reveals that the aged of this class to a great extent employ almost all the strategies, five out of six, to cope with the stresses of life, the strategy employed, probably depends upon the stress situation.

Comparison of the Coping Strategies of the Aged Amongst the Three Socio-economic Classes

1. Action Strategy: The ANOVA (Table 8.2) indicates a highly significant F value (F = 30.24, p < .01), implying that there is a significant difference in the mean action strategy scores of the aged of the three social classes. The middle social class elderly males differ significantly from the higher social class (t = 3.85) and the lower class elderly males (t = 10.18) in the use of this coping strategy. In other words, the aged of the middle class ($\bar{X}$ = 26.23) employ the Action strategy to a greater extent than the aged of the higher class ($\bar{X}$ = 21.83) and the lower class ($\bar{X}$ = 19.0). Thus, the aged from the middle class learn from their past experiences, see the challenges in the problem, and take positive action to a much greater extent than the aged of the other two classes.

2. Escapism Strategy: Table 8.2 shows that the aged from the three social classes differ significantly on the strategy of Escapism (F = 3.89, p < .05). The significant difference between mean scores reveals that the lower class aged employ this strategy more than the aged of the middle class (t = 14.43, p < .01) and the higher class (t=3.04, p < .01). The comparisons show that the elderly males of the lower social class tend to have an avoidance orientation to the greatest extent ($\bar{X}$ = 21.77), followed by the aged of the higher class ($\bar{X}$ = 18.97), and the middle class ($\bar{X}$ = 9.5). Westbrook (1979) states that the strategy of escapism implies, avoidance or lack of mastery either by emotional reaction (crying) or getting away or doing things to keep one's mind off the problem.

3. Strategy of Optimism: The ANOVA shows a highly significant F value (F = 85.28, p < .01), which indicates that the aged of the three social classes differ significantly on the strategy of Optimism. The aged of the high social class differ significantly from the aged of the middle class (t = 11.68, p < .01) and the lower class (t = 14.85, p < .01), in the use of this strategy to cope with the problems of life. Table 8.3 also shows that the elderly males of the middle class and lower class do not differ significantly in the extent to which they employ an optimistic attitude in dealing with the problems of life.

4. Strategy of Seeking Interpersonal Help: Table 8.2 shows that the F value (F = 6.22) is significant at the .01 level of significance, indicating thereby, that the aged of the three social classes differ from each other to the extent they seek help, advice, sympathy and comfort

TABLE 8.2: Mean, S.D., F Value and Response Percentage for each of the six Coping Strategies in Relation to Socio-economic Status.

Coping Strategies	Socio-economic Status Groups									
	LSES			MSES			HSES			
	$\bar{X}$	SD	%	$\bar{X}$	SD	%	$\bar{X}$	SD	%	F-Value
Action	19.00	1.05	54.29	26.23	3.74	74.74	21.83	4.95	62.37	300.24**
Escapism	21.77	3.91	72.57	9.50	2.51	31.67	18.97	3.19	63.23	3.89*
Optimism	14.83	3.79	49.43	13.30	5.80	44.33	26.27	1.79	87.57	85.28**
Seeking Inter-personal Help	17.20	1.28	86.0	15.03	3.25	75.15	16.37	2.79	81.85	6.22**
Fatalism and Passivism	12.30	2.70	82.0	10.13	3.91	67.53	7.83	2.58	52.33	16.48**
Control	8.80	3.08	44.0	10.46	2.80	52.30	14.33	5.76	71.65	13.88**

** $p < .01$ level * $p < .05$ level.

from others around them, in dealing with the problems of life. Table 8.3 shows that the middle class and lower class aged differ significantly in the use of this strategy. However, the elderly males belonging to the high social class were found not to differ significantly from the aged of the lower class and middle class on this strategy.

5. Fatalism and Passivism Strategy: The ANOVA shows a significant F value, which means that the aged males of the three social classes are significantly different to the extent they hold fatalistic and passive attitudes towards life and in dealing with the various problems of life. Significance of mean difference shows that the aged of the lower social class differ significantly on this strategy from the aged of the middle class ($t = 2.49$, $p < .05$) and high class ($t = 6.57$, $p > .01$). The middle class and high class aged also differ significantly in the use of this strategy. The aged of the lower class make the maximum use of this strategy ($\bar{X} = 12.30$), followed by the aged of the middle class ($\bar{X} = 10.13$) and the high class ($\bar{X} = 7.83$). This mean that the aged of the lower class, according to Westbrook's (1979) explanation, are prepared to expect the worst, accept that life is difficult and anticipate problems. This strategy implies a passive orientation towards life and its problems. The aged of the middle class have a more fatalistic and passive orientation towards life than the aged of the high class.

6 Control Strategy: The ANOVA shows a significant F value ($F=13.88$, $p < .01$), which implies that the aged of the three social classes are significantly different on this strategy. Tables 8.2 and 8.3 show that the aged of the high social class differ significantly in the use of this strategy from the aged of the middle class and the low social class. The middle class and the high class aged also differ significantly in the use of this strategy to cope with problems. The results show that, among the aged of the three social classes, the high social class aged employ the strategy of control to the greatest extent ($\bar{X} = 14.33$), followed by the aged of the middle class ($\bar{X} = 10.46$) and the low class ($\bar{X} = 8.80$). This mean that the aged of the high class tend to have a greater control on self and their feelings and can compromise in situations to a much greater extent than the aged of the middle and the lower class.

The findings reveal that the aged of the lower social class are more passive, fatalistic and escape oriented as compared to the aged of the other two social classes. The aged of the middle social class are the most action oriented, while the aged of the high social class are the most optimistic and control oriented. The findings of this study are indirectly consistent with the results of Dhillon and Goswami (1983), who observed that the three social classes differe significantly in the degree of satisfaction in life and emotional security. The High SES group was observed to be the most emotionally secure and satisfied in life, followed by the Middle and Low SES groups. The conclusion drawn by them was that a high level of dependency, financial insecurity, and lack of opportunities to improve their lot intensifies the feelings of emotional insecurity in the lower social class. Following the same line of reasoning it can be stated that the fatalistic, passive and escapist strategies used by the lower social class, as revealed from the results of the present study, are probably because of high emotional and financial insecurity, lack of confidence and feeling of hopelessness.

TABLE 8.3: Significance of Mean Difference of Comparison Groups on Coping Strategies: t-values

Coping Strategies	Comparison Groups		
	HSES-LSES	MSES-LSES	HSES-MSES
Action	3.04**	10.18**	3.85**
Escapism	3.04**	14.43**	12.79**
Optimism	14.85**	1.20	11.68**
Seeking Interpersonal Help	1.48	3.39**	1.71
Fatalism and Passivism	6.57**	2.49*	2.67*
Control	4.69**	2.18*	3.28**

** $p < .01$ level   * $p < .05$ level.

Thus, it can be concluded from the findings of this study that inspite of the fact that the aged in general, irrespective of social class, employ the strategy of seeking interpersonal help to deal with the problems of life, still the coping strategies used by the aged are determined significantly by the social class of the aged.

COMMENTS

The study of aging in relation to social class difference has not been an area of extensive research. The general public also views old people as being alike, when in fact they come from different social class backgrounds, have spent much of their lives in different occupations, and have had quite disparate life experiences. The results of the first study evince that different social classes and age groups of the Indian community have different meaning of the concept 'Old Age'. In other words, the perception of 'Old Age' one has is effected significantly by one's social class and age. People of the upper middle class perceive old age favourably, whereas, people of the lower middle class perceive old age unfavourably. The upper middle class perceive old age to be receptive, stable, active and of value with an average amount of strength and power. Differences in age groups, irrespective of social class, also show variations in the meaning of old age. People of age groups 20–29 years, 50–59 years and 60 years and above have neither a favourable nor unfavourable but an ambivalent perception of old age. These age groups also perceive old age with an average or more or less an average degree of receptivity, stability, activity and evaluation. On the other hand, age groups 10–19 years, 30–39 years and 40–49 years perceive old age unfavourably. The interaction effect of social class and age is also significant on the concept old age. All age groups of the upper-middle class have either a favourable or an ambivelent perception of old age, except the age group 30–39 years, which perceives old age rather unfavourably, whereas, all age groups of the lower-middle class perceive old age very unfavourably.

The results of the second study indicate that self-concept and personality traits like neurotic tendency, self-sufficiency, introversion extraversion and confidence are significantly effected by social class and age. The respondents of the high SES group exhibit less neurotic tendencies, more self-sufficiency and more confidence; the middle class respondents show more neurotic and dominance tendencies; and those of the lower class a low self concept, less self-sufficiency, confidence, sociability and extraversion. Age group 45–50 years manifest higher self concept, more neurotic and introvent tendencies, more self-sufficiency, less confidence, more sociability and more covert anxiety than the age group 57–59 years. The interaction effect of social class and age is also significant on self-concept, covert anxiety and most of the personality traits.

Significant effect of social class is observed on the life styles and religiosity of the aged 60 years and above. Aged of the high SES group use more often the normal, individualistic and conforming life-styles; those of the middle SES group use more often the domineering-authoritarian, and escapist life styles; and the aged of the low SES group have more religiousity and use more often the exploitive, pampered-spoilt and defiant-resistive life styles. Sex is another significant main effect on these psychological variables. Aged males have more an internal locus of control and use the exploitive, domineering-authoritarian and oneupmanship life styles more often than aged females, whereas, aged females have more religiosity and use the normal life style more often than aged males. The interaction effect of social class and sex is significant only on life styles.

In the last study of this section, the results show that males of the age group 60 years and above, of the different social classes, evolve diverse strategies of personal adjustment to avoid emotionally disturbing situations or to cope with stressful situations. The high social class aged, deal with day to day life problems by employing more often the strategy of optimism and control; the middle class aged, the strategy of action; and the lower class aged, the strategies of seeking interpersonal help, fatalism and escapism.

The empirical findings of these studies do establish that social class is another important variable besides age and sex in the process of aging and the lives of the aged.

PART IV

RETIREMENT AND AGING

INTRODUCTION

The dictionary meaning (*Chambers's Twentieth Century Dictionary*, 1964) of the term 'to Retire' is to withdraw: to retreat: to recede: to withdraw from society, office, public or active life, business, profession, and 'Retirement' as, 'an act of retiring: or state of being or having retired'. Since the term retirement implies withdrawal from society, active life, work and career, no wonder there are paradoxical view on it in the minds of people. As Cox (1984) states that "on one hand, retirement is viewed as a well-deserved right earned by long years of hard work in a particular occupation. On the other hand, there is the tacit feeling that one is being forced out of a chosen career and the opportunity for gainful employment." These views are held particularly, about mandatory retirement. For it is felt that chronological age, is a poor indicator of ability to perform work and mandatory retirement discriminates against older workers. The age of retirement is not the same throughout the world but varies across countries. In India, the age of retirement for government employees is 58 years, whereas, for semi-government employees it is 60 years. In America the age of retirement for all employees is 65 years. The age of retirement not only varies across countries but also across professions. In the army if a person does not get promoted beyond a Lt. Colonel by the age 48 years he is given mandatory retirement.

Retirement is viewed as a period of crises and adjustment, where a multiplicity of problems confront the individual at the time of retirement. Cox (1984) states that some of these problems are 'lowering of income; the loss of status, privilege, and power that were associated with one's position in the occupational hierarchy; a major re-organisation of life's activities since the nine-to-five work day becomes meaningless; a changing definition of self due to the fact that most individuals over time come to shape their identity and personality in line with the demands of their major occupational roles; a considerable degree of social isolation if new activities are not found to replace previous work-related activities; and a search for new identity, meaning, and value for one's life. Obviously, the major reorganisation of one's life that must take place at the time of retirement is potentially a source of adjustment problems for those individuals who must negotiate the change." However, Streib and Schneider (1971) and Schulz (1980) obtained contrary research findings to the view point stated by cox. They found that while retirees experienced a sharp drop in income, most of them stated that they were getting along well enough and did not feel a decline in status or class position.

Parnes (1985) states that some myths about retirement exist, such as it undermines physical health of the retiree and often leads to death; and it leads to disruption in family relations at it alters the balance of power and division of labour between husband and wife. However, research gives evidence of contrary effects. Longitudinal studies have found that most retirees show a slight improvement in their overall health following retirement and that there is no difference in the mortality rate of the retirees compared to those remaining in the labour market. Regarding effect on family ties, Kalish (1975) observed that retirement may actually improve family relations as couples have more time to spend together.

The, myths that retirement causes the multiplicity of problems which an individual is confronted with at the time of retirement makes a person apprehensive of and anxious about retirement. The first investigation is a study to determine the apprehensions about retirement and the level of anxiety of class I male officers, who are on the verge of retirement, as compared to those officers, who have still some years to go before retirement.

The second study investigates the social support net work and perception of life events of retirees who are re-employed and those who are not re-employed. This study determines the effect of work and career on perception of different social supports and the effect of these perceived social supports on perception of life events.

9

ANXIETY AMONG RETIRED AND WORKING CLASS I OFFICERS: A Comparative Study

PARAMJEET KAUR DHILLON and SEEMA MILBANDER

"We look before and after
and pine for what is not;
Our sincerest laughter
with some pain is fraught;
Our sweetest songs are those
that tell of saddest thoughts."

– P.B. Shelley

'Man could live longer if he was allowed to work longer' reports the Soviet Institute of Gerontology. Without activity time becomes void and meaningless. As he ages, a person can make time last longer by increasing sensory input and living to the fullest with all emotions and perceptions possible. Unless an aged person knows how to use his time meaningfully, his life becomes aimless and he feels lost in the quagmire of existence and all his time is needlessly wasted. The fact what most people take for granted, is that there are only 24 hours to a day, and this becomes even more stark when a 'busy man of yesteryears' suddenly finds that he has too much time on hand and nothing of worth to do. Retirement and after, thus, becomes devalued by the very persons who are on the verge of, or, are already going through, this compulsory retirement/compulsory 'exile' from productivity. Retirement is not a sudden event; the seed is sown from middle adult years onwards. It is a social role, that begins to unfold, requiring adjustments and assessments of previously held values, and attitudes in relation to many life events (Atchley, 1971).

Retirement is an important status passage in every society; it marks the step from the worker to non-worker, from productive maturity to seemingly non-productive old age (Maddox, 1968). However, it takes on different nuances and meanings for different people. While it is generally thought of as signalling the end of an individuals' usefulness in the work force, others may feel quite differently, especially if they have loathed the kind of work they were doing prior to retirement. Every person has his own set of choices, negotiations and coping patterns consistent with his own perceptions, meanings and social reality.

Atchley (1975) suggests that adjustment to retirement depends on what the meaning of work has been to that person. In addition, his capacity to cope with changes and his view of the role, are equally important when analysing post-retirement adjustment. Even as everyone is aware that retirement brings about some expected disruption in the life of the retired person, it is obvious that some are more affected than others. Atchley (1975) further elaborates this point, when he states that the answer lies in the relation between the amount of change introduced in this period, and the capacity of the individual to deal with change routinely.

Thus, there exist two groups of persons — flexible or adaptive and inflexible or rigid. Another important variable is the individuals' hierarchy of personal goals, which if achieved, give him a considerable self satisfaction and personal worth. While the development of personal qualities is important to some, others value material goals such as property, land, etc. The hierarchy and goals change with success or failure or substitution of new goals. For those people whose hierarchy is such that job lies at or near the top, retirement becomes more difficult. For those who stress personal qualities, the job may not be so important. Materialistic people may value the job only to the extent that it satisfies their ability to achieve their goals. Both decision-making and internal compromise are important as far as this hierarchy is considered. Interpersonal negotiations, i.e., the ability of others significant to him, to understand and accept his hierarchy, is equally vital to satisfactory adjustment.

One of the results of retirement for some people, has been termed as retirement *shock*. This refers to the uncertainties of retired life, and how to make ends meet. More frequently, it is the prospect of retirement rather than retirement itself that causes greater conflict and contributes to an unsettled state of mind. Doubts about future worth, financial worries, reduced income, standard of living one has maintained so far, all these are only some of the ramifications of this 'shock' phase.

Compulsory retirement thus, can be viewed as a clear case of discrimination against the aged. It has taken away the fundamental right to work. It has denigrated those of the older generation, most of whom are still as capable and can contribute meaningfully to society at large as well as, and perhaps more important, the immediate family, who have come to depend on him for subsistence, as well as a reasonably high standard of living, which they are used to. If on retirement, this person, who has thus far enjoyed power, prestige, status and comfort both at work and at home, is suddenly discarded as if he were a torn and tattered garment which must be shrugged off, and is made to feel 'old', it is only natural to expect the symptoms of breakdown: anxiety, depression and frustration which in turn precipitate physical stresses. This pervading impression that he is now 'old' and needs 'rest', along with his diminished sense of worth, power, and importance — all give rise to unwarranted emotional problems and shatter his self esteem, morale and feeling of worth. Traditionally, in every society, the male members have always been regarded as the bread and butter winners, although in most families, the female members are now emancipated and are working as hard as their opposite sex. This is the reason for assuming that female members of the Indian households who approach retirement do not suffer from its consequences as much as the men do. After all, is it not a fact that women in the Indian community have always been looked at as the second sex and have had to live up to the image of the 'grihaswamini'? Therefore, the tensions and anxiety associated with the loss of a job and meagre income at the time of retirement are more crucial to the males rather than the females.

Thus, the anxiety, tensions and apprehensions of the retired males, and those males who have still some years to go before retirement, is taken as more worthy of investigation. Taking the above mentioned observations into consideration, the present study was designed with the purpose to investigate the affect of retirement on the level of anxiety experienced by working and retired males and also to investigate the nature and type of tensions, apprehensions, and anxiety experienced by males in the two phases. These objectives are based on the assumption that males in both phases will experience some anxiety, tensions and apprehension but differences may be in the level, nature, and type of anxiety and tensions experienced. The study of anxiety is important firstly, because 'ours is an age of anxiety', and secondly, the anxiety of an individual, in general, is a fair indicator of his level of adjustment and adaptation.

METHODOLOGY

Sample

In order to delve into the chief areas of concern and the type of anxiety experienced by working and retired males, the sample was selectively chosen. The sample consisted of 50 class I male officers of which 25 belonged to each category: Working and Retired. The age range of working group was 52–56 years, the mean age being 55.3 years. The mean range of the retired group was 62–65 years the mean age being 63.5 years. All the officers belonged the various ministries and the UPSC and were above the rank of Under Secretary, working or retired.

Tools Used

1. A Personal Data Schedule was devised to obtain information about the respondent's age, status: Working/Retired/Working after retirement, educational level, designation, etc.
2. Anxiety was assessed by the IPAT Anxiety Scale Questionnaire (ASQ) developed by Cattell and Scheier (1963). The IPAT anxiety scale is a brief, non-stressful, clinically-valid questionnaire for measuring anxiety in adults and adolescents. This scale has primarily been designed to measure free floating, manifest anxiety level, whether it be situationally determined or relatively independent of the immediate study. The IPAT anxiety scale consists of 40 questions, distributed among five anxiety-measuring factors (or components) according to each personality component's centrality as a source or expression of anxiety. The five factors (or components) are Q3: Low self control; C: Emotional Instability; L: Suspicion; O: Apprehension and Q4: Tension. The 40 items are divided into (a) those which manifestly refer to overt or symptomatic conscious anxiety, and (b) those that refer to more covert hidden purpose cryptic anxiety. Three types of scores can be obtained from the scale: (1) Total anxiety score, (2) part anxiety scores; (1) covert and (b) overt anxiety, and (3) five anxiety component scores.

3. To probe further into the tensions and apprehensions of the retired and working males, an open-ended questionnaire was devised by the investigators. The questionnaire covered five areas of concern: (a) Concern for retirement; (b) Plans for work after retirement; (c) Satisfaction with life accomplishments; (d) Amount of change sought; and (e) Personal meaning of retirement.

Results and Discussion

The aim of this study is to compare the levels and types of anxiety of the working and retired males and supplement this objective compilation with more details gathered from an open ended questionnaire interview taken individually, whereas, they completed the ASQ forms themselves. The focus is not on coping strategies as such, but to understand the nature of the anguish and emotional upheaval that retirement or the thought of retirement brings about. Data on anxiety was analysed and the mean and SD of total anxiety, covert and overt anxiety was calculated and the results are presented in Table 9.1.

TABLE 9.1: Mean Anxiety Scores on Overt and Covert Anxiety of the Retired and Working Men

Anxiety	Working		Retired		Total
Covert anxiety	M	= 17.0	M	= 19.36	18.18
	SD	= 2.72	SD	= 2.68	
Overt anxiety	M	= 16.52	M	= 17.84	17.18
	SD	= 2.65	SD	= 2.56	
Total		16.76		18.60	

TABLE 9.1a: Two-way ANOVA Showing Working/Retired Groups and Covert/Overt Anxiety

Source of Variance	df	SS	MS	F	Significance
Working/Retired Groups (A)	1	84.64	84.64	12.02	**
Covert/Overt Anxiety (B)	1	25.0	25.0	3.55	NS
A × B	1	6.76	6.76	0.96	NS
Within cells error	96	675.36	7.035		

** $p < .01$ Level.

TABLE 9.2: Analysis of Variance on the five Components of Anxiety for the Working and Retired Groups.

Groups	Source of Variance	df	SS	MS	F	Signf.
Working group	Within	120	132.32	11.061	35.37	**
	Among	4	1565.01	391.25		
	Total	124	2892.33			
Retired group	Within	120	1931.52	16.096	70.07	**
	Among	4	4552.11	1138.03		
	Total	124	6483.63			

** $p < .01$ Level.

It is evident from Table 9.1 that retired men are more anxious than working men. The mean anxiety score of the retired group is 18.6, while the mean of the working group is 16.76. To find out if there is a significant difference in these means and whether the two groups differed significantly on the two part scores – Covert and Overt Anxiety, ANOVA was computed and presented in Table 9.1a. It is clear from Table 9.1 itself that retired men have a higher score on Covert anxiety as well as on Overt anxiety; but Table 9.1a shows that the difference is significant. The ANOVA results indicate that there is no significant difference between the two groups on Overt-Covert part scores. It means that although retirement does not bring about significant fluctuations in the amount of latent, unconscious tension or in the amount of overt, real anxiety, it does result in bringing about significant stress, worry and frustration. This shows that the retired men are on the whole, more tense, anxious and psychologically demoralised than the working men. Since the entire sample consisted of Class I officers from the various ministries, all enjoying or having enjoyed positions of power, affluence, and prestige, one can attribute this apparent anxiety to concerns associated with loss of job, which is synonymous to loss of all the correlates that the job had entailed. Also from the interviews it was evident that there was the marked feeling that "he was no longer a 'needed' person; he was totally dispensible", and this became more demoralising. At once he started feeling that he was a liability to the immediate family – which added to his inner unrest, turmoil, and resulted in greater bitterness, hopelessness and depression.

Along with this, is a drastic fall in the standard of living, irrespective of savings, which in these times of inflation, is low anyway. The way of life they were used to, is no longer a reality; this is a hard fact to reconcile to. The pressures of inadequate planning, coupled with other irreconciliable changes, makes life more of a burden than ever before. This is why, the retired men end up as casualties of their own making.

In order to determine which of the 5 components of total anxiety have contributed to the above results, the two groups were compared on each factor using the t-test of significance. Table 9.3 shows that the retired officers are significantly higher on Apprehension and Tension (Means are 18.96 and 21.08 respectively), while the working group is significantly higher on Low Self Control, Emotional Instability and Suspicion (means are 10.84, 17.36 and 12.20 respectively).

The above results show that the retired people worry more, are unable to face challenges, get morose and downhearted easily, and also they have considerably greater amount of general frustration than their working juniors. On the other hand, the working group lacks self control and tends to be disdainful of socially approved behaviour. Their insecurity, lack of foresight and preparation can be gauged from the fact that they score higher on emotional instability and suspicion. In other words, although the retirees are anxious and frustrated, they have not lost their self control, emotional equilibrium and faith. They are more tolerant, controlled, stable, trusting and do not manifest their anxiety to others, but hide it from public view. Their guilt and apparent frustration can be interpreted in the light of Erikson's (1964) theory of psycho social stages of ego development; this period corresponding to late adulthood when the social crisis facing the person is one of Ego-integrity vs Despair, and later Generativity vs Stagnation. In order to determine whether there existed any significant variation between the mean scores obtained by each subject on each of the five components, the one-way ANOVA was calculated. The results are shown in Table 9.2. From this it is obvious that the variability of scores of each subject about his subgroup mean, and the variability of the subgroup mean about the total mean, is significant at the .01 level, for both groups.

The effect of many life events depend on the meaning that an individual attaches to them. Majumdar (1985) in a survey of the elderly in Delhi found that after retirement there is a pervading feeling among the aged that others' attitudes towards them changes. Old people felt that no one said anything directly to them but they could sense the under currents. Most people tend to feel lonely and face innumerable problems financially. That financial condition is a strong predictor of life satisfaction prior to retirement and health is a strong predictor after retiring, has been seen in several studies abroad. But studies in India have shown that older people have greater problems in the areas of emotional, social, health and home adjustment in that order (Singh, Singh and Dawra, 1983; Ramamurti, 1968; 1970).

In order to investigate further the areas of concern for both the groups, individual interviews with the help of a pre-structured questionnaire were conducted and these interviews were analysed along 5 factors. The results tabulated are presented in Table 9.4. It can be seen that while 96 per cent of the working group felt more concerned about finance and housing in that order, 96 per cent of the retired group felt concerned about finance, housing and then family matters in that order. To the question of satisfaction with life accomplishments, 93 per cent of the working group emphasised that they were neither dissatisfied nor frustrated. On the contrary, 48 per cent of the retired group were satisfied with their present life style while the remaining 52 per cent were emphatic about having got a raw deal from life and hence they expressed complete dissatisfaction.

TABLE 9.3: Significance of Difference between Mean Scores of Working and Retired Groups along 5 Dimensions of Anxiety

Dimensions of Anxiety	Comparison Groups				t-value
	Working group		Retired Group		
	Mean	SD	Mean	SD	
O Apprehension	17.44	3.176	91.96	3.58	4.12**
Q4 Tension	18.28	3.397	21.08	3.97	2.10*
Q3 Low Self Control	9.84	3.255	7.82	2.14	2.17*
C Emotional instability	10.06	3.861	7.48	2.92	2.794**
H Suspicion	10.86	2.857	8.92	3.10	2.004*

** $p < .01$ level * $p < .05$ level.

They pointed out that despite years of hard work, their savings and pension was totally incommensurate with the present inflation. To the question regarding working after retirement, 78 per cent of the working group said that they would continue to work even after retirement, whilst out of a sample of 25 retired men, 72 per cent were already re-employed to 'make ends meet'. Only 12 per cent of the retired group had preferred to 'sit back and take it easy'. To the question about amount of change desired if given a choice, while 88 per cent of the working men expressed no desire to change their work or even their nature of work, 68 per cent of those retired, were very keen to change not only their life styles but also their occupations. Finally, in reply to a question regarding the personal meaning of retirement, majority of the working men were looking forward to rest and complete submission to newer hobbies, as well as carry on working at a leisurely pace; in the retired group, the majority expressed the need to withdraw from the work force but channelise energy into other areas, and domestic interests. It was only on this point that both the groups were unified in their answers.

TABLE 9.4: Responses of the Working and Retired Group on 5 Areas of Concern for Retirement

Sl. No.	Areas of Concern	Working Group		Retired Group	
1.	Concerns of Retirement	96%	a) Finance b) Housing	96%	a) Finance b) Housing c) Family
2.	Satisfaction of Life Accomplishments	93%	Neither dissatisfied not frustrated	48% 52%	Satisfied with present life completely dissatisfied frustrated, salary incommensurate with rates of inflation
3.	Plans of work after Retirement	78%	had plans to continue working	72% 12%	were already employed again preferred sedentary life style
4.	Amount of change sought given choice	88%	did not design any change in work pattern and nature of life style	68%	keen to change work and life patterns
5.	Personal meaning of Retirement	Gradual withdrawal from active involvement in geo. political & economic life. Continued social involvement. Some amount of work necessary.		Gradual withdrawal into a passive stance, complete rest and pursuance of only hobbies and passions not yet satisfied	

Conclusions

(i) Men who are retired and in the age range of 62–65 years, are significantly more anxious than their working counterparts who belong to the age group 52–56 years.

(ii) There is no significant difference between the two groups on Covert anxiety and Overt anxiety.

(iii) The working group is significantly higher on Emotional instability, lack of self control and suspicion than the retired group, whereas, the retired group is significantly higher on apprehension and tension than the working group.

10

PERCEIVED SOCIAL SUPPORT AND EFFECT OF LIFE EVENTS:
A Comparative Study of Retired Working and Non-working Males

PARAMJEET KAUR DHILLON and MADHU ARORA

A job, according to Vroom (1964) fulfills a number of motives, such as, providing wages and all economic rewards associated with the benefits of the job. It provides an opportunity for activity and expenditure of energy and also an opportunity for social interactions, which in turn lead to intrinsic satisfaction in an individual. On the other hand, Simpson *et al* (1966) give a deeper insight of the significance of work for individuals, when they state that 'work is one of the most important avenues for integrating the individual into the social system by giving him or her his or her identity, style of life, and social-participation patterns. Work places the individual, and his family in the hierarchy of the social structure'. These investigators argue that retirement undercuts the individuals major social support by removing him or her from the work world in which these supports are rooted.

Mandatory retirement therefore, is viewed as being forced out of a chosen career and gainful employment (Cox, 1984). It is dreaded as a crisis (Back, 1969) as it decreases the income, status and power of an individual as these were previously associated with the hierarchical position occupied by an individual. The 10 A.M. to 6 P.M. work schedule now seems meaningless and the individual has to search for a new identity, meaning and value for one's life.

Retirement can be viewed as an life event in which an individual almost overnight changes from an active work life to an inactive life and this requires reorganisation of life and adjustments. Similarly, other life events, whether desirable or undesirable, are conceived of as a life change that invariably requires adjustments. However, some changes in life make adjustments more difficult and consequently produce stress. Some form of stress is experienced due to changes in life from early childhood and continues all through one's life, but life events and situations that are perceived as stressors change according to the phase of life. People in later years of life, experience stress due to loss of friends and relatives, capacity to earn, failing health, and the feeling of being useless and unwanted. Changes in life events have an impact on the mental and physical health of an individual. Life event scores have been found to be related to measures of health, well being and depression (Benjanminsen, 1981; Brown and Harris, 1978; and Krause, 1986). Retirement can also be viewed as a life event, in which an able bodied individual almost overnight has to change from an active worklife to an inactive life. In order to make adjustment to life events, one needs support from society and family. People in general and retirees in particular, are emotionally, socially and sometimes financially and physically dependent on others. Thus, social support is important for the well-being of an individual, as it gives one a feeling of being loved, cared for, esteemed, valued and belonging to a network of communications and mutual belongingness (Coob, 1976). Research evidence indicates that social support also functions as a moderator of negative effects of life stresses (Brown and Harris, 1978; Coob, 1976; Eaton, 1978; and Turner, 1981).

Therefore, the study of people who have retired becomes meaningful and essential so as to get a deeper insight of their support system and the intensity of the effect of life events. This in turn would help in devising strategies for their emotional and physical health.

Objectives

The present study was designed to investigate the social support and the perceived effect of life events of retired working and non-working males.

The following hypotheses were formulated:

(i) There will be a significant difference on perceived social support between retired working and non-working males.
(ii) Retired non-working males will exhibit a greater amount of

perceived effect of life events.

(iii) There will be a significant negative relationship between perceived social support and perceived effect of life events.

Sample

The total sample of the present study comprised of 60 retired males residing in Delhi. Of these 30 males had taken up new jobs after retirement and 30 males were leading just a retired life. The sample was taken from the middle socio-economic class. The mean age of the retired working males was found to be 59 years and the mean age of retired non-working males was found to be Rs. 60.5 years.

Tools Used

1. Perceived social support was assessed by a modified version of Cohen and Hoberman's (1983) Perceived Social Support Scale (ISEL). Social support as defined by the scale, measures the way a person perceives other's provide help and assistance whenever he needs it. The scale measured perceived social support from three different sources — friends, family and neighbours.

   The scale consisted of 25 items with two response categories — 'Yes' or 'No'. The maximum score possible on the scale is 25 and the minimum is 0. Of the 25 items, 9 items measure support from friends, 10 from family and 6 from neighbours.
2. Perceived effect of life events was measured by a modified version of Holmes and Rahe's (1967) Life Events Scale. The scale measures the perceived effect of life events related to health, work, finances, family, and personal, and social spheres. The scale has 32 items and five point response categories ranging from 0–4, where 0 indicates 'No effect at all' and 4 indicates 'Severe effect'. The maximum score possible on the total scale is 128 and minimum is 0. Of the 32 items, 3 items measure perceived effect of problems relating to health, 2 to work, 4 to finances, 11 to family matters and 12 to personal and social spheres.
3. A personal data schedule was devised to obtain information regarding the respondents, age, retired: working and non-working status, income, education, place of residence, etc.

Procedure for Collection of Data

The retirees both working and non-working were approached at home and rapport was established. After gaining their confidence they were requested to answer anonymously the questionnaires alongwith the personal data schedule.

Results and Discussion

To test the first hypothesis for perceived social support the means, standard deviations and the 't' values were computed. Table 10.1 presents the mean, SD and 't' value for perceived social support. The results show that there is a significant difference on social support between retired working and non-working males. The mean score of retired working males is higher than the mean score of non-working males. This implies that working males perceive more social support than non-working males. This finding is in the expected direction, as working males because of their earning capacity perceive more social support from friends, family and neighbours as compared to the non-working males. However, the retirees in India, in general, irrespective of working and non-working status, perceive a fairly good amount of social support from friends, family and neighbours.

The results of the present study indirectly support the findings of Berg and Malmberg (1982), who reported that empirical evidence indicates that only a small minority of the aged feel socially isolated, lonely and experience a lower life satisfaction.

TABLE 10.1: Mean and Standard Deviation on Perceived Social Support for Retired Working and Non-Working Males

Social Support	Working		Non-Working		"t"
	$\bar{X}$	S.D	$\bar{X}$	S.D	
Total social support	19.18	2.16	18.02	1.82	2.27*
Friends	7.26	1.20	7.13	1.20	0.406
Family	7.86	1.46	7.23	1.64	1.146
Neighbours	4.06	1.20	3.66	0.86	1.481

* $p < .05$.

However, when the areas of social support were analysed separately, it was observed that the slight difference in the mean scores, of retired working and non-working males in these areas was not found to be significant. This means that the retirees in general, irrespective of working or non-working status, perceive almost an equal amount of support from friends, family members and neighbours. It can also be seen that the retirees, irrespective of working or non-working status, perceive a high degree of support from friends and family members as the mean scores of 7.00+ when compared with the norms, lie above the average score ($\bar{X}$ = 4.5, 5.00 respectively). They perceive an average support from neighbours as the mean scores lie near the average score of ($\bar{X}$ = 3.00). These findings are in agreement with the results of Moncini and Simon (1986) who observed that older people (aged 57–93 years) expected greater support from family members and close friends. The results of a study by Chapell (1983) on 400 Canadian elderly (aged 60 years and older) also revealed the importance of non family age peers in their lives. The explanation for no significant difference, between retired working and non-working males, in different areas of social support in this study, could be that in the Indian society the aged are provided social support, irrespective of their work status. The public pressure and traditional beliefs inculcated through tradition, culture and philosophy all contribute towards caring for the aged.

To test the second hypothesis for perceived effect of life events, data was analysed and Table 10.2 presents the mean, SD and the 't'-value for perceived effect of life events.

TABLE 10.2: Mean and Standard Deviation on Perceived Effect of Life Events for Retired, Working and Non-working Males

Life Events	Working		Non-Working		"t"
	$\bar{X}$	S.D	$\bar{X}$	S.D	
Total	83.9	12.8	84.23	13.50	1.515
Health	10.5	1.25	11.00	1.36	0.256
Work	6.4	1.47	6.30	1.66	0.246
Financial	12.5	2.57	12.30	2.68	1.052
Family	29.0	6.70	29.23	8.70	0.521
Personal and Social	25.5	11.27	25.40	5.10	0.249

The analysis indicates that there is no significant difference (t = 1.51) on perceived effect of life events between retired working and non-working males. This implies that retired working and non-working males perceive life events as almost equally stressful or unstressful. The means scores of the retired working ($\bar{X}$ = 83.50) and non-working ($\bar{X}$ = 84.30) males when compared with the norms, lie in the category marked stressful, meaning thereby, that the retires, irrespective of working/non-working status perceive a greater effect of life events, (the average score being 64.0) than the average population. This finding of the study is in consonance with Lindi and Kurt (1977) who concluded that life events for any homogeneous age group are equally stressful.

The analysis of the different areas of life events, also reveals that there is no significant difference between retired working and non-working males in the amount of perceived effect in these areas. However, the mean scores reveal that both working and non-working males perceive life events relating to health, work, family finance and personal and social spheres as stressful. However, comparing the amount of effect perceived in these areas, in relation to the general population, it is seen that the retirees, both working and non-working, perceive the life events relating to health as very stressful (average = 6.0); events related to work and finances as quite stressful (average = 4.00 and 8.00, respectively); events relating to family member and personal and social problems as stressful only to an average degree, (average score = 22.0 and 24.0, respectively). The findings that retirees perceive almost all areas of life events stressful in comparison to the norms, could perhaps also be due to the fact, that responses of all age groups in India on the life events scale are not normally distributed like the American population, and Indians in general, irrespective of age, perceive a greater effect of negative life events. This line of thought is in keeping with the results of Jahan and Hassan (1987) who reported that Indians, in comparison to Americans find all areas of life events highly stressful, particularly, areas concerning health and family.

To test the third hypothesis of relationship between perceived social support and perceived effect of life events, separately for retired working and non-working males, product-moment correlations were computed and the results are presented in Table 10.3.

TABLE 10.3: Product-moment Correlations between Perceived Social Support and Perceived Effect of Life Events for Retired Working and Non-working Males

Social Support	Life events for working males					
	Total	Health	Work	Financial	Family	Personal & Social
Total Social Support	−.87**	.05	−.08	−.29	−.84**	−.15
	Life events for non-working males					
	Total	Health	Work	Financial	Family	Personal & Social
Total Social Support	−.88**	−.45*	−.81**	−.48*	−.25	−.88**

** $p < .01$ * $p < .05$.

The correlational analysis reveals that there is a significant negative relationship between total social support and effect of total life events, for both retired working and non-working males. This means that greater the perceived soçial support less the negative effect of various life events on the retirees, both working and non-working. The results are in the expected direction for social support functions as a moderator of negative effects of life stresses (Turner, 1981) for people of all ages and particularly, for the retirees. Furthermore, the correlations reveal that there is a significant negative relationship between social support and the effect on health and work among retired non-working males but not among retired working males. This means that retired non-working males perceive that the effect on events relating to their health and work activities are consequent upon the perceived social support. The explanation for the differences in the effect of perceived social support on health and work problems, between retired working and non-working males, seems to lie mainly in the reemployment of the retirees, as it means that going to work and getting involved in some productive task makes one feel more healthy and active. Therefore, the employed retirees do not perceive that social support would have a significant effect on negative events relating to their health and work spheres.

The negative relationship between social support and effect of life events is in agreement with the results of Coob (1976), Gallor (1982)

and Krause (1987), who found that social support is an important determinant of self perceived health.

Non-working retired males perceive a significant negative relationship between social support and stress arising out of financial problems, whereas, working males do not perceive a significant relationship between the two variables. This difference between the two groups is probably again due to the job and wages of the working males. The retirees, it seems, feel that social support is very essential to lessen the stress arising out of financial problems. Bolton and Oatley (1987) also found a significant interaction between social support, employment and depression.

The retired working males perceive a significant negative relationship between social support and stress arising out of family problems. They perceive that greater the amount of social support lesser would be the perceived stress arising out of family problems, whereas, the retired non-working males do not perceive that social support would reduce the stress arising out of family problems.

Non-working retired males perceive a significant negative relationship between social support and stress arising out of personal and social problems, whereas, the working males do not perceive that social support would lessen the stress arising out of personal and social problems. This difference, could again be explained on the basis of dependence of retired non-working males on their family and relatives, to help them solve their personal and social problems, whereas, the retired working males are probably more confident of themselves and feel capable of solving their personal and social problems, as they are still active and working.

Conclusion

Thus, it could be concluded that the retirees, both working and non-working: (i) perceive a high degree of social support, particularly, from friends and family members; (ii) perceive all life events almost equally stressful, and (iii) perceive that greater the amount of social support less the effect of life events. However, retired non-working males perceive that social support decreases the negative effect of life events related to health, work, finances and personal and social problems, whereas, retired working males perceive that social support mainly decreases the negative effect of the events related to family members.

COMMENTS

Older persons are confronted with different kinds of stress. Cox (1984) states that 'one source of stress is social and begins at the time of retirement, often retirement forced on the individual by mandatory retirement rules; it has the effect of removing the individual from his or her career and the mainstream of life, thereby, bringing a sense of meaninglessness and uselessness in life, and simultaneously reducing his or her income'. The results of the first study also indicate that retirement does make a person more anxious, tense and apprehensive, but this anxiety is more unrealised, covert hidden-purpose cryptic anxiety rather than overt or symptomatic conscious anxiety. This anxiety is manifested in retired officers in the form of inability to sleep through worrying, feeling unequal to the challenges of daily life, getting easily downhearted, remorseful and depressed. The results also show that working class I officers are not without tension but anxiety arousing factors or components differ from those of the retired officers. They exhibit more low self control, emotional instability and suspiciousness, viz., working class I officers show immaturity, get easily annoyed, are dissatisfied with their family and the world situation and are high on suspicion, as compared to retired class I officers. The predominance of these trait components of anxiety in class I officers could be due to the cut throat competition and the struggles required to maintain their position in the profession and organisation.

The findings of the second study evince that retirees, in general in India, perceive a high degree of social support from friends and family members, nevertheless working status effects the amount of social support perceived. Retired working males perceive more social support from family members, friends and neighbours than retired non-working males. However, the retirees both working and non-working do not perceive any significant difference in the degree of effect of different life events. The implications of this study seems to be that, the earning capacity of an individual and his status in society, particularly in India, either actually raises the value, worth or importance of the individual in the eyes of friends, family members and neighbours that they give him more social support or the individual because of his working status, feels more self confident and self-important that he perceives that these significant others give him more social support.

Therefore, research evidence, though scanty seems to imply that even in a country like India where the family ties are still strong and the old are respected, retirement is an added source of stress, anxiety and tension to the elderly. Re-employment after retirement makes the retirees perceive more social support from significant others (*See also* Chapter 13).

PART V

INSTITUTIONALISATION AND THE AGED

INTRODUCTION

With the value system and life styles in a state of flux and with the decline of family solidarity, institutions are being established to care for the sick, the unwanted and the aged. To institutionalize means to place in or commit to the care of a specialised institutions; to accustom a person to the care and supervised routine of an institution. The characteristics generally associated with institutional life are regulation, regimentation, standardisation and impersonality (Webster, 1961). Institutionalisation, therefore, means the quality or state of being or becoming institutionalised. The institutionalised are those who are mostly forced to live under protection due to adverse circumstances and are taken care of by persons employed by the institution. The entry into an old home or institution represents a turning point in the life of the individual and is commonly thrust upon a person by unfavourable circumstances, such as lack of family support or a family unwilling or unable to take care of him/her, lack of financial resources to support himself, etc. It is observed that residents of the institutionalised homes often complain about the circumstances necessitating their entry into the home. Thus, it seems that negative factors tend to predominate the decision to enter an old home. Whatever the circumstances, however, may have been for the person to be institutionalised, the question arises, what is the effect of old homes on the well being of the elderly. Several investigators (Kart & Manard, 1976; Mendelson, 1974; Gandell, 1980) have outlined in detail the terrible living conditions and psychological deterioration that can be associated with long term residence in an institution. Liberman (1969) in a study on the institutionalised elderly found that they tend to be depressed, unhappy, intellectually ineffective, possessing a negative self image, docile, submissive and having low interest in surroundings. Cassem and Steward (1975) found that the greatest fear of the aged is abandonment by others. On the other hand, some investigators speak about the positive consequences of institutionalisation of the aged, whereby parents and children come to value each other more and new love and affection are discovered. Smith and Bengston (1979) investigated how institutionalisation of an elderly parent affected the relationship between parent and the child. The data comprised of parents whose age ranged between 70 to 92 years and children between 50 to 71 years. Open ended interviews were held and focussed on pre and post admission sessions. The results indicated six types of relationships reflecting following institutionalisation of the elderly. These are: (1) renewed closeness and strengthening of family ties (30%); (2) continuation of separatedness (20%); (3) quantity without quality interactions (10%); (4) abdication; institution as a dumping ground, discovery of new love and affection (15%); (5) continuation of closeness (25%), and (6) only about 10 per cent of parent and child combinations experienced a negative effect on their relationship.

However, old homes have come up in Delhi and other cosmopolitan cities with the will to stay and will probably increase in number in due course. But this does not necessarily mean that old people are more willing to go to them or that relatives and children are more willing to send them there. The two studies presented in this part try to examine the idea of institutionalisation and its effects upon behaviour from a psychological point of view. The study on 'Attitude towards institutionalisation of the aged', is an attempt to investigate how the older and younger generations in India, particularly in Delhi, think and feel about institutionalisation of the aged.

The second study on 'Emotional states of the institutionalised aged', investigates the mental health of the institutionalised aged and compares it those aged living with their family. The results of both the studies are discussed mainly in the light of findings from studies conducted abroad on the elderly, as there are few studies reported in India in this context.

11

ATTITUDE TOWARDS INSTITUTIONALISATION OF THE AGED

PARAMJEET KAUR DHILLON and GEETA PODUVAL

Throughout the world care of old, frail and impaired persons is generally taken by their children and family members. In the pre-industrial society, the family was a structure made up of three or four generations. The older members were either grandparents or elderly unmarried members of the family, and they had more or less well defined roles for the existence of the family. In such a system, the old were not only sustained, protected and cared for but according to their individual capabilities they also contributed to the subsistence and care of the family. With the advent of industrialisation and urbanisation there have been changes in economic and social values. The younger people move away, from their old parents for employment or higher economic prospects (business) into bigger cities and this has resulted in the break up of the joint family, with the parents being left alone. Secondly, families these days are concerned with maintaining their standard of living, by trying to keep down the number of family members in relation to their economic situation. Every member, who does not contribute financially to the existence of the family, seems an economic burden to the family (Friedburg and Weltz, 1958). Thirdly, married women who were once the caretakers of older parents have now mainly for economic reasons taken up employment outside their home. But still in India, the family ties are deep rooted, particularly, in rural India which constitutes about 70 per cent of the Indian population. However, in the urban areas family ties are loosening and old people have started feeling neglected. Sometimes, nowadays, the separation can be generated by the old themselves, when they feel self-sufficient and desire independence. The income from pension or other sources enables the old to offer some compensation (payment) for being looked after and therefore, they desire to live independently from their children.

Despite changes in the family pattern, the number of old people cared for in institutions or through community service is small, even in the western world, where majority of old people live independently from their children. The concept of institutionalisation of the aged in the Indian setting is relatively new. The number of such institutions are few (for example in Delhi: Homes for the Aged Infirm Persons, Narela, Old Home, Paharganj etc.) and people, in general are not aware of them. Whatever little is known is that only the poor aged without a family live in such homes. Empirical studies conducted to investigate the attitude of children towards institutionalisation of the aged, have been through plans the adult children have for the care of their parents when they become ill or bedridden. Such studies are very few. Tobin and Libernan (1976) administered a questionnaire, probing attitude towards caring for an aged relative, on 200 Italian Americans in Columbia and also to a sample of Italians and Poles in inner city Baltimore, enabling a comparison of urban and suburban respondents. Results indicate that a stronger reliance on family members for support was found among the urban than the sub-urban respondents. Less stress was placed on professional assistance and the role of the family in caring for the aged was reaffirmed. Broady (1978) in a study found that for most supportive families, the decision to place an aged member into a nursing home was a reluctant last alternative. Shanas (1979) conducted a survey aimed to study children's plans for the care of their parents when they become bedridden. The survey was conducted on middle aged persons, married men and women, between the age of 30 and 49 years. Slightly more than 80 per cent of the respondents said that the child or child's spouse would provide care. Less than 3 per cent answered that they were planning to depend upon resources other than family members, viz. a paid house-keeper, public home help services, nursing homes, etc. and 10 per cent answered that parents spouse would provide care. Johnson (1979) examined the family's potential to look after the elders, at that stage when their health deteriorates to the extent that some external support is required. It was found that the situational impediments which intervene, centre on job responsibilities, the care of other dependents, and higher priority on marriage and family orientation. Hence, the major family care-taker is likely to be a spouse or sibling of the aged, who is often in poor health themselves. Despite the numerous difficulties experienced, when those in poor health are being cared for by others in the same status, a high valuation on their independence prevents the search for other alternatives. Three generations of women: grandmothers, daughters and young granddaughters were interviewed to know their attitude towards family care of the aged by Broady (1981). The vast majority of all three generations of women resoundingly endorsed the traditional value of vital responsibility to the aged. Most of the women sampled, regardless of the generation thought that adult children should keep in touch with their elderly parents and should be able to depend upon adult children for help. But the grandmothers thought that adult children with their own families should not do household tasks for them and did not mind professional care (75%), more than the daughters (61%) and granddaughters (59%). Research literature reveals that there is a scarcity of studies conducted in India to assess the attitude towards institutionalisation of the aged. Keeping this in view, the present study was designed to investigate the attitude of adults of two age groups, and sexes towards institutionalisation of the aged.

METHODOLOGY

Objectives

The objectives of the present study are as follows:

(1) To assess the attitude and the differences in the attitude towards institutionalisation of the aged of two age groups: 25–45 years and 60 years and above.
(2) To investigate the attitude of the sexes towards institutionalisation of the aged.

Sample

The total sample comprised of 100 respondents, 50 respondents from each of the age groups 25–45 years and 60 years and above. (1) Each age group of 50 respondents comprised of 25 males and 25 females. (2) The mean age of the younger age group was 35 years and that of the older age group was 65 years. (3) The income of the respondents ranged from Rs. 1500 — Rs. 2700 per month. The respondents were either Government employees or had retired from Government service. The sample was selected from the residents of Middle Income (MIG) and Low Income Group (LIG) flats of the Delhi Development Authority (DDA). These flats were located in the following colonies of Delhi: Kalkaji, Saket, Prashad Nagar and Janakpuri. The data for the present study were collected during November and December 1986.

Tools Used

1. Personal data sheet seeking information about the respondents age, sex, income, area of residence, etc.
2. Attitude towards institutionalisation of the aged was assessed by an attitude scale constructed by Dhillon and Poduwal (1986). The scale based on the Likert technique consists of 21 items having statements on (1) Positive/negative effects of institutionalisation of the aged. (2) Lack of time and financial resources on the part of children for the care of the aged parents. (3) Institutionalisation would make the elderly feel unwanted and a burden, etc. The measure provides a five point response scale ranging from Strongly Agree (SA) to Strongly Disagree (SD). The maximum score is 105 and the minimum is 21. The undecided/uncertain score is 63. The scale was translated into Hindi to facilitate the respondents who did not understand English well.

The respondents were generally contacted at their home and after assuring them of confidentiality the questionnaires were administered to them. The present study was conducted to investigate the attitude towards institutionalisation of the aged in two generations of Indian males and females.

Results and Discussion

Table 11.1 depicts the mean, SD and t-values for six comparison groups on attitude towards Institutionalisation of the aged. The Table shows no significant difference in the mean scores on attitude towards institutionalisation of the aged, between respondents of the two age groups 60 years and above and 25–45 years. The mean score of respondents of the age group 60 years and above ($\bar{X}$ = 56.22) and the mean score of the age group 25–45 years ($\bar{X}$ = 53.92) indicate a slightly unfavourable attitude towards institutionalisation of the aged as the mean scores lie below the uncertain or ambivalent point of 63 on the scale. A perusal of Table 11.1 reveals that: (1) significance of mean difference, between the male and female respondents, on institutionalisation of the aged is not significant. The mean scores of both the sexes lie below the uncertain point of 63, implying an unfavourable attitude towards institutionalisation of the aged. (2) Inter group comparisons of mean scores of males and females of both the age groups, 60 years and above and 25–45 years also indicate a non-significant difference; and (3) between the mean scores of males of the two age groups and between females of the two age groups the difference is also not significant.

TABLE 11.1: Mean, SD and significance of mean difference between comparison groups on Attitude towards Institutionalisation of the aged.

Sl.No.	Comparison groups	Mean	SD	t-value
1.	Respondents of 60 years & above	N=50 56.22	11.62	1.01 NS
	Respondents between 25–45 years	N=50 53.92	11.23	
2.	Male respondents of 60 yrs & 25–45 yrs	N=50 54.92	11.54	0.14 NS
	Female respondents of 60 yrs & 25–45 yrs	N=50 55.24	11.69	
3.	Males of 60 yrs & above	N=25 55.60	11.76	0.40 NS
	Female of 60 yrs & above	N=25 56.88	11.73	
4.	Males between 25–45 yrs	N=25 54.24	11.28	0.20 NS
	Females between 25–45 yrs	N=25 53.60	11.41	
5.	Males of 60 yrs & above	N=25 55.56	11.70	0.41 NS
	Males between 25–45 yrs	N=25 55.24	11.28	
6.	Females of 60 yrs & above	N=25 56.80	11.73	1.01 NS
	Females between 25–45 yrs	N=25 53.60	11.41	

The findings of the study seem to imply that the elderly in India depend upon their children to look after them and children have also accepted the responsibility of taking care of the elderly. These findings are in line with Shanas (1979) who found that over 80 per cent of middle aged persons reported that their child or child's spouse would provide care for them. Tobin and Liberman (1976) in a study on Italian Americans in Columbia assessed attitude towards caring for an aged relative. The results indicated stronger reliance on family members for the care of the aged. Thus, the findings reveal that the middle social class respondents, males and females, of the younger generation as well as the elderly themselves, view institutionalisation of the aged unfavourably. These results could be explained partly in terms of the deep-rooted family tradition, where the aged are the responsibility of the family and therefore, the children and the family feel that it is their duty to look after the aged and partly because institutionalisation of the aged in India is still a new concept and only those aged are institutionalised who have meagre or no income and no family to look after them.

12

EMOTIONAL STATES OF THE INSTITUTIONALISED AGED

PARAMJEET KAUR DHILLON and SHALINI SAMAT

For age is opportunity no less
Then Youth itself, though in another dress
And as the evening twilight fades away
The sky is filled with stars invisible by day.

— H.W. Longfellow

Old age and its concomitant social, psychological and physiological changes, degenerative processes and the organic disturbances of the brain, create difficult problems which predispose the elderly to feeling of failure, frustration, disappointment, grief, worthlessness, apathy, resignation, loneliness or hopelessness. No wonder old age is characterised by insecurity, poor health, loneliness, depression, rigid attitudes and failing physical and mental powers (Neugarten, 1982). A study by Age Care India (1986) showed that about 80 per cent of all aged persons in India, both men and women, are lonely, depressed, shelterless and financially handicapped.

The elderly are notably vulnerable to loneliness (Baum, 1982). Loneliness among the elderly besides being associated with perceived social isolation, lack of integration into social network and role loss, is also concomitant of events such as widowhood, retirement, loss of family and age mates, which involve the disruption of supportive relationships and role sets. In addition Rosow (1976) has suggested that even one's continuing social roles (e.g. as a parent) are substantially emptied of both status and function in old age. Moreover, in advanced age physical and sensory functions decline which limit mobility (e.g. driving, walking) and communication (e.g. declining ability to see or hear a voice or the telephone) which further add to loneliness. Loneliness in older people has been found to be associated with decreased income, having fewer friends, lower satisfaction with relationships (e.g. with children, family, friends), more negative ratings of general health and life satisfaction. Loneliness creates anxiety, or depression and lonely individuals may exhibit some of the characteristic behaviours associated with these emotional states.

Depression is a common complaint of the aged and is caused by multiple factors such as biological, physical, psychological and social. Depression in old age often appears to be precipitated by adverse changes in the life and circumstances of the elderly, such as, retirement from work, bereavement or the onset of some sort of serious physical illness or defect. The depressive symptoms in the elderly, may be either severe and dramatic or simpler type of reactions which differ only in degree from the normal reactions of the elderly people to bereavement, illness or other kinds of stress. Older people with simpler depressive reactions become slower in their thoughts, words and actions, become constipated, unable to sleep, overly concerned about their physical condition and uncertain of themselves. Hopelessness or negative expectancies towards the future is another emotional state embedded in the life of the elderly (Blazer, 1982) Statements commonly made by the elderly such as, 'I have nothing to look forward to', or 'There is no sense in my doing anything for I will be dead soon' reflect futility and pessimism (Blazer, 1982). The elderly because of deterioration of physical health and sensory capacity are also likely to face more frustrating or thwarting of goal responses. Frustration in an individual may evoke either a normal response or an inadequate mode of response, depending upon his degree of frustration tolerance and the number of stressful life events experienced by him. The aforesaid observations seem to indicate that some emotional states like loneliness, depression, hopelessness, etc., are associated with old age. Therefore, review of literature on the emotional states of the elderly becomes imperative. On each emotional state: Loneliness, depression, hopelessness and frustration, research studies along with their major findings are presented as follows:

Depression: Depression is a feeling of sadness, hopelessness, worthlessness, guilt of self-reproach (Rosenfeld, 1985). Depression is by far the most common psychiatric disorder encountered in the elderly (Linn *et al*, 1980). Myers, Sheldon and Robinson (1963) reported that

45 per cent of the elderly admitted to a psychiatric hospital were diagnosed with affective disorders, and Feigenbaum (1970) reported that 52 per cent of the elderly has some type of affective disorder, the incidence of depression being higher in females than males.

Dean and Ensel (1984) in their study of socially structured depression in men and women, reviewed current knowledge of gender differences in depression, with an emphasis on the ways in which depression may be social structured. The direct effects of the following model variables on depression were assessed: parental status, marital status, work satisfaction, prior illness, competence, life events, strong tie support and depression. A total of 1091 subjects aged (17–70 years) were used. Results indicate that while depression decreased significantly over age, both for males and females, the young and older females were significantly more depressed than their male counterparts in the age groups. Strong tie support was the single best predictor of depression for females and males in young and middle age groups. Life events showed equal frequency for young females and males. For the middle age groups of females, a lesser relationship was found between stress and depression. Personal competence had a significant impact on depression, for the young and middle age group of males, and its was the single best predictor of depression in older males.

Hale and Cochran (1983) investigating sex differences in patterns of self-reported psychopathology in the married elderly, administered the Brief Symptom Inventory form of the Symptom Check List-90, to 53 male and 53 female residents (aged 63–84 years) of a retirement community. All subjects were married. The major results indicate that although no difference was found between males and females on an overall index of psychological distress, a discriminant function analysis indicated that three (Anxiety, Interpersonal Sensitivity and Paranoid Ideation) of the nine scales provided maximum separation of the two groups. Females had higher levels of anxiety and interpersonal sensitivity than males but lower paranoid ideation levels than males. It has also been suggested that higher rates of widowhood among elderly women along with the financial problems that often accompany widowhood, may .be partially responsible for the higher rates of depression among them.

Baum and Boxley (1983) for their study on depression and old age identification, selected 308 persons (mean age 75.5) from three settings, to test the relationship between psychological depression and feeling "old". Subjects were administered the Symptom Check List-90, and age indentification item and several other measures of well being (such as "Rotter's Locus of Control", "Purpose in life test", etc.). The hypothesis of the study stated that identified age and depression would be related in the direction of older identified age and greater depressive symptomology. The correlation between identified age and depression is moderately strong and significantly related at the $p < .01$ level ($r = .31$). An analysis of variance, similarly, reveals that older perceived age and depression are highly related ($F = 13.99, p < .001$), with mean differences of old age receivers ($\bar{X} = 2.26$) being significantly different from other identified mean ages: same ($\bar{X} = 1.66$) and younger ($\bar{X} = 1.57$). A multiple regression analysis ($F = 4.36, p < .01$) revealed a moderate and significant beta of $B = -.11$. When multiple regression analysis was conducted only two other variables emerged as significant predictors of depression. Physical health emerged as the strongest predictor of depression in later life ($F = 62.87, p < .01$) as evidenced by a Beta $B = .44$. The second best predictor of psychological depression was having and maintaining personal meaning in one's life ($F = 26.26$, $p < .01$) which produced a beta of $B = -.30$.

Hale (1982) investigated the relationship between numerous age related stresses and depression in the elderly. Sixty-eight residents of a retirement centre (mean age 80 years) completed a life satisfaction survey, that included a modified version of Zung Self Rating Depression Scale and assessed depression and a wide range of possible losses or stresses. Depression was found to be related to poorer financial status, fewerer and less satisfying interpersonal relationships, poorer physical health and greater concerns about health for females, and poorer physical health and lack of involvement in activities for males.

Oltman, Michals and Steer (1980) studied the prevalence and correlates of depression in elderly persons. For this 503 elderly persons (60–94 years old), living within a metropolitan area, were questioned about their socio medical characteristics and administered the Wakefield Self Assessment Depression Inventory. The distribution of scores indicated that 34.5 per cent were depressed. Stepwise regression analysis was used to examine the relationship between subject's characteristics and their depression scores. Total number of self reported symptoms, and being partially housebound, were positively associated with depression. Older persons with physical complaints and those who are partially restricted to their homes, may tend to develop levels of depression that might require psychiatric intervention. Sex was found to be significantly correlated (beyond .001 level) with total depression. Age and marital status were found not to be correlated significantly with total depression.

Weinberg (1981) studied the psychological problems experienced in old age, that are related to gradual and progressive changes during the aging process — e.g., diminished perceptual activity, memory deficits, disengagement from ongoing life activity, and increased dependency. On the basis of his research, he concludes that an individual's self image is an important factor in adopting to old age. Loss of self esteem can lead to narcisstic psychopathology, which is manifested in recurring depressions, paranoid reactions and overdependence on others. He feels that social pressure and inadequate resources cause many of the dysfunctional features of old age. Linn, Hunter and Harris (1980) studied 188 subjects aged 65 years and older who were living in the community, in terms of the relationship of recent life events to the symptoms of depression. Subjects completed the Recent Life Changes Questionnaire and the Depression Factor Score from the Hopkins Symptom Check List. Three discriminators of depression were found among the 12 events that occurred in the past year. Subjects with greater symptomatology had been involved in more arguments, experienced more deaths of relatives and friends.

Loneliness

The review of the literature on loneliness indicates that loneliness is one of the least satisfactorily conceptualised phenomena and has been subsumed under depression and treated as if it were depression. However, loneliness is a separate entity with unique characteristics that need to be identified and treated appropriately. Loneliness is a state in which one feels incomplete. The primary affect is longing, whereas, in depression the affect is anger. Unlike the depressive, the lonely individual reaches out but can never communicate and consequently never quell the longing. Loneliness is a constellation of feelings, thoughts and behaviours that arise from aversive interpersonal experience and or relational dissatisfaction. Theoretically, loneliness occurs when there is a discrepancy between one's desired and one's perceived or actual relationships (Peplau and Perlman, 1979). In this definition three points are emphasised. Firstly, loneliness results from deficiencies in the person's social relations. Secondly, loneliness is a subjective phenomenon (it is not necessarily synonymous with objective isolation, so that people can be alone without being lonely), and thirdly, loneliness is unpleasant and distressing.

Weeks, Michela, Peplau and Bragg (1980) state that research on loneliness has been hampered by its strong association with depression. The states frequently co-occur and the measures of the two states are substantially correlated. Inability to manipulate experimentally, loneliness or depression. makes it difficult to entangle the causal influence of one on the other. Measures of loneliness and depression were administered to undergraduates at two points, five weeks apart. Data from 333 subjects were correlated and analysed under a succession of structural equation models. Results indicate that loneliness and depression were correlated but were clearly different constructs; neither one was a direct cause of the other, although both probably share common origins.

Creecy, Wright and Berg (1984) examined the relationship of selected demographic, activity and social psychological variables to feelings of loneliness among a national sample of 479 non-institutionalised Blocks (aged 55–93 years). Only the activity variables had a significant relationship with feelings of loneliness.

Schultz and Moore (1984) in a study on loneliness: correlates, attributes and coping among older adults, administered a battery of measures that included the Self Report Depression Scale and scales of loneliness, anxiety, locus of control, self consciousness and satisfaction, to fifty one 55–75 year old subjects. Results showed that lonely subjects were less willing to take a risk, had more depression and experienced more anxiety than subjects who were not lonely. Loneliness was most frequently attributed to being without others, it is suggested that loneliness was aggravated by social inaction and isolation. Self descriptions of loneliness included "depressed/sad" (39%) and "anxious/restless" (30%). It was felt that loneliness among older adults as among college students is associated with anxiety, depression and low levels of life satisfaction and happiness.

Wood (1984) in her study on loneliness asked 258, 18–54 year old subjects of varying occupations, to complete a modified version of "20 statements test", a loneliness questionnaire. Multiple regression analysis showed that loneliness was greater in women than in men, greater in unmarried than in married respondents and directly related to age and inversely related to education.

Baum (1983) in the process of studying loneliness in elderly persons, administered to 75 elderly persons (mean age of 76.6 years) in

Los Angles, the UCLA Loneliness Scale and, a battery of health and psychosocial measures, including the Cornell Medical Index and Rotter's Locus of Control Scale. The correlations indicate that many factors are associated with lonely feelings in later life. Surprisingly, age (r = .09) and marriage (r = .07) were not related to feeling lonely. Death anxiety similarly was unrelated to feelings of loneliness in later life (r = .14). However, educational level (r = --.32) and purpose in life (r = –.37) were inversely related, which suggests that the more educated person feels less lonely. This is consistent with Fromm Reichman's definition of loneliness as lack of meaningful contact with others. Such a finding is consistent with the fact that better physical health (r = .36), superior emotional health (r = .49) as well as less psychological depression (r = .42) were implicated. Gender was moderately related (r = .31). Women feel lonely more than older men.

Perlman, Gerson and Spinner (1980) report an empirical study of loneliness among 158 senior citizens (average age of 70 years) of Canada, each of whom completed a self administered questionnaire. Greater loneliness was associated with less friendship contacts, fewer close friends, social anxiety, ineffectiveness in influencing others, low marital satisfaction and low life satisfaction. Lonely respondents watched more TV, and would have liked more planned activities. Furthermore, loneliness was linked with poor hearing ability, and poor health.

Rubenstein and Shaver (1980) did a study on loneliness in two cities — New York and Worcestor, using a 84 item questionnaire. Their sample consisted of people of all educational and income levels within the life group 18 to 88 years. They performed a factor analysis on the 27 feelings associated with loneliness, in order to discover whether there are clear cut feelings that define loneliness. Four factors emerged: Factor 1 — Desperation: It indicates that a large part of loneliness is anxiety about one's ability to satisfy a powerful need. It includes feelings of helplessness, panic, and hopelessness. Factor 2 — Self Depreciation: It includes feelings of being insecure, ashamed and stupid. Factor 3 — Impatient Boredom: It represents a milder form of loneliness that many people feel when they are left alone on a Saturday night or find themselves alone during an uneventful business trip. It includes feelings of uneasiness, anger, inability to concentrate, etc. Factor 4 — includes feelings of sadness, emptiness, melancholy, alienation, etc.

Bragg (1979) did a comparative study on loneliness and depression.

The sample consisted of 333 students at the University of California, Los Angeles. The subjects completed questionnaires that included Beck Depression Inventory, Profile of mood states and the UCLA Loneliness Scale. To evaluate the relationship between causal attributions for loneliness and depression, the attributions of non depressed lonely students were contrasted with those of depressed lonely subjects. Results indicated that loneliness and depression were significantly correlated (r = .49) but had different correlates. Depression was associated with anger and dissatisfaction with the non-social aspects of life but loneliness was not. Loneliness was associated with low initiation of contact with friends, but depression was not.

Hopelessness

Hopelessness has been defined by Stotland (1969) as 'negative expectancies towards oneself and towards the future. A factor analytic study was conducted by Fry (1984) to identify the major themes of hopelessness in the thoughts of the elderly. Interviews conducted with 60 elderly subjects were factor analysed and four factors emerged: Factor I: A sense of hopelessness about recovering lost physical and cognitive abilities. Factor 2: A sense of hopelessness about recovering lost personal and inter-personal worth and attractiveness. Factor 3: A sense of hopelessness about recovering spiritual faith and receiving spiritual grace. Factor 4: A sense of hopelessness about receiving nurturance and recovering respect and remembrance, both in the present and after death.

Blazer (1982) states that hopelessness and futility is embedded in the life of the elderly, and this could be because the elderly interpret the future in terms of time perspective (e.g., the consciousness of finitude of life and to the length of life that remains). Discussing the elderly's view of the future, Blazer (1982) suggests that their time perspective could be both 'very limited' and 'limitless' but with the elderly there is more oftened shortened time perspective. In the perceptions of many elderly persons, old age offers such a shortened time for resolution that it may seem pointless to find new love objects, new goals and new plans for the future.

Lehr (1983) from a study on "quality of life" in old age, reports correlates of negative and positive morale, findings from the Bonn Longitudinal Study of Aging (BLSA). Reports on studies related to consistency and change of morale (mood) in old age. In a longitudinal sample observed from 1965 to 1972 of two cohorts (born 1890-96) and (1900-1905), findings indicate consistent average increasing morale in 46.6 per cent of the cases and a slight drop in morale in 53.4 per cent of the subjects. There was no difference in the cohorts compared, but females consistently demonstrated a lower morale. Decrease in morale correlated significantly with decrease of activity and a feeling of security. The objective degree of life stress did not correlate with morale, this was true for the subjective representation of stress as well as the selection of responses to stress.

Mercer and Kane (1980) studying helplessness and hopelessness among the institutionalised, found that the most devastating effect of institutionalisation on the elderly person is the surrender of control over his or her personal life, and the resulting helplessness and hopelessness. Dicke *et al* (1980) explored the relationship between life satisfaction, health, activity level and future orientation among the institutionalised and non-institutionalised aged (65–93 years). The findings revealed that institutionalisation did not influence life satisfaction directly but rather through health variables that were associated with ins .utionalisation.

Gomathi *et al* (1984) in a study on institutionalised and non-institutionalised older male subjects (60–81 years), found that institutionalised men rated their health as poor and very poor whereas, the non-institutionalised rated their health as good and excellent. Institutionalised persons reported more physical (poor sight, crippled arms and legs, high blood pressure, etc.) and psychological problems (sleeplessness, bad dreams, nervousness, feeling blue, etc.) than the non-institutionalised persons. Institutionalised men were also found to have significantly poor adjustment as compared to non-institutionalised men. The conclusions could be drawn on the lines of Anantharaman (1981) who found that level of adjustment influences perception of one's health.

Frustration

Frustration occurs whenever the organism meets more or less surmountable obstacle or obstruction in its route to the satisfaction of any vital need and can be produced by three classes of situations: Privations, Deprivations and Conflicts (Rosenzweig, 1944). Frustration among the elderly, according to Rosenzweig's perspective, besides being caused by privations, seems more specifically to be caused by deprivations and internal conflicts. This means that frustration is caused by being deprived of something which one had, that is, less of some person, object or a specific attribute possessed by the individual and also when the person starts feeling that the obstacle is present in the individual himself/herself, by virtue of which the desired satisfaction is denied to him/her. The declining physical and sensory functions and the related consequences, such as loss of hearing, vision, mobility, etc., seems to be the loss of attributes possessed by the individual, resulting in loss of independence, and delay or obstruction in the satisfaction of a need.

Sears *et al* (1953) found that adults who have low tolerance show more frustration oriented behaviour. Gutman (1969) found that older people tend to be more passive, whereas, younger people are more aggressive. This may be because people in later life become more prone to this emotionally tinged attitude shown by cessation of activity.

Frustration during later maturity and old age can arise from a number of circumstances including: (a) adverse physiological changes and restrictions on activity, (b) occupational redundancy or failure to progress beyond the lower limit of occupational aspiration, with a consequent limitation of reduction in living standards, (c) failure to keep pace with cultural, social and scientific developments, leading to the feeling of being out of date and out of touch, (d) loss of youthful vigour and freedom, coupled with the uninviting prospect of growing old, usually reinforced by previous social attitudes, and (e) loss of valued or stabilising emotional relationship through bereavement, loss of employment or the departure of children, etc.

Review of literature on the emotional states of the elderly reveals that depression and loneliness among the elderly living alone or with their families have been a subject of more extensive research than feeling of hopelessness and frustration. However, there is a dearth of research on the emotional states of the institutionalised elderly. The above mentioned observations prompted the researchers to investigate this area, as institutions for the elderly, particularly in urban areas of India have come up and are on the increase. The present study was designed to investigate (1) the emotional states of the institutionalised and non-institutionalised aged in India, and (2) to identify some background variables associated with three of the emotional states: loneliness, depression, and hopelessness among institutionalised and non-institutionalised aged.

METHODOLOGY

Sample

The sample consisted of 120 elderly residing in Delhi, of these 120 elderly 60 were institutionalised and 60 were non-institutionalised, with an equal number of males and females. The mean age of the institutionalised aged was 60.5 years, whereas, the mean age of the non-institutionalised aged was 69.23 years. An attempt was made to match the two samples: , institutionalised and non-institutionalised elderly, as far as possible. Institutionalised aged implies those old people living in old homes for the aged run by the Government or Delhi Administration. Non-institutionalised aged implies those old people living either alone or with their children. Table 12.1 presents the description of the sample.

TABLE 12.1: Description of the Sample

Variables		Institutionalised Aged	Non-Institutionalised Aged
Sex	Males	N = 30	N = 30
	Females	N = 30	N = 30
	Total	N = 60	N = 60
Age	Range	60—82 years	60—83 years
	Mean	60.5 years	69.23 years
Income	Mean	Rs. 34.58	Rs. 562.50
Years of	Range	0—14 years	0—17 years
Education	Mean	3.73 years	6.15 years
Marital Status		22% unmarried 78% widows & widowers	16% unmarried, 63% Married and living with their spouse, 35% widows & widowers.

The table reveals that the institutionalised aged have little income, a few years of education and are either unmarried or widowed as compared to the non-institutionalised aged who are in a far better position.

Tools Used

The following tools were used in the present study:

1. Depression was assessed by the IPAT Depression Scale constructed by Krug and Langhlin (1976). This scale measures clinical depression, to differentiate normals from depressives and depressives from other types of clinical disorders, such as anxiety or psychogenic disorders. It consists of 40 items, of which 36 items give a reliable and valid estimate of the depression level, and 4 items are introduced as moderator items to reduce the relationship between scores on the Depression Scale and anxiety. For reliability two types of coefficient are reported, the Alpha coefficients and Split-half. The former were calculated for seven groups of subjects (Depressives, Prisoners, Alcoholics, Narcotic addicts, College students and Adult normals) and these range from .93 to .85. The split-half (odd-even) reliability coefficients for the same seven groups range from .95 to .89. Validity was evaluated by three approaches: (a) correlation of test score with the depression factor (r = .88); differentiation of normals from diagnosed depressives (t=13.52, df=697); and correlation of test scores with other constructs that conform to theoretical expectation.
2. Loneliness was assessed by Russell, Pepalu and Ferguson's the Revised UCLA Loneliness Scale (1980). The original scale was developed in 1978 by the same authors. The revised scale consists of 20 statements or items, half reflecting satisfaction with social relationship and half reflecting dissatisfaction. Each of the 20 statements/items have four response optionals: never lonely/rarely lonely/sometimes lonely/often lonely/. The maximum score possible is 80 and minimum is 20. High scores indicate high degree of loneliness. The reliability coefficient was .94 and concurrent validity was obtained by finding the relationship between scores on the loneliness scale and other measures of loneliness (feeling abandoned, isolated, etc.), measures of social activity and relationships, and measures of emotional states.
3. Hopelessness was measured by the Geriatric Scale of Hopelessness, developed by Fry (1984). This Scale measures hopelessness or frequency of negative expectations for the self or future. The scale covers four factors, a sense of hopelessness about (a) recovering physical and cognitive abilities, (b) recovering personal and interpersonal worth and attractiveness, (c) recovering spiritual faith and receiving spiritual grace, and

(d) receiving nurturance and recovering respect and remembrance both in the present and after death. The scale consists of 30 statements/items with two response optionals: true and false. The maximum score possible is 30 and minimum is 0. High scores indicate high degree of hopelessness. As measures of internal consistency Cronbach Alpha coefficient was computed and it was found to be .69 ($p < .01$); and Spearman-Brown split-half correlation coefficient was .73 ($p < .01$). The validity was evaluated by correlating Geriatric Scale of hopelessness scores with: (a) Brink *et al*'s (1982) Geriatric Depression Scale scores ($r = .49, p < .01$), (b) Ratings of Behavioural Depression ($r = .29, p < .05$) and Tennessee self concept scale scores ($r = -.55, p < .01$).

4. Frustration was measured by Pareek's (1968) Indian adapted version of the Rosenzweig Picture Frustration Test. This Picture Frustration test for adults was developed by Rosenzweig in 1944 and revised in 1948. The test consists of 24 cartoon like drawings, representing frustrating situations in which one character says something that causes frustration to other character depicted therein. The subject is required to write down in the space provided what the other character would say in that situation. For the internal consistency of the Indian adapted scale reliability coefficients both for matrix reliability and item reliability were calculated. The coefficient for matrix reliability ranged from .27 to .82 and for item reliability the range was .46 to .74. All the tools were translated into Hindi for the Hindi speaking subjects.

Procedure for Collection of Data

The subject of both the Institutionalised (30 males and 30 females) and Non-Institutionalised (30 males and 30 females) groups were approached individually and a good rapport was established. They were assured that their responses would remain confidential and used only for research purposes. They were also informed that there were no right/wrong or good/bad answers and that there was no time limit for answering the statements but they should give the first response (reaction) to each statement and not to think of a response which would be appropriate or desirable. The schedule consisting of a personal data sheet, measures of Loneliness, Hopelessness, Depression and

Frustration, was administered to each subject individually.

Results and Discussion

The purpose of this investigation was to study the impact of institutionalisation and non-institutionalisation on some emotional states of the aged. Two-way Analysis of Variance was computed and Table 12.2 presents the summary of the ANOVAS for the three emotional states: Loneliness, Depression, and Hopelessness. The ANOVA table shows that the main effect of institutionalisation/non-institutionalisation is significant on loneliness ($F = 95.36$, $p < .01$). A glance at the the mean loneliness scores (Table 12.3) of the institutionalised ($\bar{X} = 53.40$) and non-institutionalised aged ($\bar{X} = 35.96$) show that institutionalised aged have a higher mean score than the non-institutionalised aged. This means that institutionalised aged feel more lonely than the aged living with their children or alone. Comparing the mean scores of the institutionalised and non-institutionalised aged, with the norms of the scale, it is observed that the mean score of the non-institutionalised aged lies in the category of 'rarely lonely', whereas, the mean score of the institutionalised aged lies in the category of 'being lonely'. There could be a number of plausible explanations for the findings on Loneliness. Some of these explanations are as follows: (i) the institutionalised aged have been left in the institution by their families or relatives and they feel they have been abandoned and thus, are not needed or loved, which probably leads to a greater feelings of loneliness and depression. (ii) The institutionalised aged have low or practically no income of their own (mean income per month Rs. 34), which probably makes them feel that because of the lack of income they are institutionalised and as a result they feel more lonely than the non-institutionalised aged, who have a regular income (mean income Rs. 562) and a feeling of independence and power; and (iii) Majority of the institutionalised aged were either illiterate or had very few years of schooling (means year of schooling 3.75) as a result they could not read newspapers, magazines or novels, and therefore felt more lonely than the non-institutionalised aged who were more educated (mean years of schooling 9.15) and could spend their time reading.

ANOVA (Table 12.2) shows that the main effect of sex is significant ($F = 5.10$, $p < .05$) on loneliness. The loneliness mean scores of the sexes depict that aged females feel more lonely ($\bar{X}$ =

48.41) than aged males in general ($\bar{X}$ = 44.60). This finding is in line with the results obtained by earlier investigators, such as Wood (1980) and Baum (1982), who found females, irrespective of age, to feel more lonely than males.

However, the interaction effect of institutionalisation/non-institutionalisation and sex on loneliness has not been found to be significant.

An attempt was made to find out some determinants of loneliness among the institutionalised and non-institutionalised aged. Thus, product moment correlations were calculated between loneliness scores, income and education and these are presented in Table 12.5. The correlational analysis shows a significant negative relationship between loneliness and income both in the institutionalised (r = –.38) and non-institutionalised aged (r = –.52). This means that there is increase in loneliness consequent upon the decrease in income. Perlman *et al* (1980) also found that lower income increased feelings of loneliness. The negative relationship between loneliness and income also lends support to our argument, that institutionalised aged because of low income and its consequences feel more lonely than the non-institutionalised aged, who have more income. The results indicate a negative significant relationship between years of education and loneliness, both in the institutionalised ($r = -.33$, $p < .01$) and non-institutionalised aged ($r = -.40$, $p < .01$). This implies that there is decrease in loneliness consequent upon the increase in years of education. This finding also lends support to our argument, that institutionalised aged, because of fewer years of education cannot read and therefore, feel more lonely than the non-institutionalised aged, who have comparatively more years of education and the ability to read. The finding of a negative relationship between loneliness and education among the elderly is consistent with other research findings in this area (Baum 1983).

Depression

Table 12.2 reveals that the main effect of institutionalisation/non-institutionalisation is significant on feelings of Depression ($F = 19.15$, $p < .01$). The mean (Table 12.3) depression score of institutionalised aged ($\bar{X}$ = 28.78) is larger than that of the non-institutionalised aged ($\bar{X}$ = 23.21), which implies that institutionalised aged feel more depressed than the non-institutionalised aged. The mean depression

TABLE 12.2: Summary of the ANOVAS for Loneliness, Depression and Hopelessness

Variables	Source of Variation										
	Institutionalised/ Non-Institutionalised(A)			Sex Males/Females(B)			Institutionalised/Non-Institutionalised × Sex			Within Cells	
	df	S^2	F	df	S^2	F	df	S^2	F	df	S^2
Loneliness	1	7889.42	95.36**	1	421.87	5.10*	1	42.0	0.51	116	82.73
Depression	1	929.64	19.15**	1	1428.30	29.43**	1	3.02	.06	116	48.54
Hopelessness	1	1732.8	63.24**	1	132.3	4.83*	1	.07	.00	116	27.40

** $p < .01$ level; * $p < .05$ level.

scores of both the groups when compared with the norms show that the mean score of the institutionalised aged lies in the 'category of depressed', whereas, the mean score of the non-institutionalised aged lies in the 'category of non-depressed'.

TABLE 12.3: Mean and Standard Deviation for Institutionalised and Non-Institutionalised Aged on Loneliness, Depression and Hopelessness

Variables	Sex	Institutionalised		Non-Institutionalised		Total	
		$\bar{X}$	SD	$\bar{X}$	SD	$\bar{X}$	SD
Loneliness	30 Males	53.4	6.21	35.96	10.96	44.66	12.27
	30 females	55.93	5.67	40.9	15.7	48.41	11.87
	60 Total	54.66	4.29	38.43	13.76		
Depression	30 Males	25.34	4.21	19.76	7.45	22.55	6.66
	30 Females	32.23	5.20	26.70	9.35	29.45	8.05
	60 Total	28.78	5.84	23.21	9.18		
Hopeless-ness	30 Males	17.77	2.67	10.13	3.68	13.95	4.98
	30 Females	19.84	3.44	12.30	4.71	16.05	4.27
	60 Total	18.80	1.57	11.20	4.35		

The high level of depression in the institutionalised aged could be due to any one or all of the following reasons: (a) Lack of family and work roles among the institutionalised aged, could lead to greater feelings of depression. This reason is supported by Aneshensel *et al* (1982) who found that family and work roles tend to be associated with reduced depression; and (b) lack of a satisfying interpersonal and confiding relationship among the institutionalised aged, could be another cause of greater feelings of depression. This arguments is based on Hale's (1982) study who found depression to be related to less satisfying interpersonal relationships and Murphy's (1983) conclusions from a study, that subjects who lacked a confiding relationship were more vulnerable to depression. The majority of the institutionalised aged in this study were either widows/widowers or unmarried, thus, they lacked a satisfying interpersonal and confiding relationship in a life partner.

The results (Table 12.2) indicate that the main effect of sex on depression is significant ($F=29.43$, $p < .01$). The mean scores (Table 12.3) on depression indicate that aged females have scored higher ($\bar{X}$ = 29.45) than males ($\bar{X}$ = 22.55), implying that they feel more depressed than males. This finding is in agreement with the findings of

Aneshensel et al (1982) and Schultz and Moore (1984) who found that women in general, irrespective of age, significantly felt more depressed than men. Calvet (1983) in a survey of 133 first admission to a psychiatric hospital for loneliness and depression, observed that there were more females than males (80 vs 53). Hale and Cochran (1984) on a study of the elderly, suggested that probably higher rates of widowhood among the elderly women and the accompanying financial problems, may be partially responsible for higher rates of depression among them in comparison to elderly males.

The interaction effect of institutionalisation/non-institutionalisation and sex on depression has not been found to be significant.

To get a better understanding of the determinants of depression product moment correlations were calculated between depression and some demographic variables and these are presented in Table 12.5. The correlational analysis indicates a positive significant ($r = +.37$, $p < .01$ level) relationship between depression and age for the non-institutionalised aged, and practically no relationship between the two variables for the institutionalised aged. This implies that in the non-institutionalised aged depression is consequent upon increase in age.

A significant negative relationship is observed between depression and income, both in the institutionalised and non-institutionalised aged. This means that among the elderly, irrespective of institutionalisation or non-institutionalisation, feeling of depression is consequent upon poor finances. This findings is in agreement with Michals et al (1983) who reported that depression was related to poor financial status.

TABLE 12.4: Correlation of Psychological and Demographic Variables in the Institutionalised and Non-Institutionalised Aged

Demographic Variables		Psychological Variables		
		Loneliness	Depression	Hopelessness
Age	Institutionalised	+.12	+.02	−.16
	Non-Institutionalised	+.61**	+.37**	+.65**
Income	Institutionalised	−.38**	−.27*	−.84**
	Non-Institutionalised	−.52**	−.58**	−.50**
Years of Education	Institutionalised	−.33**	−.17	+.12
	Non-Institutionalised	−.40**	−.56**	−.50**

** $p < .01$ level; * $p < .05$ level.

TABLE 12.5: Mean and Standard Deviation on Frustration and its Dimensions

Variables	Institutionalised Aged N=60						Non-Institutionalised Aged N=60						Total			
	Males		Females		Total		Males		Females		Total		Males		Females	
	$\bar{X}$	SD	$\bar{X}$	SD	$\bar{X}$	SD	$\bar{X}$	SD	$\bar{X}$	SD	$\bar{X}$	SD	$\bar{X}$	SD	$\bar{X}$	SD
Frustration 1. Group Conformity Rating (G.C.R.)	6.92	1.05	6.93	.97	6.92	1.01	7.80	1.24	6.98	1.08	7.39	1.16	7.36	1.15	6.95	1.02
Types of Aggression																
i) E90 Defensive (E.D.)	8.00	1.57	8.16	2.04	8.08	1.82	12.35	2.35	11.68	3.02	12.01	2.74	10.17	1.96	9.92	2.53
ii) Obstacle Dominance (O.D.)	3.83	1.51	3.73	1.89	3.78	1.71	4.23	1.80	3.16	1.59	3.70	2.68	4.03	1.65	3.45	1.74
iii) Need Persistence (N.P.)	8.62	2.53	8.62	2.09	8.69	2.31	7.41	2.68	9.13	2.23	8.27	2.61	8.01	2.60	8.87	2.16
Direction of Aggression																
i) Extraggression (E.A.)	6.87	2.85	8.13	3.13	7.50	2.99	10.25	3.33	9.25	2.18	9.75	2.76	8.56	3.09	8.69	2.66
ii) Intraggression (I.A.)	9.50	2.26	8.98	1.70	9.24	1.98	8.41	1.94	8.10	1.82	8.25	1.88	8.95	2.10	8.54	1.76
iii) Imgression (M.A.)	7.63	1.39	6.76	1.65	7.20	1.52	5.26	2.61	6.61	1.17	5.94	1.89	6.45	2.0	6.64	1.41

A significant negative relationship is found between years of education and depression ($r = -.56$, $p < .01$ level) in the non-institutionalised aged but not in the institutionalised aged. However, the direction of the relationship between the two variables is same in the case of both the institutionalised and non-institutionalised aged. This implies that depression among the elderly is consequent upon poor education.

Hopelessness

The ANOVA (Table 12.2) shows the effect of institutionalisation/non-institutionalisation is significant on Hopelessness ($F = 234.16$, $p < .01$). The mean hopelessness scores (Table 12.3) show that institutionalised aged have a higher mean score ($\bar{X} = 18.80$) than the non-institutionalised aged ($\bar{X} = 11.20$). This means that the institutionalised aged have greater feelings of hopelessness, i.e., greater negative expectancies toward oneself and towards the future than the non-institutionalised aged. This finding could be explained on the basis of the personal background variables of the institutionalised aged. The personal data sheet reveals that the institutionalised aged in comparison to the non-institutionalised aged have lower income, less education and practically none or little family contact, and probably these are some of the causes for the greater negative expectancies toward oneself and the future among the institutionalised aged.

The analysis of variance (Table 12.2) reveals that the main effect of sex is significant on Hopelessness ($F = 17.95$, $p < .01$). A glance at the mean scores on hopelessness (Table 12.3) shows that females have a higher mean score ($\bar{X} = 16.05$) than males ($\bar{X} = 13.95$). This implies that aged females feel a greater sense of hopelessness than aged males. The plausible explanation for this finding seems to be, that females in comparison to males are probably more emotionally weak, and this emotional weakness among females could be the result of differences in socialisation and biological make up.

The ANOVA however, reveals no significant effect of institutionalisation/non-institutionalisation and sex on feelings of hopelessness. Further, to get a deeper understanding of the feeling of hopelessness among the elderly, product-moment correlations were calculated between demographic variables and feelings of hopelessness, both in the institutionalised and non-institutionalised aged. Table 12.5 shows a significant positive relationship between age and feelings of hopelessness in the non-institutionalised aged but not in the institutionalised aged. Infact the direction of the relationship between the variables in the institutionalised aged and the non-institutionalised aged is just the opposite. This means that among the non-institutionalised aged feeling of hopelessness is consequent upon increase in age, whereas, in the institutionalised aged feeling of hopelessness is consequent upon decrease in age.

A negative significant relationship is observed between income and feelings of hopelessness, both in the institutionalised and non-institutionalised aged. This implies that among the elderly feelings of hopelessness is consequent upon poor finances.

Feelings of hopelessness is also found to be negatively related to years of education among the non-institutionalised aged but not in the institutionalised aged. This means that among the elderly living on their own or with their families, less educated a person is greater is the possibility of his having feeling of hopelessness. Whereas, among the institutionalised aged the results show a tendency (as the correlation of + .12 in non-significant) towards greater feeling of hopelessness with higher education. This finding seems to imply, that among both institutionalised and non-institutionalised aged, the amount of education one has, plays a significant role in determining whether one would have feeling of hopelessness or not.

Frustration

Table 12.4 reveals that there is no significant effect of institutionalisation/non-institutionalisation, and sex on group conformity ratings. Group conformity rating is a measure of conformity of an individual's score to the modal response of the group as a whole or it may be regarded as a measure of the individual's adjustment to a normal group. The higher the score the greater the group conformity ratings. The results indicate that the institutionalised and the non-institutionalised aged have equal group conformity ratings.

On the types of aggression towards frustration, the ANOVA shows that the main effect of institutionalisation/non-institutionalisation is significant ($F = 8.93$, $p < .01$) only on ego defensive type of aggression. This is a type of aggression in which the ego of the individual predominates in his response to frustration. Higher the score greater the use of ego defensive responses. A glance at the mean (Table 12.5) scores shows that non-institutionalised aged use ego

TABLE 12.6: Summary of the ANOVAs on Frustration and its Dimensions

Variables	Source of Variation										
	Institutionalised/ Non-Institutionalised(A)			Sex. (B)			A × B			Within Cells	
	df	S^2	F	df	S^2	F	df	S^2	F	df	S^2
Group Conformity	1	0.39	0.14	1	10.22	3.56	1	6.80	2.36	116	2.87
Type of Aggression											
(i) Ego Defensive	1	27.50	8.93**	1	10.22	3.32	1	6.97	2.26	116	3.08
(ii) Obstacle Dominance	1	0.39	0.14	1	10.32	3.56	1	6.88	2.40	116	2.87
(iii) Need Persistence	1	5.20	1.20	1	9.33	2.14	1	15.00	3.45	116	4.35
Direction of Aggression											
(i) Extraggression	1	14.88	7.02**	1	4.15	1.96	1	15.52	7.22**	116	2.12
(ii) Intraggression	1	26.60	16.72**	1	4.22	2.65	1	.01	.01	116	1.59
(iii) Imgression	1	46.87	12.57**	1	1.64	44	1	37.41	10.03**	116	3.73

** $p < .01$ level; * $p < .05$ level.

defensive responses ($\bar{X}$ = 12.01) more than the institutionalised aged ($\bar{X}$ = 8.08) in frustrating situations, i.e., the ego of the non-institutionalised aged tends to dominate in frustrating situations. This could be because, the institutionalised aged having practically no family or relatives to fall back upon feel insecure and lack confidence and therefore, make less use of the ego defensive responses in frustrating situations in comparison to the non-institutionalised aged, who have independent income, still some status in society and some family or relatives to care for them. However, even though there is a significant difference between the institutionalised and non-institutionalised aged in the use of ego defensive responses, but if the aged population is considered in general, irrespective of institutionalisation/non-institutionalisation, and the mean ego defensive score is compared with the norms, one finds that the aged make much less use of defensive responses than the general population. The plausible explanation for this finding seems to be, that in the general population there are people of all ages and the younger age groups in order to protect their ego from being hurt, probably make more use of ego defensive responses to frustrating situations than the elderly. In the elderly population, the ego predominates less probably because of physical and biological effects of aging and other types of aggression to frustration are used more such as obstacle dominance or need persistence.

The analysis of variance indicates that institutionalisation/non-institutionalisation has no significant effect on the other two types of aggression to frustration, viz., obstacle dominance and need-persistence. This means that there is no difference between institutionalised and non-institutionalised elderly, in the emphasis of the barrier or obstacle causing frustration and of the solution to the frustrating problems, in their responses to frustration.

The ANOVA results show that the main effect of sex is not significant on any of the three types of aggression to frustration: obstacle dominance, ego defensive and need-persistence. This means that there is no difference between elderly males and females, irrespective of institutionalisation or non-institutionalisation, in the emphasis of either the obstacle or barrier causing the frustration, or ego defense or solution of the frustration, in their responses to frustrating situation.

The results shows that the interaction effect on all the three types of aggression to frustration: obstacle dominance, ego defensive and need-persistence, is also non-significant.

The ANOVA (Table 12.5) indicates that the main effect of institutionalisation/non-institutionalisation is significant on the three directions of the three types of aggression, viz., Extraggression, Intraggression and Imgression. A glance at the mean scores indicate that the non-institutionalised aged have a higher mean score ($\bar{X} = 9.75$) than the institutionalised aged ($\bar{X} = 7.50$) on Extraggression, implying that the non-institutionalised aged in a frustrating situation tend to turn the aggression more onto the environment, or on some object in the environment than the institutionalised aged. This means, that the non-institutionalised aged more frequently use the strategy of blaming the environment or some object in the environment to cope with frustrating situations than the institutionalised aged. This strategy enables them to protect their ego and self-concept and at the same time cope with the frustration. There is no significant main effect of sex on extraggression, however, the interaction effect of institutionalisation/non-institutionalisation by sex on extraggression is significant ($F = 7.22$, $p < .01$ level). The cell means reveal that the institutionalised females blame the environment as the cause of frustration more than ($\bar{X} = 8.13$) the institutionalised males ($\bar{X} = 6.87$), whereas, the non-institutionalised males blame the environment or some object in the environment as the cause of frustration more than ($\bar{X} = 10.25$) the non-institutionalised females ($\bar{X} = 9.25$).

On Intraggression a perusal of Table 12.6 shows that the institutionalised aged have a higher mean score ($\bar{X} = 9.24$) than the non-institutionalised aged ($\bar{X} = 8.25$), viz., the institutionalised aged turn the aggression more upon themselves than the non-institutionalised aged. The reason for this difference seems to lie in the adverse circumstances and the related experiences of the institutionalised aged in comparison to the non-institutionalised aged. There is no significant effect of sex on intraggression nor is the interaction of sex and institutionalisation/non-institutionalisation significant on intraggression. This means that both elderly males and females blame themselves equally for the frustrating situation. However, taking the aged population as a whole, it is observed that they use intraggression more than ($\bar{X} = 8.72$)) the general population, this may be probably because the aged feel that due to decline of abilities and activity it is their own fault for the cause of the frustrating situation. It is also observed from Table 12.5, that the institutionalised aged have a higher mean score ($\bar{X} = 7.20$) on imgression, type of direction of aggression, than the non-institutionalised aged ($\bar{X} = 5.94$), viz., the institutionalised aged make more use of imgression, that is, evading aggression in an attempt to gloss over the frustration or denying the frustration as compared to the non-institutionalised aged. There is a significant interaction effect ($F = 10.03$, $p < .01$ level) on imgression, viz., institutionalised males make more use of imgression ($\bar{X} = 7.63$) as a method of coping with frustration then institutionalised females ($\bar{X} = 6.76$). In contrast non-institutionalised females more often ($\bar{X} = 6.61$) use imgression or deny the frustration as compared to non-institutionalised males.

Conclusions

The following conclusions could be drawn from the results of the study:

1. Institutionalised aged have greater feelings of loneliness, depression and hopelessness as compared to the aged who are living either with their children or independently. They use less ego-defensive reactions to frustration and tend to direct the aggression either upon themselves or deny the existence of frustration altogether, whereas, the non-institutionalised aged use more ego-defensive reactions to frustration and tend to direct their aggression more onto the environment or some object in the environment.
2. Aged females, irrespective of institutionalisation/non-institutionalisation feel more lonely, depressed and pessimistic (feeling of hopelessness) than aged males. However, no significant differences were observed between the sexes on reactions to frustration, which implies that both males and females react more or less in a similar manner to frustrating situations.
3. The interaction effect of institutionalisation/non-institutionalisation and sex on the three emotional states: Loneliness, Depression and Hopelessness, was found to be non-significant. The interaction effect on the types of aggression was also observed to be nonsignificant. However, the interaction effect was significant on two of the three directions of frustration aggression: Extraggression and Imgression. Institutionalised females and non-institutionalised males use more extraggression, whereas, institutionalised males and non-

institutionalised females use more imgression to cope with frustration.

4. A significant positive relationship has been observed between age, loneliness, depression and hopelessness, and a negative significant relationship between income, education, and loneliness, depression and hopelessness among the non-institutionalised aged. However, among institutionalised aged:

   (a) Age is found to have no significant effect on any of the emotional states;
   (b) education is found to be related significantly and negatively to loneliness but not to the other two emotional states; and
   (c) a significant negative relationship is found between loneliness, depression, hopelessness and income.

COMMENTS

The results of the first study show that both the younger and the older generation and the sexes depict an unfavourable attitude towards institutionalisation of the aged, which indicates that probably family ties and social pressure in India, particularly, in the middle social class, are still strong. The findings of the study no doubt are limited as only the middle social class attitudes have been assessed and not of the other classes. However, on the presumption that family ties in India cut across class structure it would not be incorrect to generalise the findings to the other classes, that is, the high and low social classes. Thus, it seems that in India, it would take at least another decade or two before institutionalisation of the aged is accepted by the community at large.

Comparative studies no doubt are important and essential but because of certain methodological drawbacks they have their limitations. The comparative study on the emotional states of the institutionalised and the non-institutionalised aged is also one such study. Firstly, to get a matching sample for the institutionalised aged from the non-institutionalised aged is practically impossible and therefore, comparison may not be without methodological drawbacks. Secondly, the emotional states of those individuals, males and females, who have been institutionalised are going to be affected not only by their stay (residence) in the institution but also by the circumstances that forced them to be institutionalised, and it would not be possible to know which of the two factors is playing a greater part in influencing the mental health of the institutionalised aged. Keeping these drawbacks in consideration, the conclusions that may be drawn from the study is that institutionalisation leads to poor mental health. The institutionalised aged have been observed to have greater feelings of depression, loneliness, and hopelessness and in frustrating situations they either deny the existence of the frustrating situation or direct the aggression more upon themselves. On the other hand, the mental health of those aged living with their family is fairly good as their feelings of depression, loneliness, hopelessness when compared with the norms are found to be less than those of the average adult. Like the average adult they also direct their aggression in a frustrating situation more onto the environment than upon themselves.

However, in spite of the fact that the elderly living in families are psychologically healthy than the elderly living in institutions for the aged, old age homes have come to stay as stated by Maj. Gen. Pannu, Director General of Helpage India (1991), "Though I won't call them a necessary evil, old age homes can no longer be wished away from the Indian scene. . . ." Moreover, Sachdev (1991) has elaborated how institutional care for the aged is slowly becoming a socially acceptable option, with the joint family system breaking down and domestic help becoming increasingly difficult to find these days.

PART VI

PUBLIC VIEW OF THE AGED AND CONCLUSIONS

13

PUBLIC VIEW OF THE AGED AND AGING

Today developing countries house over 55 per cent of the world's senior citizens and in another four decades it is likely to shift to 70 per cent. The United Nations projections estimate that in India by 2001 the number of elderly is likely to swell to 7.56 crores. Indian culture while claiming reverence for age, firmly consigns older people into the sidelines, probably, because of the breakdown of family ties and changing values of the younger generation. No wonder the senior citizens are a neglected lot in our country.

Though old age is not something to fear or dread for aging is something that no human being can avoid. Therefore, while accepting the inevitable process of aging one should try and live gracefully and add years to one's life by becoming flexible, self-directed and developing a network of contacts. Scientists are finding out more and more about the aging process and way to slow it and thereby, increasing the life span drastically. But till then the society has a responsibility towards the welfare of its senior citizens. How does the society perceive their aged ? What are the views of the society about retirement, aging and the care of the aged ? In this context diverse views of the cross-section of society are reproduced.

The Rise of the Older Population

Mahinder Singh[1]

The ratio of old people to young people is now increasing dramatically all over the world together with the general increase in population. According to a United Nations publication "Demographic Indicators of Countries: Estimates and Projections", as assessed in 1980, the total population of the world in 1980 was 4432.1 million people, and that of 60 years and above was 375.8 million.

In A.D. 2000 the total world population will be 6118.9 million and people of 60 years of age and above will be 590.4 million. To a break-up of this population, the total number of people in more-developed regions including Northern America, Japan, Europe, Australia, New Zealand and USSR will be 1272.2 million and those of 60 years and above age 230.3 million. And in less-developed regions of the world including Africa, Latin America, China, other East Asia (excluding Japan), South Asia, Melanesia, and Micronesia-Polynesia, the total population will be 4846.4 million and those of 60 years and above age 360 million.

At present, on an average, every 6th or 7th person in the world belongs to the category of the elderly which is denoted by the age 60 years and above. By A.D. 2000 one out of every four people in the world will be over 60 years.

The increase in life expectancy is due to the benefits of medical technology, preventive medicine, improved sanitation, and better diet. Regular exercise, to which older people are now paying attention, is also helpful for the cardiovascular system and as a way for lowering cholesterol. People now are living to ripe old age because chronic diseases likely arthritis, hypertension, deafness, heart conditions, sinusitis, poor vision, orthopedic problems, atherosclerosis, diabetes and varicose veins, to which the elderly people hitherto were affected have now been reduced through preventive measures. In advanced countries, major causes of death now are only accidents, stroke, cancer and heart disease. Other ailments such as smallpox or tuberculosis, which have been great killers in previous years, have now been fully conquered.

. . . Scientists already in advanced countries are endeavouring to find out the codes which govern the aging process. One scientist is investigating the cell to try to figure out why it ceases some of its crucial functions after a certain point. . . . Other scientists in USA are trying to find out how external forces influence the cell's and ultimately, the body's behaviour. It is said that aging is also influenced by hormones and one hormone, dubbed the death hormone, increases as we grow older and blocks the influenced of thyroid hormone, which is crucial to the proper functioning of the metabolism. If an antidote to the death hormone exists, then health may be postponed for many years.

Another hormone, one that discourage death, decreases with time. Called dehydroepiandrosterone, or DHEA for short, it appears to have a profound influence on the immune system. If a way can be found to give its derivatives in proper doses to sufferers of chronic diseases, such as diabetes, its benefit may be enormous. Therefore, it is assumed that by the year 2000 A.D. gerontologists may be able to do these researches. The human life span then may be average 110 to 115 years. At present the oldest person on earth whose age has been authenticated is a 120 years old Japanese who, according to the "Guinness Book of World Records", says the best way to lead a long life is "not to worry" and to leave things to "God, the Sun and Budha". . . .

So, if the current population explosion in world is not curbed, by the year A.D. 2000 overpopulated countries like India may be just like a railway platform where each one will jostle each other.

Indian Express[2]

A 'grey' revolution is rocking the universe. The population of the elderly people in the age group of 60 and above is almost a global phenomenon as a consequence of advance medical sciences, modernisation, development and improvement in the health standards.

According to the United Nations projection till the year 2025 the proportion of the elderly population will register a quantum jump, aggregating to an overall increse of 13.3 per cent worldwide. It is expected to jump from 6.3 per cent to 11.9 per cent in the developing countries and from 15.8 per cent to 23.6 per cent in the developed regions of the world.

In India the number is likely to swell to 7.56 crores and beyond by the year 2001 as against 4.79 crores, according to the papers tabled at the recent meeting of the sub-group on Community Action for Social Integration.

While the developing countries are currently estimated to account for the 55 per cent of the world's elderly population the share in the next four decades is likely to shift to more than 70 per cent. . . .

The Aging Syndrome

Mahinder Singh[3]

I have noticed that since very few of our government employees plan their retirement programme, and in a country like ours as a person's position is mainly judged by his work, so retirement comes to most of our people as "a bolt from the blue."

A retired person begins to feel himself old and the ageing process, medically speaking, invites dependency in the life of elderly people. The diseases which makes the life dependent are the following:

(1) Cerebrovascular insufficiency...
(2) Parksonism...
(3) Coronary heart disease...
(4) Orthostatic hypotention...
(5) Mental confusion and Dementia...
(6) Blindness...

Thus, majority of problems of ageing population are chronic diseases which demand proper medical and nursing care. To bring these people back to their pre-illness pattern of life methodical rehabilitation is essential. This can usually be done in chronic disease hospitals or geriatric hospitals. In India geriatrics is a neglected branch in clinical medicine....

The problems of the aged can be tackled effectively by implementing policies like giving old age pension to each individual of age 60 years and above, comprehensive health care, by promoting indoor geriatric institutes, geriatric clubs and libraries and above all promotion of joint families which are best care-providers for the elderly as well as children.

Our Government should re-employ physically fit. . . . One thing more which can help our elderly people is the early decision of civil suits in our courts of law. . . . If a decision on a civil suit is not expedited, that can make an elderly person lead to stroke or heart attack etc.

A.S. Negi[4]

Old age dominates us right from the day we are born until the day we die. Society has programmed our life into definite stages. . . . The biological clock ticking within us just cannot be stopped. Forty-years old in today's world have more difficulty accepting aging because they have grown up thinking that everything can be fixed....

Like Western society, Indians too have begun to venerate youth....

After 50, a kind of acceptance grows that aging will bring change.

But growing older is generally not seen as a positive event. Most expectations about old age . . . deafness, poor vision, mental deterioration. . .hardly hit 10 per cent of the elderly people.

But age is relative. . . .athlete may be considered old at 30, a cricketeer at 35, a Supreme Court judge young at 50, a painter acts and thinks young, . . .in his 70s or even 80s. . . .

Sometimes the problems is illness, sometimes it is personality. Flexibility is now considered to be one of the keys to healthy aging. If you can change, be self-directed, develop inner resources and a network of contacts, you are likely to be happier.

The visible signs of aging start showing from out mid 20's on, as our skin starts to loose elasticity and our eyes begin to drop.

As we age, our skull becomes thinner and smaller, we lose fat under our skin and our skin becomes dry and stretchy. The tip of our nose drops. The nasal cartilages separate, causing our nose to look longer and fatter. The bones around our mouth become thin and an excess of skin overhangs. The chin starts to hang.

Most of the wrinkles and lines result from gravity pulling on our thinner, drier and less elastic skin. We get shorter because of bone and tissue loss and a narrowing of the spacers between our vertebrae. . . .

The secret of aging has yet to be discovered. But changes in our cells, tissues and organs are probably genetically programmed to occur at certain times of our life, say the researchers.

Why we age is a subject of study these days. Researchers are trying to find our why our biological clock turns off at a specific time. . . .

Generally, how fast we age depends on genetics, life style and sunlight. If your father was bald at 30, chances are you too will be. But baldness, grey hair and wrinkles should not interfere with normal activities.

An expert says that aging is not a disease. People do not usually die of old age. They die because their immune systems lose their ability to fight disease. An elderly person succumbs to influenza while a younger one survives. People who claim aging can be prevented are obscure, says a specialist. They feed into a narcissistic 20th century idea. . .that immortality is a possibility.

A reasonable goal is to ward off preventable illness, and get the best out of your genetic make-up. . . . The biggest factors in shortening life are smoking, lack of exercise, high blood pressure, inadequately controlled diabetes, obesity and a diet heavy in animal fats.

The idea is to have more people living longer, healthier lives and maintaining their creative potential. Not everyone has to play tennis. There is nothing wrong with walking, reading, playing with grand-children and so on. But improving the quality of life for the aged means eliminating some of the diseases associated with aging, Alzeimer's disease, . . .occurs in five per cent of people older than 65, and 20 per cent of people older than 80. . . .

Whatever you do, you are not likely to live past 80's or 90's (exceptions aside). Researchers say that unless there is big break-through in research, maximum life expectancies won't exceed 120.

In fact, tomorrow's elderly may benefit more from changed perceptions than an increased life expectancy. Thus, they will be less willing to accept the myth they should be infirm because they are old.

In truth, the result increased activism of seniors or elderly may be a better life, or, if attitudes of aging do not change, it may mean more disappointed people.

Preeti Singh[5]

"Is there life after 40? asked an interviewer in a radio broadcast. . . .

The implication, kidding or not was that ability, joy and hope are circumscribed by age, a proposition almost everyone seems to agree.

The opposite case is put by the existence in the past as well as the present of the artists who calmly deny the whole idea.

Titian the greatest painter of 16th century Venice, not only produced steadily through decades of what we call old age but continued to expand the range of his art (he died at 99 in a plague epidemic).

In our century several painters such as Picasso (1881-1973) and Matisse (1869-1956) have worked significantly in old age. Matisse put the finishing touches to the chapel at Venice when he was 81. Picasso produced 165 canvases the year he turned 87.

The reason: They did what they wanted when they wanted. . .the frustrations that routinely kill off humanity did not touch them. . . .

. . .Vladimir Horowitz, 82, and Claudio Arrau, 83 still perform around the world to packed houses.

Aging has always been a central human concern but as a social issue, it has never been so pressing as it is today. The phrase aging population is a journalistic common place. Demographers with a swirl of statistics can predict in no time that by A.D. 2000 old folks would become a big majority all over the world due to life-saving drugs.

That is one reason why thinking about compulsory retirement in the West has become hopelessly confused (it is beginning to affect Indians too). Making people retire, against their will is cruel and wasteful but if certain professionals do not retire they will clog the system. Is it not ironic that on the one hand we do everything medically possible to make people live longer, and on the other, we act as if we want them to go away.

In their professional lives people have responded to this great demographic change by bitterly denying that they are what their birth certificates say they are increasingly becoming addicted to youth. . . .

What counts, of course is how one perceives oneself, which often depends heavily how one is perceived by others. . . .

Those who reach middle age without distinguishing themselves in any way will grow melancholy and attribute their mood to failure. All these years and nothing to show for them. . . .

Finally a word about longetivity. A professor of Kiev University, Gennadi Berdyshev, a specialist in molecular genetics, says, "Research has shown that the ability to live long is inherited. But the genes ensure so to speak about 40 per cent of the realisation of the inherited possibility. The other 60 per cent are linked with the way of life of an individual with his general physical culture. Smoking, drinking, insufficient movement, small resistance to outer influences, irrational diet, badly organised work and psychological strains can ruin even a very good health even the most favourable heredity."

Nalini Singh[6]

. . . For a long time now I've realised at a subconscious level that we have wrapped ageing in a myth-ridden shroud. And a recent Sunday morning telephone call from Kamladevi Chattopadhyay underlined the doubt.

"I've done nothing for 3 days . . . made no progress, either on my book, or on the article on Lhasa," she grumbled.

"That sounds like a lot of work," I said . . . "It won't affect your health, will it?"

"What's wrong with me? Do a few physical problems affect the brain? Now as I was saying. . . ."

When I recounted this to my 74-year old father, he asked spontaneously, "What's special about this story? She's always been busy and alert. Do you really expect her to slow down because she's

84?" He tossed a puzzled glance in my direction, as he hurried to his car, "Am rushing to a meeting now. Let's discuss this later."

Later that week . . .

Hundred-year old Dhansar Pradhan demanded, "Teach me how to reel yarn from cocoons, I don't want to remain a rearer all my life. Rearing keeps me active for 6 months only. I must have work during the other 6 months too."

All your life, I thought silently, *might be nearly over*. But I said aloud, "You'll need to concentrate on the filament. That may be difficult. Your eyes will get tired, also fingers".

"May be. But I must try. My mind is ready to learn". . . .

. . .the senior Indian in metropolitan areas, is becoming : less dependent; less guilty about living an autonomous life; perhaps a little better-off after a lifetime of leading an organised life; fitter, with some preference for interesting and strenuous activities?

Older persons are warm, emotional, curious, capable. But in our collective consciousness they appear as death-obsessed, faded shadows whom this society ignores, although we claim reverence for age. . . .it is also a gross scientific blunder to link ageing with incompetence. In fact, middle age begins at 80 —. . .

. . .the net result is that physiological processes and systems work somewhat less effectively in older people than in the youth.

But the *decline is much less than we believe*, accept and then expect. . . .

. . .there exists a strong correlation between age and psychological factors such as outlook on life, adjustment to retirement etc. *So, the bulk of ageing is psychological* and the physical changes with age in sight, hearing or texture of the skin are modest in comparison.

Our society prescribes the most inflexible norms of behaviour for older people, . . .Older persons are supposed to conform in terms of dress, sociability, speech, visibility. . . .

. . .we live in a situation where the old are physically and physiologically much younger than society will let them be. . . . You have deteriorated, physically, physiologically and intellectually, so you should withdraw from active life. Fade more!'. . .

Yet a few persons, perhaps 2 per cent of the 60+ age group, have challenged this notion. . . and live closer to their latent potential. Their work has continued with intensity, and they've lived by a highly individual interpretation of life.

Papul Jayakar

"My body has aged, because I didn't spend time on exercise or keeping fit. But the brain's capacity for self-perception is at a peak now. "This self-perception causes new energies to be born in the brain. And energy keeps the mind young." "No, I haven't been sidelined by family or friends as I've grown older. But for me, being alone is joyous. I enjoy that as much as I enjoy being with people." (age 72 years).

L.P. Singh

In my experience there's no diminution of the cerebral processes as you age. If you keep using your mind there's no change in the abilities of reasoning, analysis, judgement, insights, perceptions."

Aruna Asaf Ali

I don't count life in terms of years, never have. Today I work 15 hours daily and that's simply not enough.

"Two things are important to me now — to finish all I've started, and to retain the capacity for self-criticism until the end." (age 78 years).

. . .Why then is life supposed to slide downhill compulsorily after 35? And who proclaimed the 'milestones' of life to be age 25, 35, 40, 50, 65, 75? Life is a continuum, and not churned out in episodes, neither marked by temporal slabstones.

"All our senses assert that they are unimpaired, are operationally efficient,. . .

. . .We recognise that each generation has a different role,. . .

But nobody says that roles determine a person's abilities. Most faculties keep improving with age. You're more able, over-all, at 75 than at 25.

Very early in life we are told it is too late. I contest that, and assert : Middle age begins at 80. . . .So be your age!

V.S. Raman[7]

By effectively shattering the myth that old age is synonymous with amnesia and deteriorating health. Nalini Singh proved her point well, that old age is to be respected and adored not be shunned or sidelined.

In her article, "Middle age begins at eighty". Singh took pains to din the dictum that one is as old or as young as he or she thinks. So long as one considers oneself independent, recognises one's own potential for society's growth, uses one's judgement and faculties to the benefit of mankind and keeps oneself physically trim through exercise, people will find their capacities improving with age.

True, age may show wrinkles on one's face. But all the acumen gained over the years, through wit and wisdom, can help people sharpen their intellect, widen their vision and deepen their perspective. If duly revered, properly cared for and treated with dignity, old people can prove a repository of values.

Bibhuti Bhushan Basu[8]

Your cover story "Middle age begins at eighty" was interesting. It enlightened the readers that the aged should not feel that they are a burden on society.

Instead of highlighting the lives of a few VIPs. I wish the writer had surveyed the lives of some downtrodden rural people. It is true that people who were held in esteem when in active service and who spend their retired lives amidst plenty, do enjoy a happier and active life even when they cross 70 or 80 years.

But there are thousands of others not so fortunate who pass their days in seclusion and in penury, but keep themselves equally active and happy in whatever surroundings they live.

During the last 25 years, I had occasion to come across quite a few people in every state who showed little or no concern that they had crossed 70 or so. They were found equally active, enthusiastic and jovial.

I am in my mid-seventies and retired about 15 years ago. Regular habits and taking everything in a lighter vein are the secret of my good health.

But the noise pollution, economic crises, instability in all spheres and lack of faith and regard for the aged. which we notice in modern society, may soon tell upon those who have refused to become a burden on society.

Dr. N.S. Subramaniam[9]

There have been a plethora of lectures, articles, talks and even a T.V.

play (in Marathi, in the serial *Bandhini*) on the heroism and nobility of the aged. Ms Nalini Singh has romanticised the aged under the encouraging heading, "Middle Age Begins at Eighty". The glorious examples of the aged which the article mentions — Kamladevi Chattopadhyay, Morarji Desai, JRD Tata and the venerable Panditji from Varanasi — achieved distinction during the early decades of their lives, and have only succeeded in maintaining a heroic hold in the evening of their lives. Ms Nalini Singh holds up these cases as typical. Considering that about a third of the nation reaches the threshold of the fifth and the sixth decades, these few luminaries don't prove that "Middle Age Begins at Eighty". These individuals were fortunate in having been born in reasonably well-do-do or affluent families. Ms Singh should have taken the millions of families without enough space to live or food too eat or proper health care to see how the aged fare in such circumstances.

I.M. Soni[10]

How strange human nature is! We forget big things and nurse the memory of trifles. For instance, I recall how as a child I wondered what I would be when I become old. I visualised myself as a man with hair a mixture of "salt and pepper", with hardly any bounce in the step, dragging my feet along a weary existence. I dreaded reaching that stage because it meant being within a hand-shaking distance from death.

Since then a whole lot of things have happened, demolishing a multitude of fallacies. I have reached that dreaded stage but the dread is simply missing. There are no over-the-fifty blues.

The future still interests me; it is brighter...

I am looking forward to the eager 60s and hope to enter the 21st century...

My attitude toward health and wealth has changed. I am determined not be a mere statistic...

I am proud of my years because these were not mere years that were ticked off the calendar. These were the years which plunged me deep into the struggle for survival...

...When you achieve success in the face of heavy odds and overcome difficulties, you develop. You grow up. You also create an anchor in your life.

I have found... two most commonly but wrongly used phrases —

"middle age" and "old age".

Both are accepted with a sign, a tinge of grief and disenchantment. Both are looked upon as sadly inevitable. According to this philosophy, life is divided into three broad sections: up-the-hill; over-the-hill and down-the-hill. People think that they are over the hill after 40 and let the poison of self-pity spread in their system. They easily slip into the slough of despondency.

One slows with age. Then what? Is not the new pace more leisurely, more rewarding and more gratifying?. . .

. . . In youth, you want to pluck flowers. In middle age, you just enjoy their fragrance.

Another factor is making this age delightful is living above the neck. I do enjoy cricket, good food and an occasional film but I enjoy reading more. . . . I watch it on TV if it telecast. . . .

I do not cling to anything which is dead. It is death-dealing. The past is gone, I cannot bring it back. Nobody can. . . . The future is today. What I do today will mould my tomorrow. Therefore, the uncertainty of future does not bother me as I am living it everyday.

One of my greatest delights is my fascination for and interest in the younger generation. . . .

One goes on maturing all life. It is a continuous process. It has nothing to do with calendar years. . . . Maturity, like modernity, is a question of outlook. . . .

You are as old as your prejudices. As such acquiring new ideas is a boon. . . . My attitude toward God has also changed. In my youth I rashly talked "to" Him. Now, I listen to Him.

S.S. Jaswal[11]

None can postpone old age and corresponding physical deterioration. Moreover, no tonics however, potent, can provide the needed strength to the worn-out tissues in old age. At the top of it, when one casts a look on one's wrinkled face and balding head, one is totally disappointed.

An old person is considered a spent force by the youngsters and sometimes they make fun. . . Old people should learn to bear with this attitude.

To keep themselves busy, some oldies start business. . . . When business fails, their condition becomes pitiable, because their life's earnings go down the chain.

When an old person has well-settled children, it is expected of him to pass his remaining time with them cheerfully. His grown up children should welcome him. . . .

I know of few old men who have taken to writing. . . for newspapers and magazines after retirement. They are doing well. . . .

I met Mr Sharma, now in his eighties,. . . He gets up at four in the morning and wakes up the temple priest at 4.30 a.m. after he has cleaned the floor of the shrine. This provides him sufficient energy for the day. During the day, he is always on the move on his cycle doing house-hold chores. He does not fear death and is ready to meet the Almighty whenever the call comes.

Old age is a curse if one is down with so many diseases like hypertension, kidney and heart ailments. To beat these, one should go for long walks in the morning. . . .

There is no point in unnecessarily worrying about old age. Even great saints like Guru Nanak Dev, Hazrat Mohammed accepted old age with a smile. They left their imprints in the form of holy hymns. . .

Always remember that we have been sent in this world to do something useful for mankind. After our exit, our work will last forever. . . .

Old age should be taken in its stride. Keeping oneself busy shall make an old man forget his aching knees, tired limbs and failing sight.

Dr. K.C. Anand[12]

A long energetic life span is a universal longing of man. He pines for it, prays for and invokes blessings for its possession. Still, he dreads old age for its link with physical and mental debility, diseases and dependence on others. The mere thought of it haunts him.

What is the factual position? Even middle-aged persons seem defeated, depressed and stagnating. However, there is a microscopic category who agree with the poet Robert Browning that, "Grow old with me, the best is yet to be". The emphasis in some cases is that life begins at sixty. There are others following Bertrand Russell who declared on his ninety-fifth birthday, "The first half of life is drawing close".

Birth, growth, decline, decay and death is an accepted phenomenon. . . . Each has its urges. Together, they goad him to action. . . .man attempts to survive, live and know the route to a prosperous, purposeful and peaceful life. In this endeavour he finds himself faced with the crucial problem of disease-free longevity. His anxiety for prolonged youth and all-round well-being is understandable. He rightly questions longevity. Is it predetermined? How far is the WHO concept for the elderly "Add years to life" practical?

The subject is, indeed, controversial. It will continue to be so. But, if man's choice lies between longevity associated with disabilities and suffering on the one hand, and the quality of life full of vigour and zest, on the other, most men, to my mind, would opt for the latter.

But is it possible to arrest the downward trend of life? Can youth be prolonged? If so, is it possible to maintain vim and vigour till a fairly advanced age — say seventy and beyond? In the story of mankind, from all available accounts, death is inevitable. None can escape it. Of course, aging gracefully is possible.

Aging is a riddle that has defied solution. Therefore, man must meekly bow to this natural phenomenon. However, only a few accept this reality joyfully. . . . Yet, it is possible to accept aging gracefully.

What is the method? Is there some talisman to ward off the decline? Of course, there is, but only for the sensible and genuinely interested. Saints, psychologists, psychotherapists, physiotherapists and nutrition experts have placed their knowledge and experience at our disposal. We are free to make use of it. . . .

It is a pity that the advanced years are associated with grey hair, brittle bones, dim eyesight, faulty hearing, dentures and depressed mind, etc. A number of bloodsucking leeches in the garb of minor and major ailments make him dependent on drugs which are certainly not to his taste. Naturally, elderly people complain and find fault with everything around, except themselves. . . . In their vocabulary, thanksgiving for the gifts of life and counting of blessings is almost missing.

Let us also not undermine the fact that there are people fairly in advanced age, though in minority, who really feel fit like a fiddle. They are always bubbling with enthusiasm. They keep themselves usefully occupied. In spite of many odds, they remain involved in contributing their best in the service of others without ulterior motives. . . .

. . .they continue on life's journey, whatever the ridicule and discouragement. They sing in unison with the poet and adopt his recipe for 'keeping old age blues at bay'.

"If you have left your dreams behind
If hope is cold, if you no longer look ahead.
If your ambition's fires are dead
Then you are old.
But, if from life you take the best
And in life you keep the just
If love you hold, no matter how the years go by,
No matter how the birthday fly,
You are not old."

Retirement

Shri S.S. Jaswal[13]

Every employee has to retire one day. But concerned person knows the date of his retirement and tells it to others. Out station persons come to know of it from the seniority list. Younger colleagues feel relieved when a person senior to them retires making a room for promotion to them.

A farewell function was arranged by the college staff on the eve of retirement. . . . Attendance was almost cent per cent. Principal, staff secretary, . . . spoke about the unblemished career of Prof Bhatia, who was really dedicated to his profession. . . .

During dinner, every one came to the main table and prayed for his long life. 'How do you feel after retirement?' one of the staff member asked Mr Bhatia, 'I feel like a free bird. Now I shall have enough time to study books other than my subject, . . .

Mr Bhatia did not open his heart to any one. In the hearts of his heart, he was sore that in spite of his fine health, he was being retired whereas he was able to work for some more years. He was critical of the government which allows the university teachers to work up to 60 years and denying this benefit to the college teachers.

. . .Mr Bhatia was too much worried about the marriage of one of his daughters. . . Then one of his sons had just joined the engineering college, . . . And with pension, it was difficult to meet day to day expenditure . . . .

It was 9 p.m. Prof Bhatia wanted to sleep but he could not because he was worried about the next day when he shall not be going to the college. . . . His daughter came to wake him up when it was past 8 a.m. Mr Bhatia said, 'let me sleep more, as I have retired from my service'.

Shri S.C. Dhall[14]

Unemployed youth generally hold retired employees who are given extension as the ones responsible for their plight. They fail to understand that a retired person has problems of his own.

It gets all the more tragic when well-meaning friends call on you and enquire about your retirement as though it was some kind of tragedy that befell you. They hardly realise that they are only reminding you that you are dud currency which has just gone out of circulation. I know of a person who died a few weeks after retirement because he could not bear the shock of sitting idle at home..

Not everyone looks forward to retirement with eagerness or pleasure. Only a few do so, and that too because they have planned it out. It is not that people are not aware that one day they will have to leave the job, yet when the time comes they experience a deep sense of hurt. Only a few manage to get another job before retiring. I know of a person's wife who, on hearing about her husband being given an extension, threw a party in celebration.

The withdrawal from office life will not be so hassh if the person has an earning son or daughter by the time the dreaded day arrives. He is lucky if he has an earning wife. The impact of retirement will be lessened.

At present, more than 15 million people in the country are over 60 years of age. If judges can be deemed fit enough to work up to the age of 65, there is hardly any reason for others in private or government service, to retire at the age of 58.

A person is fit till to work the last day of the 58th year and the next day he is cast out like a undesirable. His mental faculties become suspect overnight. Some people feel rather happy and eagerly wait for retirement so that they can enjoy the rest of their life peacefully.

The retirement age was fixed at a time when the life expectancy rate was very low. Now this is not so. Availability of medical facilities has raised the life expectancy rate sharply. No one will deny that retirement is necessary. It is corollary to life which must be accepted in a positive manner, rather than with fear and dread.

The government should evolve a pension scheme to cover all workers befitting the concept of welfare state, if only to make retirement a painless proposition.

Caring for the Elderly

Indian Express[15]

Most of the aged people in the country are a "neglected lot" and leading a "woeful" life, according to a survey.

In urban areas they have virtually been "isolated", while this process has also started in the rural areas, it says. . . .

"It was really a tough job to approach the elders for the survey. Indifferent children generally did not allow us to meet their aged parents, fearing that they may tell us about their miseries at the hands of their own children. We somehow contacted them through a group of students or under the garb of discussing matters like fund collection for religious congregations", says its senior vice-president, Mr N.L.G. Kumar.

In a majority of the cases covered by the survey, the elders suffer from basic needs including money, proper food and medical care, domiciliary services and recreation to enable them to spend "better days of the last phase of their lives for which they sacrificed their best days".

"They are regarded as a burden on the society", Mr Kumar regrets.

As the joint family system is breaking up and children are seeking employment at far-off places with the expansion of means of transport and more job opportunities, the survey says the condition of aged parents living alone is still more pathetic.

The miseries of the single aged persons, who have lost their spouse and are incapacitated due to chronic diseases, are much more aggravated, it says.

In many cases, it points out that the aged parents are forced to perform odd jobs despite their poor physique and are maltreated on one pretext or the other by their children.

The growing migration of population from rural areas to towns is also leaving behind the aged people completely neglected.

In Delhi alone, the survey discloses that the major problem is that of single old people, who account for nearly 10 per cent of the aged.

In certain cases, it says, the aged parents are living a miserable life. "They have been driven under stair-cases, in stores and backyards and do not even get a place to stretch or call their own".

Many a times, it says, they do not get proper food, which suits the digestive system of the old people.

For the "elite and rich aged people", it says, it is the problem of "good company".

This is a "gigantic task" and. . .

"We have not fully lost hope in our younger generation. We are trying to inculcate in them a feeling of respect for the elders", says Mr Kumar. . . .

Umesh M. Sharda[16]

. . .Whenever the issue of the welfare of the aged comes up, we first react by boasting of our joint family system in which the elderly enjoyed a priviledged position. In practice, we presume that the elderly need food, clothing and shelter only and our duties toward old people begins and ends in providing these bare essentials to them.

In talking about the joint family system of the old days we forget to compare the conditions of the past and those of the present. Earlier, few people reached a ripe old age and whosoever survived long enough was looked after, revered, tended and cared for. . . . The predominately agrarian economy also added to the security of the elderly. In the present circumstances, . . . a large number of people live beyond the age of 60 and the changed socio-economic conditions have exposed the older generation to various hardships. Problems faced in old age, . . . may yet differ in nature and degree as per the social status of the individual concerned. . . . According to Hindu tradition the third phase of life or *banprastha ashram* was a period when the individual should detach himself from worldly attachments. This attitude remains somewhere in a corner of peoples minds and affects their day-to-day behaviour. The concept of *banprastha* needs to be viewed at in its proper perspective; one aim for detachment but by degrees. It should not be a resignation but a gradual and mutual delegation of authority or responsibility for daily chores to the younger generation. . . .

The ever-increasing numbers of elderly people and the changing social trends necessitate a radical change in our outlook. The older generation should be considered as a class not as individuals only. . . . A futuristic outlook coupled with a proportionate balance between the resources consumed by the elderly as a class and the resources available with them in the shape of experience, expertise and time. . . .

. . .the welfare of the old is a matter of social and moral requirement as well as a national one, because if the old are neglected, uncared for and unhealthy it will add to social and subsequently national problems. To be old does not mean to forfeit one's fundamental rights. . . .while fixing priorities children and the youth will come first, but the old should not be relegated to the last ranks. They too are fully developed national resources ready to give dividends, by virtue of their experience, at the minimum cost, i.e. maintenance. The nation can ill-afford to leave such a big block of resources untapped and unutilised.

Therefore, what is needed now is the over-hauling of our thinking so that age-care is viewed in its right perspective. . . .which depends on the feeling of being wanted, useful and loved. The feeling that they are a part and parcel of the family and not a defunct part of it is a vital factor.

Baijnath Sharma[17]

Old age, disease, death, Karmas and change are the five inevitables which every one meets at different times. . . .

. . .everyone gets old, but nobody realises it. Therefore, the young do not realise that something must be done to help the aged.

The best person who can care for the old person is he himself. "Let me not, in the battlefield of life, look to my allies for help, but to my own inner self" says Rabindranath Tagore. Lord Krishna advises in the *Gita*: "Everyone is his own friend and his own enemy". "*Ayyam Main Hast Vishwa Bheshaj*" ("The medicines of the entire world are in my own hand," says the *Rig Veda*). "It is ourselves that we are thus and thus", says Shakespeare in "Othello".

So, if a person helps himself and observes moderation in diet, habits and thoughts, follows the laws of nature, avoids alcohol, smoking, narcotics, takes regular exercise and follows the simple principles of contentment, relaxation, living within means, he can enjoy a long happy life.

Despite best care that one can take of oneself, there comes a border line, beyond which one feels one's body weighted upon oneself, one is unable to do anything and stands in need of help. The sufferings of the aged at this stage are agonising in India, because of our peculiarly traditional family set-up. The aged have to depend upon their children. Sometimes there are none, and if they are, they usually regard their parents as scrap to be thrown away as early as possible. The son is lost in his wife who is generally a working girl. . . .

The year 1982 was declared as the Year of the Old and Aged. It has come and gone, but nothing tangible has been achieved. . . . The so-called philanthropists shed lacks of rupees to dodge income tax slabs and get accolades for buildings, temples, schools, colleges and ashrams. Public and private welfare organisations have not come forward to help the aged.

. . .the Red Cross. .. .set up Senior Citizens' Homes at a few places in Punjab. . . . Senior Citizens' Home . . . is available at Ludhiana at . . . subsidised rates.

Unless it is considered to wipe out this minority of about 1.5 crores through "mercy killing" for relieving the burden of over-population, it is imperative that the three-pronged drive — the state, public welfare organisations and multi-millionaires – be launched to help the aged, who have given their best in the heyday of their life.

. . . the Governor of Haryana, Mr S.M.H. Burney, . . . stated on July 10 that "his government feels strongly for the older citizens of the state." It had been decided to grant old age pension to those who had attained the age of 65 on or before June 17. . . .

. . .to know how the old are treated in other advanced countries:

Norway: . . .all Norwegian nationals are guaranteed an adequate old age pension, full sickness insurance, disablement benefit and other social welfare benefits.

Sweden: Old age pensions indexed to the cost of living have made Sweden's senior citizens comparatively well off. Municipal home helpers and special transportation services make it possible for elderly people to remain in their own homes, thus reducing their dependence on others.

Those who do not wish to live in their own homes can move to retirement houses where they are well looked after. Basic old age pension and employees pension. . .

Finland: The national pension guarantees a decent livelihood, while an additional employee pension. . .helps maintain the pensioners' standard of living. . . .

Holland (Netherlands): Old people have good accommodation and are well looked after either in old peoples' homes or in individual houses and flats with service. Index linked old age pensions at 65 play an important part in the care of the aged.

Denmark: The retiring pension is a flat rate payments to every one over the age of 67 and is equal to about 60 per cent of the average income.

Switzerland: The official retirement age for women is 62 and for men 65. The state pension scheme guarantees a basic income for old people, which contributes towards maintaining the social position they have reached over the years to follow.

Yugoslavia: Social security assures pensions pegged to income rises at 60 years for men and 55 year for women.

Indian Express[18]

The process of formulating a national policy for taking care of aged has begun, 'the Lok Sabha was informed on Wednesday. Replying to Mrs Prabhawati Gupta and others, the Welfare Minister, Mrs Rajendra Kumari Bajpai said the recently set-up inter-ministerial committee would undertake the task.

Indian Express[19]

Madras: An adoption scheme with a novel concept is being introduced in the city. Instead of children being adopted in this instance, it is the children who will do the adopting.

Twenty children from city schools will adopt an aged lady each, from the Vishranti Home in Pallavakam as their grandmother, on Sunday morning. They will visit the ladies once a month and are expected to provide the old women the emotional ties they lack.

The twenty ladies selected for the adoption scheme have no visitors and do not step outside the home, according to Vishranti trust chairperson, Mr Kalpana Ramaswamy.

Sarita Mohan[20]

According to history,. . .

The joint family system was strongly entrenched and almost all family members used to live together. . .and at times even five to seven generations living under one roof.

But now all those values are no more. The feeling of mutual tolerance and understanding is lacking. Those joint families have now split up into small nucleus families. . . .when children grow up they prefer to live separately from their parents. . . . They are rarely concerned about the welfare of their parents.

. . .Most children feel that they have discharged their duties by offering bread and butter or sending money to their parents. . . .

A question has arisen as to what kind of relationship should a son maintain with his retired parents so that mutual understanding may be sustained.

There is a generation gap between the parents and the children. . .

. . .Parents should not expect that they can mould their children according to their wishes.

On the other hand, children should also not have the feeling that their parents would join them in their new ideologies, leaving aside their old traditional values. We cannot turn the clock back. Some kind of middle path has to be adopted.

If the retired parents are financially sound and independent, . . .the magnitude of the problem is generally small. . . .because in many a case the main cause of rift is money. . . .

Some parents show their sacrifices and affection by giving all their property to their children and feel that after all their children are not so undutiful that they would not be looked after by them, even for their basic needs. This policy is wrong. . . . This leads to a lot of unhappiness and even broken families.

. . .the father. . .to make a will in favour of his wife. This would ensure to a great extent her financial independence and consequently respect from the children.

Similarly, . . .the wife should never pass on the property to the children during her lifetime. These steps would automatically help in keeping the relations cordial. . . .

Today, the general feeling is that daughters are more affectionate and responsible and there are instances where daughters and sons-in-law have taken up the responsibility of old parents or in-laws ungrudgingly.

In a nutshell, if old parents are staying with their children there has to be a cordial relationship amongst all. . . .

P.S. Walia[21]

The District Red Cross Society has decided to construct . . . a home for the aged. . . .will have accommodation for 15 inmates.

Initially the Red Cross had started a senior citizens' home in 1982 . . . known as "Youth Club". At present three aged persons, including a woman, are being given boarding and lodging facilities there at a nominal charge of Rs. 200 per month. . . .

Hindustan Times[22]

The Orient should learn from the experience of the western civilisation where there is "a move away from institutionalised care, to home and community care for the elderly", said Dr R. Pararajasegram, Regional Adviser, World Health Organisation.

Addressing a seminar on 'Management of Homes for Aged' organised by Helpage India, he said, "the Orient has prided itself on its ancient culture and traditions with its inbuilt reverence and concern for elders. However laudable these values are, there is a steady erosion of these values — partly due to social and economic pressures of development, partly through the influence of so-called 'western' civilisation".

"These effects of Western civilisation have already had an unhealthy impact on the care of the elderly in those countries, so much so, that there is already a move away from institutionalised care".

While institutionalised care is vital and imperative for a group of the elderly it is becoming obvious that if one is to add years to life then mere provision of creature comforts are inadequate — a sense of physical, social, and spiritual well-being has to be provided by caring individuals rather than those providing cure.

Today it has become increasingly apparent that mere adding life to years has little or no meaning unless the quality of life of the added years was also enhanced. The aim of "adding life to years" has thus become an imperative objective. In 1982 the theme of World Health Day was "Add Life to Years".

. . .One yardstick by which a civilisation is measured is the way in which it treats its fellow beings and. . .concerned about and caring for the elderly", he said.

Mr M.M. Sabharwal, President Helpage India, said. . . It is important for voluntary agencies like Helpage to create awareness regarding old people's problems and bringing it to the notice of the Government.

. . .favour of homes caring for the elderly than institutionalised care but if they were necessary than old age homes should create homely and family atmosphere.

Major General R.S. Pannu, Director, Helpage said. . .

It is not the amenities provided by an old age home but the number of activities it can generate of interest for the elderly and get them involved is what is important. The elderly need diversity and variety otherwise they will feel bored and indifferent, wherever the elderly are not involved in some hobby or other they are likely to create trouble.

Experiments were being done in western countries with semi-legal adoption of grand parent by children. In India also one could think in terms of a composite old age home in which ladies, children, aged could create a home like atmosphere.

In India there would continue to be a mix old age homes, some being the "pay and stay" kind and the others dependent completely on donations and government aid. . . .

Col. Gurdial Singh[23]

It is a pity that senior citizens in our country are completely a neglected lot, both by society and the government. It is high time that we learn how to take care of the aged. We must take a lesson from leading democracies in the old world like USA, Canada, U.K. and other European countries where elders are treated in a humane, respectful manner, apart from giving them various financial concessions.

In addition to the increase in old age pension, pensioners, both of the Centre and states, should get at least 75 per cent of their last pay drawn as pension (I.T. free). The increase in upper age service limit up to 60 is a must. It is equally important for the Armed Forces personnel, who retire at a much younger age than their civilian counterparts. If they have to be retired earlier to keep the forces younger, let them be paid full emoluments till the age of 60, as done for civilians.

The provision of houses at cheaper rates (if not free) on retirement to those not already in possession of will be a great help. Free travel in buses and concessional travel by rail/air, nominal charges for electricity by the Electricity Boards and no house rent/water charges by the municipal committee/corporations can be a great relief. Needless to say, free medical aid is another important requirement of theirs!

. . .I hope the recently started Senior Citizens' Home at Jalandhar functions well and does not turn out to be a 'nam ke waste' only! Every district should have such a home soon, to be followed by others at sub-divisions/tahsils and blocks.

Above all, government departments and the public should be made to realise they are duty bound towards senior citizens. They can ill-afford to stand in queues for long and should be given preference over youngsters in being attended to. They should be registered and issued with an identity card by a department set up for this purpose by the government, as is a practice in the western countries. Until such time that any proper and regular national policy is framed in the country, the government must think over these suggestions and make a start. Cutting down on wasteful expenditure in various government departments can probably meet the above requirements of senior citizens.

Indian Express[24]

The Minister of State for Health and Family Welfare, Mr Vijayendra Singh, announced a package of facilities for the aged.

Inaugurating a day's free health check-up and diabetic self-care training camp for the elders here . . . assured medical aid on top priority for the aged at all the district hospitals.

The elders will also be provided free travel facility in the mini-buses operating in the capital town for taking them to the hospitals. The minister assured the elders that all the zonal hospitals would be issued necessary instructions to knit primary health care system with geriatric clinics and also to impart proper health education for handling the aged patients.

. . .*Elders Care.* Sqn Ldr A.K. Das (retd.), Himachal Pradesh should initiate more steps for the welfare of the aged since the state had a higher percentage of persons above the age of 60.

Kanta Sharma[25]

. . .modern society seems concerned only with the welfare of the daughter-in-law and not of the mother-in-law. That is why there is an outcry when a bride is harassed by her mother-in-law. But when a mother-in-law or a father-in-law is, harassed by the "babu" and her beau, nothing happens.

. . .The old couple, deprived of their wealth and health, are condemned to a life of utter neglect in their old age. Insulted and taunted, they are denied even given proper food and medical care. In many cases, the mothers-in-law are reduced to the position of ayahs, nursing their grand-children and getting scolded for anything going amiss, even if the fault is not theirs. Still the children's parents are made out as a model son and daughter-in-law — obedient, indulging and caring.

But reality is different. The old ones are worse off than the servants, who at least get paid for their hard work and, can leave the job if they so desire. The old mother-in-law and father-in-law cannot break off a relationship in the evening of their life. They do not wish to leave behind memories of parents who brought their children down in the eyes of society — a negation of their life's mission to give their children social esteem at great personal sacrifice.

. . . how many women have been moved by the plight of an old and helpless mother-in-law at the hands of her daughter-in-law, by the "bahu's" neglect of her duty to her husband's old parents? How, many women have tried to make the "bahu" and her husband realise their mistake and correct their behaviour?. . .

Let every daughter-in-law remember that tomorrow she will be a mother-in-law. Let her the standards of behaviour she expects from the mother-in-law and be a model mother-in-law herself when her turn comes.

Sangeet Saini[26]

By the time we enter the 21st century there will be more people above sixty than under sixteen. Call it a jugglery between advanced medical science and family planning — but our senior citizens are an important part of our future society.

With the disintegration of the joint family more and more old people are dismayed when in the twilight years of their life there is no one to take care of them. Building 'Old People's Home' is no solution.

It is the duty of there children to see that they lead a comfortable life. What they require is not just a roof and four walls, but the love and warmth of a family. A feeling of belonging. They should be made to feel wanted in the house and given due respect. Our rudeness and unconcern is noticed by the children and so it really depends on us to set the proper attitude towards the elder people in the house.

After an active life when parents move in with one of their children, it requires a lot of adjustment. Do not think you are the only to do so. The parents too are adjusting to their new life style.

A little patience, love and understanding goes a long way. Put yourself in their place and think how you would like to be treated. Treat them the same way.

. . .try and spend some time with the elderly persons in the house. Listen to them. Talk to them. . . .

During family functions and gatherings making sure that they are not neglected. Leaving them alone or ignoring them can bring on a feeling of loneliness and dejection. . . .

Do not take old parents for granted. Somehow we all have set notions regarding a person past his prime, his needs and requirements. . . .

In case the lady of the house is working, let her not presume that her mother-in-law will look after her children and the house. Child rearing requires a lot of energy and they've done their share. Let them just help instead of shouldering the entire responsibility.

. . .Do not add to their problems. A happy family and social environment will not only add life to their years but years to their life.

Mamata Guha[27]

It is indeed encouraging to find that Helpage India is giving consideration to the various problems of old age (*HT*, Oct. 5).

It is a fact that the vanishing joint family system,, lack of accommodation. . .are adding to the problems of the old. ... .and more brain drain from India. As a result, the unfortunate parents are left to nobody's care, even if they have some money to support themselves. And the greatest tragedy is that the interest of organisations, both Government and non-Government, is centred around the poor and destitutes only, leaving out others who are equally helpless. . . .

In old age one needs some care and looking after. But our society is completely apathetic towards them! Nobody even bothers to think about them.

I fully agree that there is a dire necessity for "old age homes". But at the same time some "senior citizens' hostels" are equally necessary. We often hear "poverty is a curse". But I ask, "Is it a curse to have a little money? Do we not deserve a human approach to our problems?" I request old-age organisations to think of us. Unlike in western countries, the senior citizens have to live in a "no man's land" home. Following western life-style, joint families are getting obsolete. But there are no alternative institutions like senior citizens' apartments as they have in western countries.

I believe there are quite a number of senior citizens like me, facing the same problem. Since we are all in the same boat, I request them to join hands with me.

Quest for Longevity

Dr S.K. Dutt[28]

Aging is an inevitable process. Anyone born, has to age. Whether to regard aging an indication of pathology or to regard aging as a process in man, whether or not accompanied by disease, it is a *prima facie* assumption. Trends in molecular biology suggest the possibility that aging may be a phenomenon common to all living material, raises hope, that discoveries at the molecular level in any living matter may have a direct bearing on the processes in man.

The term aging signifies the progression of changes in biochemical processes which determine structural and functional alterations with age in the cells and non-cellular tissues, and hence in the whole organism.

Span of Life: As the horizons of medical sciences expand, the span of life increases, consequently the number of the aged persons increase. . . . Application of the accumulated knowledge on nutrition will help to age gracefully and remain meaningfully active when we age.

. . .Search was on for food which will delay the process of aging and preserve youth. Good nutrition continues to play its most significant role during youth and middle age in the prevention of those diseases which ultimately manifest themselves as serious disabilities among the aged. . . .

If aging as a process is examined from the nutritional point of view it will open up many facts, which can if incorporated lead to a better living. . . .

What causes aging? We are far from answering this question. Research in molecular biology might offer an answer in the recent future. The factors which cause the aging process (as is known to day) are mainly: (1) Environmental, (2) Genetic, (3) Mutation, (4) Free radical theory.

Nutrition is an environmental factor and can be controlled. Aging may be induced genetically. . . .

Others believe that aging is caused by cellular mutation resulting from external causes, such as ionising radiation, heat, chemical or perhaps viruses, such as RNA virus.

. . .A free radical is very reactive. . .damages any or every part of the cell or cell glomerulates. . . A direct inference of this theory is that, some antioxidants as vitamin 'E', ascorbic acid (Vitamin 'C') or perhaps selenium or food additive BHT, may be able to protect the polyunsaturated lipids, thus delaying the process of aging of the cell. Estimated daily Vitamin 'E' requirement is between 10 mg — 30mg. Fats of vegetable origin are rich sources of Vitamin 'E', except coconut oil, which is a poor source. Many dark green leafy vegetables are good sources. Vitamin 'C' requirements are around 50 mg daily. Fresh fruits like *amla*, guava and vegetables like cabbage, beet root, cauliflower are rich source of Vitamin 'C'.

Immune Reaction: Changes in the immune system may. . .cause the body to attack itself. The changes might be slowed by manipulating the immune system by diet, heat or other methods.

. . .Diet may affect the synthesis of neurotransmitters (such as serotonin, norepinephrine, dopamine etc.) which may affect the mechanism that regulate the aging process.

Aging is a continuous process throughout the life span. . . .

People tend to differ more as they grow older. . . . Older people therefore differ from each other more than do younger folk. This has to be given due weightage in food planning for any older person.

Functional Ability: Chronological age is a poor predictor of functional ability. Some 80 year old function as well as the 40 year old, and some 40 year old perform like the average 80 year old. Unfortunately the elderly are often the target of ageism — stereo types and discriminated because they are old. . . .

. . .changes occur practically in every part of the body. The bones decrease in density. . . . fatty tissue and connective tissue generally increase. The heart may pump blood less efficiently . . . and kidneys are less efficient in removing waste products from the blood. . . . The lenses of the eyes lose the ability to focus at near distance.

. . . Hearing loss is common specially for high tones. Smell and taste may become less acute.

Loss of teeth may make chewing difficult. So consistency of food is important. Digestion may become impaired due to decrease in gastric juice and bile secretion. . . .may result in constipation . . .

In spite of large number of changes that occur during aging, most activities in normal resting people are affected only to a modest degree by aging. Loss of function becomes more apparent during stress. . . .

Many studies of aging people have not excluded diseased persons, so there has been some confusions between changes related to age and disease. . . . Interestingly some changes related to age mimic disease states. Glucose tolerance is frequently impaired. Failure to give due consideration can result in overdiagnosis of diabetes mellitus, causing concern and unnecessary limiting the person's dietary choices.

Nutrition Factor: Nutritional factors play specific causative role in diseases, it is unlikely that dietary modifications late in life are able to halt or reverse these diseases, they may however, stabilise them. Instead nutrition is likely to play its most significant role during youth and middle age. Although these diseases are regarded as geriatric problems, their prevention may well be a pediatric concern.

As long as knowledge of aging as a process is limited as it still is today few clues exist to methods of altering the process by nutritional means. It may be safely concluded that for man the aging process cannot be substantially affected by nutritional measures. As research in molecular biology unlocks the secret of aging some more definitive role for nutrition in retarding the process may emerge. . . .

Parkash Chand Gupta[29]

Dr S.K. Dutt in his article 'Aging and Nutrition' (*HT*, Sept. 27) analyses the various factors which cause the aging process. In addition. . .there is one more which by nature is inherent in the biological system of all human and which furnishes a better scientific, logical and convincing explanation about the phenomenon of 'longevity', 'again' and 'life and death'.

Even the most advanced medical experts have accepted that as soon as a child is born, he brings with him in his body two types of germs—one of survival and the other of death. In the first instance, the germs of survival become active and they start developing in the body, while those of death remain dormant around the field of venus on our palm. The palmists call this area 'Life Line' when the germs of survival are active, we want to live life and dread death. But the natural phenomena is that after. . .65 years, the germs of survival start extinguishing gradually and come to die completely. Now the germs of death, which hitherto were lying dormant, start acting and after this, life is no more charming and death is welcome. . . .

Dr S.K. Dutt's article *inter alia* suggests an idea that it would be possible for humans to live up to a longer period by resorting to special nutritious diets, anti-aging drugs or through research in the fields of genetics, mutation, radiation, etc. But the question is whether it would be desirable to have a longer life than prescribed by nature, even presuming that all senses of right, hearing, smelling and feeling remain unimpaired? There is a natural phenomena about longevity and to extend the span of life will be an unnatural act. I am of the view that for having a full, rich and purposeful life, . . .normal diet, exercise, etc., to keep fit, let us not aspire for more than what the nature has prescribed for us.

Pravin Kumar[30]

Few things are more deflating to a person's ego than superannuation. On the day an employee crosses the age of 58 or 60, he or she is placed on the shelf.

The sharp divide between the years of utility and the years of desuetude in a person's life is artificial, for the facts of biology show a contrary picture. Different organs age at different rates. Brain cells, for example, age far more slowly than muscle cells. Brain cells are so numerous that even though some of them die every day in a mature individual, there are enough left for various kinds of activity.

"It's unfair to retire a brain worker at 58 or 60", . . .because at that age he is as active as he was at 50. If judges can give judgements at 65 years and prime ministers can functions at 75 and they take more important decision than others — we should consider increasing the retirement age for other people". . . .

The importance of studies on ageing has been recognised by the government's inclusion of the subjects as one of the "thrust areas" in biological research in the country. Biologists are now trying to frame answers to questions such as: What are the factors that make for senescence? Can adulthood be prolonged and old age put off?

Biologically and philosophically, aging is a desirable process. For, unless the old are replaced by the young, there cannot be progress. Yet for the individual, senescence poses problems such as loss of livelihood and most people would like to put if off. Aging in human beings begins shortly after maturity, that is, after the age of 25 or so. Occasionally, people live to be a 100 years old, but in certain pockets of the world, people generally live to be 110 or 120. . . .

Exercise, diet and freedom from tension can slow down the aging process. For example, muscle aging can be postponed by exercise. Brain-aging, too, can be postponed by mental activity. . . .

Can the life-span be prolonged? Experiments with fishes showed that lowering the ambient temperature prolonged the life-span. In rats, lowering the calorie intake increases the life-span by 40 per cent, but growth is retarded slightly. No such experiments have been done with humans. For one thing, humans are a relatively long-lived species. To understand the ageing process, one has to understand what happens at the level of the individual cell.

In 1959, Leo Szilard proposed that mutations in an organism's genes. . .wrong proteins go on accumulating. However, experiments in which rats. . .did not bear this theory out.

Then, in 1963, Lesley Orgel proposed the "error theory" of aging. . . .More and more defective proteins are presumably produced; eventually. . .the cell will die. But no one has shown that, in old age, wrong proteins are produced in the body.

In fact, Kanungo and his associates purified proteins from young as well as old animals and found that they were identical. However, the level or concentration of a protein does change during life, due to changes in the expression (function) of the genes coding for it. Dr Kanungo put forward his own "sequential model",. . .

To find out if indeed the expression of genes deteriorates during life, Dr Kanungo's team is now using genetic engineering and molecular biology techniques to elucidate the mechanism of expression of certain genes in rats. Hopefully, this will help unravel the basic mechanism of aging.

. . .In other words, Indians are on the whole living longer. Yet the Fourth Pay Commission has declined to recommend raising the retirement age from the present 58. Evidently, there is a political angle to this, for the Indian population above 60 is still small compared to the population below that age, which is the population that will sway the poll arithmetic.

"This is being shortsighted," comments Kanungo,"The retirement age should be raised constantly — it should be related to the average life-span. In the US, they increased the retirement age as the average life-span increased. It is now 65, and in the universities it is 70."

The increased expectancy of life is not all to the good. In conjunction with the smaller family size — due to successful family planning — by A.D. 2000 eight per cent of the Indian population will be over 60 years of age; and eight per cent of a billion is a large number. . . . Therefore, along with family planning, we should pay attention to the gerontological aspects.

B.K. Rakesh[31]

Since time immemorial the man has been engaged in the war against aging. Success has eluded him so far though claims of success have been made now and then.

The men of medicine, however, continued their quest and in the process found out effective cures for the age-old scourges such as bubonic plague, smallpox, bacterial pneumonia and even the chronic diseases from heart disease to certain kinds of cancer. As a result, the man has added a few years to his average life span. Scientists believe that another 30 years can be added to the average life span in near future.

About fifty years ago, Clive McCay successfully doubled the life span of rats by reducing their diet just after the time of waning to 60 per cent of their usual intake. The diet-restricted animals were found healthier and more mentally alert than others and they aged slowly or fell ill rarely. In human terms, the oldest among them lived for 150 years.

Researchers believe that while it was possible to extend life in the laboratory, the age seem programmed into the genes. Every organism seems to have a built-in lifespan and aging rate. Even our cells have an internal "clock" that stops ticking at a predetermined time. . . .

But this does not explain where the controlling mechanism lie. Some researchers believe there is no central mechanism. But there has to be some sort of genetic programme. . . .

Other researchers fall into two camps in their ways of looking at aging. There are some who say that aging takes place inside the cell, while others believe that the primary role is played by factors outside the cell, such as hormones which in turn bring about age changes in the cell.

The former point the finger at damage to the DNA as a major culprit in aging. . . . The DNA damage may interfere with the proper function of cells and ultimately be responsible for aging and many age-related diseases. This theory is actually a modern restatement of a very old idea, that aging stems from wear and tear on the body. The appeal of the damage theory lies in the fact that the DNA is highly vulnerable to the very factors needed to sustain life, including ultraviolet light, oxygen metabolism, substances in common foods and chemicals, both manufactured and natural. . . .

. . .Although DNA has the ability of repair itself, this repair is never complete and is also subject to the aging process. In fact, DNA repair may be a regulator of lifespan. . . .

In a key experiment in aging research a US scientist Joan Smith-Sonneborn was able to extend the life-span of one-celled paramecia by 50 per cent by raising the level of their DNA repair. This research holds out the promise of not only extending life but greatly improving the quality of life.

Some scientist, however, believe that the control mechanism lies outside the cell, most probably in the hormones and neurotransmitters. They have evidence for a "brain clock" located in the hypothalamus which controls vital functions as body temperature, appetite, thirst, sleep and wakefulness, blood-sugar levels and emotions. It has been found out that the neurotransmitters in the hypothalamus decline with age. This loss of necessary brain substances can lead to an "endocrine cascade" with adverse effects on the body.

The most dramatic evidence for a hormonal theory of aging is contained in the work of Donner Denckla. . . . By removing the pituitary, not only the 'good' hormones but one that is deadly is removed.

This hormone is called DECO (Decreasing Consumption of Oxygen). . . .

Are there any recipes for longevity? Starting right now, we could add another quarter century or more to our lifespans by applying the animal findings on diet restriction to human terms. This means that an individuals who is 1.7 meters tall and weighs 67 kg should lose nine to 13.5 kg over five to seven years. By the end of this period he should have gone from about 2,500 to 3,000 calories a day to a maintenance diet of about 1,600 following this regimen could make vigorous centenarians of all of us, and extend the upper limit of lifespan to about 120 years.

Not all gerontologists agree with the theory that lean is good and leanest is best of all. They have found just the opposite. After reviewing all the studies worldwide that looked at body weight and age at death, they found that the people who lived longest were those who were on the heavy side, about 20 per cent over what is generally considered the ideal weight.

Change the balance on your dinner plate in favour of vegetables and against meat. Specifically, one should reduce all fats to about 20 to 30 per cent of the diet, rather than the 40 per cent that makes up the average American diet. At the same time, add more complex carbohydrates so that it makes up about 45 to 55 per cent of your diet. This includes green and yellow vegetables, potatoes, rice, whole grain breads and cereals, and pasta. Gram for gram these foods deliver the most in terms of vitamins and fibre and the least in terms of fat.

While there is no general agreements as to dosage or even which nutrients should be taken in addition to the diet, most gerontologists are keeping their eye on the antioxidants. These are the substances like Vitamin E and Selenium, which protect against free radical formation. When antioxidants were added to the diet of laboratory mice, their lifespan rose up by 30 per cent. This increase is equivalent to raising the human life span from 73 to 95 years. One of the most promising anti-oxidants is beta carotena, a precursor of Vitamin A, that gives carrots and cantaloupe their orange colour. It is a powerful antioxidant, has anti cancer activity, is nontoxic, and in a study by Richard Cutler of the Gerontology Research Centre, was found to correlate with lifespan.

The major lesson to be learned from modern aging studies is that the body rusts out from inactivity rather than wears out from use. A good exercise programmes keeps the joints oiled, the muscles toned, the blood vessels dilated, and the heart pumping at maximum efficiency. It can even halt the body's downward progression for some time. At San Diego State University in U.S. a group of men who exercised regularly for a decade were as fit at 40 years of age as they were at 30.

While all sorts of aging panaceas are constantly being touted and promising compounds are now being tested in the laboratory, it is well to keep things in perspective. Just a few minor changes in your life style can add years of healthy life. (1) Don't smoke; (2) Be neither underweight nor more than 20 per cent overweight; (3) Drink alcohol moderately — no more than two or three drinks a day; (4) Exercise moderately about three times a week; (5) Don't skip breakfast; (6) Maintain regular meal schedule and (7) Get seven to eight hours of sleep a night.

Hindustan Times[32]

Experiments on animals here suggest, that man can live up to 300 years with a simple brain operation, Soviet news agency Tass has reported.

Mice with an average life span of two years lived for three years after tiny pieces of hypothalamus of new born mice or of embroys were planted in the brain,. . .

. . .Dr Ata-Murabdova told Tass that the operation not only rejuvenated the brain but also stimulated the activity of most organs in the animals. The operated animals lived longer than the others, and some of them continued breeding, she said.

R. Narayan[33]

Most people want to stay young and growing old is anathema. And who will not like to put off old age?

Now a new discovery by medical research seeks to eliminate hereditory predisposition to various diseases including tumours, which can help prevent chronic diseases later in life.

In the economically developed countries, life expectancy has almost doubled in the last 100 years. . . .

However, it has been possible to extend life expectancy not by lowering the old-age death rate. We are aging at the same rate people did a 100 years ago. But science has today made it plausible to solve the problem of extending man's active life by retarding the process of aging.

An interesting development is the new approach, scientists have worked out called the reliability approach it has long and effectively been used in technology. . . . Using the principles and the mathematical apparatus of the theory or reliability, scientists of Moscow University were able to explain the main quantitative laws regulating the dependence of death probability on human age.

In technical devices, the repair of a broken part can prolong the service life of the entire machine. But it is impossible to copy this experience and transfer it to the human body because in our "machine"—in the human organism – all its components (organs) are much closely linked with each other. And, if say, one component gets out of order, the others try to make up for its faulty work and take over its functions.

The appearance of diseases depends largely on the organism's resistance to unfavourable factors. If the predisposition is passed on to the next generation, then, as it was formerly believed, . . .and then nothing can be changed. But it turns out that the genetic programme can be "adjusted", thereby increasing the reliability of the most unreliable organ especially with respect to the processes that might have led to its failure.

In other words, it is necessary to prevent chronic diseases occurring later on in life, say, when they are still in a latent state and do not make themselves felt as yet. It is necessary to raise the resistance of the organs and tissues which are most vulnerable in a given person ever since his early childhood. Soviet biologists succeeded in mapping out an effective way of preventing chronic diseases.

According to them,. . . People inherit not the probability of developing tumours, in general, but of tumours of some definite organ.

Geneticists. . . Studying the force of tissue linkage in many mice "breeds" (strains), Soviet biologists have discovered that tumours appear only in rodents in which cell linkage in a given organ is below the value typical of that organ.

. . .Further, research made it possible to boost the tissue resistance to the development of tumours.

Natural substances were obtained from the tissues of organs of healthy animals that were capable of restoring the force of cell linkage. These substances were obtained in pure form . . . . They were called contaktins.

It is found that it was enough to administer one-billionth of a milligram of contaktin to an animal to increase cell linkage in a given organ. . . .

The question next comes up is to know its effect on organism. . . .can contaktin change the "trajectory" of the development of an organ?

A series of experiments, followed. By administering contaktin at a critical period of development researchers were able to increase cell linkage in weakened organs for a rather lengthy time, and in most animals, even for the rest of their lives, and the result was that tumour incidence was reduced by 60 or 67 per cent. This also helped to decrease the possibility of chronic pathology appearing in genetically predisposed animals.

Soviet biologists are optimistic that their discovery can be of use for the development of medicine to free people from an inherited predisposition to diseases or, considerably reduce it, thereby helping to increase life expectancy.

Indian Express[34]

A person's age is thought of as a traumatic period of life. How do you look at the problem?

Aging is no trauma. In fact it's a healthy transformation of roles from that of a son to father and on to that of grandfather. The trauma 'aspect' stems from the western concept of death as a finality. The oriental philosophy looks at death as an end of one chapter and not as the end of the book.

We all have to grow old some day and therefore we cannot turn a blind eye to the need to create a society that treats the aged in a humane manner. The old have to be looked after well. Rapidly growing populations have been of great concern to India and all other developing countries. . . .

. . .At present there are an estimated 47.5 million elderly persons in India which is about 6.3 per cent of the total population. Punjab tops among the States with 7.8 per cent old people. By A.D. 2000, there would be about 75.6 million elderly persons in India. . . .

Is it possible to slowdown aging?

In near future it may be possible to do so. Scientists. . .have found a new drug called aminoguanidine which may retard aging. . . .

Trials of the drug on human beings are still on. If successful, the drug may not actually prolong life but it will certainly improve its quality by slowing artherosclerosis, senile cataracts, kidney failure, thinning of bones, and by preventing wrinkles, thinning and breaking of skin.

Scientists suspect that processes long known to discolour and toughen foods also contribute to cell deterioration and stiffening of tissues. Research on diabetes suggests that glucose, the abundant body sugar, is a potential aging agent. . . . Unusually high amounts of glucose in the body could contribute to diabetic complications, described as 'accelerated aging'.

According to one theory undernutrition could also prolong life. . . . Both these methods were successful lengthening lives not only of young animals but also of adult animals.

It is believed that many of the immune system deficiencies that accompany aging can be avoided by undernutrition. Experiments are on to check whether the undernutrition theory – which proved so successful on animals – would also hold good for human beings or not.

During a human life time of 70 years, the cell's indomitable enzymes, which are proteins themselves may perform nearly 120 billion repair jobs. That is how the DNA (desoxyribonuacic acid) which governs cell functions is so well maintained. But the wear and tear continue, and that too at a faster rate as time wears on. As a human grows older, the undertaking of repair jobs by the body are less prompt; this leads to old age complications. If scientists were able to resolve this problem and to guard cells against attacks, they would be able to prolong life.

What are the social implications of aging?

They are both physical and economic. But what is actually overlooked is the tremendous psychological impact that the aging has on human beings. Old persons are generally lonely people; they long for company, a kind word, a cheerful smile. Letting them feel that they are welcome and wanted works better than any tonic.

The United Nation also views with concern the issues relating to the early retirement of individuals who have no productive roles for remainder of their lives and its effects on the economy, it is a disguised unemployment.

. . .In western countries, . . .a well defined social security scheme for the elderly. In India, there is no such scheme. . . .

Our Government should either increase the fixed retiring age or else let the workers choose their year of retiring according to their working capacities, a flexible retirement policy. Pension schemes should be made compulsory. . .

. . .increasing the provident fund amount even if that means more cuts from the employees' present salary. In India we cannot expect a larger contribution. . .the employer could pay a little more than the 50 per cent contribution towards the provident fund.

Another way out could be some gainful employment for the aged once they retire. . . .

There is a considerable increase in the number of women over 50 all over the world. . . .and by 1990 the number of women over 50 would rise to more than 500 million. In the developing countries where jobs are scarce, one can imagine the trauma of this growing segment of unemployed section of our society.

How do you view the performance of the day care centres?

The idea has caught on in the West but here it is yet to be accepted. There are 40 such day care centres in Maharashtra.

Let's look at the experiences of other countries. In Australia there are very systematic day care centre organisations in all the major cities. . .

The 'Home-makers' programme. . .young volunteers go to lonely elderly couples to spend time with them, sit, chat, eat with them and give them a feeling of being part of a family. They have another scheme known as 'meals on wheels'. . . .for those aged who live alone and can not cook. . . .

China has instituted old age pensions. . . . In Hong Kong, the assistance comes in the form of cash, health services, housing, community support services, residential care, leisure provisions, employment, and transport concessions. Thailand also has residential homes for aged, hostels, private houses. . . .

Indonesia, Korea and Nepal also have similar schemes for the aged. In the 8th Five Year Plan in India there is more focus on establishing day care centres, old age homes and social security to organised homes. . . .

Has the International Federation on Aging (IFA) done enough for the aged?

Why not? the IFA was set up in the last decade and. . .

One of our main objective is to draw the government's attention to the plight of the aged so that it hikes expenditure on social security schemes. . . .

Traditional obligations of structures like joint families system has been breaking. As a result the aged are finding themselves more and more alienated from family life. It is also our endeavour to strengthen the family structure, by helping to create a health psycho-social relationships.

Our federation also has an elderly adoption programme. In Bombay we run it. . . It's known as the 'Grandparent Adoption Scheme' and was launched in 1987. . .

The programme seeks to fill a void in the lives of the aged destitutes at the Dharamshala. Aged persons have been adopted by school children. These students visit their grandparents regularly to provide company to them. . . .

It's a pleasant sight to see the glow in the eyes of the aged when their 'grandchildren' visit. "We just want to see you" is a common refrain among the aged towards their young 'relatives'. That very well sums up the feeling of longing and sensitivity towards love and affection and simplicity among the aged.

Home for the Aged

Chanchal Behn[35]

The joint family system is gradually breaking up. This has put the elderly people in a difficult situation. At the fag end of their life, they need the care, affection and respect which, unfortunately, is wanting in the present social set up. What an elderly person needs is not luxury but a feeling that the society, particularly his near and dear ones, have not ignored him. The younger generation has neither the time nor willingness to discharge their obligation towards the old. Aged parents having no source of income are considered as a burden which makes them miserable. In such a situation, the only solution lies in setting up 'homes for the aged' where elderly people could lead a life of contentment with an opportunity to keep themselves engaged in their respective hobbies.

In order to give them a feeling of importance (an inherent desire among all), the long experience of these senior citizens in diverse fields could be recorded and published for the benefit of the younger generation. Their mature views could be of immense utility to bring about moral upliftment, national integration, tolerance and religious harmony. Their services could also be utilised to preach moral values, peace and brotherhood. Such homes should preferably be in rural surroundings, away from noise and pollution. Overcrowding should be avoided.

We, in the Moral Education Foundation, have a scheme to set up such homes and we solicit the attention of your readers who would be interested to help us in this venture.

Archna Sachdev[36]

Shanno Chopra, about 75, moved into the Arya Mahila Ashram more than 20 years ago on the death of her husband. She has no children and a grandnephew visits her once in a while. Basking in the winter sunshine outside her *kutiya*, she says the ashram is her home and she wouldn't change it for any other place in the world.

I.P. Verma (not his real name), a retired government official, shifted to Ozanam Home after trying various other options. Disillusioned about a society which "just does not bother" and a government that is "callous", the 74-year-old bachelor recounts how fears of the "rampant crime" in Delhi combined with practical and financial difficulties of running a household single-handed prompted him to move into an old age home.

Shanti Sodhi, 62, and Bimla Devi, 70 (not their real names) both have sons—that rain cheque to security in Indian society that is supposed to ease one's passage on earth and hereafter—but find themselves at the Arya Mahila Ashram. The latter because her sons can't afford to keep her and the former because of problems with her daughter-in law.

Shanta Gupta, a former teacher from Ferozabad, has several relatives in Delhi and back home in Ferozabad. But on her retirement, she preferred to stay independently at the Arya Mahila Ashram rather than "impose upon" any of her relations. It works out the best that way, she confides.

Then there is 70-year old Sukh Ram, who worked as a waiter in a government-owned five-star hotel for 20 years. But being a casual employee, he did not get any superannuation benefits. With his sight lost in a botched up cataract operation, he is spending the last of his helpless days in the Delhi Administration-run home for the aged and infirm. . . .

But Delhi is hardly equipped to meet the demand for old age homes, specially the demands of middle class families, which form the bulk of applicants. Ajay Sunder, communications officer with Helpage India, says he gets at least 50 queries a month from well off families asking about accommodation in old age homes. A welfare officer at Delhi Administration's Home in Narela puts the number at between 100 and 200. They ask for independent rooms and the stress is on "spacious surroundings, wholesome meals, comfortable living, peace of mind and a sense of security". One of the elderly gentlemen says he wouldn't mind paying between Rs. 2,000 to Rs. 3,000 for such accommodation. But there are no "pay and stay" homes in Delhi, at least not on a sizeable scale. There are small, private ones, but these don't accommodate more than five or six people. . . .

The bigger homes in Delhi presently accommodate under 250 people. Of these, the Arya Mahila Ashram, being run by the Arya Samaj at New Rajinder Nagar offers an interesting and successful variation to the old age homes in the city. Open to only women over 60 years, it provides a separate unit consisting of a room, a kitchenette and a bathroom to each inmate. Those who can afford it, get new units built for themselves in the complex. Those who cannot, shift into the vacant '*kutiyas*'. There are about 90 such '*kutiyas*' in the *ashram* at present. . . .

There are three homes being run by Christian missionary organisations. Of these, St. Mary's at Rajpur Road and another being run by the Delhi Christian Friend in Need Society at Fatehpur Beri can accommodate just 20 people each. Ozanam Home, at Kingsway Camp, can take upto 50 people. All of them are free of charge for those without a regular source of livelihood and take a part of the pension from those who get it. While St. Mary's is for women only and has separate rooms for them, Ozanam and Fatehpur Beri take in both men and women and put them up in separate dormitories.

At Ozanam Home, says Sister Edith, who has been in charge of the place for the past six years, preference is given to those who don't have anyone to look after them or have no income. The residents, a fairly good mix of Hindus and Christians, like going to a nearby church or temple in the mornings and evenings. Otherwise, they help in the kitchen, do gardening, watch TV, read or go for walks to the market. . . .

. . .the Home being run by Delhi Administration succinctly draws attention to the shortcomings of institutionalised care. Though a roof over the head, a meal and a sense of physical security go a long way in making old age comfortable, also important are a sense of dignity and a feeling of being needed. . . .

For those who don't have anybody to look after them, homes are the only solution. . .

NOTES

1. *Hindustan Times*, November 15, 1986.
2. *Indian Express*, November 17, 1988.
3. *Hindustan Times*, January 29, 1987.
4. *Indian Express* (Chandigarh), October 17, 1987.
5. *Indian Express* (Chandigarh), November 21, 1987.
6. *Indian Express*, April 10, 1988.
7. *Indian Express* (Chandigarh), April 24, 1988.
8. *Indian Express* (Chandigarh), April 24, 1988.
9. *Indian Express*, May 1, 1988.
10. *Indian Express* (Chandigarh), May 27, 1989.
11. *Indian Express* (Chandigarh), December 9, 1989.
12. *Indian Express* (Chandigarh), March 24, 1990.
13. *Indian Express* (Chandigarh), August 12, 1989.
14. *Indian Express* (Chandigarh), November 11, 1989.
15. *Indian Express* (Chandigarh), October 24, 1987.
16. *The Tribune* (Chandigarh), November 15, 1987.
17. *Indian Express* (Chandigarh), December 5, 1987.
18. *Indian Express*, December 10, 1987.
19. *Indian Express*, February 14, 1988.
20. *Indian Express*, May 21, 1988.
21. *Indian Express* (Chandigarh), June 17, 1988.

22. *Hindustan Times*, August 10, 1988.
23. *Indian Express* (Chandigarh), June 24, 1989.
24. *Indian Express* (Chandigarh), September 25, 1989.
25. *Indian Express* (Chandigarh), February 17, 1990.
26. *Indian Express* (Chandigarh), March 17, 1990.
27. *Hindustan Times*, November 3, 1990.
28. *Hindustan Times*, September 27, 1986.
29. *Hindustan Times*, October 17, 1986.
30. *Indian Express*, October 19, 1986.
31. *Hindustan Times*, January 29, 1987.
32. *Hindustan Times*, April 4, 1988.
33. *Indian Express*, June 3, 1988.
34. *Indian Express*, October 24, 1989.
35. *Hindustan Times*, April 4, 1988.
36. *Indian Express*, March 23, 1991.

14

CONCLUSIONS

India is greying quite rapidly during the last couple of decades and at present people over the age of 60 have crossed the 50 million mark and it is estimated that by the turn of the century there will be 76 million Indians above the age of 60. Another remarkable phenomenon is the fast pace of urbanisation. The urban-rural ratio is changing as the percentage of urban population grew from 19.9 per cent in 1971 to 23.3 per cent in 1981. Conversely, the percentage of rural population declined from 80.1 per cent to 76.7 per cent. The trend is continuing for at present (1991 Census) there are 4,689 towns and 6 lakh villages in the country against 4,029 towns in 1981. The rapid urbanisation, high inflation, and the necessity of dual incomes (couples working), is resulting in the break down of the joint family system, disruption of the traditional relationships and reordering family norms, putting the value system and life styles in a state of flux, the brunt of all this has to be borne by the ageing parents who are regarded as redundant.

The objective of this book was to study the aged in India and examine their adjustments to the social, emotional and psychological stresses and what strategies they use to cope with these stresses and make adjustments. At present Indians, particularly of the middle social class, do not have a favourable attitude towards institutionalisation of the aged and the findings of one of the studies also reveals that institutionalisation of the aged adversely effects their mental health. In spite of this, old age homes have come up in Delhi and other towns and are being occupied by old people. This fact makes it apparent that it may not be long before institutionalisation of the aged is looked upon favourably and institutions for the aged are in great demand not only in Delhi but also in other parts of India. The purpose of this book is also to highlight the various issues of the aged and aging so that policy-makers, public, and voluntary agencies, etc. should keep the care of the aged in mind not only on October 1, the Day of the Aged, but also while formulating policies and allocating funds.

APPENDIX

OLD AGE HOMES IN INDIA

Andhra Pradesh

1.1 Aram Ghar
Home for the Aged, Shivarampalli, Hyderabad - 500252

2.2 Home for the Aged
C/o Shri Shanti Ashram, Thotapalli Hills, (Via) Senkhavaram Prathipadi, East Godavari - 533202

3.3 Indian Christian Orphan Social Work Home
Thubadu Village, Chilakaluripeta - 522616

4.4 Karuna Bharathi
Home for the Aged, Near Court Buildings, Khamman - 507002

5.5 Karuna Nilayam
Mahila Seva Mandali, Kojjillipet, Machilipatnam - 521001

6.6 Little Sisters of the Poor
Home for the Aged, Secunderabad - 500003

7.7 Nirmala Hrudayam Bhavan
Home for Dying Destitutes, Vijayawada - 506002

8.8 Shanti Bhavan
St. Joseph's Home for the Aged, Autapally, Krishna District - 521286

9.9 Sneha Nilayam
Loyola Nagar, Jangaon Road, Suryapet - 508229

10.10 St. Anne's Home for the Aged
Fatima Nagar, Warangal - 506003

11.11 St. Joseph's Home for the Aged and Disabled, Karkaipetta - Shantinagar, Amalapuram P.O. East Godavari - 533202

12.12 St. Vincent De Paul Home for the Aged, Bangalore Highway, Anantapur - 515001

Assam

13.1 Mercy Home
Sisters of Charity, Convoy Road, Boiraginath P.O. Dibrugarh - 786001

Bihar

14.1 Cheshire Homes India
Meath Marg, Gari Village, Bariatu P.O., Ranchi - 834007
15.2 St. Mary's Orphanage
Fakirana Bettiah P.O., West Champaram - 845438
16.3 Swami Vivekanda Sewa Trust
Sakchi, Jamshedpur, Bihar - 831001

Chandigarh

17.1 Home for the Old
Sector 15, Chandigarh - 160016

Delhi

18.1 Arya Mahila Ashram
Near Arya Samaj Mandir, New Rajinder Nagar, New Delhi - 110060
19.2 Delhi Christian Friend-in-Need Society
3382 Christian Colony, Karol Bagh, New Delhi - 110005
20.3 Home for the Aged
Fatehpur Bari, Mehrauli Block, New Delhi - 110030
21.4 Home for the Aged Servants of People Society of India
Lajpat Bhawan, Lajpat Nagar - IV, New Delhi 110024
22.5 Nirmal Hriday Home for the Aged
1 Magazine Road, New Delhi - 110054
23.6 Ozanam Home Society
Radio Colony, Guru Teg Bahadur Nagar, Delhi - 110033
24.7 Shaheed Sainik Stri Sadan
P.B.G. Lines, Rashtrapati Bhavan, New Delhi - 110004
25.8 St. Mary's Home
6, Rajpur Road, Delhi - 110054

Goa

26.1 Asilo De Indigents
Home for the Aged Poor, Cobravaddo, Calengute, Goa - 403516

27.2 Asylum, 'Dr. Refael Pereira'
Acsona Benaulim, Salcette - 403 716

28.3 Divine Providence Convent
Home for the Aged, Cana - Benaulim, Salcette - 403716

29.4 Holy Spirit Home
AITO Pirazonas, Moira, Bardez - 403514

30.5 Home for the Aged
Convent of St. John of God, Old Goa - 403402

31.6 Home for the Aged
Sacred Heart of Jesus & Mary Asylum, Aldona, Bardez - 403508

32.7 Ishaprema Niketan
Assagao, Bardez - 403507

33.8 Ishaprema Niketan
Bairo St. Francisco, Goa Velha - 403108

34.9 Krist Raj Bhavan
Home for the Aged, Cotula, Sailgao - 403511

35.10 Mae De Deus Home for the Aged
Colula, Sailagao - 403511

36.11 Mother Mary Haven
Calangute, Bardez - 403516

37.12 St. Joseph's Home
Porto Vaddo, Siolim, Bardez - 403517

38.13 St. Mary's Guest House
Nagoa de Verna, Salcette - 403722

Gujarat

39.1 Bhavnagar Vardhashram
Bhavnagar Vardhashram Trust, Plot No. 1260/61, Bhavnagar - 364001

40.2 Sheth Dalichand Virchand Shroff Ashakta Ashram
Rampura, Surat - 395003

41.3 Sheth Megji Sojpal Jain Ashram
Nagalpur - Dhindh O.P., Mandvi (Surat) - 394160

42.4 Shram Mandir Trust
Sindhrot, Baroda - 391330

43.5 Shri Kirchandbhai Kothari Vanprasth Ashram
Near Kasturba Society, Near Broad Gauge Station
Surendranagar, Gujarat - 363001

44.6 Vana Prastha Seva Samaj
Gardhanu Ghar, Mani Nagar, Ahmedabad - 380008

45.7 Vikas Griha
Home for the aged and women, Anand Nagar P.O.,
Ahmedabad - 380007

46.8 Virdha Niketan
Home for the aged and Infirm, Narsingh Mehta Chora,
Junagadh - 362001

Haryana

47.1 Old Age Home
Yamuna Nagar, Haryana - 135001

Karnataka

48.1 Abhaya Ashraya
Konaje Village, P.O., Asaigoli - 574152

49.2 Bethany Ashram and Caring Home
Post Office Road, Channa Patna - 571501

50.3 Canara Bank Relief and Welfare Society
Mathra Chhaya, 27th Cross, Banasankari II State, Bangalore - 560070

51.4 Christa Mitra Ashram Sevamandiram
Ankola P.O., North Karnataka - 581314

52.5 Dakshina Bharath Mahila Sangham
122, 27th Cross, Jayanagar, Bangalore - 560082

53.6 Eventide Home
St. Joseph's Convent, White Field, Bangalore - 560066

54.7 Fr. Muller's Charitable Institutions
Kankanady P.O., Mangalore - 575002

55.8 Friend-In-Need Society
Home for the Aged, Bangalore - 560001

56.9 Holy Family Home for the Aged
Iranapalaya, Via Nagavara, Arabic College Post, Bangalore - 560047

57.10 Home for the Aged
Wesley Church, Benson Town, Bangalore - 560046

58.11 Jerome Home
13, Pettigrew Street, Bangalore - 560005

59.12 Little Sisters of the Poor: Home for the Aged
Chelikere Village, Doddabanswadi P.O., Bangalore - 560043

60.13 Little Sisters of the Poor: Home for the Aged
15 Hosur Road, Bangalore - 560025

62.14 Little Sisters of the Poor: Home for the Aged
Mahadeva Pura Road, Gandhinagar, Mysore - 570007

63.15 Little Sisters of the Poor: Home for the Aged
Shanti Kiran, Bajjodi, Kulshekar, Mangalore - 575005

64.16 St. Joseph's Home for the Aged Destitutes
St. Vincent de Paul Society, 16, Khanpur Road Camp, Belgaum - 519001

65.17 St. Paul's Home for the Aged
St. Paul's Church, Marikuppam, Kolar Gold Fields - 563119

66.18 Vridhashram
C/o Vallaba Niketan, 19, Kumar Kripa Road, Bangalore - 560001

Kerala

67.1 Abaya Bhavan
Keezhukunnu, Kottayam - 686002

68.2 Asha Bhavan
Nenmery, Velanilam P.O., Mundakayam - 686513

69.3 Assisi Little Flower Convent
Thalayolaparambu, Kottayam - 686605

70.4 Assisi Vinayalaya
Kottiyam P.O., Quilon District - 691571

71.5 Bethel Asram Old People's Home
Mission Quarters, Trichur - 680001

72.6 Bishop Gnanadhason Memorial "Anpu Nilayam"
Mankoodal House, L.M.S. Compound Cheruvarakonam, Parassala - 695502

73.7 Bishop Thara Yil Memorial Home for the Aged
Thellakom P.O., Kottayam - 686016

74.8 Christian Aid Movement
Kottapuram Seminary, Pulaman, Kottarakara - 686001

75.9 Christ Vilia Poor Homes
R.V. Puram P.O., Trichur - 680631
76.10 Daya Bhavan
Karoor P.O., Palai - 686590
77.11 Deya Bhavan
Chengal, Kalady, Ernakulam District - 683574
78.12 Don Bosco Poor Home
Kadanad P.O., Via Palai, Kottayam District - 686651
79.13 Home for the Aged
C/o The Bishop of Kanjirappalli, St. Dominie's Cathedral, Kottayam District, Kanjirappalli - 686507
80.14 Home for the Aged and Infirm
Chunangamvely, Erumathala P.O., Alwaye - 638105
81.15 Home for the Destitute
Perumanur, Cochin - 682015
82.16 House of Providence
Providence Road, Cochin - 682018
83.17 J.D.T. Islam Orphanage
P.O. Marikunnu, Calicut - 673012
84.18 Karunalayam
Thrikkakara B.M.C. P.O., Cochin - 682021
85.19 Little Flower Poor House
Narakal, Ernakulam - 682505
86.20 Little Lourdes Bhaghya Bhavan
Kidangoor P.O., Kottayam - 686572
87.21 Mar Thimotheous Memorial Orphanage
Kalathode, Trichur - 680005
88.22 Mercy Home
Marikunnu, Calicut District - 673012
89.23 Mercy Home
St. Teresa's Mercy Home, Banerji Road, Cochin - 682018
90.24 Mercy Home for the Aged Destitute
C/o Mercy Convent, Palghat - 678006
91.25 M.G.M. Abhaya Bhavan
Pothenpuram P.O., Pampady, Kottayam - 686502
92.26 Mutunayagam Homes for the Aged Poor
Plamood Junction, Pattam, Trivandrum - 695004
93.27 Nirmala Hospital: Home for the Aged
Marikunnu P.O., Calicut - 673012

94.28 Old Age Home
Cheenkallel, Monipallay P.O., Kottayam District - 686636

95.29 Old People's Home
Vadakkenchery P.O., Palghat District - 678683

96.30 Ozanam Society: Devadan Centre
Chethimattam, Palai - 686575

97.31 Pius XII Jubilee Memorial House of Providence
Irinjalakuda - 680121

98.32 Poor Homes Society
West Hill, Calicut - 673005

99.33 Raksha Bhavan
Maniamkulam, Chennad P.O., Kottayam - 686001

100.34 Salvation Army
Territorial Head Quarters, (South Western India), Kowdiar, Trivandrum - 695003

101.35 Santhi Bhavan
S.H. Convent, Karukutty, (via Ankamaly, Ernakulam - 683576

102.36 Santhi Nilayam
Yenthayar P.O., Mundakayam - 686513

103.37 Santhi Sadan
Irinjalakuda P.O., Trichur - 680121

104.38 Sivananda Yogavedasta
Vana Prastha Ashram, Palghat - 678001

105.39 Sneha Bhavan
Pynakulam, Mylacompu P.O., Thodupuzha, Idukki District - 685584

106.40 Snehalayam
Malayan Keezhu, Nadukani P.O., Kothamgalam - 686691

107.41 Snehalayam
Palai P.O., Karoor - 686590

108.42 Snehaniketan Social Centre
Taliparambu, Via, Pattuvam - 670143

109.43 Snehasadan
Arakuzha - 686672

110.44 Snehasadhan
Pallimala, Katoor P.O., Tiruvella - 689106

111.45 Sree Ravi Varma Destitute Home
Nelikunnu, Trichur - 680005

112.46 St. Antony's Sanketham
P.O. Pariyaram, Via Chalakudy, Trichur - 680721

113.47 St. Joseph's Asylum
Holy Family Carmelite Convent, Kothamangalam - 686691

114.48 St. Joseph's Home
Pullazhy, Trichur - 680012

115.49 St. Joseph's Home for the Aged
Puliyilakunnu, Ashtamichira P.O., Trichur District - 680731

116.50 St. Joseph's Poor Home
Peringuzha, Perumballoor P.O., Muvattupuzha, Ernakulam - 6866661

117.51 St. Joseph's Waif's Home
Veli, Cochin - 682001

118.52 St. Roch's Asylum for Women
Palai P.O., Kottayam District - 686575

119.53 St. Vincent De Paul Home for the Aged
Society of St. Vincent de Paul, P.S.C. Palai P.O. - 686575

120.54 St. Vincent Poor Home
Changanacherry - 686101

Madhya Pradesh

121.1 Asha Niketan
Kapa P.O., Raipur - 492005

122.2 Asha Nivas
Adawal P.O., Jagdalpur, Bastar District - 494001

123.3 Home for the Aged Poor
1, Queen's Road Cantt., Jabalpur - 482001

124.4 Home for the Aged
C/o The Bishop of Rajgarh, Catholic Bishop's House, Kunkari P.O., - 496225

125.5 Maria Seva Bhavan
Home for the Aged, Ganj Basoda - 464221

126.6 Mercy Home
Ananda Ashram, Risda P.O., Masturi Via, Bilaspur District - 495551

127.7 Mukti Prakash Ashram
Banjari, Bhatagaon P.O., Via Kurud, Raipur District - 493663

128.8 Pramodvan Anand Dham (Bradh Grih)
P.O. Janki Kund Chitra Koot, Satana - 210204

129.9 Social Welfare Centre
Nandanagar, Road No. 12, Indore - 452003

130.10 St. Francis Boarding Institute
Shampura P.O., Sagar Cantt. - 470 001

131.11 St. Joseph's Home for the Aged
Asha Bhavan, Chandessary, Ujjain - 456006

Maharashtra

132.1 Ashadan
Missionaries of Charity, Sankli Street, Byculla, Bombay - 400008

133.2 Ashiana All Saint's Home
Dockyard Road, Mazagaon, Bombay - 400 010

134.3 Asylum
Casa Pie-dade, Hathi Baug, Love Lane, Bombay - 400010

135.4 Hindu Women's Welfare Society
Deepmal Road, Koliwada, Vashi, Thana District - 400703

136.5 Hingne Stree Shikshan Samstha
Karve Nagar, Pune 411029

137.6 Home for the Aged and Handicapped
Uutkhanà, Medical College Road, Nagpur - 440009

138.7 Isha Anand
Home for the Aged, C/o Missionaries of Charity, Amaravati Camp P.O. - 444602

139.8 Ishaprema Niketan
972, Nana Peth, Padamji Park, Pune - 411002

140.9 Little Sisters of the Poor : Home for the Aged
Mahakali Road, Chakla MIDC P.O., Bombay - 400093

141.10 Maharashtra State Federation of the Organizations of the Aged
C/o Dr. V.K. Gokhale, Plot 11 Block 7 Jahangir Daji Street, Dadina Building, Grant Road, Bombay - 400 007

142.11 Maharogi Sewa Samiti
Maharogi Sewa Anandwan, Tah - Warora (C. Rly.), Chandrapur - 442914

143.12 Nab-Lions Home for the Aging Blind
Sudder Baug, Old-Khandala Road, Khandala - 410301

144.13 Narmada Niketan
Plot No. 2, Sector 8, C.B.D. Bela Pur, New Bombay - 400614

145.14 Nirmala Home for the Aged Society
D'Souza Shirgiri Housing Colony, Gangapur Road, Nasik Road, 422002

146.15 Panchawati Ashram
Matru Sewa Sangh, North Ambazari Road, Sitabardi, Nagpur - 440010

147.16 Poona Blind Men's Association
82, Rasta Peth, Pune - 411011

148.17 Poona Widow's Home
16, Napier Road, Poona - 411001

149.18 Poor Asylum
C/o Church of Immaculate Conception, Nanapeth, Quarter Gate, Pune - 411001

150.19 Sainani Home for the Aged
Mulund East, Bombay - 400081

151.20 Salvation Army Social Service Centre
Men's Industrial Home, 122 Maulana Azad Road, Byculla, Bombay - 400008

152.21 Shanti Avedna Ashram
15, Devaseth Road, Chowpathy, Bombay - 400007

153.22 Shanti Bhavan
Karnik Road, Kalyan - 421304

154.23 Shatayu Bhavan
Pune Vidyarthi Grihas' Vidyanagari, S. No. 44, Parvati, Pune - 411009

155.24 Shepherd Widows Home
Shepherd Road, Byculla, Bombay - 400008

156.25 Shri Gurudeo Vridhashram
Akhil Bhartiya Shri Gurudeo Sewamandal, At. P. Gurukunj Ashram, Amravati - 444902

157.26 Shi J.J. Dharamashala
District Benevolent Society of Bombay, Bombay - 400008

158.27 St. Anthony's Home for the Aged
51, Chapel Road, Bandra, Bombay - 400050

159.28 St. Vincent De Paul Society
Conference of St. Francis Xavier, St. Vincent's Street, Poona - 411001

160.29 S.V.P. Poor Home
New Modikhana, Poona - 411002

161.30 Tapovan Vradhashram, Nasik - 422003

162.31 Vridha Sevashram
Near Laxmi Nagar, Sangli - 416416

Meghalaya

163.1 Mercy Home
Dem Thring, Shillong - 793021

Orissa

164.1 Daya Ashram
Cantonment Road, Cuttack - 753001

165.2 Gram Vikas Sangha
At Nagpur, Post Balikuda, Cuttack District - 754108

166.3 Marillac Mercy Home
Daughters of Charity, St. Vincent's Provincial House, Berhampur - 760010

167.4 Vijoy Sevasadan
(St. Mary's Home for the Aged), Barbil P.O., Keonjhar District - 758035

Pondicherry

168.1 Hospice (Cluny Home)
Laporte No. 4, Pondicherry - 605001

Punjab

169.1 Apahaj Sahaik Sabha
Apahaj Ashram, Gandhi Park, G.T. Road, Jalandhar - 144008

170.2 Bhai Vir Singh Birdh Ghar
Jandiala Road, Tarn Taran, Amritsar - 143401

171.3 Fellowship Home for the Aged
Mission Compound, Brown Road, Ludhiana - 141008

172.4 Nishkam Sewa Ashram
Village Daad, Pokhowal Road, Ludhiana - 141008

173.5 Pingla Ghar
Ananth Sewa Society, T.B. Hospital Road, Jalandhar - 144008

174.6 Red Cross Home for the Aged
Sarabha Nagar, Ludhiana - 141001

175.7 Red Cross Home for Senior Citizens
Bhatinda - 151001

176.8 S.D. Kumar Sabha Yadvendra Dasondhi Ram Birji Apahaj Ashram, Patiala - 147001

Tamil Nadu

177.1 Aged's Home Trust
C/o Sri Ramakrishna Hospital, Sarojini Naidu Road, Pappanaicken Palayam, Coimbatore - 641044

178.2 Ananthammal Home for the Aged
Elarthavanachery, Perumpannaiyur (Past), Via Senmangudi, Nannilam Taluk, Tanjore District - 612603

179.3 Anbaham
Home for the aged, Besant Avenue Adyar, Madras - 600020

180.4 Bishop Agniswami Home for the Aged
Sahayapuram, Suchindram - 629704

181.5 Cheshire Home
5, Covelong, Chinglepet District - 603112

182.6 C.S.I. Mercy Home
C.S.I. Compound, Aruppukottai - 626101

183.7 C.S.I. Women's Centre
Home for the aged, Muttom - 629202, Kanyakumari District

184.8 Daya Sadan
Home for the Aged, 373 Konnur High Road, Otteri, Perambur Barracks, Madras - 600012

185.9 Friend-in-Need Society: Home for the Aged
29, E.V.R. Periyar High Road, Madras - 600003

186.10 Grace and Compassion Priory
Home for the Aged, 57, Anna Salai, Tiruvannamalai - 606601

187.11 Holy Angel's Home for the Aged
Holy Angel's Convent, Kamaraj Road, Kumbakonam - 612001

188.12 Home for the Aged
Trithuapuram, Kuzhithurai - 629163

189.13 Home for the Aged
Tzhagia Mandapam, Thuckalay, Kanyakumari District - 629702

190.14 Infant Jesus convent
Home for the Aged, Mulagumoodu, Kanyakumari District - 629167

191.15 Karunai Illam
Thirumaraiyur, Nazareth, Tirunelveli District
192.16 Little Sister of the Poor: Home for the Aged
Ettayapuram Road, Tuticorin - 628002
193.17 Little Sisters of the Poor : Home for the Aged
6, Harrington Road, Chetput, Madras - 600031
194.18 Louis Social Service Centre
Home for the Aged, R.C. Church Elappakkam, Chinglepet District, 603201
195.19 Lady Willington Home
Dresors Lane, Ootacamund - 643001
196.20 Mary Clubwala Jadhav Home for the Aged
Greenways Road, Raja Annamalaipuram, Madras - 600028
197.21 Mercy Home
64, Halls Road, Kilpauk, Madras - 600010
198.22 Monegar and Rajah of Venkatagiri Choultries
Home for the Aged, Opp. Govt. Stanley Hospital, O.P., 44, M.C. Road, Madras - 600001
199.23 Our Lady of Victory Trust
Home for the Aged, Pannaivilagam, Kangalancherry - 610101
200.24 Pope John's Garden
Home for the Aged, Leprosy Rehabilitation Centre, M.M.C. Post, Madras - 600051
201.25 Pope Paul Mercy Home
Nanjanand, Nilgiris - 643004
202.26 Rajaji Home for the Aged
Old Natham Road, Madurai - 625001
203.27 Sahaya Illam
Society of St. Vincent de Paul, St. Thomas Mount, Madras - 600016
204.28 Shanthi Gramam Kandipedu
Home for the Aged, Karigiri - 632106
205.29 Sir John D'Monte Home for the Aged
C/o Mount Carmel Church, Kovalam - 603112
206.30 Sneha Illam (Mercy Home)
St. Charles Convent, Thiruvalluvar Nagar, Madurai - 625006
207.31 St. Anne's Home for the Aged
Melapudur, Tiruchirappalli - 620001
208.32 St. Anne's Home for the Aged
Theresapuram, via, Thellar - 604406

209.33 St. Anne's Rehabilitation Society
Home for the Aged, St. Anne's Convent, Irungalur P.O., Tiruchirappalli - 621105

210.34 St. Antony's Home for the Aged
Kattur, Tiruchirappalli - 620019

211.35 St. Joseph's Charity Institute
Home for the Aged, Adaikalapuram - 628217

212.36 St. Joseph's Home for the Aged
Cluny Convent, Katpadi, Vellore - 632007

213.37 St. Joseph's Home for the Aged
Shrine Basilica, Vailankanni - 611111

214.38 St. Joseph's Home for the Aged Destitute
Samaritan Sisters, Podanur, P.O., Coimbatore - 641023

215.39 St. Thomas Mercy Home
Madurai Road, Crawford, Tiruchirappalli - 620012

216.40 Vallalar Illam : Home for the Aged
44/6-A Pillaiyar Koil Street, Velappadi, Vellore-632001

217.41 Vishranthi
Home for the Aged Destitute Women, 28, AVM Rajeswari Gardens, M.G.R. Road, Palavakkam, Madras - 600041

218.42 Vishranthi Illam
C/o Cheshire Homes India, Gandhi Nagar, Vellore - 632006

Uttar Pradesh

219.1 Arya Van Prastha Ashram
Jiwalapur, Haridwar - 249407

220.2 Dorothy Crosthwaite Homes
Off Ashok Marg, Near NCC Office, Lucknow - 226001

221.3 Home for the Aged
Methodist Hospital, Jaisinghpura, Vrindaban, Mathura - 281121

222.4 Home for the Aged : Serve Our Souls
Dignawat Village, Sarvakthani, Varanasi - 221001

223.5 Little Flower Home for the Aged
Kathgodam, Nainital - 263126

224.6 Nirmal Hriday
Missionaries of Charity, B/2/176 Shivala Ghat, Varanasi - 221001

225.7 Ramakrishna Mission Home of Service
Home for the Aged, Luxa, Varanasi - 221001

226.8 Shrimati Mungadevi Muktha Mahila Ashram
223, Patel Nagar, Nai Mandi, Muzaffar Nagar - 251001

227.9 Spreadacres
YWCA of India Project, 4, New Cantt. Road, Dehra Dun - 248001

228.10 Stranger's Home
2, Station Road, Lucknow - 226001

229.11 St. Rita's Mission
Manikpur - P.O., Banda District - 210208

230.12 Swami Jyotirmayanand Ashram
International Yoga Society, Lal Bagh, Loni - 201102

231.13 Vidur Vanprasth Ashram
Vidur Sewa Ashram, P.O., Vidurkuti, Bijnore - 246701

West Bengal

232.1 Bridha Ashram
C/o Bishop's House, Krishna Nagar, Nadia District - 741101

233.2 Harihar Sandel Home
18, Duff Street, Calcutta - 700006

234.3 Home for the Old and Infirm
Tibetan Refugee Self Help Centre, Havelock Villa, 65, Gandhi Road, Darjeeling - 734101

235.4 Little Sisters of the Poor
Home for the Aged, 2, Lower Circular Road, Calcutta - 700016

236.5 Navanir
Home for the Aged, 30, Ashoka Avenue, Calcutta - 700040

237.6 St. Lawrence D'Souza Home
138, Dharmatala Street, Calcutta - 700020

238.7 Tollygunge Homes
The East India Charitable Trust, 186, Netaji Subhash Chandra Bose Road, Calcutta - 700040

BIBLIOGRAPHY

Abammer, I.M., and Baltes P.B., 1972, Objective versus perceived age differences in personality : How do adolescents, adults and older people view themselves and each other, *Journal of Gerontology*, 27(1), p 46-51.

Abrahams, J.P. and Birren, J.B., 1973, Reaction time as a function of age and behavioural predisposition to coronary heart disease, *Journal of Gerontology*, 28, pp 471-478.

Abramowitz, S.I., 1969, Locus of control and self-reported depression among college students, *Psychological Reports*, 25, pp 149-151.

Achenbaum, W.A., 1983, *Shades of grey : Old age, American values and federal policies since 1920*, Little Brown, Boston.

Adams, G.F., 1978, *Essentials of geriatric medicine*, Oxford University Press, Oxford.

Adams, R.D., 1980, The morphological aspects of aging in the human nervous systems, *In* J.E. Birren and R.B. Sloane, eds., *Handbook of mental health and aging*, Prentice-Hall, Englewood Cliffs, N.J.

Adams, James P., Kaufman, Allan V. and Dressler, William W., 1989, Predictors of social isolation in older southern adults: A cross-racial analysis, *Journal of Applied Gerontology*, 8(3), pp 365-381.

Adams, Rebecca G., 1988, Which comes first : Poor psychological well-being or decreased friendship activity?, *Activities, Adaptation and Aging*, 12(1-2), pp 27-41.

Adelman, R.C., 1977, Macromolecular metabolism during aging, *In* C.E. Finch and L. Hayflick, eds., *Handbook of the biology of aging*, Van Nostrand Reinhold, New York.

Adelman, Ronald, D. and Albert, Rachel C., 1987, Medical student attitudes towards the elderly : A critical review of the literature, *Gerontology and Geriatrics Education*, 7(3-4), pp 141-155.

Adiseshiah, M.S., 1982, The elderly : Still contributing, *Journal of Social Welfare*, 29(1), pp 9-10.

Adler, A., 1929, *The science of living*, Greenberg, New York.

———, 1931, *What life should mean to you*, Little Brown, Boston.

Adler, W.H., 1974, A autoimmune theory of aging, *In* M. Rockstein, M.L. Sussman and J. Chesky, eds., *Theoretical aspects of aging*, Academic Press, New York.

Ad Hoc Committee of the Harvard School to Examine the Definition of Brain Death, 1968, A definition of irreversible coma, *Journal of American Medical Association*, 205, pp 85-88.

Aggarwal, A.N., 1984, A home for the homeless, *Economic Times*, January 22, p 5, col 1-4.

Aggarwal, Anju, D., 1984, Another home another time, *Economic Times*, January 22, p 4, col 1-8.

Aiken, L.R., 1978, *The psychology of later life*, W.B. Saunders Company, Philadelphia.

Ailor, J.W., 1973, The church provides for the elderly, *In* R.P. Boyd and C.G. Oakes, eds., *Foundation of practical gerontology*, 2nd ed., University of South Carolia Press, Columbia.

Ainlay, S.C. and Smith, D.R., 1984, Aging and religious participation, *Journal of Gerontology*, 39(3), pp 357-363.

Aleem, Shamin and Aleem, M.A., 1985, Age of superannuation : The need for a sound policy, *Administrator*, 30(2), pp 183-193.

Allen, Susan M., Allen, Jon G. and Weekly, Jenay, 1986, The impact of a practicum on aging and reminiscence on gifted students attitudes towards the elderly, *Roeper Review*, 9(2), pp 90-94.

Allred, Glodeen B. and Dobson, Judith, E., 1987, Remotivation group interaction : Increasing children's contact with the elderly, *Elementary School Guidance and Counseling*, 21(3), pp 216-220.

Almerico, Guna M., and Fillmer, Thompson, 1988, Portrayal of older characters in children's magazines, *Educational Gerontology*, 14(1), pp 15-31.

Amarjit, 1988, A boon for the elderly, *Social Welfare*, 35(6), September, pp 22-23.

American Psychiatric Association, 1980, *Diagnostic and statistical manual of mental disorders*, 3rd ed., American Psychiatric Association, Washington, D.C.

Ananthalakshmi, P., Vanaja, G.T., and Shalini Bhogle, 1984, *Intellectual decline in the educated aged*, Paper submitted to the 2nd National Conference on Aging, November, Tirupati.

Anantharamah, R.N., 1976, *Psychology of aging — A study in adjustment* Unpublished Ph. D. thesis, Bangalore University.

——, 1979, Adjustment and its correlates in old age, *Indian Journal of Clinical Psychology*. 6, pp 165-168.

——, 1979b, Perception of old age by two generations, *Journal of Psychological Researches*, 23(3), pp 198-199.

——,1979 c, Activity disengagement for successful aging in old age, *Journal of Psychological Researches*, 23(2), pp 110-112.

——, 1980 a, Reliability and validity of life satisfaction questionnaire, *Indian Journal of Clinical Psychology*, 7, pp 59-61.

——, 1980 b, A study of self-assessment of health status among the elderly, *Indian Journal of Applied Psychology*, 17(1), pp 11-14.

——, 1980 c, A study of institutionalised and non-institutionalised older people, *Psychological Studies*, 25, pp 31-33.

——, 1980 d, A study of stereotypes towards old age, *Journal of Psychological Researches*, 24, pp 140-143.

——, 1981 a, The concept of self among the elderly, *Indian Journal of Applied Psychology*, 18, pp 47-51.

——, 1981 b, Physical health and adjustment in old age, *Journal of Psychological Researches*, 25(1), pp 46-50.

——, 1982, The problems of the older people in a changing society, *Journal of the Madras University*, LIV, 2, pp 31-33.

——,1983, Psychology of aging, *Journal of Madras University LIV*, 1, pp 1-4.

——, 1984, Perceptional of stereotypes towards old age by two generations, *Journal of Psychological Researches*, 28, pp 170-173.

Anon, 1981, Retirement benefits in India, *Economic Times*, July 5, p 5, col 4-8.

——, 1981, Dealing with aging labour, *Eastern Economics*, 77(19), pp 869-870.

——, 1983, Age-old respect for the aged in India, *Yojana*, 27(1-2), pp 57-60.

——, 1984, *Elderly people and the environment*, Pleum Publishing Corporation, New York.

——, 1986, Aging (The) society, *Daedalus* (Cambridge), 115(1), pp 1-400.

——, 1989, Pension problems in Haryana, *Economic Times*, February, p 5, col 7-8.

Apel, Mary D.,1986, The attitudes and knowledge of church members and pastors related to older adults and retirement, *Journal of Religion and Aging*, 2(3), pp 31-43.

Arenberg, D., and Robertson-Tchabo, E.A., 1977, Learning and aging, *In* J.E. Birren and K.W. Schaie, eds., *The handbook of the Psychology of aging*, Van Nostrand Reinhold, New York.

Atchley, R.C., 1971, Retirement and leisure participation : continuity or crisis ? *Gerontologist*, 11(1), pp 13-17.

——, 1975, The life course, age grading and age-linked demands for decision-making, *In* N. Datan and L, Ginsberg, eds., *Life-span developmental psychology : Normative life crises*, Academic press, New York.

——, 1975, *The sociology of retirement*, Wadsworth, Belmont, California.

——, 1980, *Social forces in later life*, Wadsworth, Belmont, California.

Atchley, Robert C., 1989, A continuity theory of normal aging, *Gerontologist*, 29(2), pp 183-190.

Austin, Adriana G., 1989, Becoming immune to loneliness : Helping the elderly fill a void, *Journal of Gerontology*, 15(9), pp 25-28.

Avioli, Paula S., 1989, The social support functions of siblings in later life : A theoretical model, *American Behavioural Scientist*, 33(1), pp 47-57.

Avtar Singh, 1986, Predictors of life satisfaction among the urban institutionalised elderly, *Guru Nanak Journal of Sociology*, 7(1), pp 81-91.

Azin, Anwar, 1981, Old-age trepidations, *Patriot*, November 22, p 2, col 3-8.

B. Manjeshwar Dinesh and P. Hanumantha Rayappa, 1983, Caring for our aged, *Kurukshetra*, 31(9), pp 77-79.

Babchuk, Nicholas and Anderson, Trudy B., 1989, Older widows and married women : Their intimates and confidants, *International Journal of Aging and Human Development*, 28(1), pp 21-35.

Babladelis, Georgia, 1987, Young persons attitudes towards aging, *Perceptual and Motor Skills*, 65(2), pp 553-554.

Back, K.W., 1976, Personal characteristics and social behaviour : Theory and methods, *In* R. Binstock and E. Shanas, eds., *Handbook of aging and the social sciences*, Academic Press, New York.

Baltes, Margaret, M. and Schmid, Ulrich, 1987, Psychological gerontology, *German Journal of Psychology*, 11(2), pp 87-123.

Baltes, P.B. and Nesselroade, J.R., 1973, The development analysis of individual difference on multiple measures, *In* J.R. Nesselroade and H.W. Reese, eds., *Life-span developmental psychology : Methodological issues*, Academic Press, New York.

Baltes, P.B. and Schaie, K.W., 1973, *Life-span developmental psychology: Personality and socialisation*, Academic Press, New York.

——, 1974, The myth of the twilight years, *Psychology Today*, 7(10), pp 35-40.

——, and Willis, S.L., 1977, Towards psychological theories of aging and development, *In* J.E. Birren and K.W. Schaie, eds., *Handbook of the psychology of aging*, Van Nostrand Reinhold, New York.

Baltzell, E.D., 1958, *Philadelphia gentlemen : The making of a national upper-class*, Glencoe Ill., Free Press.

Barber, B., 1968, Social stratification, *In* David L. Sills, eds., *International encyclopaedia of the social sciences*, vol 15, Macmillan Company and Free Press, New York.

Barnes-Farrell, Janet L. and Piotrowski, Michael J., 1989, Worker's perceptions of discrepancies between chronological age and personal age : You are only as old as you feel, *Psychology and Aging*, 4(3), pp 376-377.

Barrow, G.M., and Smith, P.A., 1979, *Aging, ageism and society*, West, *St. Paul.*

Bartus, R.T., Dean, R.L., Beer, B. and Lippa, A.S., 1982, The cholinergic hypothesis of geriatric memory dysfunction, *Science*, 217, pp 408-417.

Bassili, T.N., and Reil, J.E., 1981, On the dominance of old age, *Journal of Gerontology*, 36(6), pp 682-686.

Bastida, Elena, 1987, Sex-typed age norms among older Hispanics, *Gerontologist*, 27(1), pp 59-65.

Baum, S.K., 1982, Loneliness in elderly persons : A preliminary study, *Psychological Reports*, 50(3), pp 1313-1318.

——— and Boxley, R.L., 1983, Depression and old age identification, *Journal of Clinical Psychology*, 39(4), pp 584-590.

———, and Sokolowski, Marica, 1984, Time perception and psychological well-being in the elderly, *Psychiatric Quarterly*, 56(1), pp 54-61.

Bayley, N., and Oden, M.H., 1955, The maintenance of intellectual ability in gifted adults, *Journal of Gerontology*, 10, pp 91-107.

Bearon, Wcille B., 1989, No great expectations : The under pinnings of life satisfaction for older women, *Gerontologist*, 29(6), pp 772-778.

Beattie, W., 1973, Designing systems of care planning : Issues and perspectives, *In* E. Pfeiffer, ed., *Alternatives to institutional care for older Americans : Practice and planning*, Centre for the study of Aging and Human Development, Durham.

Bender, M.P., 1986, The neglect of the elderly by British psychologists, *Bulletin of the British Psychological Society*, 39, pp 414-417.

Bengston, V.L., 1963, *The generation gap, differences by generation and by sex in the perception of parent-child relations*, Paper presented at Annual meeting of Pacific Sociological Associations, Seattle, Wash.

———,1973, *The social psychology of aging*, Bobbs-Merrill, New York.

———, Cuellar, J.B. and Rangan, P.K., 1977, Stratum contrasts and similarities in attitude towards death, *Journal of Gerontology*, 30(1), pp 76-89.

———, Kasschau, P.L. and Ragan, P.K., 1977, The impact of social structure on aging individuals, *In* J.E. Birren and K.W. Schaie, eds., *Handbook of the psychology of aging*, Van Nostrand Reinhold, New York.

——— and Treas, J., 1980, The changing family context of mental health and aging, *In* J.E. Birren and R.B. Sloane, eds. *Handbook of mental health and aging*, Prentice-Hall, Englewood Cliffs, N.J.

Benjaminsen, S., 1981, Stressful life events preceeding the onset of neurotic depression, *Psychological Medicine*, 2(2), pp 369-378.

Berg, J. and Malmberg, T., 1982, Loneliness, *Nordiak Psychologic*, 34(3), pp 301-311.

Berkowitz, B., 1965, Changes in intellect with age : IV. Changes in achievement and survival in older people, *Journal of Genetic Psychology*, 107, pp 3-14.

——— and Green, R.F., 1965, Changes in intellect with age-V: Differential change as functions of time interval and original score, *Journal of Genetic Psychology*, 107, pp 179-192.

Bernreuter, R.G., 1961, *The personality inventory, manual*, Stanford University Press, Stanford.

Bhatia, A., 1983, *Values and self concept of old people*, B.A.(Hons) Dissertation, Delhi University, Delhi.

Bhatia, H.S., 1983, *Aging and Society : A sociological study of the retired public servants*, The Arya's Book Centre Publishers, Udaipur.

Bhogle, Shalini, Dayalu, N., Johnson, I., *et al*, 1978, *Problems of aging among women*, IPA Convention Proceedings, Tirupati.

———, 1983, *The Problems of aging among women*, Paper submitted to the National Seminar on Psycho-social Aspects of Aging, Tirupati.

Bhushan, L.I., 1971, *The Religiosity Scale : Manual*, National Psychological Corporation, Agra.

Binstock, Robert H., 1986, Public policy and the elderly, *Journal of Geriatric Psychiatry*, 19(2), pp 115-143.

Birren, J.E., 1959, Principle of research on aging, *In* Birren, J.E., ed., *Handbook of aging and the individual : Psychological and biological aspects*, The University of Chicago Press, Chicago.

———, 1964, *The psychology of aging*, Prentice-Hall, Englewood Cliffs, N.J.

——— and Botwinick, J., 1951, The reaction of writing speed to age and to the senile psychoses, *Journal of Consulting Psychology*, 15, pp 243-249.

———, Butler, R.N., Greenhouse, S.W., Sokoloff, L. and Yarrow, M.R., 1963, *Human aging*, Public Health Service Publication No. 986, Washington.

——— and Morrison, D.F., 1961, Analysis of the WAIS subtests in relation to age and education, *Journal of Gerontology*, 16, pp 363-369.

——— and Remer, V.J., 1977, Research on the psychology of aging : Principles and experimentation, *In* J.E. Birren and L.W. Schaie, eds., *Handbook of the psychology of aging*, Van Nostrand Reinhold, New York.

——— and Sloane, R.B., 1980, *Handbook of mental health and aging*, Prentice-Hall, Englewood Cliffs, N.J.

———, Woods, A.M. and Williams, M.V., 1980, Behavioural slowing with age : Causes, organisation and consequences, *In* L.W. Poon, ed., *Aging in the 1980's : Psychological issues*, American Psychological Association, Washington, D.C.

Bishop, Sue M. and Shoemaker, Yvonne B., 1987, Married couples in later life : The ecologic transition of retirement, *Family and Community Health*, 9(4), pp 22-23.

Bishop, Dunae S., Epstein, Nathan B., Baldwin, Lawrence M., Miller, Ivan W. *et al*, 1988, Older couples: The effect of health, retirement, and family functioning on morale, *Family Systems Medicine*, 6(2), pp 238-247.

Binstock, Robert H. *et al*, 1982, *International Perspective in aging : Population and policy challenges*, U.N. Fund for Population Activities, New York.

Biswas, S.K.,1985, Dependency and family care of the aged in village India : A case study, *Journal of Indian Anthropological Society*, 20(3), pp 238-257.

———, and Mookerjee, Shyamal, 1985, *Economic activity and residential arrangements of the rural aged India*, Paper submitted to the International Seminar on population Aging in India,February, Trivandrum.

Blau, P.M., 1964, *Exchange and power in social life*, John Wiley, New York.

Blazer, D., 1980, the epidemiology of mental illness in late life, *In* E.W. Busse and D. Blazer, eds., *Handbook of geriatric psychiatry*, Van Nostrand Reinhold, New York.

——— and Palmore, E., 1971, Religion and aging in longitudinal panel, *The Gerontologist*, 16(1), pp 82-85.

Blazer, D.G., 1982, *Depression in later life* C.V. Mosby, St. Louis, MO.

Blenker, M., 1968, The place of the nursing home among community resources, *Journal of Geriatric Psychology*, 1, pp 135-144.

Bolton, A. and Oatley, B., 1987, A longitudinal study of social support and depression in unemployed men, *Psychological Medicine*, 77(2), pp 453-460.

Bondareff, W., 1980, Neurobiology of aging, *In* J.E. Birren and R.B. Sloane, eds., *Handbook of mental health and aging*, Prentice-Hall, Englewood Cliffs, N.J.

Borgatta, Edgar, F., and Mccluskey, Neil G., 1980, *Aging and society : Current research and policy perspectives*, Sage Publications, Inc., Beverly Hills, California.

Borges, M.A., and Dulton, L.J., 1976, Attitudes towards aging : Increasing optimism found with age, *Gerontologist*, 16, pp 220-224.

Bose A.B. and Gangrade, K.D., 1989, *Aging in India : Problems and potentials*, Abhinav Publications, New Delhi.

Bosse, Raymond, Aldwin, Carolyn M., Levenson, Michael R. and Ekerdt, David J., 1987, Mental health differences among retirees and workers : Findings from the normative aging study, *Psychology and Aging*, 2(4), pp 383-389.

Botwinick, I., 1964, Cautiousness in advanced age, *Journal of Gerontology*, 21(3), pp 347-353.

Botwinick, J., 1967, *Cognitive processes in maturity and old age*, Springer, New York.

———, 1973, *Aging and behaviour*, Springer, New York.

———, 1977, Intellectual abilities, *In* J.E., Birren and K.W. Schaie, eds., *Handbook of the psychology of aging*, Van Nostrand Reinhold, New York.

———, and Storandt, M., 1974, Cardiovascular states, depressive affect and other factors in reaction time, *Journal of Gerontology*, 29, pp 543-548.

———, West, R. and Storandt, M., 1978, Predicting death from behavioural test performance, *Journal of Gerontology*, 33(5), pp 755-762.

Bower, G.H., 1962, The influence of graded reduction in reward and prior frustrating events upon the magnitude of the frustration effect, *Journal of Comparative Physiological Psychology*, 55, pp 582-587.

Bowling, Ann P., Edelmann, Robert J., Leaver, Jane, and Hoekel, Theresa, 1989, Loneliness, mobility, well-being and social support in a sample of over 85 year olds, *Personality and Individual Differences*, 10(11), pp 1189-1192.

Brady, E. Michael, 1987, Patterns of learning among the active elderly : The case for elder-hostel, *Activities, Adaptation and Aging*, 9(4), pp 69-77.

Bretschneider, Judy G. and Mc Coy, Norman L., 1988 Sexual interest and behaviour in healthy 80 to 102 year olds, *Archives of Sexual Behaviour*, 17(2) pp 109-129.

Bridenstine, Janet K. and Quattrochi-Tubin, Susan, 1986, Subjective emotional responses in relation to the process of aging, *Activities, Adaptation and Aging*, 9(1), pp 25-31.

Brink, T.L., 1979, *Geriatric psychotherapy*, Human Science Press, New York.

Broady, M., Elaine, 1978, The aging of the family, *The Annals of the American Academy of Political and Social Sciences*, 438, pp 13-27.

———, 1981, women in middle and family help to older people, *The Gerontologist* 21(5), pp 471-475.

———, 1986, Filial care of the elderly and changing roles of women (and men), *Journal of Geriatric Psychiatry*, 19(2), pp 175-201.

Bromley, D.B., 1970, An approach to theory construction in the psychology of development and aging, *In* L.R. Goulet and P.B. Baltes, eds., *Life span developmental psychology : Theory and research*, Academic Press, New York.

———, 1974, *The psychology of human aging*, 2nd ed., Penguin Books, Baltimore.

Brown, C.W., and Harris, T., 1978, *Social origins of depression*, Tavistock, London.

Brown, Pat, 1982, *The other side of growing older*, The Macmillan Press Ltd., London.

Buhler, C., 1962, Genetic aspects of self, *Annals of the New York Academy of Sciences*, 96, pp 730-764.

Burkee, J.L., 1981, Young children's perception and attitudes of older adults, *The International Journal of Aging and Human Development*, 14(3), pp 86-89.

Burnside, I.M., 1980, Symptomatic behaviours in the elderly, *In* J.E. Birren and R.B. Sloane, eds., *Handbook of mental health and aging*, Prentice-Hall, Englewood Cliffs, N.J.

Busse, E.W. and Blazer, D., 1980, The theories and processes of aging, *In* E.W. Busse, and D.G. Blazer, eds., *Handbook of geriatric psychiatry*, Van Nostrand Reinhold, New York.

——— and Pfeiffer, E., eds., 1973, *Mental illness in later life*, American Psychiatric Association, Washington, D.C.

Butler, R., 1963, The life review : An interpretation of reminiscence in the aged, *Psychiatry : Journal for the study of Interpersonal Processes*, 26, pp 65-76.

Butler, R.N. and Lewis, M.I., 1977, *Aging and mental health*, C. V., Mosby, St. Louis, MO.

Bjorkstan, J., 1974, Crosslinkage and the aging process, *In* M. Rockstein, M.L. Sussman, and J. Chesky, eds., *Theoretical aspects of aging*, Academic Press, New York.

Calasanti, Toni M. and Bonanno, Alessandro, 1986, The social creation of dependence, dependency ratios, and the elderly in the United States : A critical analysis, *Social Science and Medicine*, 23(12), pp 1229-1236.

Cameron, P., 1967, Ego strength and happiness of the aged, *Journal of Gerontology*, 22(2), pp 199-202.

———, 1967, Introversion and egocentricity among the aged, *Journal of Gerontology*, 22(4), pp 465-468.

———, 1972, Stereotypes about generational fun and happiness Vs self-appraised fun and happiness, *Gerontologist*, 2, pp 120-123.

———, 1975, Mood, as an indicant of happiness, age, sex, social class and situational differences, *Journal of Gerontology*, 30, pp 216-224.

Campione, Wendy A., 1987, The married woman's retirement decision : A methodological comparison, *Journal of Gerontology* 42(4), pp 381-386.

Cappeliez, Philippe and Blanchet, Diane, 1986, Strategies of the elderly in coping with depressive feelings, *Canadian Journal on Aging*, 5(2), pp 125-134.

Canestrari, R.E., Jr., 1963, Paced and self-paced learning in young and elderly adults, *Journal of Gerontology*, 18, pp 165-168.

Cardea, Jane, M. and Tynan, Concetta M., 1987, Home safety and health : A quality of life issue for the elderly, *Lifestyles*, 8(3-4), pp 106-115.

Carp, Frances M. and Christensen, David L., 1986, Older women living alone : Technical environmental assessment of psychological well-being, *Research on Aging*, 8(3), pp 407-425.

Carpenter, J.O. and Wylie, C.M., 1974, On aging, dying and denying, *Public Health Reports*, 89, pp 403-407.

Cason, S. and Dean, L.R., 1963, A note on anger and aggression in old age, *Journal of Gerontology*, 18(3), pp 283-285.

Caven, R.S., 1962, Self and role in adjustment during old age, *In* A.M. Rose, ed., *Human behaviour and social processes*, Houghton Mifflin, Boston.

Chapell, N.L., 1983, Informal support networks among the elderly, *Research on Aging*, 5(1), pp 77-79.

Chanana, H.B. and Talwar, P.P., 1986, Implication of demographic goals in 2000 A.D. for aging population in India, *Health and Population*, 9(2), pp 67-79.

Chandra, Dave, 1983, *Some psycho-social aspects of aging*, Paper presented at the National Seminar on Psycho-social Aspect of Aging, June, Tirupati.

Chandrasekariah, K., 1985, *Problems and issues in aging—A sociological analysis*, Paper submitted to the International Seminar on population Aging in India, February, Trivandrum.

Chandrike, P. and Anatharamah, R.N., 1982, Life changes and adjustment in old age, *Journal of Psychological Researches*, 26, pp 137-141.

Chaneles, Sol, 1987, Growing old behind bars, *Psychology Today*, 21(10), pp 46-51.

Chauhan, N.S. and Tiwari, G.P., 1972, *Guide to using Frustration Test*, Agra Psychological Cell, Agra.

Chellam, Raju, 1982, Science of gerontology, *Economic Times* (Magazine), May 30, p 4, col 5-8.

Clarke, Juanne, 1987, The paradoxical effects of aging on health, *Journal of Gerontological Social Work*, 10(3-4), pp 3-20.

Cochran, C.D. and Hale, W.D., 1984, Gender differences in the relationship between health and psychological distress in the elderly, *Clinical Gerontologist*, 3(1), pp 62-64.

Cohen, D. and Dunner, D., 1980, The assessment of cognitive dysfunction in dementing illness, *In* J.O. Cole and J.E. Barrett, eds., *Psychopathology in the aged*, Raven Press, New York.

Cohen, Carl, I., Teresi, Jeanne, Holmes, Dougles and Roth, Eric, 1988, Survival strategies of older homeless man, *Gerontologist*, 28(1), pp 58-65.

Cohen, G.D., 1980, Prospects for mental health and aging, *In* J.E. Birren, and R.B. Sloane, eds., *Handbook of mental health and aging*, Prentice-Hall, Englewood Cliffe, N.J.

Cohen, J. and Hoberman, I., 1983, Positive events and social supports buffers of life change and stress, *Journal of Applied Social Psychology*, 13, pp 99-125.

Cole, J.O., and Barrett, J.E., 1980, *Psychopathology in the aged*, Raven Press, New York.

Cole, Kenneth D. and Mc Connaha, Debra L., 1986, Understanding and interacting with older patients, *Journal of the American Optometric Association*. 57(2), pp 920-925.

Colsher, Patricia L., Dorfman, Lorraine T. and Wallace, Robert, B., 1988, Specific health conditions and work-retirement status among the elderly, *Journal of Applied Gerontology*, 7(4), pp 485-503.

Comalli, P.E.; Jr., 1980, Life-span changes in visual perception, *In* L.R. Goulet and P.B. Baltes, eds., *Life-span developmental psychology : Research and theory*, Academic Press, New York.

Comfort, Alex, 1985, Geriatric medicine in India, *Journal of Indian Anthropological Society*, 20(3), pp 284-286.

Connidis, Ingrid A., 1989, Siblings as friends in later life, *American Behavioural Scientist*, 31(1), pp 81-93.

Conrad, C.C., 1976, When you're young at heart, *Aging*, 4(258), pp 11-13.

Conway, Pat, 1988, Losses and grief in old age,, *Social Casework*, 69(9), pp 541-549.

Coob, S., 1976, Social support as moderator of life stress, *Psychosomatic Medicine*, 38, pp 300-314.

Coombs, A.W. and Snygg, D., 1959, *Individual behaviour : A perceptual approach to behaviour*, Harper and Row Publishers, New York.

Corbin, David E., Metal-Corbin, Josie and Barg Cherie, 1989, Teaching about aging in the elementary school : A one-year follow up, *Educational Gerontology*, 15(1), pp 103-110.

Corso, J.F., 1976, Presbycusis as a complicating factor in evaluating noise-induced hearing loss, *In* D. Henderson, R.P. Hamernik, D.S. Dasanjh, and J.H. Mills, eds., *Effects of noise on hearing*, Raven Press, New York.

——, 1977, Auditory perception and communication, *In* J.E. Birren and K.W. Schaie, eds., *Handbook of the psychology of aging*, Van Nostrand Reinhold, New York.

Costa, F. and McCrae, B., 1975, Age differences in personality structure, *Journal of Gerontology*, 31(5), pp 564-570.

Costa, P.T., McCrae, R.R. and Arenberg, D., 1980, Enduring dispositions in adult males, *Journal of Personality and Social Psychology*, 38, pp 793-900.

Coupland, Nikolas, Coupland, Justine, Giles, Howard, Henwood, Karne *et al*, 1988, Elderly self-disclosure : Interactional and intergroup issues, *Language and Communication*, 8(2), pp 109-133.

Covey, Herbert C., 1989, Perceptions and attitudes toward sexuality of the elderly during the Middle Ages, *Gerontologist*, 29(1), pp 93-100.

Cox, H., 1984, *Later life : The realities of aging*, Prentice-Hall, Inc., New Jersey.

Cox, Harold G., 1990, Roles for aged individuals in post-industrial societies, *International Journal of Aging and Human Development*, 30(1), pp 55-62.

Craik, F.I.M., 1977, Age differences in human memory, *In* J.E. Birren and K.W. Schaie, eds., *Handbook of the psychology of aging*, Van Nostrand Reinhold, New York.

Craik, F.J., 1965, *Age differences in confidence and secondary processes*, Ph.D. Thesis, University of Boston, Boston.

Crandall, R.C., 1980, *Gerontology : A behavioural science approach*, Addison-Wesley Publishing Company, California.

Creasey, Gary L., Myers, Barbara J., Epperson, Mary J. and Taylor, John, 1989, Grand-children of grand-parents with Alzheimer's disease : Perceptions of grandparents, family environment, and the elderly, *Merrill-Palmer Quarterly*, 35(2), pp 227-237.

Crooke, James W., Myers, Kathleen, M. and Singh, Abe, 1988, The fears expressed by elderly men and women : A lifespan approach, *International Journal of Aging and Human Development*, 26(2), pp 139-146.

Cruikshank , Nelson, H., 1980, The greying of America, *Journal of Social Welfare*, 27(4), pp 14-15.

Cumming, E. and Henry, W.E., 1961, *Growing old*, Basic Books, New York.

Cunningham, W.R. and Birren, J.E., 1976, Age changes in human abilities : A 28 year longitudinal study, *Developmental Psychology*, 12, pp 81-82.

Curtis, H.J. and Miller, K., 1971, Chromosome aberrations in liver cells of guinea pigs, *Journal of Gerontology*, 26, pp 292-294.

Cutler, N.E. and Harootyan, R.A., 1975, Demography of the aged, *In* Woodruff and J.E. Birren, eds., *Aging : Scientific perspective and social issues*, Van Nostrand Reinhold, New York.

Cutter, F., 1974, *Coming to terms with death*, Nelson-Hall, Chicago.

Czaja, S.J., 1975, Age differences in life satisfaction as a function of discrepancy between real and ideal self concept, *Experimental Aging Research*, 1(1), pp 115-121.

Dail, Paula W., 1988, Prime-time television portrayals of older adults in the context of family life, *Gerontologist*, 28(5), pp 700-706.

Datan, N. and Ginsberg, L.H., 1975, *Life-span developmental psychology : Normative life crises*, Academic Press, New York.

Datta, Ella, 1988, Growing old in young India, *Times of India*, (Sunday Review) September 17, p 1, col 1-8.

Davis, J.A., 1988, A student perspective on growing old, *Educational Gerontology*, 14(6), pp 525-537.

Davis, Maradee, A., Murphy, Suzanne, P. and Neuhaus, John M., 1988, Living arrangements and eating behaviours of older adults in the United States, *Journal of Gerontology*, 43(3), pp 96-98.

Davis, R., 1967, Social influence on the aspiration tendency of older people, *Journal of Gerontology*, 22(4), pp 510-516.

Davis, Richard H. and Westbrook, G. Jay, 1985, Television in the lives of the elderly : Attitudes and opinions, *Journal of Broadcasting and Electronic Media*, 29(2), pp 209-214.

de Beauvoir, S., 1966, *A very easy death*, G.P. Putnam's Sons, London.

de Beauvoir, Simone, 1985, *Old age*, Penguin Books, London.

Delong, A.J., 1970, The microspatial structure of the older person, *In* L.A. Pastalan and D.H. Carson, eds., *the spatial behaviour of older people*, University of Michigan Press, Ann Arbor.

Dennis, Helen, 1986, Retirement preparation programs : Issues in planning and selection, *Journal of Career Development*, 13(2), pp 30-38.

Denselow, Robin, 1984, The rising sun and the setting sun, *Times of India* (Sunday Review), January 1, p 5, col 1-8.

Depner, Charlene E. and Ingersoll-Dayton, Berit, 1988, Supportive relationships in later life, *Psychology and Aging*, 3(4), pp 348-357.

Desai, K.G. and Naik, R.D., 1970, *Problems of the retired people in Greater Bombay*, Tata Institute of Social Sciences, Bombay.

———, 1983, *Aging in India*, Tata Institute of Social Sciences, Bombay.

———, 1985, *Planning for retirement*, Paper submitted to the International Seminar on Population Aging in India, February, Trivandrum.

———, 1985, Situation of the aged in India, *Journal of Indian Anthropological Society*, 20(3), pp 201-209.

———, 1986, Age imprints more wrinkles on the mind than on the face, *Social Welfare*, 33(3), p 4-10.

De'Souza, Alfred, 1981, Aging among the urban poor : Theoretical and policy issues, *Economic Times*, July 5, p 4, col 1-4.

———, 1981, *The social organisation of aging among the urban poor*, Indian Social Institute, New Delhi.

——— and Fernandes, Walter, 1982, *Aging in South Asia : Theoretical issues and policy implications*, Indian Social Institute, New Delhi.

Deva, R.C., 1982, *Manual for Deva's social adjustment inventory,* National Psychological Corporation, Agra.

Devries, H.A., 1975, Physiology of exercise and aging, *In* D.S. Woodruff and J.E. Birren, eds., *Aging : Scientific perspectives and social issues,* Van Nostrand Reinhold, New York.

Dewit, David, J., Wister, Andrew V. and Burch, Thomas, K., 1988. Physical distance and social contact between elders and their adult children, *Research on Aging,* 10(1), pp 56-80.

Dhaon,, J.K., *et al,* 1983, Some bio-social characteristics of pensioners of Lucknow city, *Health and Population,* 6(2), pp 119-27.

Dharanendriah, A.S., Madgaonkar, J.S. and Dayal, N.M., 1983, *A study of adjustment of aged men and women to their day to day activities,* Paper submitted to the National Seminar on Psycho-Social Aspects of Aging, June, Tirupati.

Dhillon, P.K. and Goswami, A., 1983, Poverty and its psychological dimensions, *In,* M.G. Hussain, ed., *Psycho-ecological dimensions of poverty,* Manohar Book Services, New Delhi.

Dhumal, S.S., 1981. *Socio-psychological study of menopause,* Paper presented on the National Conference in Applied Psychology, December, Bombay.

Diamond, M.C., 1978, The aging brain : Some enlightening and optimistic results, *American Scientist,* 66, pp 66-71.

——, Rosenzweig, M.R., Bennett, E.L., Lindner, B. and Lyon, L., 1972, Effects of environmental enrichment and impoverishment on rat cerebral cortax, *Journal of Neurobiology,* 3, pp 47-64.

Die, Ann E., Steelbah, Wayne C. and Sherman, Ginny, D., 1987, Achievement motivation, achieving styles, and morale in the elderly, *Psychology and Aging,* 2(4), pp 407-408.

Dipti Oza, J., 1984, *The effect of old age, sex and socio-economic status on the adjustment problems,* Paper submitted to the 2nd National Conference on Aging of the AGI, November, Tirupati.

Dixit, S.A., 1984, *The effect of age and repression—sensitisation on depression,* Paper presented at the Twenty seventh annual Conference of Applied Psychology, May.

Dobrosky, Barbara, J. and Bishop, James M., 1986, Children's perceptions of old people, *Educational Gerontology,* 12(5), pp 429-439.

Doka, K.J., 1985, Adolescent attitudes and beliefs toward aging and the elderly, *The International Journal of Aging and Human Development,* 22(3), pp 173-187.

——, and Mertz, Mary E., 1988, The meaning and significance of great-grand-parenthood, *Gerontologist,* 28(2), pp 192-197.

Dollard, J. and Miller, N.E., 1950, *Personality and psychotherapy* McGraw-Hill, New York.

Doppelt, J.E. and Wallace, W.L., 1955, Standardisation of the Wechsler Adult Intelligence scale for older persons, *Journal of Abnormal and Social Psychology,* 51, pp 312-330.

Domino, George, 1986, Sleep in advanced age : A comparison of mexican American and Anglo American elderly, *Hispanic Journal of Behavioural Sciences,* 8(3), pp 259-273.

Dorfman, Lorraine T. and Hill, Elizabeth A., 1986. Rural housewives and retirement : Joint decision-making matters. *Family Relations : Journal of Applied Family and Child Studies,* 35(4), pp 507-514.

———, and Moffett, Mildred M., 1987, Retirement satisfaction in married and widowed rural women, *Gerontologist*, 27(2), pp 215-221.

Douglas, K. and Arenberg, D., 1978, Age changes, cohort differences, and cultural change on the Guilford-Zimmerman Temperament Survey, *Journal of Gerontology*, 33, pp 737-747.

Dowd, J.J., 1975, Aging as exchange : A preface to theory, *Journal of Gerontology*, 30, pp 584-594.

Dusek, J.B., 1977, *Adolescent development and behaviour*, Science Research Associates, Palo Alto, California.

Dwarka Pershad, 1983, *Some experiences on WAIS-R Verbal scale with aged cases*, Paper presented at the National Seminar on the Psycho-Social Asnects of Aging, Tirupati.

Eaton, W.W., 1978, Life events, social supports and psychiatric symptoms : A reanalysis of New Haven data, *Journal of Health and Social Behaviour*, 19, pp 230-234.

Edward, A.L., 1959, *Manual for Edwards Personal Preference schedule*, The Psychological Corporation, New York.

Edinberg, Mark A., 1985, *Mental health practice with the elderly*, Prentice Hall, Inc, New Jersey.

Eisdorfer, C., 1963, The WAIS performance of the aged : A retest evaluation, *Journal of Gerontology*, 18, pp 169-172.

———, 1980, Paranoia and Schizophrenic disorders in late life, *In* E.W. Busse and D. Blazer, eds., *Handbook of geriatric psychiatry*, Van Nostrand Reinhold, New York.

———, and Friedel, R.O., 1977, *Cognitive and emotional disturbances in the elderly*, Year Book Medical Publishers, New York.

———, and Lawton, M.P., 1973, *The psychology of adult development and aging*, American Psychiatric Association, Washington, D.C.

———, Nowlin, J. and Wilkie, F., 1970, Improvement of learning in the aged by modification of autonomic nervous system activity, *Science*, 170, pp 1327-1329.

———, and Stotsky, B.A., 1977, Intervention, treatment and rehabilitation of psychiatric disorders, *In* J. Birren and K.W. Schaie, eds., *Handbook of the psychology of aging*, Van Nostrand Reinhold, New York.

———, and Wilkie, F., 1977, Stress and disease aging and behaviour, *In* J.E. Birren and K.W. Schaie, eds., *Handbook of the psychology of aging*, Van Nostrand Reinhold, New York.

Engen, T., 1977, Taste and smell, *In* J.E. Birren and K.W. Schaie, eds., *Handbook of the psychology of aging*, Van Nostrand Reinhold, New York.

Erickson, R.P., 1963, Sensory neural patterns and gastation, *In* Y. Zotterman, eds., *Olfaction and taste*, Pergamon Press, Elmsford, New York.

Erikson, E.H., 1963, *Childhood and society*, W.W. Norton and Co., Inc, New York.

Estes, Corroll L., 1986, The politics of ageing in America, *Ageing and Society*, 6(2), pp 121-134.

Etholm, B. and Belal, A., Jr., 1974, Senile changes in the middle ear joints, *Annals of Otology, Rhinology, and Laryngology*, 83, pp 49-54.

Everitt, A.V. and Huang, C.Y., 1980, The hypothalamus, neuroendrine and autonomic nervous systems in aging, *In* J.E. Birren and R.B. Sloane, eds., *Handbook of mental health and aging*, Prentice-Hall, Englewood Cliffs, N.J.

Featherman, David L. and Petersen, Trond, 1986, Markers of aging : Modeling the clocks that time us, *Research on aging*, 8(3), pp 339-365.

Federal Council on Aging, 1978, *The frail elderly*, Federal Council on Aging, Washington, D.C.

Feifel, Herman and Strack, Stephen, 1987, Old is old is old? *Psychology and Aging*, 2(4), pp 409-412.

Finch, C.E. and Hayflick, L., 1977, *Handbook of the biology of aging*, Van Nostrand Reinhold, New York.

Fiske, M., 1961, Geriatric mental illness : Methodologic and social aspects, *Geriatrics*, 16, pp 306-310.

——, 1980, Tasks and crises of the second half of life : The interrelationship of commitment, coping and adaptation, *In* J.E. Birren and R.B. Sloane, eds., *Handbook of mental health and aging*, Prentice-Hall, Englewood Cliff, N.J.

Flavell, J.H., 1970, Cognitive changes in adulthood, *In* L.R. Goulet and P.B. Baltes, eds., *Life-span development psychology : Research and theory*, Academic Press, New York.

Foner, A., 1975, Age in society : Structure and change, *American Behavioural Scientist*, 2, pp 144-165.

Fountain, Douglas E., 1986, How to assimilate the elderly into your parish : The effects of alienation of church attendance, *Journal of Religion and Aging*. 2(3), pp 45-55.

Foulds, G.A., and Ravens, J.C., 1948, Normal changes in the mental abilities of adults in age advances, *Journal of Mental Science*, 94, pp 133-142.

Fozard, J.L., 1980, The time of remembering, *In* L. Poon, ed., *Aging in the 1980 : Psychological* issues, American Psychological Association, Washington, D.C.

——, and Costa, P.T., 1984, Age differences in memory and decision making in relation to personality, abilities and endocrine function : Implications for clinical practice and health planning policy, *In* M. Marios, ed., *Aging : A challenge for science and social policy*, Oxford University Press, London.

——, Wolf, E., Bell, B., Mcfarland, R.A. and Podolsky, S., 1977, Visual perception and communication, *In*, J.E. Birren and K.W. Schaie, eds., *Handbook of the psychology of aging*, Van Nostrand Reinhold, New York.

Friedman, H. and Garnick, T., 1962, Adjustment to retirement, *American handbook of psychiatry*, Van Nostrand Reinhold, New York.

Fries, J.F. and Crapo, L.M., 1981, *Vitality and aging*, W.H. Freeman and Company, San Francisco.

Fry, P.S., 1984, Development of a Geriatric Scale of Hopelessness : Implications for counselling and intervention with the depressed elderly, *Journal of Counselling Psychology*, 31(3), pp 322-331.

Furstenbery, Anne-Linda, 1988, Expectations about outcome following hip fracture among older people, *Social Work in Health Care*, 11(4), pp 33-47.

Gail, S., 1974, Cateh-30 and other predictable crises of growing up adult, *New York Magazine*, February 18, p 36.

Gaitz, C.M. and Varner, R.V., 1980, Preventive aspects of mental illness in late life, *In*, J.E. Birren and R.B. Sloane, eds., *Handbook of mental health of aging*, Prentice-Hall, Englewood Cliffs, N.J.

Galloway, G.G., 1956, The philosophy of *religion*, T and T Clark, Edinberg.

Galper, A. and Seefeldt, C., 1980, The child's concept of age and aging, *The International Journal of Aging and Human Development*, 12(2), pp 149-153.

Gans, H., 1964, *The urban villagers : Group and class in the life of Italian-Americans*, Free Press, New York.

Garner, H.H., 1977, Somatopsychic concepts, *In* R.P. Marinell and A.E. Dellorto, eds., *The Psychological and social impact of physical disability*, Springer, New York.

Garg, B.S. *et al*, 1980, To be aged, sick and disabled in a city, *Journal of Social Welfare*, 27(4), pp 6-8.

Gatz. M., Smyer, M.A. and Lawton, M.P., 1980, The mental health system and the older adult, *In* L.W. Poon, ed., *Aging in the 1980s : Psychological issues*, American Psychological Association, Washington, D.C.

Geddie, W., 1964, *Chamber's Twentieth Century Dictionary*, W and R Chamber, Ltd., London.

Gfellner, Barbara M. and Finlayson, Coleen, 1988, Loneliness, personality and well-being in older widows, *Perceptual and Motor Skills*, 67(1), pp 143-146.

Gekoski, William L. and Knox, V. Jane, 1990, Ageism or healthisum? Perceptions based on age and health status, *Journal of Aging and Health*, 2(1), pp 15-27.

Geldard, F.A., 1966, *The human senses*, John Wiley and Sons, New York.

Gelfand, D.E. and Olsen, J.K., 1980, *The aging network : Programe and Services*, Springer, New York.

George, L.K., 1978, The impact of personality and social status factors upon levels of activity and psychological well-being, *Journal of Gerontology*, 33(6), pp 840-847.

Ghosal, B.C., 1982, Care of the aged, *Yojana*, 26(10), pp 9-10.

———, 1982, The gentle art of ageing, *Economic Times* (Magazine), May 30, p 5, col 4-8.

———, 1982, Facts about old persons, *Yojana*, 26(10), pp 7-8.

Gilbert, J.G., 1941, Memory loss in senescence, *Journal of Abnormal and Social Psychology*, 36, pp 73-86.

Glass, J. Conrad, Mustain, R. David and Carter, Lois R., 1986, Knowledge and attitudes of health-care providers towards sexuality in the institutionalised elderly, *Educational Gerontology*, 12(5), pp 465-475.

Glock, C.Y., 1962, On the study of religious commitment, *Religious Education*, 57, pp 98-110.

Golant, Stephen M., 1987, Residential moves by elderly persons to U.S. central cities, suburbs and rural areas, *Journal of Gerontology*, 42(5), pp 534-539.

Gold, Deborah T., 1989, Sibling relationship in old age : A typology, *International Journal of Aging and Human Development*, 28(1), pp 37-51.

Gomatinayagam, V., 1987, The problems of the aged in Urban India — A study in the Union Territory of Pondicherry, *Indian Journal of Community Guidance Service*, 4(1), pp 71-88.

Gomathi, S., Sitharathan, T. and Anantharamah, R.N., 1981, A study of institutionalised and non-institutionalised older people, *Journal of Psychological Researches*, 25, pp 125-128.

Gore, H.S., 1981, Health care of the elderly, *Indian Journal of Social Work*, 42(1), pp 87-89.

Gotestam, K.W., 1980, Behavioural and dynamic psychotherapy with the elderly, *In* J.E. Birren and R.B. Sloane, eds., *Handbook of mental health and aging*, Prentice-Hall, Englewood Cliffs, N.J.

Goulet, L.R. and Baites, P.B., 1970, *Life span developmental psychology : Research and theory*, Academic Press, New York.

Graham, Ian D. and Baker, Paul M., 1989, Status, age and gender : Perceptions of old and young people, *Canadian Journal of Aging*, 8(3), pp 255-267.

Granick, S. and Patterson, R.D., 1971, *Human aging, II : An 11 year biomedical and behavioural study,* Government Printing Office, Washington, D.C.

Grau, Lois, 1988, Mental health and older women, *Women and Health,* 14(3-4), pp 75-91.

Gray, Denis and Calsyn, Robert, J., 1989, The relationship of stress and social support to life satisfaction : Age effects, *Journal of Community Psychology,* 17(3), pp 214-219.

Gray, R.M. and Moberg, D.O., 1970, The church and the older person, *In* A.M. Hoffman, ed., *The daily needs and interests of older persons,* Charles C. Thomas Press, Springfield.

Grotjohn, M., 1955, Analytic therapy with the elderly, *Psychoanalytic Review,* 42, pp 419-427.

Gruenberg, E.W., 1967, The social breakdown-Some origins, *American Journal of Psychiatry,* 123, pp 481-489.

Guarnera, Sharvan and Williams, Robert L., 1987, Optimism and locus of control for health and affiliation among elderly adults, *Journal of Gerontology,* 42(6), pp 594-595.

Gupta, S.P., 1988, The aged parents : Where will they go ? *Social Welfare,* 35(5), August, pp 28-31.

Gurland, B.J., 1980, The assessment of the mental health status of older adults, *In* J.E. Birren and R.B. Sloane, eds., *Handbook of mental health and aging,* Prentice Hall, Englewood Cliffs, N.J.

Gutmann, D.L., 1964, An exploration of ego configurations in middle and later life, *In* B.L. Neugarton, *et al. Personality in middle and late life,* Atherton Press, New York.

———, 1971, Dependency, illness and survival among Navajo men *In* E. Palmore and F.C. Jeffers, eds., *Predication of life-span,* D.C., heath, Lexington, Massachusetts.

———, 1975, Parentalhood : A key to the comparative study of the life cycle, *In* N. Datan and L. Ginsberg, eds., *Life-span developmental psychology : Normative life crises,* Academic Press, New York.

———, 1977, The cross-cultural perspective : Notes towards a comparative psychology of aging, *In* J.E. Birren and K.W. Schaie, eds., *Handbook of the Psychology of aging,* Van Nostrand Reinhold, New York.

Haber, Carole, 1983, *Beyond sixty-five : The dilemma of old age in America's past,* Cambridge University Press London Cambridge.

Habot, B. and Libow, L., 1980, The interrelationship of mental and physical status and its assessment in the older adult : Mind-body interaction, *In* J.E. Birren and R.B. Sloane, eds., *The handbook of mental health and aging,* Prentice-Hall, Englewood Cliffs, N.J.

Hale, W.D. and Cochran, C.D., 1983, Sex differences in patterns of sex reported psychopathology in the married elderly, *Journal of Clinical Psychology,* 39(5), pp 647-650.

Hall, Beverly A., 1984, *Mental health and the elderly,* Grune and Stratton, Inc., New York.

Hann, Judith, 1984, Is there a life after wrinkles ? *Times of India,* Sunday Review, June 10, p III, Col 1-4.

Hansson, Robert O., 1986, Relational competence, relationship and adjustment in old age, *Journal of Personality and Social Psychology,* 50(5), pp 1050-1058.

Hansson, Robert O. and Remondet, Jacqueline H., 1988, Old age and widowhood : Issue of personal control and independence, *Journal of Social Issues,* 44(3), pp 59-174.

Harris, Julainne and Fiedler, Charles M., 1988, Preadolescent attitudes towards the elderly : An analysis of race, gender and contract variables, *Adolescence,* 23(90), pp 335-340.

Harris, L., 1975, *The myth and realities of aging in America,* National Council on Aging, Washington, D.C.

Harris, Marry B., Page, Polly and Begay, Cynthia, 1988, Attitude towards aging in a South-Western Sample : Effects of ethnicity, age and sex, *Psychological Reports,* 62(3), pp 735-746.

Hartford, M.E., 1980, The use of group methods for work with the aged, *In* J.E. Birren and R.B. Sloane, eds., *Handbook of mental health and aging,* Prentice-Hall, Englewood Cliffs, N.J.

Hartley, J.T., Harker, J.O. and Walsh, D.A., 1980, Contemporary issues and new directions in adult development of learning and memory, *In* L.W. Poon, ed., *Aging in the 1980s : Psychological issues,* American Psychological Association, Washington, D.C.

Harwood, E. and Naylor, G.F.K., 1969, Recall and recognition in elderly and young subjects, *Australian Journal of Psychology,* 21, pp 251-257.

Havighurst, R.J., 1952, Roles and status of older people, *In* A.I. Lansing, ed., *Cowdry's problems of aging,* Williams and Wilkins Company, Baltimore.

———, 1957, The social competence of middle-aged people, *Genetic Psychology Monographs,* 56, pp 297-375.

———, 1961, Successful aging, *The Gerontologist,* 1, pp 8-13.

———, 1968, Personality and patterns of aging, *The Gerontologist,* 8, pp 20-23.

———, 1973, History of developmental psychology : Socialisation and personality development through the life span, *In* P.B. Baltes and K.W. Schaie, eds., *Life-span developmental psychology : Personality and socialisation,* Academic Press, New York.

Hawkins, Charles H., 1989, Residents power in retirement homes, *Journal of Housing for the Elderly,* 5(2), pp 51-63.

Hawley, Peggy J. and Klanber, Melville R., 1988, Health practices and perceptions of social support in persons over age sixty, *Journal of Applied Gerontology,* 7(2), pp 205-230.

Hayflick, L., 1977, The cellular basis for biological aging, *In* C.E. Finch and L. Hayflick, eds., *Handbook of the biology of aging,* Academic Press, New York.

Healy, Judith M., 1988, Elderly couples and the division of household tasks, *Australian Journal of Sex, Marriage and Family,* 9(4), pp 203-214.

Heller, Peter S., 1986, *Aging and social expenditure in the major industrial countries, 1980-2025,* IMF, Washington.

Hema Krishnan, 1983, Too old to live? *Time of India,* Sunday Review, July 24, p 6, Col 1-4.

Hemalatha, P., and Suryanarayana, M., 1984, *Study of the aged in Rural and Urban settings,* Paper presented at the 2nd National Conference on Aging of the AGI, Tirupati.

Hemant Kumar, 1986, Health status of the aged in a Uttar Pradesh village, *Social Welfare,* 33(3), pp 19-23.

Hendricks, Jon., Calasanti, Toni M. and Turner, Howard B., 1988, Foodways of the elderly : Social research considerations, *American Behavioural Scientist,* 32(1) pp 61-83.

Herbert, Lisa and Teague, Michael L., 1988-89, Exercise adherence and older adults : A theoretical perspective, *Activities, Adaptation and Aging,* 13(1-2), pp 91-105.

Herr, J.J. and Weakland, J.H., 1979, *Counseling elders and their families,* Springer, New York.

Hickey, T., 1980, *Health and aging,* Brooks/Cole, Monterey, California.

——— and Kalish, R.A., 1968, Children's perception of the elderly, *Journal of Genetic Psychology,* 112, pp 227-235.

———; Rakowski, William and Julius, Mara, 1988, Preventive health practices among older men and women, *Research on Aging,* 10(3), pp 315-328.

Hicks, R., Funkenstein, H.H., Davis J.M., and Dysken, M.W., 1980, Geriatric psychopharmacology, *In* J.E. Birren and R.B., Sloane, eds., *Handbook of mental health and aging,* Prentice-Hall, Englewood Cliffs, N.J.

Hinton, I., 1967, *Dying,* Penguin Books, Baltimore.

Hoch, Carolyn C., Reynolds, Charles F., Kupfer, David J., Houck, Patricia R. *et al.*, 1987, The superior sleep of healthy elderly nuns, *International Journal of Aging and Human Development,* 25(1), pp 1-9.

Holahan, Carole K., 1988, Relation of life goals at age 70 to activity participation and health and psychological well-being among Terman's gifted men and women, *Psychology and Aging* 3(3), pp 286-291.

Holcomb, W.L., 1975, Spiritual crises among the aged, *In* M.G. Spencer and C.J., Dorr, eds., *Understanding aging : A multidisciplinary approach,* Appleton Century-Crofts, New York.

Holmes, T.H. and Rahe, R.H., 1967, The Social Readjustment Rating Scale *Journal of Psychosomatic Research,* 11, pp 213-218.

Horn, J.L., 1970, Organisation of data on life span development of human abilities, *In* L.R. Goulet and P.B. Baltes, eds., *Life-span developmental psychology : Research and theory,* Academic Press, New York.

——— and Donaldson, G., 1976, On the myth of intellectual decline in adulthood, *American Psychologist,* 31, pp 701-719.

———, 1980, Cognitive development II : Adulthood development of human abilities, *In* O.G. Brim and J. Kagan, eds., *Constancy and change in human development : A volume of review essays,* Harvard University Press, Cambridge, Massachusetts.

Horney, K., 1937, *The neurotic personality of our times,* Norton, New York.

Hornykiewicz, O., 1975, Parkinson's disease and its chemotherapy, *Biochemical Pharmacology,* 24, pp 1064-1065.

Hubert, Ryan J. and Lens, Wiley, 1988, Time and self-identify in later life, *International Journal of Aging and Human Development,* 27(4), pp 293-303.

Hultsch, D.F. and Deutsch, F., 1981, *Adult development and aging,* McGraw-Hill, New York.

Indira, Jai Prakash, 1983, *Age related changes in marital satisfaction,* Paper presented at the National Seminar on Psycho-Social Aspects of aging, June, Tirupati.

——— and Harini Kumari, R., 1984, *Age differences in psychological morbidity and life events,* Paper presented at the 2nd National Conference on Aging of the AC November, Tirupati.

——— and Murthy, V.N., 1981, Psychiatric morbidity and the menopause, *In Journal of Psychiatry,* 23, pp 242-246.

———, 1982, Menopausal Symptoms in Indian women, *Journal of Personality and Group Behaviour,* 2, pp 54-58.

Indira, S.N., and Murthy, V.N., 1980 a, A factor analytical study of menopausal symptoms in middle aged women, *Indian Journal of Clinical Psychology,* 7, pp 125-128.

———, 1980b, Nature of Psychiatric disturbances in menopausal women, *Journal of clinical Psychology,* 7, pp 7-11.

Ingvar, D., Brun, A., Johansson L. and Samuelsson, S.M., 1978, Survival after severe cerebral anoxia with destruction of the cerebral cortex : The apallic syndrome, *In* J. Korein, ed., Brain death : International medical and social issues, *Annals of the New York Academy of Sciences,* 315, pp 184-214.

Insel, P.M. and Moose, R.H., 1974, *Health and the social environment,* D.C. Heath, Lexington, Mass.

Isaacs, B., 1977, comprehensive care of the cognitively imaired elderly, *In* C. Eisdorfer and R.O. Freidel, eds., *cognitive and emotional disturbance in the elderly,* Year Book Medical Publishers, Chicago.

Isaacs, Leora W. and Bearison, David J., 1986, The development of children's prejudice against the aged, *International Journal of Aging and Human Development,* 23(3), pp 175-194.

Ivester, C. and King, K., 1977, Attitudes of adolescents towards the aged, *the Gerontologist,* 17, pp 85-89.

Jackson, Linda A. and Sullivan, Linda A., 1988, Age stereotype disconfirming information and evaluations of old people, *Journal of Social Psychology,* 128(6), pp 721-729.

Jackson, M. and Wood, J.L., 1976, *Aging in America : Implication for the black aged,* National Council on the Aging, Washington, D.C.

Jacobs, E.A., Alvis, H.J. and Small, S.M., 1972, Hyperoxygenation : A central nervous system activator ? *Journal of Geriatric Psychiatry,* 5, pp 107-121.

Jacobs, J., 1974, *Fun city : An ethnographic study of retirement community,* Holt, Rinehart and Winston, Inc., New York.

Jahan, M. and Hassan, M., 1987, A comparative study of stressfulness of certain life events for Indians and Americans, *Advances in Psychology,* 2(1), pp 1-7.

Jamuna, D., 1984 a, *A study of some factors related to adjustment of middle aged and older women,* Doctoral Dissertation, S.V. University, Tirupati.

———, 1984 b, *Role activity and general adjustment of middle aged and older women,* Paper presented at the 2nd National Conference on Aging of the AGI, Tirupati.

———, 1985, Self-concept among middle aged and older women, *Journal of the Indian Academy of Applied Psychology,* 11, pp 16-20.

———, 1987 Self and care givers perceptions of needs and problems of elderly women : A case for guidance and counselling, *Indian Journal of Community Guidance Service,* 4(3), pp 25-31.

——— and Ramamurti, P.V., 1984 c, Age, adjustment and husband-wife communication of middle aged and older women, *Journal of Psychological Research,* 28, pp 145-147.

——— and Ramamurti, Sujatha., 1984 d, Coronary prone behaviour as a function of age. *Psychological Studies,* 29, pp 165-169.

Jarvik, L.F. and Blum, J.E., 1971, Cognitive decline as predictors of mortality in twin pairs : A twenty-year longitudinal study of aging, *In* E. Palmore and F.C. Jeffers, eds., *Prediction of lifespan,* D.C. Heath, Lexington, Mass.

Jarvik, L.F. and Falek, A., 1963, Intellectual stability and survival in the aged, *Journal of Gerontology,* 18, pp 173-176.

Joe, V.C., 1971, A review of internal-external control construct as a personality variable, *Psychological Reports,* 28, pp 619-640.

Johnson, B., 1979, Impediments to family support to depressed elderly, *The Gerontologist,* 19, pp 5-6.

Johnson, Robert J., Lund, Dale A. and Diamond, Margaret F., 1986, Stress, self esteem and coping during bereavement among the elderly, *Social Psychology Quarterly,* 49(3). pp 273-279.

Johoda, M., 1958, *Current concepts of positive mental health,* Basic Books, New York.

Jones, H.E. and Conrad, H.S., 1933, The growth and decline of intelligence : A study of homogenous population between the ages of ten and sixty, *Genetic Psychology Monographs,* 13, pp 233-298.

Joseph, Joni C., 1988, Interaction between the old and the young, *Social welfare,* 35(6), September, pp 17-19+.

Kahl, J.A., 1957, *The American class structure,* Rinehart, New York.

Kahn R.L., 1977, Perspectives in the evaluation of psychological mental health programmes for the aged, *In* W.D. Gentry, ed. *Geropsychology : A model of training and clinical services,* Ballinger, Cambridge, Massachusetts.

——— and Miller, N.E., 1978, Adaptational factors in memory function in the aged, *Experimental Aging Research,* 4, pp 273-290.

Kalish, R.A., 1969, *The dependencies of old people,* University of Michigan Division of Gerontology, *Ann Arbor, Michigan.*

———, 1970, The onset of the dying process, *Omega,* 1, pp 57-59.

———, 1975, *Late adulthood : Perspectives on human development,* Brooks and Cole, Monterey, California,

———, 1976, Death and dying in social context, *In* Robert, B. and Ethal, Shanas, ed., *Handbook of aging and social sciences,* Behavioural Publication, Inc., New York.

———, 1979, The new ageism and the failure models : a polemic, *The Gerontologist,* 19(4), pp 398-402.

——— and Reynolds, D.K., 1976, *Death and ethnicity : A psychocultural study,* University of Southern California Press, Los Angeles.

Kamerman, Jack B., 1988, *Death in the midst of life,* Prentice — Hall, Englewood Cliffs, New Jersey.

Kanbargi, Romesh., 1985, Old age security and fertility behaviour : Some research issues, *Journal of Indian Anthropological Society,* 20(3), pp 226-237.

Kansal, Kamla, 188, Geriatrics and homeopathy, *Yojana,* 32(17), September 16, pp 27-29.

Kaplan, Giora, Barell, Vita, and Luksy, Ayala, 1988, Subjective state of health and survival in elderly adults, *Journals of Gerontology,* 43(4) pp 114-120.

Kaplan, O.J., 1940, *Studies in the psychopathology of later life,* University of California Press, Berkeley.

Kapnick, P.L., 1978, Organic treatment of the elderly, *In* M. Storandt, I. Siegler and M.F. Elias, eds., *Clinical psychology of aging,* Plenum Press, New York.

Karp, David A., 1988, A decade of reminders : Changing age consciousness between fifty and sixty years old, *Gerontologist,* 28(6), pp 727-738.

Kart, C.S., Metress, E.S. and Metress, J.F., 1978, *Aging and health : Biologic and social perspectives,* Addison-wesley, Menlo Park, California.

Kasl, S.V., 1974, The health belief model and behaviour related to chronic illness, *Health Education Monographs,* 2, pp 433-454.

Kastenbaum, R., 1976, The realm of death : An emerging area in psychological research, *Journal of Human Relations*, 13, pp 538-552.

———, 1975, Is death a life crisis ? On the confrontation with death in theory and practice, *In* N. Datan and L. Ginsberg. eds., *Life-span developmental psychology : Normative life crises*, Academic Press, New York.

———, 1977, *Death, society and human experience*, C.V. Mosby, St. Louis.

———, 1978, Personality theory, therapeutic approaches and the elderly client, *In* M. Storandt, I. Siegler and M.F. Elias, eds., *The clinical psychology of aging*, Plenum Press, New York.

———, 1979, Growing old : Years of fulfillment, *In* L. Kristal, ed., *Life cycle series* Harper and Row, New York.

——— and Aisenberg. R., 1972, *The Psychology of death*, Springer, New York.

Katwal, Indira, 1984, Health problems of the aged, *Economic Times*, January 22, p 3, col 1-8.

Kaufman, Allan V. and Adams, James P., 1987, Interaction and loneliness : A dimensional analysis of the social isolation of a sample of older southern adults, *Journal of Applied Gerontology*, 6(4), pp 389-404.

Kaufman, M.R., 1940, Old age and aging, *American Journal of Orthopsychiatry*, 10, pp 73-84.

Kausler, D.H., 1982, *Experimental psychology and human aging*, John Wiley and Sons, New York.

Keily, M.C. and Dudek, S.Z., 1977, Attitudes towards death in aging persons, *Psychiatric Journal of the University of Ottawa*, 2(4), pp 181-184.

Keith, Pat, M., 1986, The social context and resources of the unmarried in old age, *International Journal of Aging and Human Development*, 23(2), pp 81-96.

——— and Lorenz, Prederick O., 1989, Financial strain and health of unmarried older people, *Gerontologist*, 29(5), pp 684-691.

Kelkar, Vasundhara, 1974, *A psychological study of the problem of old age adjustment*, M.A. Dissertation, S.P. College, Pune.

Keller, J.W., Sherry, D. and Piotrowski, C., 1984, Perspectives on death : A developmental study, *Journal of Psychology*, 116(1), pp 137-142.

Keller, Mary L., Leventhal. Elaine A. and Larson, Barbara. 1984. Aging : The lived experience, *International Journal of Aging and Human Development*, 29(1), pp 67-82.

——— *et al* 1989, Beliefs about aging and illness in a community sample, *Research in Nursing and Health*, 12(4), pp 247-255.

Kelly, Lynn, E., Knox, V. Jane, Gekoski, William I. and Evans, Kathryn, M., 1987, Age-related humor as an indicator of attitudes and perceptions, *Journal of Social Psychology*, 127(3), pp 245-250.

Kendig, Hal L., Coles, Rita, Pittelkow, Yvonne, and Wilson, Sue, 1988, Confidants and family structure in old age, *Journals of Gerontology*, 43(2), pp 31-40.

Kenshalo, D.R., 1977, Age changes in touch, vibration, temperature, kinesthesis and pain sensitivity, *In* J.E. Birren and K.W. Schaie, eds., *Handbook of the psychology of aging*, Van Nostrand Reinhold, New York.

———, 1986, Somethetic sensitivity in young and elderly humans, *Journal of Gerontology*, 41(6), pp 732-742.

Kercher, Kyle, Kosloski, Karl D. and Normoyle, Janice, B., 1988, Reconsideration of fear of personal aging and subjective well-being in later life, *Journal of Gerontology*, 43(6), pp 170-172.

Khatoon, M., Hagen, M., Akhtar, S.S and Rizvi, R., 1984, *The psychological correlates of aging among Indian females*, Paper presented at the Ist National Conference of the AGI, October, Varanasi.

Kieffer, Jarold, A., 1986, Kicking the premature retirement habit, *Journal of Career Development*, 13(2), pp 39-51.

Kimmel. Douglas, C., 1988, Ageism, psychology, and public policy, *American Psychologist*, 43(3), pp 175-178.

Kirchman, Margaret, M. and Schulte, Kay, 1989, A study of morale in the elderly, *Physical and Occupational Therapy in Geriatrics*, 7(4), pp 29-41.

Kirikae, I., 1960, Auditory function in advanced age with reference to histological changes in the central auditory system, *International Audiology*, 8, pp 221-230.

Kir-Stimon, W., 1977, Counseling with the severely handicapped : Encounter and commitment, *In* R.P. Martinelli and A.E. Dell Orto, eds., *The psychological and social impact of physical disability*, Springer, New York.

Kite, Mary E. and Johnson, Blaire, T., 1988, Attitudes toward older and younger adults : A meta-analysis, *Psychology and Aging*, 3(3), pp 233-244.

Kivett, V.R., 1979, Religious motivation in middle age : Correlates and implications, *Journal of Gerontology*, 34(1), pp 106-115.

Kleemeier, R., 1962, Intellectual changes in the senium, *In proceedings of the social statistics section of the American Statistical Association*. American Statistical Association, Washington, D.C.

Kleiman, Michael B. (Tampa, Fla), 1983, *Social gerontology*, S. Karger Publishers, Inc., New York.

Knipscheer, Kees, 1987, Sociological research on age, aging and the aged in the Netherlands, *Tijdschrift Voor Gerontologie on Geriatrie*, 18(2), pp 130-138.

Koenig, Harold G., 1986, Depression and dysphoria among the elderly : Dispelling a myth, *Journal of Family Practice*, 23(4), pp 383-385.

——, 1988, Religious behaviours and death anxiety in later life, *Hospice Journal*, 4(1), pp 3-24.

——, George, Linda K. and Siegler, Ilene C., 1988, The use of religion and other emotion-regulating coping strategies among older adults, *Gerontologist*, 28(3), pp 303-310.

——, Kvalve, James N. and Ferrel, Carolyn, 1988, Religion and well-being in later life, *Gerontologist*, 28(1), pp 18-28.

Kohn, R.R., 1977, Heart and cardiovascular system, *In* C.E. Finch and L. Hayflick, eds., *Handbook of the biology of aging*, Van Nostrand Reinhold, New York.

Kopac, Catharine, A., Robertson-Tchabo, Elizabeth A. and Holt, Robert W., 1988, A study of the relationship between personal characteristics, life events, the Type A behaviour pattern, and well-being in older adults, *Psychological Reports*, 62(2), pp 667-671.

Koestenbaum, P., 1976, *Is there an answer to death* ? Prentice-Hall, Englewood Cliffs, N.J.

Kragie, Evelyn R., Gerstein, Martin and Lichtman, Marilyn, 1989, Do Americans plan for retirement ? Some recent trends, *Career Development Quarterly*, 37(3), pp 232-239.

Kramer, M., Taube, C.A. and Redick, R.W., 1973, Patterns of use of psychiatric facilities by the aged : Past, present and future, *In* Eisdorfer and M.P. Lawton, eds., *Psychology of adult development and aging*, American Psychiatric Association, Washington, D.C.

Krause, Daniel and Chapin, Rachel, 1987, An examination of attitudes about old age in a sample of elementary school children, *Gerontology and Geriatrics Education,* 7(3-4), pp 81-91.

———, Neal, 1986, Stress and sex differences in depressive symptoms among older adults, *Journal of Gerontology,* 41(6), pp 727-731.

———, 1986, Life stresses as correlates of depression in the adult, *Psychiatry Research,* 18(3), pp 227-237.

———, 1987, Chronic strain locus of control and distress in older adults, *Psychology and Aging,* 2(4), pp 374-382.

———, 1987, Satisfaction with social support and self rated health in older adults, *The Gerontologist,* 27(3), pp 301-308.

———, 1988, Positive life events and depressive symptoms in older adults, *Behavioural Medicine,* 14(3), pp 101-112.

Kremer, John F., 1988, Effects of negative information about aging on attitudes, *Educational Gerontology,* 14(1), pp 69-80.

Krosnick, Jon A. and Alwin, Duane, F., 1989, Aging and susceptibility to attitude change, *Journal of Personality and Social Psychology,* 57(3), pp 461-425.

Krout, John A., 1988, Rural versus urban differences in elderly parents contact with their children, *Gerontologist,* 28(2), pp 198-203.

Krug, S.E. and Laughlin, J.E., 1976, *The I P A T Depression Scale and manual,* Institute for personality and Ability Testing, Champaign, Illinois.

Kuber-Ross, E., 1969, *On death and dying,* Macmillan, New York.

———, 1975, *Death : The final stage of growth,* Prentice-Hall, Englewood Cliffs, N.J.

Kullai, Reddy L. and Ramamurti, P.V., 1988, Attitude towards aged and adjustment towards aging, *Journal of Psychological Researches,* 32(1-2), pp 82-84.

Kuppuswamy, E., 1962, *Socio-Economic Status Scale : manual* (Urban), Manasayan, Delhi.

Kunzru, Hrudayanatha B. and Reddy, Suryanarayana M., 1984, *Study of the aged in Tirupati, Chittor District, Andhra Pradesh,* Paper submitted to the 2nd National Conference on Aging of the AGI, November, Tirupati.

Kurlycheck, R.T. and Trepper, T.S., 1982, Accuracy of perception of attitude : An Intergenerational Investigation, *Perceptual and Motor Skills,* 54(1). pp 271-274

Kurup, V., 1982, Make evening life happy, *Patriot* (Magazine), August 1, p 1, col 1-5.

Kuypers, J.A. and Bengtson, V.L., 1973, Social breakdown and competence : A model of normal aging, *Human Development,* 16, pp 181-201.

Lachman, J.L. and Lachman, R., 1980, Age and the actualisation of world knowledge, *In,* L.W. Poon, J.L. Fozard, L.S. Cermak, D. Arenberg and L.W. Thompson, eds., *New directions in memory and aging : Proceedings of the George A. Talland Memorial Conference,* Lawrence Erlbaum, Hillsdale, N.J.

La Greca, Anthony J., Akers, Ronald L. and Dwyer, Jeffery W., 1988, Life events and alcohol behaviour among older adults, *Gerontologist,* 28(4), pp 552-558.

Laksham, Nirmala, 1987, A marginal people, *Hindu,* July 26, pp 18, col 1-6.

Langone, J., 1974, Vital signs : *The way we die in America, Little,* Brown, Boston.

Larson, R., 1978, Thirty years of research on the subjective well being of older Americans, *Journal of Gerontology,* 33, pp 109-125.

La Rue, A., 1978, *An overview of measures of cognitive functioning Comparative performance of depressed, organic and normal and patients,* Paper presented at the Annual Meeting of the Gerontological Society held in Dallas, November, Texas.

Lauer, R.H. and Rance, T., 1976, An comparative analysis of the psychological consequences of change, *Human Relations*, 29(3), pp 239-248.

Lawton, M.P., 1980, Psychosocial and environmental approaches to the care of senile dementia patients, *In* J. O. Cole and J.E., Barrett, eds., *Psychopathology in the aged*, Paven Press, New York.

——, Moss, Miriam and Fulcomer, Mark, 1986-87, Objective and subjective uses of time by older people, *International Journal of Aging and Human Development*, 24(3), pp 171-188.

Lee, A., Barry, J., Tamkin, A. and McConatha, D., 1984, Coping in later life : An optimistic assessment, *Journal of Applied Gerontology*, 3(1), pp 82-96.

Lee, Gray R. and Ishii-Kuntz, Masako, 1987, Social interaction, loneliness, and emotional well-being among the elderly, *Research on Aging*, 9(4), pp 459-482.

—— and Shehan, Constance L., 1989, Social relations and the self-esteem of older persons, *Research on Aging*, 11(4), pp 427-442.

Lefcourt, H.M., 1967, Effects of cue explication upon persons maintaining external control expectancies, *Journal of Personality and Social Psychology*, 5, pp 372-378.

Lehman, H.C., 1977, The use of medication to prevent custodial care, *In* C. Eisdorfer and R.O. Freidel, eds., *Cognitive and emotional disturbances in the elderly*, Yearbook Medical Publishers, Chicago.

Lengrand, Paul, 1982, The challenge of old age, *National Herald*, July 4, p 7, col 1-4

Lesnoff-Caravaglia, G., 1980, *Health care of the elderly : Strategies for prevention and intervention*, Human Sciences Press, New York.

Levin, William C., 1988, Age stereotyping : College student evaluations, *Research on Aging*, 10(1), pp 134-148.

Lewis, H., 1967, Culture, class and the behaviour of low income families, *In culture, class and poverty*, Health and Welfare Council of the National Capital Area, Washington.

Libow, L.J., 1977, Senile dementia and pseudosenility : Clinical diagnosis, *In* C. Eisdorfer and R.O. Friedel, eds., *Cognitive and emotional disturbance in the elderly*, Yearbook Medical Publishers, Chicago.

Lieberman, M.A., 1965, Psychological correlates of impending death : Some preliminary observations, *Journal of Gerontology*, 20, pp 181-190.

——, 1966, Observation on death and dying, *Gerontologist*, 6, pp 70-72.

Light, K.C., 1975, Slowing of response time in young and middle aged hypertensive patients, *Experimental Aging Research*, 1, pp 209-227.

——, 1978, Effect of mild cardiovascular and cerebrovascular disorders on serial reaction time performance, *Experimental Aging Research*, 4, pp 3-22.

Link, Mary S., 1987, The grandparenting role, Lifestyles, 8(3-4), pp 27-34.

Linn, Benard S. and Zeppa, Robert, 1987, Predicting third year medical students attitudes towards the elderly and treating the old, *Gerontology and Geriatrics Education*, 7(3-4), pp 167-175.

Linn, M.W., Huner, K. and Harris, R., 1980, Symptoms of depression and recent life events in the community elderly, *Journal of Clinical Psychology*, 36(3), pp 675-682.

Lomranz, Jacob Bergman, Simon, Eyal Nitza and Shmotkin, Dov, 1988, Indoor and outdoor activities of aged women and men as related to depression and well-being, *International Journal of Aging and Human Development*, 26(4), pp 303-314.

Louis, Harris and Associates, 1975, *The myth and reality of aging in America* National Council on the Aging, Washington, D.C.

Lowenthal, M.F., 1977, Toward a sociopsychological theory of change in adulthood and old age, *In* J.E. Birren and K.W. Schaie, eds., *Handbook of the psychology of aging*, Van Nostrand Reinhold, New York.

Lowy, L., 1979, *Social work with the aging*, Harper and Row, New York.

———, 1980, Mental health services in the community, *In* J.E. Birren and R.B. Sloane, eds., *Handbook of mental health and aging*, Prentice-Hall, Englewood Cliffs, N.J.

Lozier, J., 1975, Accommodating old people in society : Examples from Apalachia and New Orleans, *In* N. Datan and L. Ginsberg, eds., *Life-span developmental psychology: Normative life crises*, Academic Press, New York.

Luken, Paul C., 1987, Social identity in later life : A situational approach to understanding old age stigma, *International Journal of Aging and Human Development*, 25(3), pp 177-193.

Lumpkins, J.R., 1985, Health versus activity in elderly person's locus of control, *Perceptual and Motor Skills*, 60(1), pp 288-292.

Mac Brayer, C.T., 1960, Differences in perception of the opposite sex by males and females, *Journal of Social Psychology*, 52, pp 309-314.

Mc Cluskey, Neil G., 1989, Retirement and the contemporary family, *Journal of Psychotherapy and the Family*, 5(1-2), pp 211-224.

Mc Conatha, Jasmin T. and Mc Conatha, P. Douglas, 1988-89, The study of the relationship between wellness and life satisfaction of older adults, *Activities, Adaptation and Aging* 13(1-2), pp 129-140.

Mc Crae, R.R. and Costa, P.T., 1983, Psychological maturity and subjective well-being: Towards a new synthesis, *Developmental psychology*, 19(2), pp 243-248.

Mc Crae, Robert R. and Costa, Paul T., 1988, Age, personality and the spontaneous self-concept *Journals of Gerontology*, 43(6), pp 177-185.

Mc Donald, J., 1973, Religious needs of older Americans, *In* John G. Cull and Richard E. Hardy, eds., *The neglected older American*, Charles C. Thomas, Springfield.

Mc Gloshen, Thomas H. and O'Bryant, Shirley L., 1988, The psychological well-being of older, recent widows, *Psychology of Women Quarterly*, 12(1), pp 99-166.

Mc Hale, M.C., Mc Hale, J. and Streatfield G.J., 1979, *Children in the world*, Population Reference Bureau, Washington, D.C.

McKee, M. and Robertson, I., 1975, *Social problems*, Random House, New York.

Mc Mahon, Margaret A., 1987, The value of intergenerational relationships, *Journal of Gerontological Nursing*, 13(4), pp 25-29.

Mc Lean, Michael J. and Chown, Sheila M., 1988, Just world beliefs and attitudes toward helping elderly people: A comparison of British and Canadian University Students, *International Journal of Aging and Human Development* 26(4), pp 249-260.

Mac Mahon, B. and Pugh, J.J., 1970, *Epidemiology: Principles and methods*, Little, Brown, Boston.

Maddox, G.L., 1964, Disengagement theory: A critical evaluation, *Gerontologist*, 4, pp 80-82.

Maddox, G.L., 1968, Persistence of life style among the elderly: A longitudinal study of patterns of social activity in relation to life satisfaction *In* B.L. Neugarten, ed., *Middle age and aging*, Chicago University Press, Chicago.

———, 1970, Themes and issues in sociological theories of human aging, *Human Development*, 13, pp 17-27.

Mahajan, A., 1986, Problems of the aged in unorganised sector: A case study of old age pensioners in Haryana state, *Guru Nanak Journal of Sociology* 7(2), pp 93-109.

Mahajan, P. Mani, 1980, Probing the mind of the old, *Journal of Social Welfare*, 27(4), pp 4-6.

Mahadevan, K., 1985, *A system of policy for welfare of the elderly citizen*, Paper presented at the International Conference on Population Aging in India, February Trivandrum.

———, 1986, A system of policy for welfare of the elderly citizens, *Indian Journal of Social Work*, 46(4), pp 497-505.

Majumdar, Bhaswati, 1984, The problem of ageing in rural Bengal, *Economic Affairs*, 29(1), pp 63-69.

Majumdar, Vandana, 1985, The end of the road, *Hindustan Times* (Magazine), October 6, p 1, Col 1-8.

Makinodan, T., 1977, Immunity and aging, *In* C.E. Finch and L. Hayflick, eds., *Handbook of the biology of aging*, Van Nostrand Reinhold, New York.

Malinowski, B., 1948, *Magic, science and religion and other essays*, Free Press, New York.

Mangum, Wiley P., 1985, But not in my neighbourhood: Community resistance to housing for the elderly, *Journal of Housing for the Elderly*, 3(3-4), pp 101-119.

Mangammal Chari, S.K., 1980, Friendly societies for the aged, *Journal of Social Welfare*, 27(4), pp 8-9.

Manicini, J.A. and Simon, J., 1984, Older adults expectations of support from family and friends, *Journal of Applied Gerontology* 3(2), pp 150-160.

Mannes, M., 1977, *Last rights*, William Morrow, New York.

Markides, Kyriakos S., Levin, Jeffrey S. and Ray, Laura A., 1987, Religion, aging and life satisfaction: An eight-year, three-wave longitudinal study, *Gerontologist*, 27(5), pp 660-665.

Marsh, G.A., 1980, Perceptual changes with aging, *In* E.W. Busse and D.G. Blazer, eds. *Handbook of geriatric psychiatry*, Van Nostrand Reinhold, New York.

Marshall, V.W., 1980, *Last chapters: A sociology of aging and dying*, Wadsworth, Belmont, Calif.

Mass, H.S. and Kuypers, J.A., 1975, *From thirty to seventy*, Jossey-Bass, San Francisco.

Mathiasen, G., 1955, *Guide to development of protective service for older people*, Charles C. Thomas, Springfield.

Mathur, Deepa and Sen, Anima, 1989, Depression in the elderly and some of its psychosocial concomitants: A study of the efficacy and age-care centers, *Indian Journal of Community Guidance Service*, 6(1), pp 27-39.

Mattila, Vilho J., Matti, Joukamaa and Salokangas, Raimo K., 1987, Retirement, ageing and adaptation, The TURVA project, : 1. Theoretical frame of reference, *European Journal of Psychiatry*, 1(4), pp 37-43.

Mausner, J.S. and Bahn, A.K., 1974, *Epidemiology*, Philadelphia, W.B. Saunders.

Meddin, Jay and Vaux, Alan, 1988, Subjective well-being among the rural elderly population, *International Journal of Aging and Human Development*, 27(3), pp 193-206.

Medvedev, Z.A., 1974, Caucauses and Altay longevity: A biological or social problem? *The Gerontologist*, 14, pp 381-387.

Meissner, W.W., 1976, Normal psychology of the aging process, revisited (1) social learning and self-image in aging: Discussion, *Journal of Geriatric Psychiatry*, 9, pp 151-161.

Mellor, Karen S. and Edelmann, Robert J., 1988, Mobility, social support, loneliness and well-being amongst two groups of older adults, *Personality and Individual Differences*, 9(1), pp 1-5.

Menachery, George E., 1983, *Changes in life-satisfaction over the years among the retired*, Paper presented at the National Seminar on Psycho-Social Aspects of Aging, Tirupati.

———, 1984, *Adjustment and socio-economic status among the urban retired*, Paper presented at the 2nd National Conference on Aging of the AGI, Tirupati.

———, 1985, *Retirement: A psycho-social study*, Doctoral Dissertation, University of Poona, Poona.

———, 1986, Adjustment and socio-economic status among the urban retired, *Indian Psychological Review*, 30(5), pp 31-34.

Menon, L., 1980, Helping the retired to lead active life, *Journal of Social Welfare*, 27(4), pp 12-12.

Mercier, Joyce M., Paulson, Iori and Morris, Earl W., 1989, Proximity as a mediating influence on the perceived aging parent-adult child relationship, *Gerontologist*, 29(6), pp 785-791.

Meyers, J.M., Sheldon, D. and Robinson, S.S., 1963, A study of 138 elderly first admissions, *American Journal of Psychiatry*, 120, pp 244-249.

Milindapanha, 1890, Reprint, Translated by T.W. Rhys Davids, *Sacred books of the East series*, translated by various scholars and edited by F. Max Muller 1969, Nos. 35, 36, Motilal Banarsidas, Delhi.

Milinsky, Tova S., 1987, Stagnation and depression in the elderly group client, *Social Casework*, 68(3), pp 173-179.

Miller, J.H. and Shock, N.W., 1953, Age differences in the renal tubular response to antidiuretic hormone, *Journal of Gerontology*, 8, pp 446-450.

Miller, Marilyn J., 1986, Elderly persons as intergenerational child care providers, *Journal of Employment Counseling*, 23(4), pp 156-162.

Miller, S.M., 1984, Child and the aged: Attitudes, contact and discriminative ability, *The International Journal of Aging and Human Development* 19(1), pp 47-53.

Miller, W.B., 1958, Lower class culture as a generating milieu of gang delinquency, *Journal of Social Issues*, 14, 3(1), pp 5-19.

Minkler, Meredith and Ianghauser, Carol, 1988, Assessing health differences in an elderly population: A five-year follow-up, *Journal of the American Geriatrics Society*, 36(2), pp 113-118.

Mishra, Saraswati, 1988, *Social adjustment in old age*, B.R. Publications, Delhi.

Mitchell, Jim and Mathews, Holly F., 1987, Perceptions of older adults: Differences by age and sex among children in a Costa Rican community, *International Journal of Aging and Human Development*, 25(3), pp 223-238.

Moberg, D.O., 1970, Religiosity in old age, *The Gerontologist*, 5(2), pp 78-87.

Molinari, V. and Neiderche, G., 1984-85, Locus of control, depression and anxiety in young and old adults: A comparison study, *International Journal of Aging and Human Development*, 20(1), pp 41-52.

Monahan, Deborah J. and Greene, Vernon L., 1987, Predictors of early retirement among university faculty, *Gerontologist*, 27(1), pp 46-52.

Monge, R. and Haltsch, D., 1971, Paired-associate learning as a function of adult age and the length of the anticipation and inspection interval, *Journal of Gerontology*, 26, pp 157-162.

Monge, R.H., 1973, Developmental trends in factors of adolescent self-concept, *Developmental Psychology* 8, pp 382-393.

———, 1975, Structure of the self from adolescence through old age, *Experimental Aging Research*, 1(2), pp 281-291.

———, and Gardner, E.J., 1972, *A program of research in adult differences in cognitive performance and learning: Background for adult education and vocational retraining, A Final Report*, Department of Health, Education and Welfare, Washington, D.C.

Mongia, J.N., 1981, Problems of older workers: Work and retirement, *Indian Labour Journal*, 22(11), pp 1599-1612.

Monk, Abraham, 1988, Aging, loneliness and communications. *American Behavioural Scientist*, 31(5), pp 532-563.

Monte, C., 1980, *Beneath the mask: An introduction to theories of personality*, Holt Rinehart and winston, New York.

Montepare, Joann M. and Lachman, Margie E., 1989, You're only as old as you feel: Self-perception of age, fears of aging life satisfaction from adolescence to old age, *Psychology and Aging*, 4(1) pp 73-78.

Moody, R.A., 1976, *Life after life*, Bantan Books, New York.

Moore, Pat, 1986, *Disguised*, World Books.

Moos, R.H. and Isu, V.D., 1977, The crisis of physical illness: An overview, *In* R.H. Moss, ed., *Coping with physical illness*, Plenum Medical Book Company, New York.

Morgan, Leslie A., 1986, The financial experience of widowed women: Evidence from the LRHS, *Gerontologist*, 26(6), pp 663-668.

Morgan, Kevin, Dallosso, Helen Arie, Tom, Bryne E., Jane *et al*, 1987, Mental health and psychological well-being among the old and the very old living at home, *British Journal of Psychiatry*, 150, pp 801-807.

Morrow-Howell, Nancy and Leon, Joel, 1988, Life-span determinants of work in retirement years, *International Journal of Aging and Human Development*, 27(2), pp 125-140.

Morse, Donald R., 1988, Aging: Causes and control, *International Journal of Psychosomatics*, 35(1-4), pp 12-42.

Moss, Sidney Z. and Moss, Miriam S., 1989, The impact of the death of an elderly sibling: Some considerations of a normative loss, *American Behavioural Scientist*, 33(1), pp 94-106.

Mukherjee, D.P., 1985, Population aging: An emergent issue for biosocial research, A review article, *Journal of Indian Anthropological Society*, 20(3), pp 287-306.

Mukhopadhyaya, Nilanjan, 1984, In the evening of their lives, *Hindustan Times*, Magazine, September 2, p 4, Col. 1-8.

Muller, H.F., Grad, B. and Engelsmann, F., 1975, Biological and psychological predictors of survival in a psychogeriatric population, *Journal of Gerontology*, 30, pp 47-52.

Mullins, Larry C. and Mc Nicholas, Neil, 1986, Loneliness among the elderly: Issues and considerations for professionals in aging, *Gerontology and Geriatrics Education*, 7(1), pp 55-65.

———, Woodland, Amanda and Putnam, Jean, 1989, Emotional and social isolation among elderly Canadian seasonal migrants in Florida: An empirical analysis of a conceptual typology. *Journal of Gerontological Social Work*, 14(3-4), pp 111-129.

Munnichs, J.M. and Diesfeld, H.F., 1987, Psychology of ageing: An overview of research in the Netherlands, *Tijdschrift Voor Gerontologie en Geriatrie*, 18(2), pp 117-129.

Muriel, Skeet, 1982, Nursing at every stage, *Journal of Social Welfare*, 29(1), pp 13-16.

Murray, R., Huelskoetter, M.M. and O' Driscoll, D., 1980, *The nursing process in later maturity*, Prentice-Hall, Englewood Cliffs, N.J.

Myers, Jane E. and Blake, Richard H., 1986, Preparing counselors for work with older people, *Counselor Education and Supervision*, 26(2), pp 137-145.

Nalini Singh, 1988, Middle age begins at eighty, *Indian Express* (Magazine), April 10, p 1, col 1-6.

Nadkarni, M.M., 1981, Aging: Yet unexplained, *Economic Times*, July 5, p 4, col 1-3.

Narayanan, S., 1983, *Probabilistic orientation and death anxiety among elders*, Paper presented at the National Seminar on Psychosocial Aspects of Aging, Tirupati.

Nash, J., 1978, *Developmental psychology: A psychobiological approach*, Prentice-hall, Englewood Cliffs, N.J.

Natarajan, V.S., 1987, Geriatrics: A new discipline in India, *Indian Journal of Community Guidance Service*, 4(1), pp 63-70.

———, Balakrishnan, S. Eswaran, and John C.A., 1982, *Geriatric patients: An in-patient study*, Paper presented to the Ist National Conference of the AGI, October, Varanasi.

———, and Sridharan, 1982, *A study of autonomic dysfunction in the elderly*, Paper submitted to the Ist National Conference of the AGI, October, Varanasi.

———, *et al.*, 1984, *Anthropometric indices in elderly*, Paper submitted to the 2nd National Conference of Aging of the AGI, November, Tirupati.

Nayar, P.K.B., 1985, *Population aging in India: The background*, Paper presented at the International Seminar on population aging in India, February, Trivandrum.

Nayar, P.K.B., 1987, Aging and society, *Social Welfare*, 34(3), pp 28-31.

Nehrke, M.F., Hulicka, I.M. and Morganti, J.B., 1980, Age differences in life satisfaction, locus of control and self concept, *International Journal of Aging and Human Development*, 15(1), pp 54-59.

Nelson, Patricia B., 1990, Intrinsic/extrinsic religious orientation of the elderly: Relationship to depression and self-esteem, *Journal of Gerontological Nursing*, 16(2), pp 29-35.

Nesselroade, J.R. and Harkins, S.W., 1980, Introduction to methodological issues, *In* L.W. Poon, eds., *Aging in the 1980's: Psychological issues*, American Psychological Association, Washington, D.C.

Neugarten, B.L., 1971, *The awareness of middle age and aging*, University of Chicago Press, Chicago.

———, 1977, Personality and aging *In* J.E. Birren and K.W. Schaie, eds., *Handbook of the psychology of aging*, Academic Press, New York.

———, 1982, *Age or need*, Sage Publication, Inc., California.

———, and Datan, N., 1973, Sociological perspectives on the life cycle, *In* P.B. Baltes and Schaie, K.W., ed., *Life span in developmental psychology: Personality and socialisation*, Academic Press, New York.

———, and Weinstein, K.K., 1964, The changing American grandparent, *Journal of Marriage and the Family*, 26, pp 199-204.

———, *et al.*, 1968, Personality and patterns of aging, *In* B.L. Neugarten, ed., *Middle age and aging*, University of Chicago Press, Chicago.

———, *et al*, 1964, *Personality in middle and late life*, Atherton Press, New York.

———, and Neugarten, Dail A., 1986, Age in the aging society, *Daedalus*, 115(1), pp 31-49.

Newman, B.M. and Newman, P.R., 1980, *Personality development through the life span*, Books/cole, Monterey, California.

Norris, Fran H. and Murrell, Stanley A., 1987, Older adult family stress and adaptation before and after bereavement, *Journal of Gerontology*, 42(6), pp 606-612.

Nussbaum, Jon F. and Robinson, James D., 1984, Attitudes towards aging, *Communication Research Reports*, 1(1), pp 21-27.

O'Bryant, Shirley L., 1988, Self-differentiated assistance in older widows support systems, *Sex Roles*, 19(1-2), pp 91-106.

Oden, M.H., 1968, The fulfillment of promise: 40-year follow up of the Terman gifted group, *Genetic Psychology Monographs*, 77, pp 3-93.

Ogilvie, Daniel M., 1987, Life satisfaction and identity structure in late middle-aged men and women, *Psychology and Aging*, 2(3), pp 217-224.

Ohuche, Nancy M. and Littrell, John M., 1989, Igho students attitudes toward supporting aged parents, *International Journal of Aging and Human Development*, 29(4), pp 259-267.

Oltman, A.M., Michlas, T.J. and Steer, R.A., 1980, Structure of depression in older men and women, *Journal of Clinical Psychology*, 36(2), pp 672-674.

Okun, M.A., 1976, Adult age and cautiousness in decision: A review of the literature, *Human Development*, 19, pp 220-233.

———, Siegler, I.C. and George, L.K., 1978, Cautiousness and verbal learning in adulthood, *Journal of Gerontology*, 33, pp 94-97.

Orbach, H.L., 1961, Aging and religion: Church attendance in the Detroit Metropolitan Area, *Geriatrics*, 16, pp 530-540.

Orgel, L.E., 1963, The maintenance of the accuracy of protein synthesis and its relevance to aging, *Proceedings of the National Academy of Sciences*, 49, p 517.

O' Rourke, Kevin, 1988, Developing in younger physicians an ethical perspective towards geriatric patients, *Journal of the American Geriatrics Society*, 36(6), pp 565-568.

Osgood, C.E., Suci, E.J. and Tannenbaum, P.H., 1957, *The measurement of meaning*, University of Illinois Press, Urbana.

Overton, W.J. and Reese, W.W., 1973, Models of development: Methodological implications, *In* J.R. Hesselroade and H.W. Reese, eds., *Life span developmental psychology: Methodological issue*, Academic Press, New York.

Owens, W.A., 1953, Age and mental abilities: A longitudinal study, *Genetic Psychology Monographs*, 48, pp 3-54.

———, 1966, Age and mental ability: A second follow up, *Journal of Educational Psychology*, 57, pp 311-325.

Paintal, Harinder Kaur, 1970, *A study of adjustment among aged medical men*, Doctoral Dissertation, All India Institute of Mental Health, Bangalore.

———, 1976, Engagement theory and successful aging, *Indian Journal of Clinical Psychology*, 3(2), pp 101-109.

Palmore, E.B., 1968, The effects of aging on activities and attitudes, *The Gerontologist*, 8, pp 259-263.

———, 1969, Physical, mental and social factors in predicting longevity, *Gerontologist*, 9, pp 103-108.

———, 1970, *Normal Aging*, Duke University Press, I. Durbam, N.C.

——, and Cleveland, W., 1976, Aging, terminal decline and terminal drop, *Journal of Gerontology*, 31, pp 76-81.

Pal, Roma, 1985, Gerontology: Viewpoint of Hindu Psychology, *Indian Psychological Review*, 28(1), pp 36-40.

Pan, J.S., 1954, Institutional and personal adjustment in old age, *Journal of General Psychology*, 85, pp 391-394.

Pandey, Ram Sajiwan and Thakur, Giridhar P., 1984, *A study of the influence of modality and meaningfulness on age related changes in recall experiments*, Paper submitted to the 2nd National Conference on Aging, November, Tirupati.

Pareek, U., 1968, *An adaptation of Rosenzweig P-F (adult form) Test manual*, Mansayan, Delhi.

Pareek, U.N., 1964, *Development patterns in reaction to frustration*, M.A. Dissertation, Delhi University, Delhi.

Parida, S., 1983, Responsibility of industry towards retiring employees, *Personnel Today*, 4(2), pp 21-26.

Parkinson, C., Northcote *et al*, 1985, *Retirement: Plan now for your last years*, Indian Books, Bombay.

Parnes, H.S., 1981, *A longitudinal study of men, work and retirement*, MIT Press, Cambridge, Mass.

Pathak, J.D., 1978, *Our elderly: Some effects of aging in Indian subjects*, Medical Research Centre of the Bombay Hospital Trust, Bombay.

——, 1982, *Incidence of diseases and disorders in elderly Indian subjects*, Paper submitted to the 1st National Conference of the AGI, Varanasi.

——, 1985, *Trends in incidence of disorders and illnesses in Indian women patients of upper age (40+)*. Paper presented at the International Seminar on Population Aging in India, February, Trivandrum.

——, Joshi, S.D. and Mehrotra, P.P., 1983, *Reaction time in the elderly Indian subjects*, Paper presented at the National Seminar on Psychosocial Aspects of Aging, June, Triputi.

Pat-Horenzyk, Ruth, 1988, Attitudes of psychotherapists towards diagnosis and treatment of depression in old age, *Israel Journal of Psychiatry and Related Sciences*, 25(1), pp 24-37.

Patrick, Linda F. and Moore, Janet S., 1986, Life-event types and attributional styles as predictors of depression in elderly women, *Journal of Geriatric Psychiatry*, 19(2), pp 241-262.

Pattison, M., 1977, *The experience of dying*, Prentice-Hall, Englewood Cliff, N.J.

Payne, Barbara, 1988, Religious patterns and participation of older adults: A sociological perspective, *Educational Gerontology*, 14(4), pp 255-267.

Peck, R.C., 1968, Psychological development in second half of life, *In* J.E. Anderson, ed., *Psychological aspects of aging*, American Psychological Association, Washington, D.C.

Peplau, L. and Perlman, D., 1982, *Loneliness: A source book of current theory, research and therapy*, John Wiley, New York.

Peretti, Peter O. and Lowrey, Beverly, 1984-85, Intimacy in the confidant role in closest friendships of non confined aged males, *Psychology and Human Development*, 1(2), pp 75-79.

——, and Tero, Linda, 1984, Closest friendships of nonconfined aged males, *Psychology and Human Development*, 1(1), pp 25-31.

Perlman, D., Gerson, A.C. and Spinner, B., 1978, Loneliness among senior citizens: An empirical report, *Essence*, 2, pp 239-248.

Peters, George R., Hoyt, Danny R., Babchuk, Nicholas, Kaiser, Marvin, *et al*, 1987, Primary-group support systems of the aged, *Research on Aging*, 9(3), pp 392-416.

Peterson, Candida C., Hall, Lesley C. and Peterson, James L., 1988, Age, sex and contact with elderly adults as predictors of knowledge about psychological aging, *International Journal of Aging and Human Development*, 26(2), pp 129-137.

Pfeiffer, E., 1980, Pharmacology of aging, *In* G. Lesnoff-Carovaglia, eds., *Health care of the elderly*, Human Sciences Press, New York.

———, 1980, The psychosocial evaluation of the elderly patient, *In* E.W. Busse and D. Blazer, eds., *Handbook of Geriatric Psychiatry*, Van Nostrand Reinhold , New York.

Phares, E.J., 1973, *Locus of control : A personality determinant of behaviour*, General Learning Press, Morriston, New Jersey.

Phillips, B.S., 1961, Role changing, subjective age and adjustment : A correlational analysis, *Journal of Gerontology*, 16(4), pp 347-352.

———, 1975, A role theory approach to adjustments in old age, *American Sociological Review*, 22, pp 212-217.

Pillai, A.K.B., 1985, The Asian Indian model of the elderly : A study in anthropological gerontology, *Journal of Indian Anthropological Society*, 20(3), pp 210-25.

Pinge, N.D., 1982, The bogey of retirement, *Economic Times* (Magazine), May 30, p 4, col 1-4.

Poon, L., ed., 1980, *Aging in the 1980's; Psychological issues*, American psychological Association, Washington, D.C.

Post, F., 1980, Paranoid, Sz-like and schizophrenia states in the aged, *In* J.E. Birren and R.B. Sloane, eds., *Handbook of mental health and aging*, Prentice-Hall, Englewood Cliffs, N.J.

Prager, Edward, 1986, Components of personal adjustment of long distance elderly movers, *Gerontologist*, 26(6), pp 676-680.

Pratte, C.P., 1976, Attitudinal predictors of devaluation of old age in a multigenerational sample, *Journal of Gerontology*, 31(2), pp 193-197.

Preston, D.B. and Mansfield, P.K., 1984, An exploration of stressful life events, illness and coping among the rural elderly, *Gerontologist*, 24(5), pp 490-494.

Proller, Norman L., 1989, The effect of an adoptive grand parent programme on youth and elderly participants, *Journal of children in contemporary society*, 20(3-4), pp 195-203.

Pukan, G.C., 1985, The sorry plight of pensioners, *Times of India*, November 27, p 8, col 7-8.

Purohit, C.K. and Sharma, R., 1973, A study of aged 60 years and above in social profile, *Indian Journal of Gerontology*, 4, pp 71-83.

Quint, J.C, 1967, *The nurse and the dying patient*, Aldine, Chicago, Ill.

Rabbitt, P., 1977, Changes in problem solving ability in O.A. *In* J.E. Birren and K.W. Schaie, eds., *Handbook of the psychology of aging*, Van Nostrand Reinhold, New York.

Rabins, P.V., Mace, N.L. and Lucas, M.J., 1982, The impact of dementia on the family, *Journal of the American Medical Association*, 248, pp 333-335.

Rainwater, L., 1966, Crucible of identity : The Negro lower-class family, *Daedalus*, 95, pp 172-216.

Raja, R.K., 1982, Problems of the aged, *Yojana*, 26(3), pp 14-15.

Ramamurti, P.V., 1956, *Interest in music among the young and the elderly,* Paper presented at the Regional Conference of Psychology, Mysore University, Mysore.

———, 1968 a, *A study of some factors related to the adjustment of urban aged men,* Doctoral Dissertation, S.V. University, Tirupati.

———, 1968 b, An adjustment inventory for the aged, *Indian Journal of Psychology,* 43, pp 27-29.

———, 1969, A problems inventory for older people, *Journal of Psychological Researches,* 13, pp 162-163.

———, 1970a, Problems of older people, — An analysis of age trends, *Psychological Studies,* 15, pp 128-130.

———, 1970b, A study of certain socio-economic variables related to adjustment in aging, *Journal of Psychological Researches,* 14, pp 94-99.

———, 1970 d, Life satisfaction in the older years, *Indian Journal of Gerontology,* 2, pp 68-70.

———, 1976 a, Adjustment in later maturity — A follow up study, *Psychological Studies,* 21, pp 41-44.

———, 1976 b, Disparity in self-signficant other perceived role activity and its relation to adjustment among older people. *Indian Journal of Applied Psychology,* 13, pp 91-94.

———, 1978. *The sixth decade and after,* S.V. University Press, Triputi.

———, 1982: Age, work efficiency and retirement, *Bombay Psychologist,* 4(2), pp 34-36.

——— and Reddy, K.L., 1986, A study of the attitudes of different generations towards aging, *Psychological Studies,* 31(2), pp 127-129.

———, and Parameswaran, E.G., 1963, A study of bilateral transfer on a mirror drawing task in the old and the young, *Journal of Psychological Researches,* 7(2), pp 7-13.

Ramanathan, Jaya, 1983, Homes for the aged, *Urban India,* 2(4), pp 23-26.

Ram Kumar, 1985, Retired citizens on the go, *Times of India,* November 6, p 8, col 7-8.

Ranade, S.N., 1985, *Social aspects of aging in India,* Paper presented at the International Seminar on Population Aging in India, February, Trivandrum.

Randhawa, Maninder and Bhatnagar, G.S., 1985, Changing attitudes and beliefs of the retired people, *Journal of Sociological Studies,* 4, pp 120-127.

Rangaswamy, K., Ramani, P. and Anatharamah, R.N., 1982, A study of menstrual distress, *Journal of Psychological Researches,* 26, pp 84-87.

Rangnekar, Sharu S., 1989, Planning for retirement, *Indian Management,* 28(10), pp 4-12.

Rao, Venkoba., 1979, Gero-Psychiatry in Indian Culture, *Canadian Journal of Psychiatry,* 24, p 431.

———, 1981, Mental health and aging in India, *Indian Journal of Psychiatry,* 23, pp 11-30.

——— and Madhavan, T., 1981, 'Late paraphrenia' : A report from the geropsychiatric clinic, Madurai India, *Indian Journal of Psychiatry,* 23, pp 291-297.

———, 1982, Geropsychiatric morbidity survey in a semi-urban area near Madurai, *Indian Journal of Psychiatry,* 24, pp 258-267.

———, and Ram R., 1984, *Suicide behaviour in the elderly,* Paper presented at the 2nd National Conference, AGI, November, Tirupati.

———, Virudhagirinathan, B.S. and Malathy, R., 1972, Mental illness in patients aged fifty and over : A psychological and sociological study, *Indian Journal of Psychiatry,* 14, pp 319-332.

——— *et al*, 1984, *Health care of the rural aged — A study near Madurai : A preliminary communication*, Paper presented at the 2nd National Conference on Aging, AGI, November, Tirupati.

Rappoport, Leon and Peters, George R., 1988, Aging and the psychosocial problematics of food, *American Behavioural Scientist*, 32(1), pp 31-40.

Raskin, A., 1979, Signs and symptoms of psychopathology in the elderly, *In* A., Raskin and L.F., Jarvik, eds., *Psychiatric symptoms and cognitive loss in the elderly*, Hemisphere, Washington, D.C.

——— and Jarvik, L.F., 1979, *Psychiatric Symptoms and cognitive loss in the elderly*, Hemisphere Washington, D.C.

Raskind, M.A. and Storrie, M.C., 1980, The organic mental disorders, *In* E.W. Busse and D. Blazer, eds., *Handbook of geriatric psychiatry*, Van Nostrand Reinhold, New York.

Rastogi, G.D., 1984, *Psychological problems of aging*, Paper presented at the 2nd National Conference on Aging of the AGI, November, Tirupati.

Ray, Diane C., McKinney, Kelly A. and Ford, Charles V., 1987, Differences in psychologists ratings of older and younger clients, *Gerontologists*, 27(1), pp 82-86.

Reed, C.I., 1966, Suggestions for revision of nomenclature on aging, *The Gerontologist*, 6(4), pp 188-190.

Reddy, Gangi D., 1971, *A study of certain factors related to attitudes to future and death*, M.A., Dissertation, S.V. University, Tirupati.

Reddy, Kullai L., 1984, *A study of the attitudes towards aging and their relation to the problems of adjustment of older people*, M. Phil Dissertation, S.V. University, Tirupati.

Reddy, Narasimha, K.L., 1985, *Inter-generational preferences as a function of values and interests*, M. Phil. Dissertation, S.V. University, Tirupati.

Reddy, Siva Sankara K., 1983, *Attitudinal difference between the young and the old — A study of generation gap*, Doctoral Dissertation, S.V. University, Tirupati.

———, 1985, Difference in morals between young and old, *Journal of the Indian Academy of Applied Psychology*, 11, pp 11-15.

Regestein, Quentin R. and Morris, John, 1987, Daily sleep patterns observed among institutionalised elderly residents, *Journal of the American Geriatrics Society*, 35(8), pp 767-772.

Reichard, S., Livson, F. and Peterson, P.G., 1962, *Aging and personality : A study of 87 older men*, John Wiley and Sons, New York.

Reiff, T.R., 1980, Biomedical aspects of aging and their relation to geriatric care, *In* G. Lesnoff-Caravaglia, ed., *Health care of the elderly*, Human Science Press, New York.

Reimanis, G. and Green, R., 1971, Imminence of death and intellectual decrement in the aging, *Developmental Psychology*, 5, pp 270-272.

Reisberg, B., Ferris, S.H. and Gershon, S., 1980, Pharmacotherapy of senile dementia, *In* J.O. Cole and J.E. Barrett, eds., *Psychopathology in the aged*, Raven Press, New York.

Reitan, R.M., 1955, The relationship of the Trail-Making Test to organic brain damage, *Journal of Consulting Psychology*, 19, pp 393-395.

Reker, Gary., Peacock, Edward J. and Wong, Paul T., 1987, Meaning and purpose in life and well-being : A life-span perspective, *Journal of Gerontology*, 42(1), pp 44-49.

Retsinas, Joan, 1989, Functioning and perceived distress, *Clinical Gerontologist*, 8(4), pp 46-47.

Rhudick, P.J. and Dibner, A.S., 1961, Age, personality and health correlates of death concerns in normal aged individuals, *Journal of Gerontology,* 16(1), pp 44-49.

Rice, Susan, 1989, Single, older childless women : Differences between never-married and widowed women in life satisfaction and social support, *Journal of Gerontological Social Work,* 13(3-4), pp 35-47.

——— and Kelly, James, J., 1987, Love and intimacy needs of the elderly : Some philosophical and intervention issues, *Journal of Social Work and Human Sexuality,* 5(2), pp 89-96.

Richard, J., 1985, Family type and the aged, *Journal of Family Welfare,* 31(4), pp 31-38.

Riegel, K.F., 1971, The prediction of death and longevity in longitudinal research : A twenty-year longitudinal study of aging, *In* E. Palmore and F.C. Jeffers, eds., *Prediction of life span,* D.C. Heath, Lexington, Mass.

———, 1973 (a), Developmental psychology and society : Some historical and ethical considerations, *In* J.R. Nesseloade and H.W. Reese, eds., *Life span developmental psychology : Methodological issues,* Academic Press, New York.

———, 1973 (b), Dialectic operations : The final period of cognitive development, *Human Development,* 16, pp 346-370.

———, 1973 (c), An epitaph for a paradigm, *Human Development,* 16, (1-2), pp 1-7.

———, 1977, History of psychological gerontology, *In* J.E. Birren and K.W. Schaie, eds., *Handbook of the psychology of aging,* Van Nostrand Reinhold, New York.

Riegel, K.F., Riegel, R.M. and Meyer, G., 1967, A study of the drop-out rates in longitudinal research on aging and the prediction of death, *Journal of, Personality and Social Psychology,* 4, pp 342-348.

Riley, J.W., Jr., 1970, What people think about death, *In* O.G. Brim, Jr., H.E. Freeman, S. Levine and N.A. Scotch, eds., *The dying patient,* Russell Sage Foundation, New York.

Riley, M.V. and Foner, A., 1968, Parish clergy and the aged : Examining stereotypes, *Journal of Gerontology,* 31(3), pp 340-345.

———, 1968, *Aging and society, Vol. I, An inventory of research findings,* Russell Sage Foundation, New York.

——— Johnson M. and Foner A., 1972, *Aging and society : A sociology of age stratification,* Vol. 3, Russell Sage Foundation, New York.

Roberto, Karen A. and Kimboko, Priscilla J., 1989, Friendships in later life : Definitions and maintenance patterns, *International Journal of Aging and Human Development,* 28(1), pp 9-19.

Robinson, Lillian H., 1989, Grand parenting : Intergenerational love and late, *Journal of the American Academy of Psychoanalysis,* 17(3), pp 483-491.

Robinson, P.J. and Keith, W., 1983, Fear of death and physical illness : A personal construct approach, *Death Education,* 7(2-3), pp 213-228.

Robertson-Tchabo, E.A., Arenberg, D. and Costa, P.T., 1979, Temperamental predictors of longitudinal change in performance on the Benton revised visual retention test among seventy-year old men : An exploratory study, *In* F. Hoffmeister and C. Muller, eds., *Brain function in old age : Evaluation of change and disorders,* Springer-Verlag, New York.

Rockstein, M., Chesky, J. and Sussman, M., 1977, Comparative biology and evolution of aging, *In* C.E. Finch and L. Hayflick, eds., *Handbook of the biology of aging,* Van Nostrand Reinhold, New York.

——— and Sussman, M., 1979, *Biology of aging,* Wadsworth, Belmont, California.

Rodeheaver, Dean, 1987, When old age became a social problem, women were left behind, *Gerontologist,* 27(6), pp 741-746.

Rodin, Judith, 1986, Aging and health : Effects of the sense of control, *Science,* 233(4770), pp 1271-1276.

Rogalski, Sharon, and Paisey, Timothy, 1987, Neuroticism versus demographic variables as correlates of self-reported life satisfaction in a sample of older adults, *Personality and Individual Differences,* 8(3), pp 397-401.

Rogers, T.W., 1980, Ingroup-outgroup distinctions : The case of the aged American society, *Indian Journal of Social Research,* 21(2), pp 77-85.

———, 1980, Ascribed and episodical deviance among the American aged, *Journal of Social and Economic Studies,* 8(1), pp 31-54.

Rose-Colley, Mary and Eddy, James M., 1988, Interactions of university students with elderly individuals : An investigation into the correlates, *Educational Gerontology,* 14(1), pp 33-43.

Rosenfield, A.H., 1985, Depression : Dispelling dispair, *Psychology Today,* 19(6), pp 28-34.

Rosengarten, Lucy, 1986, Creating a health-promoting group for elderly couples on a home health care programmes, *Social Work in Health Care,* 11(4), pp 83-92.

Rosow, I., 1967, *Social integration of the aged,* Free Press, New York.

Rotenberg, Ken J. and Hamel, Jocelyn, 1988, Social interaction and depression in elderly individuals, *International Journal of Aging and Human Development,* 27(4), pp 305-318.

Rotter, J.B., 1986, Generalized expectancies for internal versus external control of reinforcement, *Psychological Monograph,* 80(1), pp 609-614.

Roth, M., 1980, Senile dementia and its borderlands, *In* J.O., Cole and J.E. Barrett, eds., *Psychopathology in the aged,* Raven Press, New York.

Rowe, Alan, 1986, Retirement of emeritus medical professors of the University of Chicago and the University of Wisconsin, *Psychological Reports,* 59(2), pp 721-722.

Rowe, John, W. and Kahn, Robert L., 1987, Human aging : Usual and successful, *Science,* 237(4811), pp 143-149.

Roy, S. Guha, 1985, Demography of ageing : Indian experience, *Journal of Indian Anthropological Society,* 20(3), pp 251-283.

Rubenstein, C. and Shaver, P., 1980, Loneliness in two northern cities, *In* Hartog, J.R. Andy and Y.A. Cohen, eds., *The anatomy of loneliness,* International University Press, New York.

Rubio Herrera, R., 1981, The problem of death in old age : From a psychological perspective, *Revista de Psicologia General Ablicado,* 36(4), pp 719-727.

Rubenstein, Robert L., 1986, *Singular Paths : Old men living along,* Columbia University Press, New York.

Ruhm, Christopher J., 1989, Why older Americans stop working, *Gerontologist* 29(3), pp 294-299.

Russell D., Peplau L. and Cutrona, C., 1980, The revised UCLA loneliness scale : Concurrent and discriminant validity evidence, *Journal of Personality and Social Psychology,* 39, pp 427-480.

Russell, Ruth V., 1987, The importance of recreation satisfaction and activity participation to the life satisfaction of age-segregated retirees, *Journal of Leisure Research,* 19(4), pp 273-283.

Ryan, J., 1984, Silent barter, *Journal of Death and Dying,* 14(2), pp 145-154.

Ryckman, R.M. and Malikiosi, M.X., 1975, Relationship between locus of control and chronological age, *Press Reports*, 36, pp 655-658.

Sahayam, M. Deva, 1988, Aged females, The most deprived among the deprived, *Indian Journal of Social Works*, 49(3), pp 61-69.

Saibaba, G. and Vijaylakshmi, R., 1984, Aging population : Impact on rural labour force, *Economic Times*, August 8, p 5, col 3-6.

Salthouse, T.A., 1980, Age and memory : Strategies for localising the loss, *In* L.W. Poon, J.L. Fozard, L.S. Cermak, D. Aronberg, and L.W. Thompson, eds., *New Directions in memory and aging : Proceedings of the George Talland Memorial Conference,* Lawrence Erlbaum, Hillsdale, N.J.

Sampson, Anthony and Sampson, Sally, 1985, *The Oxford book of ages,* OUP, Oxford.

Sanders, Gregory, F., 1988, Family contributions of older persons, *Activities, Adaptation and Aging,* 11(1), pp 53-60.

——— and Pittman, Joe F., 1987, Attitudes of youth towards known and general target elderly, *Journal of Applied Gerontology,* 6(4), pp 464-475.

Santak, B.D., 1984, With the aged in Fiji, *Journal of Social Welfare,* 30(2), pp 16-22.

Sargent, S.S., 1984, Reactions to frustration — A critique and hypothesis, *Psychological Review,* 55, pp 108-114.

Saraswathi, T.S. *et al,* 1982, Recovering a lost paradise, *Journal of Social Welfare,* 29(1), pp 5-9.

Sasi, P.T. and Sanandaraj, H. Sam., 1982, Old people living in home for the aged : A study of certain variables of adjustment, *Psychological Studies,* 27(2), pp 77-80.

Saunders, C., 1965, The last stages of life, *American Journal of Nursing,* 65, pp 70-75.

Saxena, Hina and Gon, Manjuli, 1985, *A comparative study of the effects of age, sex difference and sex roles on locus of control,* Private Communication, University of Baroda, Baroda.

Saxena, Poonam, 1987, The unquite years, *Indian Express,* March 15, p 1, col. 1-8.

Sears, R.R., 1943, Survey of objective studies of psychoanalytic concepts, *Social Science Research Council,* 51, pp 76-104.

Seefeldt, C., 1984, Children's attitudes towards the elderly : A cross-cultural comparison, *The International Journal of Aging and Human Development,* 19(4), pp 319-328.

Seeman, Teresa E. and Berkman, Lisa, 1988, Structural characteristics of social networks and their relationship with social support in the elderly : Who provides support, *Social Science and Medicine,* 26(7), pp 737-749.

Seligman, M.E.P., 1975, *Helplessness : On depression, development and death,* W. H. Freeman, San Francisco.

Selye, H., 1956, *The stress of life,,* McGraw-Hill, New York.

Sen, Anima and Ochaney, Madhu, 1983, *Some psychological antecedents of depression in senescence,* Paper presented at the National Seminar on Psycho-Social aspects of Aging, June, Tirupati.

Sethi, Patanjali, 1982, New harijans, *Economic Times,* Magazine, May 30, pp 4, col 6-8.

Schaie, K.W., 1955, Cross-sectional methods in the study of psychological aspects of aging, *Journal of Gerontology,* 10, pp 91-107.

———, 1958, Rigidity-flexibility and intelligence : A cross sectional study of the adult life span from 20 to 70 years, *Psychological Monographs : General and Applied,* 72(9), pp 1-26.

———, 1973, Methodological problems in descriptive research on adulthood and aging, *In* J.R. Nesselroade and H.W. Reese, eds., *Life-span developmental psychology : Methodological issues,* Academic Press, New York.

———. 1974 Translations in gerontology-From lab to life : Intellectual functioning, *American Psychologist,* 29, pp 802-807.

———, 1980, Intelligence and problem-solving, *In* J. Birren and R. B. Sloane, eds., *Handbook of mental health and aging,* Prentice-Hall, Englewood Cliffs, N.J.

———, 1988, Ageism in psychological research, *American Psychologist,* 43(3), pp 179-183.

——— and Labouvie-Vief, G., 1971, Generational vs. Ontogenetic components of change in adult cognitive behaviour : A 14 year cross-sequential study, *Developmental Psychology,* 10, pp 305-320.

——— and Strotics, C.R., 1964, *A cross-sectional study of age changes in cognitive behaviour,* Paper presented at the meeting of the midwestern Psychological Association, MO. St. Louis.

Scheidt, Rick, J., 1986, Mental health of small-town kansas elderly : A report from the Great Plains, *American Journal of Community Psychology,* 14(5), pp 541-554.

Schiffman, S., 1977, Food recognition by the elderly, *Journal of Gerontology,* 32(5), pp 586-592.

——— and pasternak, M., 1979, Decreased discrimination of food odors in the elderly, *Journal of Gerontology* 34(1), pp 73-79.

Schogt, Barbara and Sadavoy, Joel, 1987, Assessing the protective service needs of the impaired elderly living in the community, *Canadian Journal of Psychiatry,* 32(3), pp 179-184.

Schonfield, A.E.D., 1980, Learning, memory and aging, *In* J. Birren and R.B. Sloane, eds., *Handbook of mental health and aging,* Prentice-Hall, Englewood Cliffs, N.J.

Schulz, J., 1980, *The economics of aging,* Wadsworth, Belmont, California.

Schulz N.R. and Moore, D., Loneliness : Correlates, attributions and coping among older adults, *Personality and Social Psychology Bulletin,* 10(1), pp 67-77.

Schulz, R., 1978, *The psychology of death, dying and bereavement,* Addison-wesley, Reading, Mass.

Schwalb, Susan J. and Sedlacek, William E., 1990, Hewe college students attitudes toward older people changed ? *Journal of College Student Development,* 31(2), pp 127-132.

Schwartzman, Alex E., Gold, Dolores, Andres, David, Arbuckle, Tannis Y., *et al*, 1987, Stability of intelligence : A 40 year follow-up, *Canadian Journal of Psychology,* 41(2), pp 244-256.

Scott, Jean P. and Robert, Karen A., 1987, Informal supports of older adults : A rural-urban comparison, *Family Relations : Journal of Applied Family and Child Studies,* 36(4), pp 444-449.

Shah, Rajiv, 1986, When will Soviet villages stop, 'ageing' ? *Link* 28(48) July 6, pp 24-25.

Shanas, Ethel, 1979, The family as a social support system in old age, *The Gerontologist,* 19(2), pp 169-172.

——— and Maddox, G.L., 1977, Aging, health and organisation of health resources, *In* R.H. Binstock and E. Shanas, ed., *Handbook of aging and the social sciences,* Van Nostrand Reinhold, N.Y.

Sharma M.L. and Dak, T.M., 1987, *Aging in India-Challenge for society,* Ajanta Publication, Delhi.

Sharma, O.P., 1986, Aged population. Do they need more attention ? *Economic Times,* May 1, p 5, col 3-6 +.

———, 1989, India is greying : 12 M. elderly work for a living, *Economic Times,* April 15, p 5, col 3-6.

———, 1989, We are not paying our grandmothers their due, *Economic Times,* April 26, p 5, col 7-8.

Sharma, P.S., 1980, Treat them with dignity and love, *Journal of Social Welfare,* 27(4), pp 1-3.

Sharp, G.L., Butterfield, W.H.J. and Keen, H., 1964, Diabetic survey in Bedford, *Proceedings of the Royal Society of Medicine,* 57, pp 193-202.

Shebani, Bashir L., Wass, Hannelore, and Guertin, Wilson, H., 1986-87, Correlates of life satisfaction for old libyans compared with the judgements of libyan youth, *International Journal of Aging and Human Development,* 24(1), pp 19-28.

Sherwood, S. and Mor, V., 1980, Mental health institutions and the elderly, *In* J. Birren and R.B. Sloane, eds., *Handbook of mental health and aging,* Prentice-Hall, Engle Wood Cliffs, N.J.

Shock, N.W., 1977 (a), Biological theories of aging, *In* J.E. Birren and K.W. Schaie, eds., *Handbook of the psychology of aging,* Van Nostrand Reinhold, New York.

———, 1977 (b), Systems integration. *In* C.E. Finch and L. Hayflick, eds., *Handbook of the biology of aging,* Van Nostrand Reinhold, New York.

Shneidman, E.S., 1980 (a), The death certificate, *In* E.S. Shneidman, ed., *Death : Current perspectives,* Mayfield, Palo Alto, Calif.

Shute, George E., Fitzgerald, Stephen G. and Haynes, Stephen N., 1986, The relationship between internal attentional control and sleep-onset latency in elderly adults, *Journal of Gerontology,* 41(6), pp 770-773.

Siddaiah, Marula, H.S., 1970, *The older people of Makunti,* Karnataka University, Dharwar.

Siddhantalankar, Satyavrata, 1983, *From old age to youth,* Chandravati Trust Society, New Delhi.

Siegler, I.C., 1975, The terminal drop hypothesis: Fact or artifact? *Experimental Aging Research,* 1, pp 169-185.

———, 1980, The psychology of adult development and aging, *In,* E.W. Busse and D. Blazer, eds., *Handbook of geriatric psychiatry,* Van Nostrand Reinhold, New York.

Sinic, Andrei, 1987, Ethnicity as a career for the elderly : The Serbian-American case, *Journal of Applied Gerontology,* 6(1), pp 113-126.

Simmons, L.W., 1945, *The role of the aged in primitive societies,* Yale University Press, New Haven Conn.

Simon, A., 1980, The neuroses, personality disorders, alcoholism, drug use and misuse, and crime in the aged, *In* J.E. Birren and R.B. Sloane, eds., *Handbook of mental health and aging,* Prentice-hall, Englewood Cliffs, N.J.

Simon, Jolene M., 1990, Humor and its relationship to perceived health, life satisfaction, and morale in older adults, *Issues in Mental Health Nursing,* 11(1), pp 17-31.

Simpson, I.H., Back K.W. and McKinney, J., 1966, Work and retirement, *In* I.H. Simpson and J.C. McKinney, eds., *Social aspects of aging,* Duke University Press Durham N.C.

Singh, J.G., Singh S. and Dawra, V., 1983, Adjustment problems of old people, *Indian Journal of Clinical Psychology,* 10(1), pp 127-131.

Singh, R.P. and Malik, A.K., 1984, *Life span as related to role stress and mental health problems*, Paper submitted to the 2nd National Conference on Aging of the AGI, Tirupati.

Singh, Y. and Bhargava, M., 1984, *Emotional maturity scale : manual*, National Psychological Corporation, Agra.

Singhleton, Jerome F., 1985, Activity patterns of the elderly, *Society and Leisure*, 8(2), pp 805-819.

Sloane, R.B., 1980, Organic brain syndrome, *In* J.E. Birren and R.B. Sloane, eds., *Handbook of mental health and aging*, Prentice-Hall, Englewood Cliffs, N.J.

Slotrick, H.B., Reichelt, Carolyn R. and Gardner, Russell, 1985, Gifted students meet the institutionalised elderly : Learning about aging and the aged in a rural nursing home, *Journal for the Education of the Gifted*, 9(1), pp 45-58.

Smith, J.M., 1970, Age differences in achievement motivation, *British Journal of Social and Clinical Psychology*, 9(2), pp 175-176.

Smyer, Michael A. and Gatz, Margaret, 1983, *Mental health and aging: Programmes and evaluations*, Sage Publications, Inc., Beverly Hills.

Snygg, D., 1941, The need for a phenomenological system of psychology, *Psychological Review*, 48, pp 404-434.

Spieth, W., 1965, Slowness of task performance and cardiovascular diseases, *In* A.T. Welfond and J.E. Birren, eds., *Behaviour, aging and nervous system*, Charles C. Thomas, Springfield, Ill.

Spirduso, W.W., 1975, Reaction and movement time as a function of age and physical activity level, *Journal of Gerontology*, 30, pp 435-440.

Soodan, K.S., 1975, *Aging in India*, Minerva Associates, Calcutta.

Sridhar, M.J., 1986, *Age influence on accident rate*, NIRD, Hyderabad.

Srivastava, R.S., 1983, *The aged and the society*, C.D.S., New Delhi.

Stack, Steven, 1982, Aging and suicide: A cross-national study, *International Journal of Contemporary Sociology*, 19(3-4), pp 125-133.

Stankov, Lazar, 1988, Aging attention and intelligence, *Psychology and Aging*, 3(1), pp 59-74.

Steitz, Jean, A. and Verner, Betty S., 1987, What adolescents know about aging, *Educational Gerontology*, 13(4), pp 357-368.

Stenback, A., 1980, Depression and suicidal behaviour in old age, *in* J.E. Birren and R.B. Sloane, eds., *Handbook of mental health and aging*, Prentice-Hall, Englewood Cliffs, N.J.

Stevens, S.J., Cooper, P.E. and Eugene, T.L., 1980, Agra norms for Templer's death anxiety scale, *Psychological Reports*, 46(1), pp 205-206.

Stine, Elizabeth L., 1986, Attribute-based similarity perception in younger and older adults, *Experimental Aging Research*, 12(2), pp 89-94.

Stini, William A., 1984, The significance of body composition in human aging, *Journal of Indian Anthropological Society*, 19(1), pp 80-91.

Stoland, E., 1969, *The psychology of hope*, Jossey-Boss, San Francisco.

Stones, Michael J. and Kozme, Albert, 1989, Happiness and activities in later life : A propensity formulation, *Canadian Psychology*, 30(3), pp 526-537.

Storandt, Martha, Siegler, Ilene C. and Elias, Merrill F., 1978, *The clinical psychology of aging*, Plenum Press, New York.

Story, Marilyn D., 1989, Knowledge and attitudes about the sexuality of older adults among retirement home residents, *Educational Gerontology*, 15(5), pp 515-526.

Streib, G.F. and Schneider, C.J., 1971, *Retirement in American society*, Cornell University Press, Ithaca and London.

Strehler, B.L., 1976, *Introduction : Aging the human brain*, in R.D. Terry and S. Gershon, eds., *Neurobiology of aging*, Raven Press, New York.

Struyk, Raymond J. and Katsura, Harold M., 1987, Aging at home : How the elderly adjust their housing without moving, *Journal of Housing for the Elderly*, 4(2), p 192.

Sukumaran, V., 1981, Catching up on age, *Economic Times*, July 5, p 4, col 4-8.

Surwillo, W.W., 1963, The relation of simple response time to brain wave frequency and the effects of age, *Electroencephalographic Clinical Neurophysiology*, 15, pp 105-114.

Swan, James H., Fox, Patrick J. and Estes, Carroll L., 1986, Community mental health services and the elderly : Retrenchment or expansion: *Community Mental Health Journal*, 22(4), pp 275-285.

Swenson, W.M., 1959, Attitude towards death among the aged, *Minnesota Medicine*, 42, pp 399-402.

Szinovacz, Maximiliane E., 1986-87, Preferred retirement timing and retirement satisfaction in women, *International Journal of Aging and Human Development*, 24(4), pp 301-317.

Talland, George A., 1968, *Human aging and behaviour*, Academic Press, Inc., New York.

Tangavelu, M., 1984, *Community base action plan for the welfare of the elderly*, Paper presented at the 2nd National Conference of Aging of the AGI, November, Tirupati.

Tarbox, Arthur R., Connors, Gerard I. and Faillace, Louis A., 1987, Freshman and senior medical students attitudes toward the elderly, *Journal of Medical Education*, 62(7), pp 582-591.

Taves, M.J. and Hanson, G.D., 1963, Seventeen hundred elderly citizens, *In* A.M. Rose, ed., *Aging in Minnesota*, Minneapolis Press, Minnesota.

Taylor, Robert J., 1986, Religious participation among elderly blacks, *Gerontologist*, 26(6), pp 630-636.

Taylor, Debbie, 1982, Head over heels at 60, *Economic Times*, May 23, p 4, col. 5-8.

Taylor, Robert J. and Chatters, Linda M., 1986, Church-based informal support among elderly blacks, *Gerontologist*, 26(6), pp 637-642.

Templer, D.I., 1972, Death anxiety in religiously very involved persons, *Psychological Reports*, 31(2), pp 361-362.

Terpstra, Tammy L., Terpstra, Terra L., Plaweeki, Henry, M. and Streeter, Jean, 1989, As young as you feel: Age identification among the elderly, *Journal of Gerontological Nursing*, 15(2), pp 4-10.

Terry, R.D. and Gershon, S., 1976, eds., *Neurobiology of aging*, Raven Press, New York.

———, and Wisniewski, H., 1977, Structural aspects of aging in the brain, *In* C. Eisdorfer and R.O. Friedel, eds., *Cognitive and emotional disturbance in the elderly*, Year Book Medical Publishers, Chicago.

Tesing, D.J., Newman, E.I. and Brockett, R.G., 1978, *Basic adult services: A model curriculum*, School of Social Welfare, Albany, New York.

Teski, M.P., Arcuri, A.F. and Lester, D., 1980, Locus of control in elderly women who have worked and those who have not, *Psychological Reports*, 46(3), pp 1304-1308.

Tikku, Vinati, 1981, Old age, *Hindustan Times*, Magazine, January 11, p 1, col 1-5.

Tiwari. S.K. and Tripathi, N.K., 1981, Socio-economic status of subjects and locus of control, *Psychologia: An International Journal of Psychology in the Orient*, 24(4). pp 223-227.

Thomae. H., 1980, Personality and adjustment to aging, *In* J. Birren and R.B. Sloane. eds., *Handbook of mental health and aging*, Prentice-Hall, Englewood Cliffs, N.J.

Thomas. E.J. and Biddle, B.J., 1966, Role theory : Concepts and research, John Wiley, New York.

Thomas, Jeanne L., 1989, Gender and perceptions of grandparenthood, *International Journal of Aging and Human Development*, 29(4), pp 269-282.

Thomas, P.D. and Hooper, E.M., 1983, Healthy elderly : Social bonds and locus of control, *Research in Nursing and Health*, 6(1). pp 11-16.

Thompson, J. Victor, 1989, The elderly and their informal social networks, *Canadian Journal on Aging*, 8(4), pp 319-332.

Tilak, Sriniwas, 1989, Religion and aging in Indian tradition, State University of New York Press, Albany, New York.

Tobin, Joseph J., 1987, The American idealisation of old age in Japan, *Gerontologist*, 27(1), pp 53-58.

Tobin, S.S. and Neurgarten, B.L., 1961, Life satisfaction and social interaction in the aging, *Journal of Gerontologist*, 16(4), pp 344-346.

Toch, H., 1953, Attitudes of the 'Fifty Plus' age group : Preliminary considerations towards a longitudinal study, *Public Opinion Quarterly*, 17, pp 391-394.

Togonu-Bickersteth, Funmi, 1984-85, Multi-generational residence and perception of old age by Nigerian youth, *Psychology and Human Development*, 1(2), pp 81-86.

———, 1988, Perception of age among Yoruba aged, *Journal of Comparative Family Studies*, 19(1), pp 113-122.

———, and Akinnawo, Ebenezer O., 1987-89, Perception of the old by young adults in Nigeria, *Psychology and Human Development*, 2(2), pp 85-88.

———, 1989, knowledge about aging and perception of the old by Nigerian nurses, *Archives of Gerontology and Geriatrics*, 9(2), pp 137-146.

———, and Henderson, G., 1976, Some quantitative cerebral findings in normal and demented old people, *In* R.D. Terry and S. Gershon, eds., *Neurobiology of aging*, Raven Press, New York.

Topalova, Velina, 1986, Value system of the aged, *Studia Psychologica*, 28(2), pp 113-124.

Treanton, J., 1961, Comments, symposium on attitude towards death in older persons, *Journal of Gerontology*, 16(1), pp 63-67.

Treichel, J.A., 1980, Its never too late to start living longer, *In* Harold, C., ed., *Focus Aging*, Dushkin Publishing Group, Inc., Guilfort, Ct.

Troll, L.E. and Bengston, V.L., 1982, Inter-generational relations throughout the life span, *In* Wolman, B.B. Stricker, G., Ellman, S.J., Spiegel, P.K. and Palermo, D.S., eds., *Handbook of Developmental Psychology*, Prentice-Hall, Englewood Cliffs, New Jersey.

———, Miller, S.J. and Atchley, R.C., 1979, *Families in later life*, Wadsworth, Belmont, Calif.

Turner, B.F., 1979, The Self-concepts of Older women, *Research on Aging*, 1, pp 464-480.

Turner, R.J., 1981, Social support as a contingency in psychological well being, *Journal of Health and Social Behaviour*, 22, pp 357-67.

Upton, A.C., 1977, Pathobiology, *In* C.E. Finch and L. Hayflick, eds., *Handbook of the biology of aging*, Van Nostrand Reinhold, New York.

United Nations, 1975, Guidelines for national policy, *In The aging : Trends and policies*, United Nations, New York.

United States of America, Department of Commerce, 1979, Social and economic characteristics of the older population, *Current Population Reports*, 85, (a).

———, Department of Commerce, 1979, *Population profile of the U.S.: 1981* U.S. Bureau of the Census, 1979, Washington, D.C.

———, Department of Health, Education and Welfare, 1977, *Health United States 1976-77*, Public Health Service, Washington, D.C.

———, 1978, *Health United States 1978*, Public Health Service, Washington, D.C.

———, 1980, *Health United States, 1980*, Public Health Service, Washington, D.C.

U.S. Health Resources Administration, Division of Long-Term Care, 1974, *Guidelines and definitions for day care centres under PL 92-603*, Government Printing Office, Washington, D.C.

Usha, V., 1985, *Attitude to future and death of cancer patients, non seriously ill and normals*, M.Phil Dissertation, S.V. University, Tirupati.

Ushasree S. and Sunanda, Y., 1988, Education, adjustment and self confidence of the middle aged women, *Indian Journal of Community Guidance Service*, 5(3), pp 49-52.

Van Haitsman, Kim, 1986, Intrinsic religious orientation: Implications in the study of religiosity and personal adjustment in the aged, *Journal of Social Psychology*, 126(5), pp 685-687.

Verma, V.S., 1988, *A handbook of population statistics: Census of India 1981*, Samrat Press, New Delhi.

Verwoerdt, A., 1975, *Clinical geropsychiatry*, Williams and Wilkins, Baltimore.

Viegas Savita, 1981, Ageing in the west, *Economic Times*, July 5, p 5 col 1-3.

Vinod Kumar, 1986, Ageing and role of hormones, *Yojana*, 30(12) July, pp 30-32.

Vinokur-Kaplan, Diane, and Bergman, Simon, 1986, Retired Israeli social workers: Work, volunteer activities and satisfaction among retired professionals, *Journal of Gerontological Social Work*, 9(4), pp 73-86.

Vlasov, N.A. and Yadgarov, I.S., 1986, The structure of nocturnal sleep in sleep disorders in middle-aged and elderly people, *Soviet Neurology and Psychiatry*, 19(3), pp 71-79.

Vroom, V., 1964, *Work and motivation*, John Wiley, New York.

Walford, R.L., 1969, *The immunological theory of aging* Williams and Wilkins, Baltimore.

———, 1983, *Maximum life span*, W.W. Norton and Company, New York.

Walker, J.I. and Brodie, H.K., 1980, Neuropharmacology of aging, *In* E.W. Russe and D. Blazer, eds., *Handbook of geriatric psychiatry*, Van Nostrand Reinhold, New York.

Warty, M.S., 1970, *A study of the attitudes of young towards the aged*, Doctoral Dissertation Baroda University, Baroda.

———, 1988, *Dynamics of senile dementia in old age*, Paper presented at the National Seminar on Psychosocial Aspects of Aging, June, Tirupati.

Watts, Thomas D., 1981, The growing needs of the aged disabled: Some considerations, *Indian Journal of Public Administration*, 27(3), pp 629-636.

Warren, H.C., 1962, *Dictionary of psychology*, Houghton Mifflin Company, Massachusetts.

Warren, L.R., Wagener, J.W. and Herman, G.E., 1978, Binaural analysis in the aging auditory system, *Journal of Gerontology*, 33(5), pp 731-736.

Waskel, Shirley A. and Powell, F.C., 1987-88, Use of words to describe aged or elderly: A factor analysis, *Gerontology and Geriatrics Education*, 8(1-2), pp 123-131.

Wattis, J.P., Smith, C.W. and Binns, V., 1986, Medical students attitudes to old people and career preference: A comparison of two universities, *Medical Education*, 20(6), pp 498-501.

Waugh, N.C. and Barr, R.A., 1980, Memory a mental tempo, *In* L.W. Poon, J.L. Fozard, L.S. Cermak, D. Arenberg, and L.W. Thompson, eds., *New directions in memory and aging*, Lawrence Erlbaum, Hillsdale, N.J.

Webb, Lynne, Delaney, Judith J. and Young, Lorraine R., 1989, Age, interpersonal attraction and social interaction : A review and assessment, *Research on Aging*, 11(1), pp 107-123.

Wechsler, D., 1939, *The measurement of adult intelligence*, Williams and Wilkins, Baltimore.

Weeks, D.G. *et al*, 1980, Relation between loneliness and depression: A structural equation analysis, *Journal of Personality and Social Psychology*, 39, pp 1238-1244.

Weg, R.B., 1975, Changing physiology of aging: Normal and pathological, *In* D.S. Woodruff and J.E. Birren, eds., *Aging: Scientific perspectives and social issues*, Van Nostrand Reinhold, New York.

Weisman, A.D., 1972, *Death and denial*, Behavioural Publications, New York.

———, 1980, Common fallacies about dying patients, *In* E.S. Shneidman, ed., *Death : Current perspectives*, Mayfield, Palo Alto, Calif.

Weizman, R. and Hart, J., 1987, Sexual behaviour in healthy married elderly men , *Archives of Sexual Behaviour*, 16(1), pp 39-44.

Welford, A., 1980, Sensory, perceptual and motor processes in older adults, *In* J.E. Birren and R.N. Sloane, eds., *Handbook of mental health and aging*, Prentice-Hall, Englewood Cliffs, N.J.

Welford, A.T., 1977, Motor performance, *In* J.E. Birren and K.W. Schaie, eds., *Handbook of the psychology of aging*, Van Nostrand Reinhold, New York.

Werthner, Penny and Orlick, Terry, 1986, Retirement experiences of successful olympic athletes, *International Journal of Sports Psychology*, 17(5), pp 337-363.

West, G.E. and Simons, R.L., 1983, Sex differences in stress, coping resources and illness among the elderly, *Research on Aging*, 5(2), pp 235-268.

Whall, Ann L., 1987, Self-esteem and the mental health of older adults, *Journal of Gerontological Nursing*, 13(4), pp 41-42.

Whanger, A.D., 1980, Treatment within institution, *In* E.W. Busse and D. Blazer, eds., *Handbook of geriatric psychiatry*, Van Nostrand Reinhold, New York.

Williamson, J.B., Munley, A. and Evans, L., 1980, *Aging and society*, Holt, Rinehart and Winston, New York.

Willis, Lee, Thomas, Paula, Garry, Philip J. and Goodwin, James S., 1987, A prospective study of response to stressful life events in initially healthy elders, *Journal of Gerontology*, 42(6), pp 627-630.

Willoughby, R., 1935, Emotionality as a function of age, sex and conjugal conditions, *Psychological Bulletin*, 32(5), pp 325-335.

Windle, Michael, 198[illegible], Sex role orientation, cognitive flexibility and life satisfaction among older adults, *Psychology of Women Quarterly*, 10(3), pp 263-273.

Wingrove, C.R. and Alston, J.P., 1971, Age, aging and church attendance, *The Gerontologist*, 11(4), pp 356-358.

Winokur, G., Behar, D. and Schlesser, M., 1980, Clinical and biological aspects of depression in the elderly, *In* J.O. Cole and J. Barret, eds., *Psychopathology in the aged*, Raven Press, New York.

Wohlwill, J.F., 1973, *The study of behavioural development*, Academic Press, New York.

Wolff, K., 1959, Group psychotherapy with geriatric patients in a state hospital setting: Results of a three year study, *Group Psychotherapy*, 12, pp 218-222.

———, 1961, A coordinated approach to the geriatric problem, *Journal of American Geriatric Society*, 9, pp 573-580.

Wolfsen, Connie R., Barker, Judith C. and Mitteness, Linda S., 1990, Personalisation of formal social relationships by the elderly, *Research on Aging*, 12(1), pp 94-112.

Wolinsky, Mary A., 1986, Marital therapy with older couples, *Social Casework*, 67(8), pp 475-483.

Wong, Paul T., 1989, Personal meaning and successful aging, *Canadian Psychology*, 30(3), pp 516-525.

Wood, Linda A. and Johnson, Julia, 1989, Life satisfaction among the rural elderly: What do the numbers mean? *Social Indicators Research*, 21(4), pp 379-408.

Woodruff, D.S., 1972, *Biofeedback control of the EEG alpha rythmn and its effect on reaction time in the young and old*, Dissertation University of Southern California, California.

———, 1975, A physiological perspective of the psychology of aging, *In* D.S. Woodruff and J.E. Birren, eds., *Aging: Scientific perspectives and social issues*, Van Nostrand Reinhold, New York.

Wrong, D.H., 1977, *Population and society*, 4th ed., Random House, New York.

Young, John B., 1989, Effects of retirement on aspects of self-perception, *Archives of Gerontology and Geriatrics*, 9(1), pp 67-76.

Young, Katherine K., 1989, Foreword, In Shrinivas, Tilak *Religion and aging in Indian tradition*, State University of New York Press, Albany, New York.

Yu, Lucy C., Yu, Yanju and Mansfield, Phyllis, K., 1990, Gender and changes in support of parents in China: Implications for the one-child policy, *Gender and Society*, 4(1), pp 83-89.

Zarit, S.H., 1977, Gerontology: Getting better all the time, In Zarit, S.H., ed., *Reading in aging and death*, Harper and Row, New York.

———, Miller, N.E. and Kahn, R.L., 1978, Brain function, intellectual impairment and education in the aged, *Journal of the American Geriatrics Society*, 21(2), pp 58-67.

Zung, W.W.K., 1980, Affective disorders, *In* E.W. Busse and D. Blazer, eds., *Handbook of geriatric psychiatry*, Van Nostrand Reinhold, New York.

INDEX

Achievements, 70
Action strategy, 174
Across age and sex, 81
Activity, 117
 factors, 107
 theory assumption of, 51
Adaptation, 188
Adler, A., 32
Adolescents, 64, 104
Adulthood, 61
Affiliation, 70, 77, 78, 95
Age Care India, 215
Age categories, 55
 devaluation of, 105
 distribution, 38
 non-institutionalised, 237
 parents problems, 113
 problems, 34
 public view of, 245
 religiosity of, 137
 social interaction of, 132
 stratification model, 52
Age group, 43, 108
Aging, 45, 245
 activity theory, 50-51
 aspects, 134
 continuity theory, 52-53
 criteria of, 31
 disengagement theory, 49-52
 exchange theory, 53-56
 factors, 103
 inevitable process of, 245
 labelling theory, 54-55
 multidirectional approaches, 57-58
 natural phenomenon, 258
 personality theory, 55-57
 phenomenological theory, 57-58
 problems of, 258-49
 role theory, 56
 secondary, 46
 stereotypes, 34
 subculture theory, 55
 syndrome, 247
 theoretical approaches, 49-50
Aggression, 74, 78
Aggressiveness, 151
Agreement, 154, 199, 279
Ainley, S.C., 145
American society, 34
Anand, K.C., 257
Anantharaman, R.N., 223
ANOVA, 70, 86, 108, 149, 163, 190, 228, 230, 236, 237
 results, 84, 116
Antithesis, 50
Anxiety, 119, 137, 185, 187
 basic, 122
 concept of, 122
 types of, 188-89
Anxiety Scale Questionnaire (ASQ), 188
Arya Mahila Ashram, 285, 286
Ashram Dharma, 15
Assam, 292
Atchley, R.C., 49, 185, 186
Attitude towards institutionalisation, 211-12, 290
Australia, 246
Authoritarian life style, 157

Bajpai, Rajendra Kumari, 265
Banprastha Ashram, 262
Ballot power, 17
Barber, B., 99
Baltzell, E.D., 99
Bassili, T.N., 105
Baum, S.K., 217

Bengtson, V.L., 54, 62
Benjaminsen, 196
Bhargava, M., 148, 151
Bhusan, L.I., 84
Bible, 145
Bihar, 292
Biological age, 14, 53
Birren, J.E., 31, 32, 45, 63, 167
Blazer, D.G., 81, 82, 83, 216, 222
Borges, M.A., 105
Botwinick, J., 63
Bower, G.H., 66, 119
Brain clock, 278
Breathing problems, 32
Broady, M. Elaine, 211
Brown, C.W., 196
Browning, Robert, 33, 257
Bureaucracy, 21
Burkee, J.L., 104
Burney, S.M.H., 264

California, 222
Cameron, 138, 151
Campbell, Joseph, 33
Cancer, kinds of, 277-78
Capitalism, 14
Cardiovascular system, 246
Carpenter, J.O., 140
Cell functions, 282
 regeneration of, 22
Cell means, 155
 examination of, 132-35, 155, 161
Central nervous system, 138
Challenges, 119, 191, 203, 252
Chandigarh, 292
Chauhan, N.S., 68
Children's Attitudes Towards the Elderly (CATE), 104
Chhabra, Seema, 167
Chi-square test, 67
Christian missionary, 286
Chronological age, 31, 45, 46, 61, 73
Cluster analytic approach, 123
Clyde Mood Scale, 168
Cochran, C.D., 154
Cohen, J., 197
Coin, 15
Collter, 121, 124, 135
Comeron, P., 65, 104
Communication, 216
Communism, 14
Community, 106, 147, 217
 facilities, 41
Comparing death anxiety, 85
Components, 127
 social adjustment, 65
Concept of Old age, 108
 age and social class on, 114
 comparison means of, 111
 different dimensions of, 110-14
 favourable meaning, 112
Conceptualisation, 145
Conforming life style, 159
Control strategy, 172, 176
Coob, S., 196, 201
Coping strategies, 162, 171, 186
Cornell medical index, 221
Corollary, 16
Corrective mechanisms, 19
Cosmopolitan cities, 208
Costa, P.T., 123
Covert anxiety, 133
Cox, H., 183, 203
Craik, F.J., 168
Crises, 130, 195
Criticism, 51, 123
Cumming, E., 46, 63, 67, 123, 133
Czaja, S.J., 122, 135

Dampared-spoiled style females, 161
Data, 64, 119, 189, 208, 220
 collection of, 227
  procedure of, 172-73, 198
Davis, R., 64
Death, causes of, 246
Death anxiety, 81, 83, 89-92, 137-38, 140-41, 148, 161, 221
 scale, 85
Decreasing power resources problems, 54-55
Delhi, 126, 292
Delhi Christian friend, 286
Demographic variable, 105, 232
Demonstration, 18

Denmark, 264
Dependency, 168
  ratio, 41
Depression, 216-18, 226-28, 230-32
  high level of, 231
  sector score, 219
Destruction, 151
Deterioration, 32
Devaluation, 105
Dhall, S.C., 260
Dhillon, P.K., 63, 81, 103, 119, 137, 167, 176, 185, 195
Dichotomistic societies, 13
Different age group, interaction effect of, 96
Discrepancy, 122
Discriminant function, 217
Diseases, 246, 274, 280
  free crucial problems, 258-59
Disharmony, 16
Divorced, 43
Dixit, S.A., 137
Doka, K.J., 105
Dollard, J., 69
Domineering authoritarian style, 157, 161
Douglas, K., 65
Dowd, J.J., 53
Dramaturgical model, 56
Drug, 282
D'Souza, Sheila, 63
Dual income, 290
Dutt, S.K., 272, 274

Economic burden, 209
  restraints, 16
Education, 15, 42, 84, 92, 147, 197
Eighth Five Year Plan, 284
Elastic tissues, 32
Emotional adjustment, 68, 76, 78, 95
  insecurity, 132, 177
  instability, 203
  maturity, 138, 149, 153, 155
    dimensions of, 148-49
    scale, 148
  problems, 130, 187
  regression, 151
    dimension of, 153
  security, 81
  states, 216
Empirical reality, 21
Employment, 18, 209
Eric Erikson, 139
Europe, 246
Evaluation, 107, 117
  dimension, 112-14
  factor, 107
Exchange processes, 53
Expectancy, 280
Extraversion, 130, 179
Eysenck extraversion scale, 65

Family problems, 202
Family support services, 20
Fear of Death Scale (FODS), 85
Female, socialisation of, 70
Financial security, 105
Finland, 264
Fonner, A., 82
Fourth Pay Commission, 276
Friedman, H., 168
Frustration, 66, 71, 78, 96, 216, 224, 227, 235, 236
  mean and standard deviation of, 233
  modes of, 69-74
  reaction of, 63
  situation, 241
Functional activity, 273

Gainful employment, 183, 195
Galloway, G.G., 144
Gans, H., 99
Gerontology, 33, 44
  field of, 36
Global anxiety, 125
Gomathi, S., 232
Good exercise programmes, 279
Government employees, 183, 212
Grant parent adoption scheme, 284
Gratification, 63
Grey revolution, 247
  power movements, 17
Grey Skill Bank, 20
Grihaswamini, 187
Guha, Mamata, 271

Guiness Book of World Records, 247
Gujarat, 293
Gupta, Anita, 103
Gupta, Parkash Chand, 274
Gurdial Singh, 268
Guru Nanak Dev, 257
Gutmann, D.L., 130, 224

Hale, W.D., 217
Harris, L., 62, 145
Haryana, 294
Havighurst, R.J., 50
Hazrat Mohammed, 257
Henry, W.E., 49
High Court, 126
Higher socio-economic group, 126, 173
Hindustan Petroleum, 126
Holcomb, W.L., 82, 91
Holland, 264
Home-makers programmes, 283
Hopelessness, 222, 226, 228, 230, 235
Hoppins-Ville Community College, 85
Hostility, 168
Human development, stage of, 33
    ingenuity, 14
Hypotheses, 67, 73, 78, 124, 146

Illiteracy, 22
Illogical human desire, 14
Implementing policies, 248
Implications, 203
India, elderly population growth, 36
Indian adult males, 130
Individualistic life style, 157
Industrial revolution, 13, 62
Industrialisation, 34
Infant mortality rates, 39-40
Interaction effect, 87
Institutionalised aged, 215, 225, 229, 231, 237-38
Institutionalisation, 207, 209, 211, 241
    concept of, 210
    consequences of, 207
    impact of, 210
    interaction effect of, 232, 238
International Federation Aging (IFA), 284
Introversion, 130, 133, 179
Irritation decline, 67
Ivestes, C., 105
Iyer, P.N., 13

Jacobs, J., 81
Jackson, M., 64
Jamuna, D., 170
Japan, 246
Jasra, Anju, 119
Jaswal, S.S., 256, 259
Jayakar, Papul, 253
Joe, V.C., 143
Johnson, B., 52
Johnson, R., 210
Joint family system, 106, 265, 284

Kahl, Beverly A., 99
Kalish, R.A., 141, 163, 184
Kaplan, O.J., 138
Karnataka, 294
Kastenbaum, 104, 140
Keller, Mary L., 141
Kerala, 295
Krause, D., 202
Krug, S.E., 226
Kubler-Ross, E., 140
Kuder-Richardson method, 127
Kumar, N.L.G., 261
Kumar, Roma, 137
Kuppuswamy, E., 107
Kurlycheck, R.T., 142
Kutiyas, 286

Languages, 15
Larson, R., 151
Lee, Gary R., 168
Lefcourt, H.M., 142, 143
Lieberman, M.A., 207
Life cycle, 52, 119
Life events, 199
    effect of, 195, 201
    different areas, 200
    perspectives, 14
Life expectancy, 18, 37
Life styles, 138, 139, 148, 155
    analysis of, 156
    reformulation, 14

Linguistic affinity, 14
Living arrangement, 41
Locus of Control, 142, 148, 161, 163, 218
Logos, 44
Loneliness, 219, 222, 226, 228, 230
Longevity, quest for, 272
  recipes for, 278
Longfellow, H.W., 215
Longitudinal study of Aging, 222
Lord Krishna, 263
Low Income Group (LIG), 212
Lower-class subculture, 100
Lower-middle class, 114
Lower socio-economic groups, 126, 172
Lumpkins, J.R., 143

Maddox, G.L., 186
Madhya Pradesh, 298
Maharashtra, 299
Majumdar, Vandana, 191
Malinowski, B., 62
Mandatory retirement, 183
Manifestation, 133, 135
Marital status, 42
Marshall, V.W., 141
Masculine mid-life crisis, 119-20
  population, 41
Mass transportation, 41
Materialism, ascendancy of, 14
Mathiasen, G., 81
Mathur, Deepa, 81
Maturity, 137, 145
McCrae, R.R., 138, 168
McDonald, J., 81
McKee, M., 33
Mean anxiety scores, 189, 190
Mean hopelessness scores, 234
Mean personality disintegration scores, 154
Mean and standard deviation, dimensions, 233
Medical facilities, 41
  problems, 35
Meghalaya, 301
Mercier, Joyee, M., 233
Methodology, 124, 146
Metropolitan area, 145
Mid-life crises, 130-33
Middle age criteria, 51
  definitions of, 120
Middle Income Group (MIG), 212
Middle-socio-economic group, 126, 173, 197
Milbander, Seema, 185
Miller, W.B., 35, 100
Miller, S.M., 104
Moberg, D.O., 81, 82
Moderately integrated personality category, 151
Modern complex societies, 139
Modernisation, 34, 247
Modification, 52, 274
Molinari, B., 143
Monge, R.H., 122, 135
Moral education foundation, 285
Mortality rate, 37, 39
Motivational determinant, 63, 66
  factors, 63
Multiple regression, 220
  analysis, 141, 218

Narayan, R., 280
Negi, A.S., 248
Negotiation, 186
Neugarten, B.L., 45, 63, 65, 139
Neurotic tendency, 135, 179
Neuraticism, 133
New cultural ethos, 13
Newman, B.M., 139
New Zealand, 246
Non-institutionalisation, 228, 232
  aged, 225, 229, 238
Non-working males, 200, 202
  status, 197-99
Northern America, 246
Norway, 264
Nurturance, 68, 70, 78
Nutrition, 39, 272, 274
  factors, 274

Occupation, 83, 84, 91, 92, 147, 183, 193
Old age, ambivalent perception, 110-12, 179-80
  biosystemic changes of, 14

homes, 291
negative concomitant, 105
pensions, 284
perception of, 108, 173, 179
problems of, 32
unfavourable perception, 113, 117
Old homes, effect of, 207
Older population, 245
Oltman, A.M., 218
Optimism, 173
strategy of, 174
Orbach, H.L., 145
Organisation, 286
Orissa, 301
Osgood, C.E., 107
Ozonam Home, 285

Paintal, Harinder Kaur, 124
Palmore, E.B., 51
Parnes, H.S., 184
Parrivism strategy, 176
Pension, 192, 284
Perceptions, 108, 113, 173, 179, 186
Perceived social support scale, 196
Perlman, D., 221, 229
Personal data schedule, 188
income, 91
information schedule, 84
problems, 113
Personality, 119, 127, 179
disintegration, 151, 153, 155
traits, 127, 131, 135
Peterson, Candida C., 55
Phillips, B.S., 66
Physical decline, 32
Picasso, 250
Pillai, A.K.B., 137
Pollution, 285
Pondicherry, 301
Population, 17, 37
changing age-structure of, 19
composition of, 41
distribution of, 44
trends in, 40
Potency, 107, 117
dimension of, 112
factor, 107
Poverty, 135, 172, 271
Pratte, C.P., 105
Pravin Kumar, 275
Preeti Singh, 250
Pre-illness pattern, 248
Preston, D.B., 169
Primary aging, 46
Psychological age, 46
tension, 64
Psychopathological problems, 122
Punjab, 301
Punjab National Bank, 126
Puranas, 15

Rainwater, L., 100
Rakesh, B.K., 277
Ramamurti, P.V., 170
Raman, V.S., 253
Ramifications, 187
Recent life changes questionnaire, 219
Receptivity, 114, 117
Regression, 69, 73, 74
Reichard, S., 168
Religiosity, 81, 91, 96, 144, 161, 165
relationship of, 89
Remaining young, 14
Reserve Bank of India, 126
Resource crunch, 17
Restrictions, 103
Retired non-working male, 199, 201
overt and covert anxiety of, 189
perceived social support for, 198
Retirement, 183, 185, 219, 259
age, 260
compulsory, 187, 251
impact of, 260
mandatory, 195
personal meaning, 193
responses, 193
results of, 186
shock, 186
system, 196
time of, 203
Rig Veda, 15, 263
Riley, J.W., 52, 83
Robertson-Tchabo, E.A., 33
Robinson, P.J., 141

Rose-Colley, Mary, 55
Rosenfield, A.H., 216
Rosow, I., 215
Rotter, J.B., 65, 142, 221
Rosenzweig Picture Frustration Test, 223, 227
Rubenstein, C., 221
Rubio Herrera, R., 142
Rural community, 105
Russel, Bertrand, 257
Russel, D., 226
Ryan, J., 163

Sachdev, Archna, 285
Saini, Sangeet, 270
Saints, 257
Sargent, S.S., 66
Sarita Mohan, 265
Secondary aging, 46
Self concept inventory, 126
  investigation of, 120
  scores, 121
Self-criticism, 253
Self depreciation, 221
Self-hate, 168
Self-perception, 253
Self report depression scale, 220
Self sufficiency, 133, 179
Semi-Government employees, 183
Sex ratio, 39, 41
Shakespeare, 263
Shelley, P.B., 185
Shanas, Ethel, 210, 213
Sharda, Umesh M., 262
Sharma, Baijnath, 263
Sharma, Kanta, 269
Singh, L.P., 253
Singh, Nalini, 251
Singh, Vijayendra, 269
Smith, J.M., 64, 208
Snygg, D., 57
Social adjustment, 63, 74
  age, 46
  gerontology, 45
  maturity, 68, 78, 95
  participation, 195
  restrictions, 53
  scripts, 56
  stratifications, 99
Socialisation, 57, 154
Societal classification scheme, 14, 16
Socio-economic status, 107, 131, 134, 143, 159, 165
  classes, 167, 171
  impact of, 137
  rating scale, 107, 147
  significantly, 117
Socio-psychological problem, 14
Son, I.M., 255
Spiritual freedom, 16
Statland, E., 222
Stevens, S.J., 142
Stratification model, 57
Strategies, 101, 168
Subramaniam, N.S., 254
Suburban, 210
Succorance, 70, 77
Superannuation policy, 18
Sweden, 264
Swenson, W.M., 81
Switzerland, 264
Synonymous, 34

Tagore, Rabindranath, 263
Tamil Nadu, 302
Templer, D.I., 85
Terichel, J.A., 46
Theoretical approaches, 57
Thomas, P.D., 56, 165
Thyroid hormone, 246
Tissues, 281
Tiwari, S.K., 143, 163
Tobin, Joseph J., 213
Tobin, S.S., 210
Tools, 107, 147
  used, 188, 197
Towards institutionalisation, 212
Treanton, J., 82, 88
Turner, B.F., 201
Typical aged females, 65

Unemotionality, 111
Upper middle class, 114
Urbanisation, 34, 209, 290

Values, 198
  systems, 13, 14
Vasculo-circulatory system, 22
Vayovriddha, 20, 22
Vegetables, 279
Verma, I.P., 285
Victims, 14
Vladimir, Horowitz, 250
Vroom, V., 195

Walia, P.S., 266
Weeks, D.G., 220
Welford, A., 138
West Bengal, 305
West, G.E., 169
Westbrook, 171, 176
Western Societies, 14, 15, 34, 35
Widowhood, 21
Wingrove, C.R., 81, 87, 91
Willoughby, R., 63, 66
Wolff, K., 144
Wood, Linda A., 220
Work opportunities, 36
World Health Organisation, 267

Yeats, W.B., 137
Young, adults, 53
  females, 65
Younger age group, 73
Youth club, 266

Zarit, S.H., 45
Zung self rating, 218